Westermanns Monatshefte. Nobody has dared tackling the Science taboo so forcefully before. Henceforth, vivisectionists will have a hard time to find even a single argument in favor of animal experimentation.

SWITZERLAND

Nebelspalter. A tremendous persuasiveness and exceptional competence emanates from this book.

La Suisse. With this book, Hans Ruesch, the novelist, launches a bomb that unfortunately is not fictional. He denounces the crimes of vivisection in terms that for the first time might convince even people who don't care one whit about animals.

GREAT BRITAIN

Daily Express. ...It's a view I'd always taken myself—until I read Hans Ruesch's book. It's an appalling indictment of much modern-day vivisection, as cruel and largely useless....As the first nation to restrict vivisection by law in 1876, it's time we looked again at our dubious record.

FRANCE

Lyon-Matin. The book demonstrates that the claims of vivisection are a monstrous fraud, due to the coalition of an almighty pharmaceutical industry and a certain medicine which has turned its back on Hippocrates.

Hans Ruesch is an English-writing, Swiss author of many novels, including *Top of the World* (which has sold almost 3 million copies worldwide and was made into a film starring Anthony Quinn), *The Racer* (made into a film starring Kirk Douglas), *South of the Heart, The Game, The Stealers,* and *Back to the Top of the World.* He has also written short stories for many leading American and European magazines. Mr. Ruesch was once editor of a series of medical books in Italy and has been a scholar in zoology and sociology for some time. He lives in Switzerland. *Slaughter of the Innocent* was his first non-fiction book. He also recently published *Naked Empress*.

Hans Ruesch

SLAUGHTER
OF
THE
INNOCENT

Civitas Publications

Reissued in 1983 by CIVITAS Publication,
Copyright © 1983 by Hans Ruesch.

All rights reserved
ISBN   0-9610016-0-7

For information, address:
CIVIS, Tal-Str. 40, CH-7250 Klosters, Switzerland
or CIVITAS, P.O. Box 26, Swain, N.Y. 14884.

Printed in the United States of America

Previously published in the United States by
Bantam Books in 1978 (ISBN 0-553-11151-5)

Second printing, 1985

Library of Congress Cataloging in Publication Data

Ruesch, Hans, 1913–
    Slaughter of the Innocent

    Revised translation of: Imperatrice nuda.
    Reprint. Originally published: New York, N.Y.:
Bantam Books, 1978.
    Includes index.
    1. Medical research.   2. Medicine, Experimental.
3. Animal experimentation.   4. Vivisection.   I. Title.
R850.R8313   1983   619   83–1910
ISBN 0–9610016–0–7

Leonardo da Vinci, Mark Twain, Queen Victoria, George Bernard Shaw, and Albert Schweitzer are just a few of the eminent thinkers and world leaders who have opposed vivisection. If you are against the mindless and brutal exploitation of animals, you're in good company.

"A day will come when the world will look upon today's vivisection in the name of science the way we look today upon witch hunts in the name of religion."

—Henry J. Bigelow
formerly Professor of Physiology
Harvard University

CONTENTS

FOREWORD

by Robert S. Mendelsohn, M.D.
Author of Confessions of a Medical Heretic

In the Religion of Modern Medicine, the rite of vivisection is central.

The medical student acolyte, early in his preclinical years in the seminary called medical school, learns live animal dissection in physiology and pharmacology classes. The religious significance of this practice is implanted deeply into his unconscious by his teachers, who train him, at the end of each experiment, not to kill the animal, nor to dispose of it, but to "sacrifice" it.

Although never explicitly spelled out, the purpose of that "sacrifice" is tacitly shared by the student-acolyte and his doctor-priest teacher. That word — and the positive image it evokes — obviates any serious deliberation of the pros and cons of vivisection. Thus, the highly charged, human emotion inevitably aroused by vivisection, carried out in sacred precincts, far from public view, blessed by its bishops and archbishops, becomes incorporated, subliminally, almost instinctively, into the belief system of every medical student.

Without any perceived need for reflection, thought, debate or evidence, the medical student, in his formative years, is indoctrinated with the value of vivisection in teaching, testing and experimenting. If pressed, he/she may defend its use in highly limited circumstances; but in accord with a basic ethic of the Religion of Modern Medicine — "the extreme always becomes the mean" — he/she will soon sanction vivisection on a large, indeed massive, scale. How else can penicillin, a wonderful drug for meningitis and severe pneumonia, be applied to the

i

common cold? How else can cortisone, a miracle for life-threatening Addison's disease, be prescribed for sunburn?

The payoff of this early religiously-sanctioned blood-letting in seminary training is an insatiable blood-lust — or tolerance for the spilling of blood — during the student's later tenure as a lifetime physician-priest. How else can the doctor be trained to do big operations (e.g., radical mastectomy) when smaller ones (lumpectomy) are scientifically demonstrated over and over to kill fewer and cure more? How else can he accept, indeed defend, the ever-increasing epidemic (now 25% of all births) of Caesarian sections? How else can he learn to mouth the catechism of surgery? *"When in doubt, cut it out." "Big surgeon, big incision; little surgeon, little incision." "Your uterus is just a sac for cancer." "Your husband loves you for yourself, not for your breasts."* And the all-powerful *"Just trust me."* It is that litany that proves Modern Medicine is not a science, but a religion.

The physician's blood-lust demands laboratory tests on patients to the point of exsanguination. The risk of excessive blood tests to little babies is so well recognized that a special diagnostic category now exists — "iatrogenic (Greek for *doctor-produced)* anemia."

Other religions also have their blood rituals. The American Indians require a drop from the fingertip. We Jews demand several drops from circumcision ("bris"). But the Religion of Modern Medicine, in its blood-bank drives, calls for pints and quarts and gallons. There is never enough blood in the hospital-temples of Modern Medicine to satisfy the surgeon's desires as he seduces his victims — primarily women, virgins and otherwise — to mount the holy altar so he can carry out his ritual mutilations.

This wild blood-lust, starting with animal vivisection and proceeding to human mutilation, stamps Modern Medicine as the most primitive religion ever known to mankind.

Like other false religions, Modern Medicine is now exposed as death-oriented. The antibiotics kill more than they cure. When studied statistically, surgical mortality is twice as high as the surgeons verbally claim. The body-count from vaccine-induced encephalopathy is now reaching public view. The hatred of doctors for a normal birth is reflected in their automatic response to women complaining about dangers of The Pill — "It's safer than a pregnancy." While the death-rate from pregnancy drops, that from doctor-sanctioned contraception (oral contraceptive, IUD, vasectomy, tubal ligation, hysterectomy, multiple abortions) skyrockets.

Of course, not all doctors carry out the death-oriented atrocities of the Church of Modern Medicine. Some do. The rest, by condoning and protecting the actions of their colleagues, are equally guilty. I refer to the latter as the "good Germans" of Modern Medicine.

Modern Medicine mocks religion. Readers of the Old Testament will remember the many Biblical restrictions surrounding animal sacrifices — animals brought by the citizen, sacrified in his presence in public view, by a member of a hereditary caste (the priestly class) who did not later become a surgeon. Contrast this careful ritual with the secret vivisection by students and doctors of the Religion of Modern Medicine.

Regarding human sacrifice, the Jewish patriarch, Abraham, was prohibited from sacrificing his own son to his God. Contrast this to the surgical slaughter and mayhem — the millions of deaths from unnecessary operations — permitted, indeed required, by the god of the Religion of Modern Medicine. No wonder the surgeon is masked!

Modern Medicine tries to replace the 8th day "bris" with the dangerous hospital circumcision right after birth. In sharp contrast to Jewish ethics, the Religion of Modern Medicine sanctions, indeed delights in, abortion-on-demand.

I have made my choice. I have rejected as idolatrous the Religion of Modern Medicine and its fundamental sacrament — vivisection. For years I have encouraged my medical students to surreptitiously photograph animal conditions in their laboratories, to keep diaries, to leak the truth to the media. This sabotage serves not only to inform the public, but also helps save the integrity — indeed the souls — of the students.

For myself, I cling to the Sabbath commandment prohibiting even animals from being worked seven days a week. Every human being whose religion is derived from the Old Testament (and Eastern religions as well) knows the laws protecting animals. Only Modern Medicine, in its arrogant idolatry, sanctions cruelty to animals as the norm.

Hans Ruesch's magnificent book washes away the thin excuses of doctor-apologists for animal testing. Comprehensively and carefully documented, objective, yet emotionally compelling, it serves as the steel battering ram that can dislodge the cornerstone of Modern Medicine — vivisection. All of us — including future generations — are in his debt.

Robert S. Mendelsohn, M.D.
June 1982

PREFACE

to the 1983 reissue of Slaughter of the Innocent
by Hans Ruesch

AN ONGOING BATTLE

Under the headline "Antibiotics: Trouble Ahead," the *International Herald-Tribune* of August 24, 1981 carried a *Washington Post* story that began:

> Doctors from 25 nations have warned that the "flagrant misuse" of antibiotics has caused a "world-wide public health problem." Their statement will come as a surprise to many— including American doctors . . . .

Those who read *Slaughter of the Innocent* when it first came out in English, in 1978, understand this problem with antibiotics, since it was discussed there. They also knew about the oncoming DES tragedy before it became widely known, as the book had predicted that cases of a new type of cancer, induced by this synthetic estrogen, were bound to increase. The same goes for *Slaughter*'s prediction that malformed births would be increasing — not in spite of, but because of the intensification of animal tests after the Thalidomide horror; such malformations have indeed been increasing. No particular prophetic gift was required for making these predictions — only some basic knowledge and common sense.

All of which calls to mind what Dr. Anna Kingsford, Britain's first woman physician, wrote over a century ago: "The spiritual malady which rages in the soul of the vivisector is in itself sufficient to render him incapable of acquiring the highest and best knowledge. . . . He finds it easier to propagate and multiply disease than to discover the secret of health. Seeking for the germs of life, he invents only new methods of death."

v

AN ILLUMINATING HISTORY

This book is a photographic copy of the 1978 edition, with the Appendix to the British edition (1979) added. The work had first appeared in an Italian version, in 1976. The history of the publication of this book provides some valuable and frightening insight into the methods and power wielded by vivisectionists and their allies; how they were able to squelch a book already printed and make it disappear — at least for a time.

In America. Bantam Books of New York, one of the biggest publishing houses in the world, was preparing to print *Slaughter* in 1976, with an enthusiasm I had not seen in 40 years as a writer in some 20 countries. On November 23, 1976, Roger F. Cooper, one of the senior editors at Bantam, wrote to me in Switzerland:

> I am particularly pleased to be involved with your book.... It is a controversial work, and we therefore felt that it was important to have the manuscript reviewed by outside legal counsel.... I am enclosing the legal report, and as you see it concludes that there are some points in the book that will require either rewording or substantiation of some sort. I'd very much like to talk to you about the feasibility of your coming to New York for further discussion.... Until then, I would simply like to reiterate the enthusiasm we all feel about being the publisher of *Slaughter of the Innocent,* and our confidence that these legal questions can be easily cleared up.

The following January, I flew to New York to meet with Cooper and the lawyer whom Bantam had called in, to clear up the various points in question. After that, the manuscript went into production, and I kept receiving reassurances from Cooper that Bantam expected the book to be one of its top sellers in 1978, and that everyone there was fully committed to a major effort for Spring 1978, when it would appear. But when Spring came, there was only silence from Bantam.

While I was in New York, I had told the Bantam people that Rizzoli, Italy's largest publisher, had been forced to suppress the book shortly after its publication in 1976. Excerpts from the book, which had appeared in various magazines and newspapers in the Rizzoli chain, had stirred public opinion to the point of prompting discussions in Parliament. But a few weeks after publication, Italian bookstores were advised that the title was out of print (although I had personally seen thousands of copies held back in Rizzoli's warehouse). At the time, Rizzoli was financially dependent on Italy's largest chemical concern, Montedison, which comprised the country's major pharmaceutical firms. So the publisher's decision to withdraw the book was understandable.

Bantam's position differed only in external appearance. It is not generally known that the major media are subject to influence by the Drug Trust, often without being aware of it. In *The Drug Story* (1949), former Maryland news editor Morris Bealle revealed how the Drug Trust had all news about drugs and therapies in America censored, under the pretext that the average newsperson knows nothing about medicine and thus needs guidance from experts — which the Drug Trust obligingly provided.

Knowing this, I had advised Bantam not to advertise the book beforehand and not to circulate advance chapters to the media before publication, but to launch the book by surprise. They said it could not be done that way, and went ahead distributing advance copies. The first American review was also the last. On February 27, 1978, five weeks before publication, a review appeared in *Publishers Weekly* which read in part:

> This study of vivisection aroused a storm of outrage in Italy, where it was originally published. It could receive the same reaction here, for Ruesch's findings are shocking and deeply disturbing. A medical editor and novelist, Ruesch conducted his research throughout Europe and the U.S..... Medical knowledge, he claims, is not only not helped by laboratory experiments on animals but can actually be hindered.... Ruesch builds a well-documented argument and certainly a controversial one.

The *Chicago Tribune* had been so impressed by the advance copy that they sent their Bonn correspondent, Alice Siegert, to see me in Switzerland, to prepare a feature interview for the Sunday edition, April 2, 1978 (the eve of the book's publication). Siegert arrived, interviewed me, and telexed her story to Chicago on time — but it never appeared.

Bantam had also fallen into silence, which persisted long after publication. When I finally flew over to find out what was happening, the same people who had held long trans-Atlantic telephone conversations with me the year before had no time to answer a few simple questions in person:

1. Why had Brentano's, one of America's most famous bookstores (on Fifth Avenue, New York City), not received a single copy of *Slaughter*?

2. How many copies, of the 200,000 initially scheduled, had actually been printed?

3. Why were the principal antivivisection (AV) societies, which had ordererd several thousand copies and were running ads in the major newspapers, advised by Bantam not to advertise the book, as it would soon be out of print, permanently?

Bantam did not reply to my charges that they were deliberately suppressing the book — until three years later, when an executive stated that it had been allowed to go out of print "because it wasn't selling." Yet Bantam's Fall 1978 catalogue listed *Slaughter* among their bestsellers. How could a publisher of such prominence be so pressured?

A change of ownership had taken place at Bantam during the 18 months between acceptance of the manuscript and publication. Agnelli, the Italian automobile tycoon, had sold his majority stock in Bantam to Bertelsmann Corporation, a huge West German publishing conglomerate headed by Reinhard Mohn. Mohn's string of magazines made him dependent on advertising which, in Europe as in America, came largely from petrochemicals and derivatives: drugs, cosmetics, plastics, dyes, rubber, oil, etc. Earlier, Bertelsmann had turned down the German version of *Slaughter*. At the time, it had just been forced to withdraw *Weisse Magier* (White Magicians) by Kurt Bluchel, a shattering expose of West Germany's pharmaceutical industry. Bertelsmann had learned its lesson — no more attacks on the Drug Trust. Now it was in control of Bantam, which had been getting ready to publish *Slaughter* in an English language version in America.

So in our Western democracies, no public book-burnings are necessary; there are subtler and more effective ways to stifle information unfavorable to the industrial powers-that-be.

In England. Bantam had told me that they could not find a British publisher for *Slaughter* (although they had their own publishing firm in London). One of my British paperback publishers, Futura Publications Ltd., finally took on the project. *Slaughter* came out in Great Britain exactly a year after the Bantam edition had appeared. What followed was a rerun of the American experience, with some fascinating frills added by Dr. Christiaan Barnard, the famous heart surgeon from Cape Town.

The weekly *Observer* sent a reporter to interview me when I flew to London shortly after the publication, in April 1979. The article she showed me was supposed to run the following Sunday; it never appeared.

After Peter Grosvenor had given the book a big plug in his literary column in the daily *Express,* not another word appeared in the British press, which in the past had devoted quite a number of articles to my other books. Even without publicity and without advertising from the publisher, over 11,000 of the 20,000 copies printed were gone by the end of 1979, and almost 3,000 more went in the first two months of 1980 — this according to a letter (March 10, 1980) from Futura's director, Nicholas Chapman, which stated: "We find this a satisfactory rate of sales, and so, I hope, do you."

But just three weeks later, Futura suddenly withdrew all copies from the market and declared the book out of print. The publisher had thus committed a breach of contract, which contained a clause that the author had to be informed before any such action were taken, giving him the option to take over any remaining copies. Ignoring their own letter of March 10, Futura claimed that the book had been withdrawn because it wasn't selling. I informed the company that I considered this a fraudulent statement, but that I would buy up all remaining copies. Eventually, after threats of a lawsuit, Futura delivered 1,000 copies to my representative in Great Britain. They were unable to account for the rest, and they refused my request to buy the printing plates (I was already planning a reissue).

Contact with a British law firm convinced me that I could never afford the legal costs of suing a major publisher. So I sent out circulars which appeared in various British and American AV publications, appealing for funds to reprint the book.

Soon, a new obstacle appeared—

Dr. Christiaan Barnard. On October 30, 1980—two and a half years after *Slaughter* first appeared in English and six months after it had been withdrawn by Futura—a London law firm "representing Prof. Christiaan Barnard, the heart surgeon of international repute" informed me that their client felt libeled by statements in *Slaughter,* and that they would institute proceedings against me unless they received within a week my proposal for "payment of damages," a public apology and confirmation that all unsold copies of the book would be immediately withdrawn from circulation.

Similar notices were sent to the publisher and even the printers of the book. Futura's law firm wrote to me and asked: "Are you in a position to justify the allegations against Dr. Barnard that have been made?" I replied that I was prepared to back up what I had written. The main points concerning Barnard were:

1. A June 1977 article from *Blick*, quoted verbatim (p. 413) which alleged that Barnard had excised a baboon's heart without anesthetizing the animal (the same story was reported in other major European newspapers); and

2. The doubts I had expressed (pp. 24–25) about the

medical wisdom of some of Barnard's experiments on humans, and the questions they raised about his mental make-up.

In fact, I had merely reported what had already appeared in print by some of Barnard's medical colleagues. At that, I had been restrained in my selection of published comments:

I had *not* quoted Italy's weekly *Stop*, which, on July 7, 1977, reported that according to some of Barnard's colleagues, "he was on the verge of a psycho-physical collapse" at the time of his ill-advised experiment on a young Italian woman.

I had *not* cited a scathing article by Dr. Lothar Reinbach in West Germany's *Neue Revue*, which listed an international string of medical authorities who had publicly criticized Barnard's morality and medical judgment (one Nobel laureate speaking of "criminal operations").

I had *not* mentioned an interview in the Afrikaans-language Sunday newspaper *Rapport*, in which Barnard himself advocated that South Africa "should murder its enemies," and stated that he had given to his government a list of people who, in his opinion, should be "eliminated."

I sent all the evidence I had to Futura and informed them that I would be collecting more. In the face of such evidence, could any British judge have found me guilty of libel? Would Barnard even want to go through with a suit that would bring these things to light? Hearing nothing more about the case for several months, I assumed that Barnard had been convinced to drop his suit.

So I was astonished when I received a letter (March 2, 1981) from Futura's attorneys advising me that the publisher had agreed to make a public apology to Dr. Barnard, along with payment of £4,000 in damages and £1,000 in costs—and that Futura expected me to reimburse them for these amounts.

I answered that I would not reimburse them, and that I would consider any indemnity they might pay to Dr. Barnard as a defamation of my own professional integrity. I wanted a British court to judge the case on the merit of the evidence I could provide—most of which Futura's lawyers had not even asked to see before settling with Barnard's lawyers. But an open trial was exactly what the powers-that-be wanted to avoid.

It seems unlikely that Barnard had not heard of *Slaughter* before this time, and even less likely that he hadn't seen any of the uncomplimentary newspaper and magazine articles that had appeared about him, only some of which were mentioned in the book. Yet he did nothing until late 1980, with this threat of a libel suit against me. Could it be that Barnard was just being used to discourage other publishers from reissuing the book, by making it seem as if a lawsuit had been lost—which, in fact, had never taken place?

Indeed, the *Sunday Times* of South Africa reported that "Prof. Barnard was awarded a 'substantial' sum by the London High Court for allegations in a book." This was a total untruth. Since there was no trial, no court had awarded any sum to Barnard. Whatever payment may have been made represented a private settlement to which the publisher had unnecessarily agreed. The protests I addressed to the South African newspapers were ignored.

One aspect of the case deserves special note. The story about the unanesthetized baboon, which had appeared in *Blick*, had originated with Claus E. Boetzkes (a staff writer at Munich's *Abend-Zeitung*) who had interviewed a nurse who claimed to have been present at the operation. But in their October 30, 1980 letter to me, Barnard's lawyers wrote: "The baboon's heart was [removed] by another doctor in a separate operating theatre. Our client did not remove the baboon's heart, nor was he even present at that operation." Note that this does not dispute that the procedure took place as described. And whether or not Barnard did it himself, he was in charge over-all. In a way, it hardly matters. Worse things than surgery without anesthesia take place daily at the hands of vivsectors, and Barnard himself has described worse things, such as his

xii

attempt to reverse the birth process, a technique he tried on dozens of helpless pregnant dogs (pp. 25-27).

Now retired from the transplant business, Barnard's next venture was an endorsement of a Swiss clinic that specialized in a lucrative fad which also happens to involve cruelty to animals: obtaining live fetal cells, usually by Caesarian section from pregnant, unanesthetized ewes and cows, for implantation into sick or aging people. This medical nonsense—outlawed in America and branded as dangerous quackery in many countries—had been around for years. It was supposed to restore the sick to health and the old to youthful vigor. (However, it was not too successful in the case of Pope Pius XII, who died in 1958, shortly after receiving this "therapy.") Switzerland's largest-circulation periodical, *Der Beobachter*, reported (December 31, 1979):

> There have been cases of serious and even fatal diseases ensuing from the therapy of transplantation or injection of cells .... It is a doubtful procedure, based on the hope of naive people who age normally or are gravely ill .... If the benefits of these therapies for the patients are doubtful, the benefits for the doctors and clinics leave no doubt at all: one patient from Zurich was billed by her doctor 13,680 francs for 10 applications. (About $6,500.)

FOES OF ABOLITION—
EXPECTED AND UNEXPECTED

The futility and cruelty of vivsection as a method of medical research may surprise the average person, but medical professionals are less likely to fall for the propaganda about its alleged benefits to human health.

After *Slaughter* appeared, many medical doctors joined antivivisectionists in demanding a radical change in the current methods of research. But the book also outraged some of the very people and institutions who might have been expected to welcome it—for it attacked some vested interests that have developed in some of the animal protection and antivivsection societies.

For example, I state that vivisection can only be abolished by force of law, after its uselessness and horrors have been made public; and that it can never be eliminated, or even substantially reduced, by supporting what is called Alternative Research, a search for means other than vivisection to obtain the same information—unfortunately, the animal experimentation goes on unchecked during the search. Although societies which raise funds for alternative research may do so in good faith, the idea is based on a totally false notion: the alleged need for an alternative falsely implies that experiments with animals are necessary and scientifically valid.

Infiltration. Infiltration into animal protection groups is widespread. This may be surprising, but it should not be. Large corporations routinely practice political corruption and industrial espionage; those with a vested interest in vivisection infiltrate the protection societies to paralyze any concerted action by their members.

Sometimes, a physician writes an article denouncing vivisection. As this happens rarely, animal protection groups will rush to recruit him as a scientific advisor. In that capacity, as a medical authority who is also, supposedly, an outspoken antivivisectionist, he will typically say that vivisection is horrible and unnecessary *in many cases* —thereby implying, falsely, that it is necessary in other cases. How can the society then dispute its own "expert"?

Of course, not all scientific advisors are deliberate infiltrators from the opposition. But considering the large number of medical authorities who confirm the uselessness of all animal experimentation, one must question the competence or the sincerity of any scientific advisor who refuses to concede that vivisection could be abolished today without cost to human health.

On the Continent, in past decades, some self-styled AV societies were actually founded by vivisectionists who then, posing as animal defenders, collaborated with the official vivsectors to establish laws supposedly designed to regulate vivisection—and actually designed to protect the vivisectors.

After *Slaughter* appeared, I debated Dr. Joseph König, a well-known Viennese veterinarian, on Austrian television. President of Vienna's recently founded AV league, he turned out to be a vivisectionist, who had been instrumental in setting up the laws that for the first time legalized vivisection in Austria.

At an abolitionist rally in Great Britain, a doctor who had been hailed as an antivivisectionist asserted that some important medical discoveries came out of vivisection. When he was challenged to name just one such discovery—with the promise that he would be refuted on the spot—he said he couldn't, and that he would first have to search the medical literature. He was requested to do so and to put his findings in writing so that they could be answered in writing, for the edification of each member of the audience who had heard his claim. His answer: "Sorry, I have no time for that."

This professor had earned the respect of antivivisectionists with a book which denounced its horrors; he toured and gave lectures on the subject; he wrote articles for newspapers and pamphlets for AV societies; and he had won a reputation for sincerity by admitting to having conducted animal experiments at one time, and stating that all the suffering he had inflicted had taught him nothing. So when this repentant sinner claimed that vivisection was useful in some cases, how many in the audience would have reason to doubt his word?

That is why phony or incompetent medical "authorities" within the AV movement represent a greater obstacle to achieving abolition than undisguised vivisectors.

INFLUENCE OF *SLAUGHTER OF THE INNOCENT*

A book of this sort cannot hope to be a runaway bestseller; yet its influence has been felt in many ways.

In Italy. The book's initial publication caught the pharmaceutical-medical establishment by surprise, so large excerpts could appear in the nation's leading newspapers and magazines. The subject was debated on radio and television, and even in Parliament. When Rizzoli's papers and the state's radio and television stations turned silent, other papers and the free broadcasters kept public attention alive.

The mayor of Voghera in Northern Italy signed an ordinance that forbade, for the first time, the delivery of dogs from the city pound to experimental laboratories "in view of the recognized cruelty and uselessness of such experimentation"—and the ordinance listed the drugs named in *Slaughter* (p. 8) as examples of products proven harmful to humans after tests on animals had indicated they were safe. Similar ordinances followed in Milan and then in hundreds of other towns.

Italy's National AV League, founded as a direct result of the publication of *Slaughter*, pulled off an unprecedented coup. League president Luigi Macoschi, armed with testimony from a number of doctors at Italy's largest medical center (Careggi, Florence), got its entire vivisection laboratory closed down, and 32 well-known doctors indicted for cruelty and embezzlement. The three-billion lire (about $3 million) annual grant to the laboratory was cut off. (Experimentation at the Careggi lab has since resumed, but operations must be conducted under total anesthesia, and the AV League has permission to make unannounced inspections at any time.)

In Switzerland and West Germany. After the German version of *Slaughter* appeared in Spring 1978, many daily newspapers and illustrated weeklies revived the vivisection issue, though few dared to condemn it. An editor of Mohn's *Stern,* Germany's top illustrated weekly, obtained my collaboration and photographs for a lengthy article, promising that vivisection would be condemned and not condoned. Instead, the article concluded that the defeat of cancer, diabetes, and rheumatism depends on animal experimentation.

A German psychiatrist, Dr. Herbert Stiller, founded an abolitionist league, Doctors Against Animal Experimentation, in the Federal Republic. A similarly named league was founded in Switzerland by a general practitioner, Dr. Balz Widmer; he was surprised by the large number of medical colleagues who joined. *Slaughter* had apparently impressed a great many sincere and knowledegable physicians.

On the other hand, Switzerland's prosperous establishment press—a puppet moved by the Big Three drug manufacturers in Basel (Ciba-Geigy, Hoffman-La Roche, and Sandoz)—either followed the American example of ignoring the book entirely or excoriated it.

An interesting case was the Animal Protection League of Basel. Its president, Dr. Rudolph Schenkel, professor of ethology, criticized the revival of antivivisectionist feeling in Switzerland. Thereafter, the establishment press could write that "even the animal defenders disapprove of the antivivisectionists' views." A closer look at Schenkel revealed that:

1. His League had received a donation of 200,000 Swiss francs (about $100,000) from Hoffman-La Roche, "for its animal shelter"—with no questions asked.

2. His own wife was experimenting on animals in the endocrinology department of Ciba-Geigy.

When my CIVIS organization brought out these facts, Schenkel dropped all pretense of being an animal protectionist: at the next convention of Swiss animal protection groups (SPCAs), he argued that "since laboratory animals are a product of human enterprise, we can do with them as we please."

Meanwhile, Ciba-Geigy engaged another self-styled animal defender, a German journalist, Dr. Horst Stern, to make a film on its premises for the German state television network. Aware of the resurgent public concern about vivisection, the press campaign promised to reveal the full truth, praising Ciba-Geigy and Dr. Stern for their frankness and courage. But all the film series showed was the evisceration of a totally anesthetized rat, some sprightly cats snuggling up to an affectionate lab employee, a monkey convulsed by epileptic-like seizures, and some paraplegic patients whose only hope for recovery—so Dr. Stern told the viewers—lay in more animal experimentation.

In June 1980, Franz Weber, a Swiss journalist famous for his ecological and humane campaigns, founded a committee which included several doctors, and launched a drive to collect the 100,000 signatures required to insure a referendum demanding the abolition of all vivisection and all painful experiments on animals in Switzerland. His initiative was immediately disavowed by the country's central SPCA, which directed its more than 60 affiliated societies *not* to support the drive (because abolition would mean loss of jobs in animal experimentation!). The establishment press voiced doubts that so many signatures could be obtained.

Nevertheless, despite the hostility of the press and the central SPCA, 155,000 signatures were collected within a few months. It was the German version of *Slaughter* that had convinced Weber (and the doctors on his committee) that animal experimentaiton should—and could—be abolished at once, and he recommended the book as a reference. (The Swiss government has stalled in fixing a date for the referendum, and rumors are rife that the pharmaceutical-medical establishment is preparing a counter-proposal to forestall the referendum.)

"Charges must be pressed, not only against the manufacturers, but against the health authorities who have authorized the sale of drugs that cause human malformations and cancers after having been proved safe for animals. . ." (p. 409). This direction has been put into practice.

In March 1981, Mrs. Milly Schär-Manzoli, president of one of the most active Swiss AV leagues, the ATA of Lugano, brought criminal charges against Switzerland's Intercantonal Office of Drugs Control, analogous to the American Food and Drug Administration (FDA). Officially a government agency, it is dominated by the drug industry. Through lavish donations to medical faculties, the industry secures their obedient collaboration and designates the "experts" whose opinions are considered binding. This agency, in fact, allows the manufacturers to sell their drugs without liability—on the grounds that "all the prescribed tests had been undertaken" (i.e., meaningless animal tests).

The ATA has charged "multiple homicides due to the adoption of a method of research that a great number of responsible medical people have declared erroneous and that only have an alibi function." The damage caused by these drugs is real, not hypothetical, as demonstrated by the readiness of the manufacturers to pay huge sums in damages to the victims in order to avoid criminal prosecution. A legal system that allows monetary payment to replace criminal liability proves itself beholden to the industry's interests. It was on this basis that the first charges were brought by ATA against the Swiss health authorities; more charges are being prepared against the manufacturers. Soon, strong pressure was being applied on Mrs. Schär-Manzoli to withdraw her charges. Instead, she publicized them in a book meaningfully entitled *J'Accuse* (February 1982). Although the book was irrefutably documented, the Swiss establishment press either ignored it or ridiculed it.

The first half of the book is a factual listing of drugs that had all been safety-tested on animals but caused sickness or death to tens of thousands of consumers (an expansion of the list in *Slaughter,* p. 8). It condemns the pharmaceutical industry and the Swiss government, which allowed the continued sale of these products, some even after they had been ordered withdrawn in other countries because of their fatal effects.

The second half of *J'Accuse* is an equally harsh indictment of Switzerland's central SPCA, which uses its influence to favor the drug industry at the expense of the animals they are paid to protect. The president of the Swiss SPCA in Basel, Richard Steiner, and its general secretary, Hans Peter Haering, went to Lugano, where ATA is based, to find a district judge of their liking. They found one in Giuseppe Greppi. On the contention that these two "respected citizens" had been slandered in *J'Accuse*, Greppi issued a court order on April 20, 1982, ordering Mrs. Schär-Manzoli as the author, and ATA as the publisher, to withdraw all copies of the book from stores and newsstands, and prohibiting any further distribution, even privately or by mail—on penalty of a fine of up to 40,000 Swiss francs (about $20,000) and a possible jail sentence.

Whereupon, the ATA president distributed to the press and public a hastily assembled dossier entitled *The Fifth Column,* which contained photocopies of letters from SPCA officers and other principals in the case, documenting her charges; it also contained the Lugano court's injunction. This new publication unleashed Judge Greppi's anger. On May 13, he signed another injunction, imposing a fine of 10,000 Swiss francs on the ATA and its president, and ordering the seizure of all existing copies of *J'Accuse* and *The Fifth Column.*

In his own commentary, designed to justify this new order, Judge Greppi admitted the truth of ATA's charges: that the SPCA viewed vivisection as being beneficial to both medical research and the national economy (so that the continued sacrifice of animals was indispensable); that the SPCA had been opposing Franz Weber's drive for abolition; that dogs and cats had been shipped to Swiss laboratories from outside the country, by dealers connected with the SPCA; that dogs and cats had been shipped from SPCA shelters to unknown destinations. Greppi admitted all of this—and then came to the startling conclusion that it was all irrelevant, representing a series of "sporadic episodes or fortuitous coincidences" which the author of *J'Accuse* had "skillfully exploited" in order to discredit the SPCA and its directors.

This scandalously partisan injuction violated, among other things, the European Convention on Human Rights, which guarantees freedom of speech and of expression to all. An earlier case involving the Convention established a useful precedent on which to base an appeal In 1972, London's *Sunday Times* had started a series of articles on the Thalidomide horror (another instance of how the drug industry's stubborn adherence to animal tests results in human tragedy). But Distillers Company, the British licensee for this drug, quickly obtained an injunction prohibiting continuation of the series on the grounds that indemnity payments to the victims' families were then being negotiated. The journalists appealed the injunction but were rebuffed. So they took their case to the Convention. On April 26, 1979, the Strasbourg court decreed that the injunction of the British court had been illegal because it violated Article 10 of the European Convention, and the British government was ordered to pay an indemnity to the journalists that had been muzzled.

CIVIS will take the *J'Accuse* case to the Convention's Strasbourg court. What makes Greppi's decision particularly deplorable is that he acted without even troubling to read the book—he just followed the request of the SPCA. In fact, the Lugano press quoted him, in the course of the only hearing he had granted Mrs. Schär-Manzoli, as saying, "Who has time to read this sort of stuff?" The very fact that the judge's decision was of such obvious illegality demonstrates the tactics employed by the Drug Trust in its efforts to hide the truth, with the complicity of some animal protection groups and a servile, industry-beholden magistrature.

In Great Britain. The oldest British AV society, the London-based British Union for the Abolition of Vivisection (BUAV), tried to denigrate *Slaughter* in its magazine, but the effort backfired.

John Pitt, editor of BUAV's *Animal Welfare*, wrote that the book "destroyed any lingering illusion of credibility" for him when he read its description of the Horsley-Clarke stereotaxic device (p. 4), which is designed to facilitate the implantation of a cannula into an animal's brain. According to Pitt, the inventors were "distinguished antivivisectionist surgeons," and he went so far as to quote a description of the instrument as "a highly ingenious and valuable tool, a consummate technical achievement."

Actually, it was one of the worst torture devices ever created. From the *Journal of Physiology* (1954; Vol. 123, pp. 148–167), this description of fully conscious cats immobilized in the Horsley-Clarke device, each with a perforated skull and a cannula in the brain: the researchers noted "...retching, vomiting, defaecation, increased salivation, greatly accelerated respiration, spastic paresis or convulsions..." From the same journal (1965): "In unanesthetized cats, nicotine injected into the central ventricles through a chronically implanted Collison cannula produced various effects—blinking, narrowing of palpebral fissures, retching, vomiting, laboured respiration followed by panting and salivation...There was, further, torticollis [spasm of the neck muscles—H.R.], ataxia [loss of control over movements—H.R.], and blind charging sometimes terminating in clonic-tonic convulsion." This was the consummate technical achievement admired by John Pitt.

He failed to publish my documented reply and redoubled his attack on *Slaughter,* citing a vivisectionist science writer, J.H. Benson, who had written in the *New Scientist:* "It would be good to see no more volumes like *Slaughter of the Innocent,* a highly emotive attack on vivisection by someone who would like to see it abolished, not merely restricted." The *A* in BUAV stands for *Abolition.* Its constitution directs that it may not be connected with any group which seeks merely to reform. Therefore, Pitt's denunciation of *Slaughter* for advocating abolition is, to say the least, odd.

Many BUAV members had already read the Bantam edition of *Slaughter* long before the British Futura edition—and Pitt's attacks on it—appeared. They didn't like having their dues and donations squandered in an attempt to slander a book that had made thousands of converts to abolition the world over. Their indignation was such that at the following General Assembly an unprecedented event took place: instead of renewing the mandate of BUAV's long-time president, Mrs. Betty Earp, the members elected a new president. In subsequent assemblies, the executive committee also was renewed, Pitt was ousted, and BUAV eventually became the most militant of the British societies. However, the situation within each league can change, and what was true yesterday does not necessarily apply today, as this is written.

Animal Aid, Britain's youngest and fastest-growing antivivisection society, was not known to me when I listed the AV organizations in that country.

DEMAND FOR ACTION

The American societies I had listed in *Slaughter* (p. 420) are not the only existing ones. Unknown to me at the time were the very active Society for Animal Rights (421 So. State Street, Clarks Summit, PA 18411) and the Society Against Vivisection (P.O. Box 206, Costa Mesa, CA 92626).

Meanwhile, a growing number of Britons who are tired of waiting for the Home Office to take action, are supporting the Animal Liberation Front, a group of doubtful legality but unquestionably high morality. ALF-style raids on vivisection laboratories have been spreading to other countries, as well, including France, West German, Italy, America, and even staid old Switzerland. *The Animals Film,* a production depicting the activities of the Animal Liberation Front, created a furor when it was shown at the London Film Festival in 1981.

A great change is in the offing. People cannot and will not tolerate vivisection once they learn about it.

But as the movement for abolition grows, so does the opposition. Where intimidation and media hostility fail to silence critics, economic pressure is applied.

Morris Bealle found that he had to publish *The Drug Story* at his own expense and could distribute it only by mail.

Franz Weber is being harassed by Swiss internal revenue agents, a method used against critics of the American government during the Nixon administration.

Futura Publications is trying to get me to refund the amount they paid (unnecessarily) to Christiaan Barnard.

And the Lugano court is trying not only to muzzle but

also to crush financially Mrs. Schär-Manzoli and her sensationally successful ATA with a dictatorially imposed fine they cannot afford and the threat of imprisonment.

But meanwhile, CIVITAS Publications in the USA and the Buchverlag CIVIS in Switzerland will continue to supply unadulterated information about the vivisectionist organization and those who keep it alive.

Hans Ruesch
CIVIS
Klosters, Switzerland
February 1983

Part One

SCIENCE OR MADNESS?

A dog is crucified in order to study the duration of the agony of Christ. A pregnant bitch is disemboweled to observe the maternal instinct in the throes of pain. Experimenters in an American university cause convulsions in dogs and cats, to study their brain waves during the seizures, which gradually become more frequent and severe until the animals are in a state of continual seizure that leads to their death in 3 to 5 hours; the experimenters then supply several charts of the brain waves in question, but no idea how they could be put to any practical use.

Another team of "scientists" submits to fatal scaldings 15,000 animals of various species, then administers to half of them a liver extract that is already known to be useful in case of shock: As expected, the treated animals agonize longer than the others.

Beagles, well-known for their mild and affectionate natures, are tortured until they start attacking each other. The "scientists" responsible for this announce that they were "conducting a study on juvenile delinquency."

Exceptions? Borderline cases? I wish they were.

Every day of the year, at the hands of white-robed individuals recognized as medical authorities, or bent on getting such recognition, or a degree, or at least a lucrative job, millions of animals—mainly mice, rats, guinea-pigs, hamsters, dogs, cats, rabbits, monkeys, pigs, turtles; but also horses, donkeys, goats, birds and fishes—are slowly blinded by acids, submitted to repeated shocks or intermittent submersion, poisoned, inoculated with deadly diseases, disemboweled, frozen to be revived and refrozen, starved or left to die of thirst, in many cases after various glands have been entirely or partially extirpated or the spinal cord has been cut.

The victims' reactions are then meticulously recorded, except during the long weekends, when the animals are left unattended to meditate about their sufferings; which may last weeks, months, years, before death puts an end to their ordeal—death being the only effective anesthesia most of the victims get to know.

But often they are not left in peace even then: Brought back to life—miracle of modern science—they are subjected to ever new series of tortures. Pain-crazed dogs have been seen devouring their own paws, convulsions have thrown cats against the walls of their cages until the creatures collapsed, monkeys have clawed and gnawed at their own bodies or killed their cage mates.

This and much more has been reported by the experimenters themselves in leading medical journals such as Britain's *Lancet* and its American, French, German and Swiss counterparts, from which most of the evidence here presented derives.

But don't stop reading just yet—because the purpose of this book is to show you how you can, and why you should, put a stop to all that.

THE REFINEMENTS

Each new experiment inspires legions of "researchers" to repeat it, in the hope of confirming or debunking it; to procure the required tools or to devise new, "better" ones. Apart from a long series of "restraining devices," derived from the "Czermak Table," the "Pavlov Stock" and other classic apparatuses which decorate those pseudoscientific laboratories the world over, there exist some particularly ingenious instruments, usually named after their inventors.

One is the *Noble-Collip Drum,* a household word among physiologists since 1942, when it was devised by

two Toronto doctors, R. L. Noble and J. B. Collip, who described it in *The Quarterly Journal of Experimental Physiology* (Vol. 31, No. 3, 1942, p. 187) under the telltale title "A Quantitative Method for the Production of Experimental Traumatic Shock without Haemorrhage in Unanesthetized Animals": "The underlying principle of the method is to traumatize the animal by placing it in a revolving drum in which are projections or bumps . . . The number of animals dying showed a curve in proportion to the number of revolutions . . . When animals were run without having their paws taped they were found to give irregular results, since some would at first jump over the bumps until fatigued, and so protect themselves . . ."

There is the *Ziegler Chair,* an ingenious metal seat described in *Journal of Laboratory and Clinical Medicine* (Sept. 1952), invented by Lt. James E. Ziegler of the Medical Corps, U.S. Navy, Johnsville, Pa. One of the advantages claimed in the descriptive article for the apparatus is that "the head and large areas of the monkey's body are exposed and thus accessible for various manipulations." The uses of the chair include perforation of the skull with stimulation of the exposed cortex, implantation of cranial windows, general restraint for dressings, and as a seat for the monkey in various positions on the large experimental centrifuge for periods that may last uninterruptedly for years, until death.

There is the *Blalock Press,* so named after Dr. Alfred Blalock of the famed Johns Hopkins Institute in Baltimore, Md. Constructed of heavy steel, it resembles an ancient printing press. But the plates are provided with steel ridges that mesh together when the top plate is forced against the bottom plate. Pressure of up to 5,000 pounds is exerted by a heavy automobile spring compressed by tightening four nuts. The purpose is to crush the muscular tissue in a dog's legs without crushing the bone.

There is the *Collison Cannula,* designed to be implanted into the head of various animals to facilitate the repeated passage of hypodermic needles, electrodes, pressure gauges, etc., into the cranial cavity of the fully conscious animal—mostly cats and monkeys. The cannula is permanently fixed to the bone with acrylic cement anchored by four stainless-steel screws screwed into the skull. After undergoing this severe traumatic experience, the animal must be given at least a week to recover before the experiments proper can begin—as described in *Journal of Physiology,* October 1972. (In time, in an unsuccessful attempt to reject it, a purse of pus grows around the firmly anchored cannula and seeps into the victims' eyes and sinuses, eventually leading to blindness and death—sometimes one or two years later.)

There is the *Horsley-Clarke Stereotaxic Device,* so named after the two doctors who designed it to immobilize small animals during the implantation of the aforementioned cannula, for the traditional brain "experiments" that have never led to any other practical result than procuring the Nobel Prize for Prof. Walter R. Hess of Zurich University in 1949, and fat subsidies for various colleagues all over the world.

It may as well be pointed out right now that Nobel prizes in biology, physiology and medicine—as well as the various grants for "medical research"—are conferred on the recommendations of committees of biologists, physiologists and doctors, who have either been similarly favored by the colleagues they recommend, or who hope to be repaid in kind.

WHAT IS VIVISECTION?

The term vivisection "is now used to apply to all types of experiments on living animals, whether or not cutting is done." So states the Encyclopedia Americana (International Edition, 1974). And the large Merriam-Webster (1963): ". . . broadly, any form of animal experimentation, especially if considered to cause distress to the subject." Thus the term also applies to experiments done with the administration of noxious substances, burns, electric or traumatic shocks, drawn-out deprivations of food and drink, psychological tortures leading to mental imbalance, and so forth. The term was employed in that sense by the physiologists of the last century who started this kind of "medical research," and so it will be used by me. By "vivisection-ist" is usually meant every upholder of this method; by "vivisector" someone who performs such experiments or participates in them.

The "scientific" euphemism for vivisection is "basic research" or "research on models"—"model" being the euphemism for laboratory animal.

Though the majority of practicing physicians defend vivisection, most of them don't know what they are de-fending, having never set foot in a vivisection labora-tory. Conversely, the great majority of vivisectors have never spent five minutes at a sick man's bedside, for the good reason that most of them decide to dedicate them-selves to laboratory animals when they fail that most important medical examination, the one that would al-low them to practice medicine. And many more take up "research" because that requires no formal study-ing. Any dunce can cut up live animals and report what he sees.

The number of animals dying of tortures through the practice of vivisection is estimated at around 400,000 a day world-wide at the time of this writing, and is growing at an annual rate of about 5 percent. Those experiments are performed in tens of thousands of clinical, industrial and university laboratories. All of them, without exception, deny access to channels of in-dependent information. Occasionally, they take a jour-nalist, guaranteed "tame," on a guided tour of a laboratory as carefully groomed as one of Potemkin's villages.

Today we no longer torture in the name of the Lord, but in the name of a new, despotic divinity—a so-called Medical Science which, although amply demonstrated to be false, successfully uses through its priests and min-isters the tactics of terrorism: "If you don't give us plenty of money and a free hand with animals, you and your children will die of cancer"—well knowing that modern man does not fear God, but fears Cancer, and has never been told that most cancers, and maybe all, are fabricated through incompetence in the vivisection laboratories.

In the past, humanity was trained to tolerate cruelty

to human beings on the grounds of a widespread super-stition. Today humanity has been trained to tolerate cruelty to animals on the grounds of another superstition, equally widespread. There is a chilling analogy between the Holy Inquisitors who extracted confessions by torture from those suspected of witchcraft, and the priests of modern science who employ torture trying to force information and answers from animals. Meanwhile, the indifferent majority prefers to ignore what is going on around them, so long as they are left alone.

Vivisectors indignantly reject charges that their driving motive is avarice, ambition, or sadism disguised as scientific curiosity. On the contrary, they present themselves as altruists, entirely dedicated to the welfare of mankind. But intelligent people of great humanity—from Leonardo da Vinci to Voltaire to Goethe to Schweitzer—have passionately declared that a species willing to be "saved" through such means would not be worth saving. And furthermore there exists by now a crushing documentation that vivisection is not only an inhuman and dehumanizing practice, but a continuing source of errors that have grievously damaged true science and the health of humanity at large.

If such a sordid approach to medical knowledge were as useful as advertised, the nation with the highest life expectancy should be the United States, where expenditures for vivisection are a multiple of those in any other country, where more "life-saving" operations are performed, and whose medical profession considers itself to be the world's finest, besides being the most expensive. In fact, "Among the nations that measure average life expectancy, America ranks a relatively low 17th—behind most of Western Europe, Japan, Greece, and even Bulgaria," reported *Time* Magazine, July 21, 1975, after having reported on December 17, 1973, that "The US has twice as many surgeons in proportion to population as Great Britain—and Americans undergo twice as many operations as Britons. Yet, on the average, they die younger."

All this in spite of Medicare and Medicaid and the formidable therapeutic arsenal at the disposal of American doctors and patients.

Science or Madness? 7

MAN AND ANIMALS

Many of the medical men who have denounced the practice of vivisection as inhuman, fallacious and dangerous have been among the most distinguished in their profession. Rather than a minority, they ought to be called an élite. And in fact, opinions should not only be counted—they should also be weighed.

The first great medical man who indicated that vivisection is not just inhuman and unscientific, but that it is unscientific *because* it is inhuman was Sir Charles Bell (1774–1824), the Scottish physician, surgeon, anatomist and physiologist to whom medical science owes "Bell's law" on motor and sensory nerves. At the time the aberration of vivisection began to take root in its modern form, he declared that it could only be practiced by callous individuals, who couldn't be expected to penetrate the mysteries of life. Such individuals, he maintained, lack real intelligence—sensibility being a component, and certainly not the least, of human intelligence.

Those who hope to find remedies for human ills by inflicting deliberate sufferings on animals commit two fundamental errors in understanding. The first is the assumption that results obtained on animals are applicable to man. The second, which concerns the inevitable fallacy of experimental science in respect to the field of organic life, will be analyzed in the next chapter. Let us examine the first error now. Already the Pharaohs knew that to find out whether their food was poisoned they had to try it on the cook, not on the cat.

Since animals react differently from man, every new product or method tried out on animals must be tried out again on man, through careful clinical tests, before it can be considered safe. *This rule knows no exceptions.* Therefore, tests on animals are not only dangerous because they may lead to wrong conclusions, but they also retard clinical investigation, which is the only valid kind.

René Dubos, Pulitzer Prize-winner and professor of microbiology at the Rockefeller Institute of New York, wrote in *Man, Medicine and Environment* (Praeger, New York, 1968, p. 107): "Experimentation on man is usually an indispensable step in the discovery of new therapeutic procedures or drugs . . . The first surgeons who operated on the lungs, the heart, the brain were by necessity experimenting on man, since knowledge deriving from animal experimentation is never entirely applicable to the human species."

In spite of this universally recognized fact, not only the vivisectors, but also health authorities everywhere, having been trained in the vivisectionist mentality, which is a throwback to the last century, allow or prescribe animal tests, thus washing their hands of any responsibility if something goes wrong, as it usually does.

This explains the long list of products developed in laboratories, *and* presumed safe after extensive animal tests, which eventually prove deleterious for man:

Due to a "safe" painkiller named Paracetamol, 1,500 people had to be hospitalized in Great Britain in 1971. In the United States, Orabilex caused kidney damages with fatal outcome, MEL/29 caused cataracts, Metaqualone caused psychic disturbances leading to at least 366 deaths. Worldwide Thalidomide caused more than 10,000 deformed children. Chloramphenicol (Chloromycetin) caused leukemia, Stilbestrol cancer in young women. In the sixties a mysterious epidemic killed so many thousands of asthma sufferers in various countries that Dr. Paul D. Stolley of Johns Hopkins Hospital—who in July 1972 finally found the killer in Isoproterenol, packaged in England as an aerosol spray—spoke of the "worst therapeutic drug disaster on record." In the fall of 1975, Italy's health authorities seized the anti-allergic Trilergan, responsible for viral hepatitis. In early 1976 the laboratories Salvoxyl-Wander, belonging to Switzerland's gigantic Sandoz enterprise, withdrew their Flamanil, created to fight rheumatisms, but capable of causing loss of consciousness in its consumers—certainly one effective way to free them of all pains. A few months later, Great Britain's chemical giant, ICI

(Imperial Chemical Industries), announced that it had started paying compensations to the victims (or their survivors) of its cardiotonic Eraldin, introduced on the market after 7 years of "very intensive" tests; but hundreds of consumers had then suffered serious damages to the eyesight or the digestive tract, and 18 had died.

The Great Drug Deception by Dr. Ralph Adam Fine (Stein and Day, New York, 1972) is just one of the many books published in the last decade on the subject of dangerous and often lethal drugs, but it achieved no practical results. Health authorities, as well as the public, stubbornly refused to take cognizance of the fact that all those drugs had been okayed and marketed after having been proved safe for animals. Actually it is unfair to single out just a few dangerous drugs, since there are thousands of them.

Of course the fallacy works both ways, precluding the acceptance of useful drugs. There is the great example of penicillin—if we want to consider this a useful drug. Its discoverers said they were fortunate. No guinea pigs were available for the toxicity tests, so they used mice instead. Penicillin kills guinea-pigs. But the same guinea pigs can safely eat strychnine, one of the deadliest poisons for humans—but not for monkeys.

Certain wild berries are deadly for human beings, but birds thrive on them. A dose of belladonna that would kill a man is harmless for rabbits and goats. Calomelan doesn't influence the secretion of bile in dogs, but can treble it in man. The use of digitalis—the main remedy for cardiac patients and the savior of countless lives the world over—was retarded for a long time because it was first tested on dogs, in which it dangerously raises blood pressure. And chloroform is so toxic to dogs that for many years this valuable anesthetic was not employed on patients. On the other hand a dose of opium that would kill a man is harmless to dogs and chickens.

Datura and henbane are poison for man, but food for the snail. The mushroom *amanita phalloides,* a small dose of which can wipe out a whole human family, is consumed without ill effects by the rabbit, one of the most common laboratory animals. A porcupine can *eat* in one lump without discomfort as much opium as a human addict *smokes* in two weeks, and wash it down with enough prussic acid to poison a regiment of soldiers.

The sheep can swallow enormous quantities of arsenic, once the murderers' favorite poison.

Potassium cyanide, deadly for us, is harmless for the owl, but one of our common field pumpkins can put a horse into a serious state of agitation. Morphine, which calms and anesthetizes man, causes maniacal excitement in cats and mice, but dogs can stand doses up to 20 times higher than man. On the other hand, our sweet almonds can kill foxes and chickens, and our common parsley is poison to parrots.

Robert Koch's Tuberkulin, once hailed as a vaccine against tuberculosis because it cured TB in guinea pigs, was found later on to *cause* TB in man.

There are enough such instances to fill a book—all proving that it would be difficult to find a more absurd and less scientific method of medical research.

Moreover, the anguish and sufferings of the animals, deprived of their natural habitat or habitual surroundings, terrorized by what they see in the laboratories and the brutalities they are subjected to, alter their mental balance and organic reactions to such an extent that *any* result is a priori valueless. The laboratory animal is a monster, made so by the experimenters. Physically and mentally it has very little in common with a normal animal, and much less with man.

As even Claude Bernard (1813–1878), founder of the modern vivisectionist method, wrote in his *Physiologie opératoire* (p. 152): "The experimental animal is never in a normal state. The normal state is merely a supposition, an assumption." (*Une pure conception de l'esprit.*)

Not only do all animals react differently—even kindred species like rat and mouse, or like the white rat and brown rat—not even two animals of the identical strain react identically; furthermore, they may be suffering from different diseases.

To counter this disadvantage, somebody launched the idea of breeding strains of bacteriologically sterile laboratory animals—mass-born by Caesarean section in sterile operating rooms, raised in sterile surroundings and fed with sterile foods—to provide what the researchers called a "uniform biological material," free of diseases.

One delusion spawned another. Consistent failures made certain of those misguided scientists realize—some haven't realized it yet—that organic "material" raised under such abnormal conditions differs more than ever from normal organisms. Animals so raised never develop the natural defense mechanism, the so-called immunological reaction, which is a salient characteristic of every living organism. So it would be difficult to devise a less reliable experimental material. Besides, animals are by nature immune to most human infections —diphtheria, typhus, scarlet fever, German measles, smallpox, cholera, yellow fever, leprosy, and bubonic plague, while other infections, such as TB and various septicemias, take up different forms in animals. So the claim that through animals we can learn to control human diseases could seem a sign of madness if we didn't know that it is just a pretext for carrying on "experiments" which, however dangerously misleading for medical science, are either intimately satisfying for those who execute them, or highly lucrative.

The Swiss nation illustrates well to what extent the profit motive promotes vivisection: With a population of less than 6 million, Switzerland uses up annually many times as many laboratory animals as does all of Soviet Russia with its 250 million inhabitants, but where there is no money in the making of medicines.

EXPERIMENTAL RESEARCH

Experimental research has brought about all human inventions and most discoveries—except in medicine.

When speaking of modern invention, the first name that comes to mind is Thomas Edison. His case is particularly interesting because Edison attended school for only three months, whereafter he had to start making a living. Thus Edison was not a well-educated man. But it was just this lack of formal education—the lack of notions blindly accepted by most educated people, including the scientists, inculcated into them at an early stage by rote—that enabled Edison to accomplish the extraordinary series of inventions that altered man's way of life.

For instance, in trying to perfect the first electric light bulb Edison wanted a wire that would remain incandescent for a reasonable length of time. No university professor, no metallurgical expert was able to help him. So Edison resorted to pure empiricism. He started trying out *every type of wire* he could think of—including the least likely ones, such as, say, a thread of charred cotton. Over a period of years, Edison spent $40,000 having his assistants trying out one material after another. Until he found a wire that remained incandescent for 40 consecutive hours. It was a charred cotton thread . . .

However, experimental science had started modifying the face of the earth two and a half centuries before Edison went about lighting up the nights. The beginning took place in 1637 with the publication of that *Discourse on Method* by Descartes which taught man a new way of thinking, and led to modern technology. But, who could foresee in this New World being born in the midst of widespread enthusiasm the danger of an exclusively mechanistic knowledge? Hardly Descartes, who was himself a negation of the arts and all human sentiments—his private life was a failure—and who believed in a mechanistic biology, establishing the basis for what may well be mankind's greatest error.

In his thirst for knowledge through experimentation, Descartes also practiced vivisection, making it a symbol of "progress" to succeeding mechanists. Descartes himself, of course, had learned nothing from this practice, as demonstrated by his statement that animals don't suffer, and that their cries mean nothing more than the creaking of a wheel. Then why not whip the cart instead of the horse? Descartes never troubled to explain that. But he gave as "proof" of his theory the fact that the harder one beats a dog, the louder it howls. Through him a new science was born, deprived of wisdom and humanity, thus containing the seed of defeat at birth.

Rid at last of the yoke of medieval obscurantism, man went all out for experimentation. The sensational conquests of technology led some doctors of limited mental power to believe that experimental science would bring about equally sensational results in their own field; that living organisms react like inanimate matter, enabling medical science to establish absolute, mathematical rules. And today's vivisectionists still cling to that belief, no matter how often it has proved tragically wrong.

The experiment Galileo made from Pisa's leaning tower, demonstrating that a light stone and a heavy stone fall at one and the same speed, established an absolute rule because it dealt with inanimate matter. But when we deal with living organisms, an infinity of different factors intervene, mostly unknown and not entirely identifiable, having to do with the mystery of life itself. It is difficult to disagree with Charles Bell that callous, dehumanized individuals are the least likely ever to penetrate these mysteries.

In his book *La sperimentazione sugli animali* (2nd ed., 1956,), Gennaro Ciaburri, one of Italy's antivivisectionist doctors, provides among many others the following insight: "Normally, pressure on one or both eyeballs will slow down the pulse . . . This symptom has opened up a vast field for vivisection. Experimenters squashed the eyes of dogs to study this reflex, to the point of discovering that the heartbeat was slowing down—owing to the death of the animal . . ."

That such vivisectionist divertissements achieve nothing more than to provide a measure of human stupidity, has been declared repeatedly. The famed German doctor Erwin Liek—of whom the major German encyclopedia, *Der Grosse Brockhaus,* says, "he advocated a medical art of high ethical level, which takes into consideration the patient's psyche"—gives us the following information:

"Here is another example that animal experimentation sometimes can't answer even the simplest questions.

I know personally two of Germany's most authoritative researchers, Friedberger of the Kaiser Wilhelm Institute for Nutritional Research and Prof. Scheunert of the Institute of Animal Physiology at Leipzig. Both wanted to investigate the simple question as to whether a diet of hardboiled eggs or of raw eggs is more beneficial. They employed the same animals: 28-day-old rats. Result: over an observation period of three months, Friedberger's animals prospered on a diet of raw eggs, while the control animals which got hardboiled eggs pined, lost their hair, developed eye troubles; several died after much suffering. At Scheunert's I witnessed the identical experiments, with exactly opposite results." (From *Gedanken eines Arztes,* Oswald Arnold, Berlin, 1949.)

Of course any disease deliberately provoked is unlike any disease that arises spontaneously.

Let's take the case of arthritis, a degenerative disease causing painful inflammation of the joints, and bringing about lesions or destruction of the cartilage. Overeating is one of its causes, regular exercise at an early stage of the malady is the only reliable cure we know to date. And yet the drug firms keep turning out "miracle" remedies based on animal tortures: mere palliatives that mask the symptoms, reducing the pain for a while but in the meantime ruining the liver or the kidneys or both, thus causing much more serious damage than the malady they pretend to cure—and eventually aggravating the malady.

While no solution to any medical problem has ever been found through animal experimentation, so on the other hand one can prove practically anything one sets out to prove using animals, as in the following case reported in the monthly *Canadian Hospital* (Dec. 1971): In the Montreal Heart Institute are thousands of cages full of rats used to determine the effects of specific diets on animals. One of the "researchers" in charge, Dr. Serge Renaud, "took one of the animals from its cage; its hair had fallen out; its arteries had hardened and it was ripe for a heart attack. This rat, with a normal life span of two years, was old at two months. 'We kill them with pure butter,' said Dr. Renaud."

So butter is poison! Science or idiocy?

Sometimes it is neither one nor the other, but a highly profitable business gimmick, as the cyclamate and the saccharin cases demonstrate. In the mid-sixties the new artificial sweeteners known as cyclamates had become a huge commercial success because they cost 5 times less than sugar and had 30 times the sweetening power, besides being non-fattening. So the American Sugar Manufacturers Association set about financing "research" on cyclamates, as did the sugar industries in some other countries. To "prove scientifically" what the sugar industry was determined to prove from the start—that cyclamates should be outlawed—hundreds of thousands of animals had to die painfully.

They were force-fed such massive, concentrated doses of the product that they were bound to become seriously sick, developing all sorts of diseases, including cancer. To consume the equivalent amount of artificial sweetener a human would have to drink more than 800 cans of diet soda every day of his life. In 1967 the British Sugar Bureau, a public relations organization set up by the sugar industry, was pressuring members of Parliament about the deadly dangers of cyclamates. The same was happening in the United States—the sugar lobby besieging the politicians. I am not saying that money changed hands, because I don't know. All I know is that in 1969 both the American and British Governments banned the sale of cyclamates. It wasn't banned in Switzerland, however, where there is no powerful sugar lobby, but a powerful chemical lobby instead. In Switzerland, cyclamates are still on sale, 8 years after they were taken off the shelves in America and Britain.

Then there was a repeat performance of the whole three-ring scientific circus in 1976 in regard to saccharin—and once more uncounted thousands of in-

nocent animals were caught in the crossfire of
embattled industrial giants.

*   *   *

Financed by a grant of $641,224 for 1971–72, re-
searchers at the Center for Prevention and Treatment
of Arteriosclerosis at Albany Medical College experimented with an initial group of 44 pigs. One by one
these animals were made to die of induced heart disease resulting from arteriosclerosis. Using an extreme
form of diet known to be injurious to the vascular
system, the process was further speeded up by X
rays that damage the coronary arteries. Personnel
were always on hand when an animal dropped dead;
they hoped to pinpoint precisely what happens to
the heart of a pig at this critical moment. Such, in
essence, was a report in the *Times Union* of Buffalo,
New York, Oct. 24, 1971.

Except for the money angle, the whole thing appears
sophomoric. Yet similar programs utilizing various
experimental animals were in progress at the same
time at 12 other medical institutions all over the U.S.
All of them proved adept at creating a wide range of
diseases in animals, but were notable failures at coming up with a solution. Research of this nature has
been practiced for decades, and millions of animals
have died in the process, while the cures are still pies
in the sky.

Today's pseudoscience proceeds similarly on all
fronts. In the "fight against epilepsy," monkeys are
submitted to a series of electroshocks that throw them
into convulsions, until they become insane and manifest symptoms that may outwardly resemble epileptic
fits in man—frothing at the mouth, convulsive movements, loss of consciousness, and such. Obviously the
monkeys' fits have nothing to do with human epilepsy,
as they are artificially induced, whereas man's epilepsy arises inside from reasons deeply rooted in the
individual's organism or psyche, and not from a series of electroshocks. And by trying out on these
insane monkeys a variety of "new" drugs—always the
same ones, in different combinations—vivisectionists

promise to come up with "a remedy against epilepsy" some time soon, provided the grants keep coming. And such methods sail today under the flag of science —which is an insult to true science, as well as to human intelligence. Small wonder that epilepsy is another disease whose incidence is constantly increasing.

* * *

One of the latest shifts devised by medical research to make quick money is the invention of drugs that promise to prevent brain hemorrhages. How is it done? Easy. By now any attentive reader can do it. Take rats, dogs, rabbits, monkeys, and cats, and severely injure their brains. How? Our laboratory "Researchers" brilliantly solve that problem with hammer blows. Under the broken skulls, the animals' brains will form blood clots, whereafter various drugs are administered to the traumatized victim. As if blood clots due to hammer blows were the equivalent of circulation troubles which have gradually been building up in a human brain that is approaching the natural end of its vital arch, or has grown sclerotic through excessive intake of alcohol, food, tobacco, or from want of exercise, of fresh air, or mental activity. Everybody knows what to do to keep physically and mentally fit. But it is less fatiguing to swallow, before each rich meal, a couple of pills, and hope for the best.

Anybody suggesting that these pills are of no use would be in bad faith. They *are* useful: They help increase the profits of the world's most lucrative industry—and further ruin the organism, thus creating the necessity for still more "miracle" drugs.

THE SOLID GOLD SOURCE

The cancer bogy has become the vivisectionists' most powerful weapon. Dr. Howard M. Temin, a well-known scientist, said in a recent address at the University of Wisconsin that scientists are also interested in money, power, publicity and prestige, and that "some promise quick cures for human diseases, provided they are given more power and more money." He added that there is a tremendous advantage in the assertion that "If I am given 500 million dollars for the next five years, I can cure cancer," pointing out that if a rainmaker puts the time far enough in the future, no one can prove him wrong.

But so far as cancer is concerned, the rain may not come in our lifetime. It is obvious to anybody who has not been brainwashed in the western hemisphere's medical schools that an experimental cancer, one caused by grafting cancerous cells into an animal, or in other arbitrary ways, is entirely different from cancer that develops on its own and, furthermore, in a human being. A spontaneous cancer has an intimate relationship to the organism that developed it, and probably to the mind of that organism as well, whereas cancerous cells implanted into another organism have no "natural" relationship whatsoever to that organism, which merely acts as a soil for the culture of those cells.

However, the ably exploited fear of this dread disease has become an inexhaustible source of income for the researchers. In the course of our century, experimental cancer has become a source of solid gold without precedent.

*   *   *

It all started in France in 1773, when the Academy of Science in Lyon offered a prize for the best original essay on the subject: "What is Cancer?" The prize went to Bernard Peyrilhe, who described the first cancer experiment on record in which he inoculated a dog with "cancer fluid" from a breast cancer patient.

In the more than two centuries since then, during which not millions but billions of animals of every known species have been sacrificed to cancer research, the so-called scientists have not only failed to come up with any solution, but the problems have multiplied, the doubts proliferated. The results add up to the greatest confusion medical "science" has ever been able to create.

We know that filling our lungs with smoke, our stomachs with chemicals, and subjecting our tissues to various irritants can lead to cancer. And we know that carnivorous animals have short bowels, designed to expel the digested meat promptly, whereas man has the long bowels of herbivores, in which meat and animal fats stagnate causing toxic fermentations which are most likely responsible for the steady increase of the cancers of the lower bowels, as demonstrated by the sharp rise of such cancers among mainly vegetarian populations who have suddenly taken up meat consumption. We know that an exclusive meat diet is deleterious and in the long run deadly for man, while an exclusive vegetable diet is not, as many of the Japanese Olympic medalists who were vegetarians have demonstrated.

Indeed, we know a great many things about cancer, as about other diseases. This knowledge was acquired through clinical observation, without animal experiments. But there is little money in this. Extensive experimentation is a prerequisite for securing grants.

A few years ago, the Sloan-Kettering Institute decided to "solve the cancer problem once and for all" and tested no less than 40,000 different substances and combinations on millions of animals, with new methods —and the usual results.

At irregular intervals, every country in the world is shaken by a report that the nation's researchers have found a "cure" for cancer. So in September 1972, according to a United Press dispatch, Michael Hanna, Jr., immunologist at National Laboratory of Oak Ridge, Tennessee, had "definitely" found a cancer cure. Eventually the scientists found out once more that human beings don't react quite like guinea pigs.

In 1973, the American Cancer Society, a private organization, awarded $23,052,737 to 525 applicants.

But there has never been any lack of money in the fight on cancer—only a lack of brains. In England, many years ago, assurance was given in the House of Commons that if ever money was needed to do *effective* research on cancer, such money would be forthcoming. Mr. Molson went on record as saying

(April 29, 1952): "At the present time there is no reason to suppose that greater expenditure of money would produce greater results."

For 1976, the new French Minister for Health, Madame Simone Veil, decided to reduce her government's subsidies to scientists, with a special view to cancer research. There were loud outcries of despair and dismay from the science corner, but Simone Veil remained unflustered: "You can well mention the hundreds of millions of dollars given to the American National Cancer Institute, but they have brought no results. The deaths by cancer have not diminished—on the contrary. We are not willing to spend any more money on futile research, but only on prevention: We campaign against alcohol, for early diagnoses, for improvement of housing. This is the kind of support the nation's health can expect from this Ministry."

And in fact it doesn't seem far-fetched to regard all the "Defeat Cancer" drives undertaken by public and private organizations as evidence of ignorance, if not outright fraud.

An essay in *Newsweek* (Jan. 26, 1976) titled "What Causes Cancer?" reported what that magazine apparently believed to be big news: "Cancer may be a man-made disease." The article went on to say: "Already the World Health Organization estimates that up to 85 percent of all cancer cases are a direct result of exposure to environmental factors of one kind or another—in many instances almost fatalistically self-inflicted by such habits as overeating, smoking, overdrinking and excessive exposure to sunlight and dangerous chemicals in the factories . . . Despite all the warnings, the majority of Americans continue to indulge themselves in the potentially harmful pleasures that their opulent society provides, and so far they are apparently content to take the perils along with the pleasures. 'Right now we've decided that this is the way we want to live and die,' says Dr. David Baltimore, who won a 1975 Nobel Prize for basic cancer research."

Basic cancer research, of course, consists mostly of inflicting cancer upon millions of scapegoats, justifying the expenditures of huge grants—a sizeable portion of which may go into the indulgences mentioned above.

On March 26, 1975, an article by the NEA-London Economist News Service, titled "Is Cancer Research Worth Cost?" appeared on the editorial page of *The Galveston Daily News*. It said in part:

"The sums that are being spent [on cancer research] are enormous—$600 million in the present financial year—and the fear of getting the disease universal. One million Americans have it. Recently Dr. James Watson, who is listened to because he helped to discover the molecular structure of life's genetic material, derided the national cancer program as a fraud. Dr. Watson said that the government's newly created cancer research centers around the country are institutions that are 'starting out lousy and will stay lousy.' "

Dr. James Watson is thus one more medical authority who recognizes the fraudulent motives behind the cancer research, but apparently fails to understand—or to denounce—what makes the fraud possible: animal experimentation, which has been the backbone of all cancer research uninterruptedly over the past 200 years.

We shall return to the cancer question toward the end of this treatise, which unfortunately has bad news for us all.

OPERATION SUCCESSFUL, PATIENT DEAD

News of heart transplants appears to be falling into the same oblivion as the grafts of monkey glands by which Prof. Serge Voronoff had promised to restore youthful sexuality to the aged—a bit of news that shook the world in the twenties no less than the announcement of Christiaan Barnard's first heart transplant less than fifty years later. One of America's leading heart surgeons, Michael DeBakey, announced a few years ago that he was giving up heart transplants entirely, because "the results obtained don't justify by far the sacrifices made." This was an elegant euphemism for failure, without having to specify who he considered to have been sacrificed—the patients who had been deluded and made to suffer additional pains, or the thousands of dogs on which the experimenters had exercised their transplant skill.

The failure of heart transplants had been clearly predicted. Many surgeons could have performed a heart transplant before Christiaan Barnard. If they hadn't done so it was not for technological reasons. But because of that powerful defense mechanism, the immunological reaction, with which all organisms are endowed by nature. This mechanism opposes the entry of any foreign material, including organs and foreign tissues. As a result, tissues transplanted into a body from any other organism (except sometimes an identical twin) are rejected by the host: The grafted tissue dies, killed by the body's immunological reaction. (Corneal transplants are an exception; that part of the eye has scant blood supply, so only small amounts of the complex, and to us almost totally unknown, substances produced by the body's defense mechanism reach it; thus survival of cornea grafts is quite common.)

To prevent the rejection of a transplanted organ, various ways have been devised to suppress the immunological reaction; in other words, to thwart the body's natural power to eliminate any foreign matter —thus enabling the body to destroy harmful microbes and stay healthy. It is when the natural immunological reactions are weakened that diseases manifest themselves, and infectious bacteria may gain the upper hand and kill the organism. So even minor and trivial infections like herpes simplex (the blisters often caused by a common cold) may prove fatal in a patient in whom the immunological reaction has been suppressed, for this interference opens the door to *all* diseases, including cancer.

British Dr. H. M. Pappworth states clearly in his now famous *Human Guinea Pigs* (Pelican Books, London, 1969, p. 302): "Immunosuppressive drugs may cause cancer—five cases have been recorded of cancer developing later in recipients of kidney transplants. It is significant that in each case the tumor symptoms started a considerable time after the transplant. Even more significant, and virtually eliminating the possibility of mere coincidence, is the fact that in all five cases the cell structure of the tumor was the same (malignant lymphoma)."

It is not generally known that Philip Blaiberg, Barnard's most famous heart transplant patient, who survived for 18 months, had two severe bouts of heart failure, a severe episode of jaundice due to drugs, and meningitis due to lowered resistance after the transplant, as reported in *Hospital Medicine,* July 1969. No one can say whether Blaiberg would not have survived just as long without the transplant. Surely he would have suffered less. Says Dr. Pappworth: "I am far from convinced that this state of affairs is any more tolerable to the patient than the disease for which the transplant was done."

The American College of Surgeons/National Institutes of Health's organ-transplant registry studied more than 8,000 transplant patients and found 77 cases of cancer, 17 of which were a bone-marrow malignancy called reticulum cell sarcoma. Significantly, that disease occurs about 100 times more frequently in transplant patients than it does in members of the general population, according to a report by doctors at the Medical College of Virginia of the Virginia Commonwealth University (*Time,* Mar. 19, 1973). Immunosuppression, presently the mainstay of transplant surgery, reduces the body's ability to resist both infection and cancer.

Thus medical research once more is faced with a self-created dilemma—another Hydra's head that presents new problems whenever we think we have resolved the preceding ones. The transplant surgeons regularly boast that the transplant was successful, and that the patient died from other causes, such as pneumonia or kidney failure. That is grossly misleading. The complications are an inevitable consequence of the immunosuppressive treatment designed to prevent rejection. Responsible for this new aberration of modern medicine were the experiments Christiaan Barnard had conducted on dogs: Far more resistant than man, those dogs aroused hopes in Barnard, and in his hapless patients, that the facts proved unjustified.

"The public is being misled into believing that the problem of rejection either has been solved or will be solved in a very near future," wrote Dr. Pappworth. "This is wishful thinking . . ." (p. 303) And further on: "No doctor, however experienced, can balance precisely the expected period of survival without transplant against the period of the apparent acceptance of the transplant before it is finally rejected . . . The public should know that transplant surgery never cures the original disease and never makes the recipient into a healthy person . . . No organ of the body exists in complete isolation, independent of other organs. For example, a patient who undergoes a heart transplant because of coronary disease is likely to have incipient vascular disease of other organs such as the kidneys."

Dr. Pappworth further states: "All transplant surgery is a confession of failure, of unsuccessful early diagnosis and treatment. Would it not be wiser to spend the energy and money involved on research into the early diagnosis, prevention and better treatment of disease?"

"Money involved on research" means, of course, money spent on vivisection, mostly. And who would want to renounce *that?*

After Christiaan Barnard's 11th heart transplant, a spokesman for the South African Medical Association declared that its members "were having second thoughts about heart transplants." (*Messaggero,* Rome, Dec. 13, 1973.) And when, a year later, Barnard implanted a second heart next to a patient's existing heart, making him the first human being with two hearts, disapproval from his colleagues became louder. "A civilized world should not stand for this," Prof. Guido Chidichimo, heart surgeon-in-chief at Rome's San Camillo Hospital, was quoted as saying by Rome's daily *Messaggero* (Nov. 26, 1974). "What sense does it make to implant a heart in a poor devil who hopes for resurrection and then is forced to resign himself to a fate that perhaps he had already accepted? This is a juggler's stunt. It's cruelty without bounds. It's cynicism."

It was simply the result of two centuries of stolid acceptance of the experimental method, begun on helpless animals and increasingly extended to human beings. In spite of widespread, authoritative disapproval, transplant "experiments" on animals continue the world over, although they are nothing but laboratory exercises, in which teachers try to display before awed students their alleged surgical skill. The result can regularly be summed up in the immortal phrase of the legendary German surgeon, "The operation was a success, but the patient died."

Less than four months after the operation, the first man with two hearts was dead. The news was withheld for over a week. How much he suffered we were never told. All we learned was the surgeon's predictable alibi, from an article in *Time* (May 5, 1975):

"Barnard is still satisfied that his surgical spectacular was a success. The death, he explained last week, was not directly related to the operation. Taylor died not because his body rejected the new heart but as a result of a blood clot in his lung."

It was announced that same autumn that Barnard was going to use live baboons for "storing" human hearts to have them "ready" whenever another transplant would be undertaken.

For men like Christiaan Barnard, experimentation on men and animals would seem to have become a hypnotic preoccupation, a paranoid fixation, that he would perform at any cost or personal sacrifice, and without any rational basis. This is my belief, especially after reading Barnard's autobiography, *One Life* (Howard Timmins, Cape Town, 1969).

Barnard's claim that an experiment he performed using more than forty dogs and their puppies led to a new life-saving technique appears totally unconvincing, not only to me but also to surgeons I asked to read that account. Apparently, Barnard merely succeeded, like so many other experimenters, in duplicating in an animal a diseased condition that occurs in humans—though in man it is not caused by the arbitrary surgical intervention to which Barnard subjected his dogs. The condition known as intestinal atresia.

Some babies are born with a gap in the bowel; there is an obstruction, and unless this condition can be quickly corrected they die. Barnard set out to reproduce this condition in dogs, wanting to prove a widely held theory that the gap in the bowel was due to the fact that in the fetus the blood supply to that segment of the bowel was cut off. To prove this point, Barnard set off to block off surgically the blood supply to a segment of the bowel in dogs before birth.

As he puts it in his book, "I had to open up a pregnant dog and expose its uterus. After that, the uterus had to be opened and the puppy removed. Then the puppy had to be opened up in order to tie off a portion of blood supply to the bowel—and so create an infarct which would disappear and create a gap, proving that intestinal atresia came from this defect. Then the whole process had to be done in reverse— the fetus closed and replaced in the uterus, then the uterus closed and replaced in the dog and, finally, the dog itself closed up. All of it had to be done in a way which would not kill or abort the fetus, allowing for its natural growth in the womb until the day of birth —hopefully with a bowel defect."

It seems quite obvious to me that if the blood supply is interrupted to any part of the fetus, that part will fail to develop. But then I am a layman and not a vivisectionist doctor.

Barnard could not finish the operation with the first half dozen dogs. Upon opening the uterus the fluid escaped, the uterus contracted, and the puppy could not be returned because there was no room for it. So Barnard devised for his next operation a skillful way to do the intervention without removing the fetus, but extracting the uterus through a long incision in the mother, for easier handling. Thus, after obstructing the blood flow to a section of the small intestine of the fetus, the uterus was sutured and replaced.

How the bitch felt after she awoke from all this, with ten more days of pregnancy before her, seemed clearly unimportant to the surgeon, who merely stated that "we waited anxiously for birth." Vast was his surprise when the bitch finally brought forth her manhandled puppy—and promptly ate it up, before Barnard could get to it and cut it open to see whether the experiment had worked.

"Impossible!" cried he, according to his own account, when his assistant told him the bad news. "Dogs aren't cannibals."

But even dogs can become cannibals after the experimenters are through with them—probably for the same reason some baboon mothers decapitate their babies on the way to your laboratories at Groote Schuur.

Barnard added a complaint: "We had to be opposed by the mother, too. I could see her doing it: the tongue licking its offspring one by one until it felt one with the black silk stitches. Sensing something was wrong, the mother had eaten it up—rather than allow it to take milk into a blocked intestine and eventually die."

After 43 such experiments Barnard finally obtained a live puppy with a devascularized bowel as it appears in newborn infants suffering from intestinal atresia. But he had no suggestions to offer as to how such malformations could be prevented. (The strict avoidance of laboratory-perfected drugs may be one step in the right direction, I daresay.) And when surgeons sometimes succeed in eliminating the defective segment in a newborn's bowel and joining together the healthy parts, they did not learn how to do it from Barnard's experiments related above. None the less, on seeing that he had been able at last to produce a defective puppy, Barnard declared (p. 157): "It was the promise of life for thousands of babies."

THE PORK BARREL

For all its inconceivable savagery and utter uselessness, animal experimentation keeps running wild in the medical schools of the so-called civilized world, increasing from year to year. How is it possible?

The foremost reason is pecuniary gain. Vivisection is the type of "research" that enables "scientists" to obtain huge subsidies from government and private sources on the assumption—plausible to the incompetent—that the more animals used in an experiment the more reliable the results may be.

Let us examine the consequence of this assumption in the light of a single case—the experiment involving 15,000 animals scalded to death, to retest the already well known effectiveness of a liver extract for the victims of shock.

The experiment was reported in two standard medical publications, *Journal of the American Medical Association* (July 10, 1943) and *Journal of Clinical Investigation* (Sept. 1944), by Myron Prinzmetal, Oscar Hechter, Clara Margoles and George Feigen, of the research laboratory of Cedars of Lebanon Hospital and the University of Southern California Medical School. It was known in advance that practicing physicians had tried and approved the liver extract, but the afore-named wanted to affirm in their report that they had used "a sufficient number of animals to yield results of statistical significance."

Thus they disclosed their own ignorance of elementary statistics. It is a statistical fact that if you flip a coin 6 times, it may come up heads all 6 times. But if you go on flipping, it will start to come up tails. If you continue flipping up to a total of some 300 times, the "law of averages" will definitely assert itself. This law operates in such a fashion that if you go on flipping a coin, heads will turn up half the time within very narrow limits. At 150 flips or at 1,500 flips the 50:50 ratio will still be off by only a few flips, getting ever closer to the ideal difference between heads and tails of 0.5. In other words, the law of averages is a mathematical law, not theoretical fancy. At 500 flips, the heads-tails average is close to 50:50, and stays so even if one goes on flipping to a total of 1,000 or 10,000 or 100,000. In short, assuming that a point is worth proving statistically, it can be thus proven in fairly short order.

Now a question arises: Is it possible that not one among the numerous "scientists" who knew about this giant experiment—which lasted a number of years—was aware of this simple rule known to most schoolboys? And permitted not 50, not 150, not 1,500, but 15,000 animals to be scalded to death in order to prove a point already known? Everything is possible. But one thing is sure: The sacrifice of 15,000 animals makes it much easier to explain where a large sum of money went than if only 50 animals had been used.

In fact it wouldn't be possible to spend the billions of dollars the U.S. government gives to medical research at home and abroad if the researchers didn't constantly think up new experiments, besides repeating the old classical standbys. In other words, *first* there is the money, *then* means must be found to spend it.

This explains why some of the American "studies" have included: 1) facial expressions; 2) the anal temperatures of the Alaskan sled dog; 3) the nervous system of the Chilean squid; 4) the dental arches of Australian aborigines. Bilking the taxpayer, the U.S. government granted $100 million in 1940 for "research" at home and abroad, $1 billion in 1949, $8 billion in 1960, $15 billion in 1970—and an estimated $25 billion in 1975—and the temperature keeps rising. Here's how some of this tax money was squandered:

$30,000 to turn rats into alcoholics, under the pretext of curing human alcoholism, although in man alcoholism has deep psychological roots, whereas rats are by nature well-balanced teetotalers.

$1,000,000 to study the mother love of monkeys.

$500,000 to study the love life of the flea.

$148,000 to find out why chickens grow feathers.

$1,000,000 to study the mating call of the mosquito.

$102,000 to study the effects of gin compared to the effects of tequila administered to Atlantic fish.

$500,000 to find out why monkeys clench their jaws in anger. The money grant for this idiocy went to Dr. Ronald Hutchinson of Kalamazoo State Hospital in Michigan, whom Senator William Proxmire consequently proposed for the Golden Fleece Award of the month (*Congressional Record,* Apr. 18, 1975).

$525,000 in grants from the National Institutes of Health (between 1950 and 1963) to help Dr. S. C.

Wang of New York's Columbia University induce vomiting in dogs and cats by various methods (swinging, drugs, electrical stimulation of the brain, etc.) in order to find out the differences in the vomiting mechanism between the two species.

$92,000,000 for the costliest failure of them all, when Bonny, a small chimpanzee, was launched on an abortive space flight. No less than the National Aeronautical and Space Administration planned and conducted with federal money this abysmal flop, involving America's top scientists and physicists. With dozens of electronic sensors implanted in her brain and catheters in her arteries, Bonny was launched inside a biosatellite into an earth orbit programmed to last 30 days. But she soon became sick and was brought back to earth— dead. The big team of medical specialists on the space program were unable to find out why. A reasonable assumption would be that Bonny died of fear, misery, loneliness and despair. And certainly in pain. Body functions surely do not become inoperative without acute physical distress—something too difficult to be understood by the pseudo-scientists of our day.

On July 10, 1969, the *New York Daily News* reported: "Col. John (Shorty) Powers, who resigned five years ago from Nasa, today criticized the abortive flight of Bonny, the space monkey, as 'a complete and total waste of $92 million of my money.' Powers, who kept the public informed about previous space efforts as the 'voice' of mission control, said, 'You can learn more from a computer than a monkey. We finished with monkeys five years ago.' "

* * *

While government subsidies everywhere represent one major incentive to vivisection, another comes from the pharmaceutical companies. The vivisectionist method enables them to flood the world with their products—usually the same ones, in new combinations and with different names—which promise to repair the damages caused by the earlier products that have meanwhile been withdrawn, having proven to be useless or harmful. The new products will be replaced sooner or later by other "new" products (different labels, same ingredients), equally useless or harmful—except to the world's most lucrative industry.

Federal funds spent annually in the U.S. for research and development in industry and science amount to an estimated $25 billion. It isn't enough, say the rich beggars, who never give a thought to the poor, the sick, and the underprivileged. One microbiologist at a science writers' seminar even suggested that Social Security taxes be increased to get more money for "biomedical research," namely vivisection. Every day they come, literally thousands of them, palms up, to the coffers of government, presenting their "project" papers, all filled out according to bureaucratic stipulations.

To the huge sums the U.S. government and drug manufacturers spend for research—to which the taxpayers contribute willy-nilly—must be added the donations of individual citizens, most of whom don't remotely know how their donations are really being used.

If pecuniary gain is the principal incentive to vivisection, another incentive is careerism, the cousin of greed—the desire to obtain, without effort or talent, a university degree, a professorship, or a sliver of pseudo-scientific notoriety. Usually this is achieved through the performance of some traditional experiment, described in every treatise on physiology, which has as much scientific value as if somebody proceeded to reinvent the umbrella. With one difference: making an umbrella would be far more difficult.

* * *

A further powerful push to vivisection comes from a category that perhaps should have been mentioned in the first place, for they originated the senseless experiments that in the course of the last century became accepted as a demonstration of intelligence: the sadists. If it is a mistake to believe that all vivisectors are sadists, it would be a far bigger mistake to think that sadism doesn't loom very large in this practice.

Experimenters who crush dogs' legs in the Blalock Press—repeating an exercise in shock that has been done in all American medical schools hundreds of thou-

sands of times, or hammer the testicles of cats to a pulp
in order to see once again how that will affect their sex
lives, done for 14 consecutive years up to 1976 at the
New York Museum of Natural History—will always
claim that they want to satisfy their "scientific" curiosity. Many people would call it sadistic curiosity.

Sadism exists. Psychologists assure us that there are
traces of it in all of us. We see it in the child who pulls
the wings from an insect, or locks the kitten in the
washing machine. At such times education should intervene. Through the realization of what these actions
do, the child may be able to nip such sadistic tendencies in the bud. These feelings may change to compassion.

But when sadism manifests itself in an adult, taking
forms that make us shudder with disgust and indignation, it is a sign of sickness, of a serious mental disorder.

The psychologists assure us that this pathological
state is not as rare as most people imagine. Could there
be a more convenient activity for a sadist than vivisection? It enables a person to satisfy those tendencies,
and even to gain a slice of "scientific" glory in the
process, or at least an easy income.

THE SCAPEGOAT CONCEPT

The scapegoat concept—the idea of getting rid of
one's sins, vices, diseases, misfortunes and other troubles by transferring them to some guiltless man or animal—has always been widespread in human society.
The Babylonians used to behead a ram for this purpose. The ancient Greeks scourged two human scapegoats out of the city every year—a criminal, or
deformed, man and woman.

Today the scapegoat transference is usually psychological rather than physical, and consists in blaming
other persons or groups for one's own shortcomings and
frustrations.

The scapegoat concept looms importantly in the
whole vivisectionist practice. Although usually the
choice of a scapegoat is arrived at through an irrational
process, the vivisectors have "rational" reasons for

their practice: monetary gain or personal satisfaction. But the scapegoat concept has certainly contributed to the tacit acceptance of the vivisectionist practice by large segments of the public.

To obtain "scientific confirmation" of the well-known fact that overcrowding leads to nervousness, hostility and violence, experimenters like to confine great numbers of rats in such cramped quarters that they will eventually attack and kill one another. To get "scientific proof" that motherly warmth and love are important for the child, newborn primates are snatched from their mothers and kept for years in solitary confinement, some of them, furthermore, in total darkness —a punishment generally considered too cruel even for hardened criminals.

To the same category of experiments belong those designed to turn animals into drug addicts. When they get cramps or convulsions after the sudden withdrawal of the drug, soothing medicines can be tried out on them. But then, of course, the researchers still don't know whether those medicines will have the same effect on man, or whether they are going to poison men —in view of the fact that strychnine, for instance, is a deadly poison for man but not for monkeys.

Although worldwide statistics have conclusively proved that heavy smoking can lead to lung cancer, the researchers—especially those in the employ of the tobacco companies—obstinately claim that "there is no scientific proof" that tobacco smoking causes lung cancer, since it has not yet been possible to produce lung cancer in animals. Actually, if researchers succeed in causing lung cancer in an animal through heavy smoking, it would only prove that smoking can give cancer to that particular species, not to man. We already know that smoking may give lung cancer to man: through statistics and clinical observations.

Yet millions of animals, mainly dogs and rabbits immobilized in restraining devices, are subjected to smoking treatments lasting a lifetime for the sake of theories that the experimenters keep calling "scientific" but which, in actual fact, are an insult to real science and to every thinking man and woman.

The American press recently reported experiments on sleep that one Dr. William Dement of Stanford University was making, depriving cats of sleep until they went out of their minds—in order, so he claimed, to understand better the mechanism of human sleep. The usual nonsense.

The nervous system of animals, especially of cats, has very little in common with ours. A cat normally snoozes 22 hours out of 24, practically anywhere and even standing up. So perhaps does Dr. Dement, but most people don't. To deprive cats of sleep, without having to keep awake himself, Dr. Dement has hit on a bright idea: He places his experimental cat, electrodes in its head, on a brick surrounded by water. When the cat goes limp with sleepiness its nose slips into the water. Dr. Dement has thus kept hundreds of cats awake for up to 70 days—not hours, but days. Whereafter he reported that the brain waves revealed "definite personality changes," which in "scientific" jargon means "madness." Many sane people have expressed the view that scientists of Dr. Dement's ilk are definitely victims of personality changes.

* * *

In her book *Intelligence and Personality* (Pelican, 1970) Dr. Alice Heim, an eminent British psychologist working as a member of the Medical Research Council, denounced other experiments in sleep deprivation, which speak very poorly for the mental balance of the experimenters in her own country as well. Rats were deprived of sleep for 27 consecutive days, by means of placing them in a continuously rotating wheel, two-thirds submerged in water. The rats, when exhausted, fell from the wheel into the water and were unable to remount the wheel. Some found ways of resting by hanging on food trays and, in one case, climbing on top of the cubicle and sleeping while hanging with front teeth hooked in the cloth top. *Modifications were introduced to prevent this.*

Thus in every field of science innocent animals are made to serve as scapegoats for man's vices and faults. We smoke, animals don't: So we force animals to smoke, although for them it's torture, for us pleasure.

We drink alcohol, animals don't: So we cause liver cirrhoses in animals by funneling alcohol into them. We drug ourselves, animals don't: So we turn animals into drug addicts. We suffer from insomnia owing to our daily excesses, animals don't: So we force animals to stay awake until they go crazy. We suffer from stress owing to our unnatural way of living, animals don't: So we traumatize them in rotating drums to put them in a state of stress. We cause car accidents through incompetence or carelessness, animals don't: So we fasten animals to vehicles and send them crashing against walls. We contract cancer by consuming the wrong foods and toxic drugs, and through pollution caused exclusively by ourselves: So we inflict cancer upon millions of animals and continue torturing them while we watch them slowly waste away through the cruelest malady mass-produced by man.

* * *

Now we have had a first glimpse of what passes today for Medical Science. Speculating upon the ignorance and suffering of countless people, their constant fear of pain and disease, and with the help of the mass media, this pseudo-science has created the illusion—like the shamans of the primitive tribes who promise rain—that she wields mysterious and unlimited powers on which mankind's salvation depends. So the peoples of the western hemisphere have prostrated themselves in awe and servility at her feet, imagining her as an almighty goddess of peerless beauty, shining with gold and brocades, to whom common mortals may not even raise their eyes, lest they be blinded. But if they dared to do so, they would discover that their empress hasn't got a stitch on and is gruesome to behold.

Greed, cruelty, ambition, incompetence, vanity, callousness, stupidity, sadism, insanity are the charges that this treatise levels at the entire practice of vivisection. The evidence is in the coming parts. They exaggerate nothing, for the simple reason that in matters of vivisection any exaggeration is not only superfluous, but impossible.

However, to understand fully how grievously this "science" sins, we must first see who she sins against.

Part Two

THE VOICELESS

If a newborn ant is left alone, it lets itself die. Two newborn ants proceed at once to build a nest.

*   *   *

According to his biographer Jean Pierhal, Albert Schweitzer was about to admit into the lofty chambers of philosophy, hitherto reserved for man, all four-legged and winged creatures, when death interrupted his long life entirely dedicated to showing the meaning of humanity to his fellow men.

There is a far cry between men like Albert Schweitzer and the confraternity of vivisectors, who on one hand compare the animals' physiological, nervous and psychological reactions to man's, but on the other hand claim that they can do with them whatever they please because animals don't suffer. What could be more ridiculous, more hypocritical, than to say that animals don't reason, feel, or suffer, and then to use them for experiments allegedly designed to "explain" human behavior? But it is possible, and highly significant, that for all their continual contacts with animals those individuals don't seem to notice that all of them are endowed with an exquisite sensitivity, and with a kind of intelligence that, although in many respects different from man's, is not necessarily "inferior" to ours.

Voltaire wrote in his *Philisophical Dictionary:* "To say that the animals are machines without knowledge and sentiment, that they always do everything in the same way, without learning and perfecting anything, is

36

a sign of obtuseness. The bird which builds its nest in a half circle against a wall, in a quarter circle in a corner, and in a full circle on a tree top—does this bird do everything the same way? And when you want to teach a melody to a canary, haven't you noticed that he first goes wrong and then corrects himself? And the dog that whines in anguish looking for its lost master in the street, rushes into the house worried and agitated, runs upstairs and downstairs and from one room to the next, and finally finds his beloved master, and demonstrates his joy jumping and yelping. Some brutes seize this dog, which so surpasses us in loyalty and friendship, they nail him to a table and vivisect him to show us the mesenteric veins—and find in him the same organs of feeling that we have. Answer me, mechanicist! Has nature endowed this animal with the well-springs of sentiment so that he should not feel? Has he got nerves in order to be insensitive?"

Whenever we can do something that the animals can't, we credit our superior intelligence for it. But animals can do a lot of things we are incapable of; in that case we attribute it not to their superior intelligence but to some alleged, not well defined "instinct."

If a man is left to his own devices even close to home in unknown territory, he is unlikely to find his way back without asking directions, although he has been taught that the movement of the sun can provide valuable information. But since we have not yet discovered how the animals manage to find their bearings over a distance of thousands of miles, we think they don't know either.

One needn't go as high as the vertebrates to find intellective qualities in animals. Even the simplest forms show intelligence of sorts. This is a rather recent discovery. Robert Macnab and Daniel Koshland, biochemists from California University (Berkeley), have recently discovered that even microbes are endowed with something that can only be defined as memory—a kind of intelligence. As a rule in a solution, microbes move erratically, by fits and bounds. If a nutrient such as sugar is added to the solution, the microbes move more calmly for a while, in a straight line, before returning to their usual erratic way of swimming. This variation was considered an indication of some rudimentary intelligence by the two scientists. So they transferred the microbes suddenly from a sugared solution to one without sugar—and noticed that the microbes immediately moved in an extremely agitated way, as if trying to find the way back to the sugary solution. Evidently, the microbes "remembered" their sweet paradise lost. (*Time & Life Nature/Science Annual* for 1973.)

Pasteur's biographer, René Dubos, Professor of Microbiology at New York's Rockefeller Institute and Pulitzer Prize-winner for his science books, had already related a similar discovery: "One of these primitive unicellular protozoans was exposed to an acid concentration so weak as not to affect its behavior; then the acid concentration was raised to an injurious level. After the experiment had been repeated several times, the protozoan learned, and remembered from prior experience, that contact with a solution not injurious in itself foretold exposure to a stronger, dangerous acid concentration. The experienced protozoan took advantage of this awareness to escape in advance of the approach of danger. The faculty to learn is so developed even among the most primitive unicellular creatures that it prompts them to react to the symbols of danger as vigorously as to the danger itself." (From *Man, Medicine and Environment,* Praeger, New York, 1968.)

If scientists of Dubos' standing have come to the conclusion that even unicellular protozoans don't lack intelligence, it may be assumed that the life of more complex animals, insects for example, is not regulated merely by blind instinct.

The studies of Karl von Frisch in the fifties have given us new knowledge about the bees, whose organizational talents already fascinated the ancient philosophers—as the scientists used to be called in antiquity. Summarily, everybody knows something about the bees' social structure: The queen bee, the workers, the warriors; their strict discipline, their altruism. Today, thanks to Frisch, we know a great deal more.

Frisch discovered that the young honeybees go through a routine of education, and that they have a language. They could not have achieved their high level of integration unless the individual members could communicate with each other. Speech is not the only means of communication. Many animals use other ways, not all of which we have discovered. Frisch discovered that the bee language consists in an elaborate series of signals. Scouts, for example, inform the hive in detail of new areas of nectar, of which they can indicate the exact location, by means of a food dance on the comb. If the food is 50 meters or less from the hive, the scout performs a turning dance, first in one direction and then in the other direction. If the distance is between 50 and 100 meters, the dance includes a short straight run between the turns, and the abdomen is wagged during the straight run. At distances greater than 100 meters, the number of turns decreases per unit of time while the wagging motions increase in intensity. If the food is toward the sun, the straight run is vertically upward on the comb. A downward run indicates a direction away from the sun. A deviation of 10° to the right of the vertical indicates the direction of the food 10° to the right of the sun. Any angle to the right or left of the vertical corresponds to the angle to the right or left of the sun.

The complexes of the beehives form cooperative colonies that are thoroughly social.

Another example of the typical ignorance of certain scientists can be found in the Encyclopedia Britannica. When speaking of bees it says that "the conduct of the colony is so harmonious that some are inclined to attribute high intelligence to bees." But that copywriter does not, for he or she promptly adds: ". . . there is little improvement from practice, hence it is clear that the behaviour is instinctive."

This is exactly what St. Thomas of Aquinas said of the birds, arousing the ire of Voltaire, whose brightness illumined more than his own century.

Anybody who knows the ants' history and way of life and refuses to credit them with prodigious intelligence, casts doubts on his or her own intellectual facul-

ties. All social insects evolved from solitary insects
which in warm climates used to build their nests in the
open.

Occasional examples of this primitive nidification
still occur. So it is not true that insects are unable to
progress: They built their highly organized societies.
So far, more than 1,000 species of social wasps and far
more than 10,000 of social bees have been identified,
each species with its own social peculiarities. If they
have not changed their mode of building and of living
since early or mid-Tertiary, it is because they had
achieved perfection already as long ago as that. And
that applies to most animals in their natural habitat, if
not to all. Only man keeps changing continuously, and
mostly thoughtlessly, getting further and further from
the perfection that he allegedly seeks, and in the process only promoting the decadence of his own species.

Naturalist Verlaine had observed in the Belgian
Congo a solitary wasp that was trying to build a cell of
clay in which to lay its eggs. The wasp brought various
alterations to the cell in the course of its construction,
for example the roof was repeatedly set up but then
taken off again for modifications. New situations elicited distinct inventiveness. When the cell collapsed, the
wasp built a new cell using one wall that was left over.
Verlaine was impressed not only by the constant variations in this insect's behavior, but also by its memory.
One repair was done after a delay of four hours, during
which the wasp had not been able to visit its cell. Four
hours in an ant's life equal months in a man's life.

Ants and termites have an organization even more
complex than bees. Both have reached the level of
farming—they cultivate fungi. The ants' abundance in
practically all parts of the world, even in desert and
swampy regions, is due to their successful exploitation
of all sources of food as well as to their social organization. Very careful housekeepers, they establish garbage piles in abandoned areas, where they carry all
household refuse and the bodies of their dead. They
discovered millions of years before Pasteur that no
great congeries of animals can live together in health
without cleanliness of the habitation.

Some Oriental and African ants construct their arboreal nests of leaves sewn to one another by means of silk spun from the salivary glands of the larvae. Some workers hold the leaf edges together while other workers hold silk-secreting larvae in their jaws and weave them back and forth between one leaf and the other.

Certain "human" traits can be found in the ants and termites, which Maurice Maeterlinck—the Nobel laureate who is to ants what Frisch is to bees—considered organizatorially superior not only to all other insects but to man himself. Certain widespread forms of ants (*formica sanguinea*) live as slavers, kidnapping the larvae of related forms of ants and rearing them into slavery. Slaves have to chew the masters' food and feed them. Other ant species are successful on a pastoral level: they rear and tend great herds of completely domesticated "ant cows" (aphids) from which they "milk" the honeydew they contain.

*   *   *

Proof of outstanding architectural inventiveness are the dams of mud, stones and tree trunks the beavers build, rendering the water in which they live of sufficient depth to prevent it from freezing to the bottom of the streams, and the lodges which open underwater to keep predators out. They attained their architectural perfection millions of years before the first *Homo erectus* walked the earth.

Clear signs of intelligence and organizational talent are also the birds' strictly disciplined flight formations.

Herring gulls lift sea urchins and clams in their bills and drop them on the rocks to break open their shells and get at the contents.

Usually, man holds up the ostrich as a symbol of the birds' alleged stupidity—hiding its head in the sand in the hope of not being seen. Hunters in Africa have told me a different story. When a flock of ostriches is being chased, one of the birds separates from the others and limps conspicuously, pretending to be wounded, in the hope of drawing the pursuers away from the rest of the group. Blind instinct?

And what about the vixen that drops her litter in a freshly sown field, knowing the farmer will keep away from it—long enough for the cubs to learn running?

We can't say that the bear is stupid only because he can't type. This defect certainly rules him out as an office worker; on the other hand he knows how to survive a severe winter without stove and food. He plugs his rectum in autumn by eating dry pine needles, which get digested very slowly, and finally stop the exit, to retain whatever food the bear eats afterwards, so that its nutritive value gets fully exploited during hibernation. Who taught the bear this? And who taught the polar bear, who has no mirror in which to study his makeup, to whiten his nose with snow before approaching a seal, so as to eliminate the only black spot that might reveal his presence on the ice field?

Some animal species, such as rat and elephant, have a larger brain-to-body ratio than man's, who prides himself on the weight of his brain. But while it is futile to compare the intelligence of entirely different species, we can compare the intelligence of the non-human primates or anthropoid monkeys—chimpanzees, orangutans, rhesus monkeys, baboons, marmosets, lemurs—to our own. But taking into account that individual intelligence varies: Each species has geniuses and idiots.

*   *   *

Monkeys can communicate with each other, with gestures similar to ours and words of which so far some 80 have been identified. The intelligence of the average adult ape is comparable to that of a human between the ages of 5 and 9. But the monkey's nervous system is more delicate and fragile than ours, which makes them able to suffer as much or more than we do. Newborn humans have little or no sensitivity, even at the age of 6 months. But we wouldn't dream of authorizing experiments on newborn babies (even though the maniac experimenters in the hospitals keep doing them without authorization). So why do we authorize them on grown monkeys?

Man's physical and mental development is extremely slow compared to most animals. Man doesn't reach his full physical efficiency until he is about 20—when some kinds of monkey have already died of old age—and his full mental development well after 40. If it's true that a few humans can reach very high intellectual development, it is equally true that among all animals man is the slowest learner. Most animals can walk at birth—from chickens to quadrupeds to monkeys.

British Prof. Richard D. Ryder, who experimented on animals both in Britain and the U.S. before becoming Senior Clinical Psychologist at Warneford Hospital in Oxford, has declared: "I have seen some human individuals in many respects less intelligent than a clever chimpanzee—and I say that as a psychologist." Prof. H.W. Nissen, an American vivisector who specialized on monkeys, stated that "there are no fundamental or qualitative differences between the emotions and motivations of man and other primates." (*Human Biology*, Vol. 26, 1954.)

And Prof. Harry F. Harlow of the University of Wisconsin's Primate Center wrote in *Lessons from Animal Behavior for the Clinician* (1962), "The rhesus monkey is the most useful animal for analyzing the learning processes . . . It can solve many problems similar in type to the items used in standard tests of human intelligence."

Prof. Harlow points out the advantages in working on monkeys: "It is much more mature intellectually than a human at birth, and it has a degree of motor control that a child takes months to acquire . . . Most individuals can be tested for several hours week after week, year after year . . . We can submit them to conditions that cannot be imposed upon human beings. We can expose them to long periods of social and sensory deprivations . . . We can also damage their brains."

Though fully aware of their similarity to man, Dr. Harlow relentlessly subjects the primates in his care to surgical mutilations, traumatic, electric and psychological shocks, and other experiences that, if he did them on humans, would brand him as a monstrous criminal. He thought up the series of experiments in which dozens of baby chimpanzees—the closest in nature to man—were taken away from their mothers at birth and kept isolated in bare wire cages for periods varying from 5 to 8 years. Others were housed in solitary confinement, in cubicles with solid walls, seeing no living being for years. Their behavior was observed through one-way screens. Many developed stereotyped, compulsive manners: They stared fixedly ahead, or clasped their heads in their hands and rocked for long periods of time. Or "the animal may chew and tear at its body until it bleeds."

Commented a scientist of a quite different ilk, Dr. Catherine Roberts, a California-born microbiologist and author of *The Scientific Conscience* (1973): "That these experiments are conducted to attain a knowledge of love makes them not only ludicrous but revealing as well. For they reveal a grave lack of understanding of the subject that is believed to be under investigation."

Of the nearly $2,000,000 granted to Dr. Harlow in 1961, $1,664,540 was for the construction of a primate center or monkey farm. The remainder was earmarked for his experiments. Under his "expert" directions, records were kept of awkward mating attempts of naive male monkeys, and "trained" monitors kept tab on the number of times baby monkeys turned in their cages, whether or not they sucked their thumbs, or licked their genitals when deprived of their favorite food. So the professor knew what he was saying when he stated in *Journal of Comparative and Physiological Psychology* (Dec. 1962) that "most experiments are not worth doing, and most data obtained are not worth publishing." Clearly, those in charge of dishing out federal funds didn't read the professor's profound thought: Grants in his name that year totaled $708,300.

The professor evidently considers his work of the utmost importance, an opinion most people who don't worry inordinately about the condition of their own brain find difficult to share. But although he is allowed to damage their brains, Prof. Harlow has no great affection for monkeys. An interview in *Psychology Today* (Apr. 1973) reveals interesting insights into his character as well as into the nature of his almost life-long experimentation with monkeys. Asked whether he didn't consider it cruel to take infant monkeys away from their mothers, especially as the results didn't seem very useful, Dr. Harlow replied: "I think that I am a soft-hearted person, but I never developed a fondness for monkeys. Monkeys do not develop affection for people, and I find it impossible to love an animal that doesn't love back."

This professor—whose next endeavor, incidentally, was to create schizophrenic monkeys by dint of electric shocks—probably rates top grades in vivisection but, for all his experiments on brains, pretty low grades in psychology and intelligence, if he expects monkeys to fall in love with their torturer. And anybody who has had such long-standing contacts with primates and fails to realize their immense potential for affection, reveals an obtuseness that is worrisome in one who presumes to form the future generations, and who furthermore defines himself "soft-hearted."

ON AFFECTIVITY

Man's fondness for animals is a natural, inborn feeling, which manifests itself early in life. Once the child has outgrown the unconscious stage of pulling off a fly's wings or a lizard's tail, this same child will feel fondness for animals, will want to pet, to feed them. In all zoos feeding time is conspicuously advertised, as it is one of the children's main pleasures. Parental and environmental influences can develop this natural inclination or destroy it. It takes some doing to subvert it into hatred.

The desire to protect animals derives inevitably from better acquaintance with them, from the realization that they are sensitive and intelligent creatures, affectionate and seeking affection, powerless in a cruel and incomprehensible world, exposed to all the whims of the master species. According to the animal haters, those who are fond of animals are sick people. To me it seems just the other way around, that the love for animals is something more, not something less.

As a rule, those who protect animals have for them the same feeling as for all the other defenseless or abused creatures: the battered or abandoned children, the sick, the inmates of penal or mental institutions, who are so often maltreated without a way of redress. And those who are fond of animals don't love them for their "animality" but for their "humanity"—their "human" qualities. By which I mean the qualities humans display when at their best, not at their worst.

Man's love for the animal is, at any rate, always inferior in intensity and completeness to the love the animal has for the human being that has won its love. The human being is the elder brother, who has countless different preoccupations, activities and interests. But to the animal that loves a human being, this being is everything. That applies not only to the generous, impetuous dog, but also to the more reserved species, with which it is more difficult to establish a relationship without personal effort and plenty of patience.

But once a relationship is established, it is very rare that a naturally diffident animal will shift its affection to a new master. There have been a great many cases of cats that let themselves die of starvation when they changed hands, even if the new hands were good ones. In them the attachment was stronger than their instinct.

The animals' great potential for affection for human beings never ceases to surprise those who experience it. French writer Serge Golon had such an experience with a gorilla baby that had been orphaned in the course of a hunt in the Belgian Congo.

Already the sight of the dying mother had filled Golon with remorse. Shot in the chest, she had touched her wound, and on seeing the blood on her hand had burst into tears, like a human being. She looked at the hunters with pleading eyes; she had hidden her baby in the forest. The natives found it. It was a male suckling, and Golon took him to his farm and raised him with the bottle. The little one soon developed a strong attachment to his adoptive father, took food only from him, and refused to play with anybody else. He lived at the house; from time to time he jumped on Golon's lap demanding to be petted. Every time Golon went out, the little one cried like a child. A year later Golon had to go to Brazzaville for several weeks and confided the little gorilla to the local veterinary. But while Golon was away the little one died.

He had refused to eat after Golon's departure, and had to be force-fed. The veterinary was convinced that the little gorilla had died of heartbreak. He used to spend hours on end looking at the road where his adoptive father had left, while in Golon's house he would always look toward the forest that had been his homeland. One day he had escaped from the veterinary's house and had been found dead on the road to Brazzaville.

*　　*　　*

The dolphins are the latest category of animals that have attracted the vivisectors' fancy. There again the poets have preceded by many centuries today's self-styled "scientists." Ancient legends told of friendships between children and dolphins, of dolphins that saved drowning people and carried them to shore. Today we know those weren't merely legends. Dolphins are particularly fond of human beings and, like most animals, they are easily trained.

A dolphin could kill a man with a single blow of its pointed snout—their method of dispatching sharks— or by cutting him in two with its sharp-toothed, powerful jaws. But there has never been a report of a dolphin attacking a man, not even in legitimate defense—with a harpoon in its side, for example, or when, with the usual electrodes in its skull, it has been massacred in the name of science. In fact, ever since it became known that the dolphin is very intelligent and that its relative brain weight per unit of body length is similar to man's, the "researchers" can't leave the dolphins alone: They try to "communicate" with them. So now also this species is on the way to extinction.

Is it really necessary to point out that any child who, swimming in the Aegean Sea, ever struck up a friendship with a dolphin, knows more about dolphins than any vivisector ever will?

*　　*　　*

A few years ago Farley Mowat, a Canadian biologist and naturalist, was hired by the Dominion Wildlife Service to investigate charges of the hunting associations that the wolves were responsible for the scarcity of deer—the hunters' idea being that the government should exterminate the wolves so that the hunters might have more deer to shoot. At Brochet, the northern Manitoba base for Farley Mowat's winter studies, the local people complained that they had been able to kill as many as 50,000 caribou each winter as recently as two decades past, whereas nowadays they were lucky if they killed a couple of thousand, even though some of them hunted from low-flying planes. Mowat settled down for a long, lonely vigil in the desolate wastes of the subarctic Keewatin Barren Lands, beyond the western shore of Hudson Bay, and for many months observed the doings of wolf families with a high-powered periscopic telescope. He reported his findings in his book *Cry Wolf*.

Mowat discovered that the animal that man had chosen since ancient times as a symbol of treachery and wickedness is just the opposite. The wolf couple he studied in particular could be a model for its human counterparts—loyal, affectionate, hospitable, and exemplary child-rearers. They even displayed a great sense of humor, were strictly monogamous, and highly responsible parents.

They never left their young alone. Whenever the male or the female came back from an absence, even a short one, they effusively demonstrated their joy at the reunion. And yet the wolf's sexual activity is limited to 3 weeks a year. Once when a nearby fox family dug up a meat cache made by the wolves, the wolves merely watched them from afar, amusedly as it were, without interfering. The wolves, Mowat remarked, could easily have destroyed the marauders and their litter—as we have seen man do all too often in the course of his long, bloody history.

Mowat established that the wolves, whose main staple was mice, could have nothing to do with the scarcity of deer, because any healthy deer could outrun the fastest wolf. The only time Mowat saw a few deer pass by, the wolves made a half-hearted attempt at attacking them, but even the young deer had no trouble avoiding them. In the wild the wolves contribute to the health of the caribou herds by keeping them on the run; they can catch only the sick, the old or the wounded ones. In the zoos, wanting strenuous exercise, the caribou get sick.

The hunters were furious about Mowat's report, especially as he pointed out that wolves had been preying on caribou, without decimating the herds, for some 10,000 years before the white man appeared in the North with his firearms, and they called him "wolf-lover."

In spite of Farley Mowat's report, the Canadian Wildlife Service, in pursuance of its continuing policy of "wolf control," employed several Predator Control officers to patrol the Keewatin Barrens in ski-equipped aircraft and set out cyanide "wolf getters" around the dens that appeared to be occupied.

At present, the wolf belongs to the endangered species—and soon it will be the caribou's turn.

HATE

Each loom has its reverse, if there were no light we wouldn't recognize the shade, and perhaps there couldn't be love if there were no hatred.

The hatred against animals, which is at least as widespread as the love for them, is an atavistic hangover, dating back to the primordial times when the beasts of the forest endangered man's survival. Today this hatred is mostly based on ignorance—mother of fear and cowardice. That's why animal hatred is rampant mainly among uneducated people, and in culturally retarded regions or countries where the adults instill into their offspring their own blind fear of anything alien, until they have changed their children's natural sympathies into traditional hatred. The hatred of animals is transmitted in the same deliberate manner in which racial hatred is transmitted. Most animal haters come from animal-hating parents.

The fear of dogs felt by intellectually underdeveloped people can be at least partially explained by their terror of hydrophobia or rabies—in the western world one of the rarest of all infections. The much more widespread hatred against the cat is harder to explain. But it is surely not a coincidence that the victims of particularly cruel and senseless experiments in the laboratories are usually cats.

I had not yet been awakened to the countless abuses animals are made to suffer at the hands of man when one of my fellow students at Zurich University, an otherwise quite civil young man, baffled me with the revelation that he hated cats so much that whenever he got hold of one he would bind it between his car bumper and a tree and tear it apart. He couldn't explain what caused this hatred, which he defined "instinctive."

The cat is a complex animal, more difficult to understand, and therefore to appreciate, than the dog, whose love for man is so boundless that he willingly submits to any injustice at the hands of his master. Some people like to own a dog mainly because having someone to order around flatters their ego. But cats don't pander to man's vanity. For George Bernard Shaw, man may consider himself civilized in the measure that he understands cats.

Many people can't forgive a cat its independent spirit, its refusal to adulate man and lick the boot that kicks it. But the cat considers itself a guest, not a slave. Its affection cannot be bought with food, only with friendship and respect.

The centuries of obscurantism were the somberest not only for man's intellect and humanitarian ideals, but for the animals as well, and the cats were made to suffer more than others. Once idolized by the Nubians and then by the Egyptians, adored by the Greeks, pampered by the Romans, the cats became in the Middle Ages accursed creatures, destined for the stake. In 1494 they were exterminated by the tens of thousands on orders of Pope Innocent III, and their owners, accused of witchcraft, had to get rid of their pets lest they meet the same fate.

The hatred for animals is widespread and has many facets.

The London *Daily Telegraph* of August 23, 1974 had a story about the illegal dogfights that still take place in the U.S.—approximately 1,000 each year. The spectacle of dogs, usually Staffordshire bull terriers, trained by man to fight each other to the death, is sadistic and cruel enough, but the method of training the killer instinct in those dogs is even worse. One enthusiast used kittens to train fighting dogs. "Now, you don't want to throw a kitten in there with the puppy right away for it to kill. It'll just go crazy for more," this expert told the newspaperman. He suggested placing the kitten in a sack with its paws poking out of holes, having first clipped the kitten's claws off. The bag is then hung on a spring just out of the dog's reach so that the dog will worry it until exhausted. "If the cat gets pretty mauled up in the bag, just take it down and keep it till the next day and then throw it in and let the dog kill it."

In the far north, in man's relentless pursuit of the wolf, light aircraft are often employed to spot and chase the wolf on an open space or a frozen lake, making the duel between man and animal even more uneven. The flyers pursue their prey until it collapses and sometimes dies, even before a blast of buckshot kills it. Farley Mowat reported that one pilot had become so adept at this sport that he was able to hit the wolf with the skis of his aircraft. But once the harassed wolf turned, leaped high into the air, and snapped at one of the skis. The wolf died in the ensuing crash, but so did the two men on board. The incident was described in a sportsman's magazine as an example of the cunning and dangerous nature of the wolf, and of the great courage of the men who match themselves against it. "This," commented Mowat, "is of course a classic gambit. Whenever and wherever men have engaged in the mindless slaughter of animals (including other men), they have attempted to justify their acts by attributing the most vicious or revolting qualities to those they would destroy—and the less reason there is for the slaughter, the greater the campaign of vilification." In fact, hatred for animals always goes hand in hand with mental denseness.

It is difficult to become familiar with animals without becoming fond of them, provided one doesn't wish to domineer them. I have never heard that love for animals has changed to hate, but many cases where the opposite happened. Many hunters, obliged to observe the animals while stalking them, in time grow increasingly reluctant to kill them, and finally wish to become wardens in the national parks, to help protect them.

Very few vivisectors seem to be hampered by this natural evolution that leads to the love and respect of the animals through a deeper knowledge of them.

Dr. Harry F. Harlow, the already mentioned head of the University of Wisconsin primate laboratory, has at least one great quality: candor. In contrast to his Swiss colleagues, who all claim to be great animal lovers and to suffer more than the victims themselves from the pains they are obliged to inflict on them, Dr. Harlow didn't conceal his real feelings when he declared to the *Pittsburg Press* (Oct. 27, 1974):

"The only thing I care about is whether the monkeys will turn out a property that I can publish. I don't have any love for them. Never have. I really don't like animals. I despise cats. I hate dogs. How can you like monkeys?"

Just as the love for animals has conditioned many antivivisectionists—animal lovers don't like to think of the dog that licks its torturer's hand—so a deep-seated hatred against animals becomes often evident in vivisectionists. Some have admitted to me in private, as Harlow has done publicly, that they have an aversion to animals. Two are Italian journalists who write articles in praise of the drug industry. "I don't give a damn what happens to them," admitted one of them to me. And the other: "I couldn't care less about animals sufferings. Why shouldn't they suffer? My only interest is whether they are good to eat."

One thing seems sure to me: For a sadist, who at the same time happens to be an animal hater, what a godsend is vivisection!

COMPASSION

Dr. George Hoggan, the English physiologist, related an incident he had witnessed in Claude Bernard's laboratory. A small mongrel dog, whose hind quarters were paralyzed as a result of an operation, had been removed from the operating table and left on the floor. He started dragging himself painfully toward a retriever that had been blinded a few days earlier for another experiment and was kept under observation. Its eyes had begun to putrefy. The blind dog managed to pick itself up, tottered toward the half-paralyzed little mongrel and wagged its tail. Nobody else in that laboratory seemed to notice the scene, which prompted Dr. Hoggan to write: "The pathetic gesture of mutual sympathy put the human race to shame."

Vivisectors have revealed sides of the human soul that few sane people believed to exist. Some try to justify themselves with such sophisms as "the real pity is the pity for man"—proving how alien the concept of pity is to them; as if there were different kinds of pity.

Nobody has ever explained why pity for one's own species should be more admirable than for other species. If we want to discriminate, it could be considered *less* deserving, for it can be suspected of utilitarianism, ultimately of taking into account the convenience of group solidarity, maybe unconsciously. But mostly whoever advocates compassion for animals doesn't do so in the belief that this is more important than to advocate compassion for humans, but because animals have neither voice nor vote, because the foulness is too deep, the hypocrisy that hides it is too shameful for the human race. And at the end it will emerge that by helping the animals we shall also have helped mankind.

In all nations where animals are better protected, such as Sweden, Denmark, Great Britain, the sick, the old, the unwed mothers and abandoned children are also better protected. There is only one kind of compassion. But it is not surprising that the champions of vivisection don't seem to know that whoever has compassion for animals is equally able to pity their fellow-men, provided they deserve pity. A vivisector who weeps in despair because the grants for more experiments have been denied him can hardly expect pity from our quarter.

Many antivivisectionists distinguished themselves for services to humanity. Charles Bell went to Europe expressly to tend the wounded of the battle of Waterloo. Albert Schweitzer dedicated the longest part of his existence curing the destitute blacks in his jungle hospital, meanwhile undertaking strenuous tours of concerts and lectures to raise funds for his philanthropic activity. Of British Cardinal Manning, who was among the starters of the first antivivisection movement, even the Italian Encyclopedia notes "Very great was his love for the poor and most fruitful his social work." And so the first committee that founded in Great Britain the Society for the Prevention of Cruelty to Animals included mostly names already known for other humanitarian causes, such as William Wilberforce, chiefly associated with the abolition of the slave trade, and the two penal reformers, Fowell Buxton and James Macintosh.

*   *   *

My father used to point out to me ants that were carrying dead companions between their jaws. He would say: "Look, they don't abandon them. Who knows if they don't bury them with some ritual?" Today we know that maybe those ants removed their dead for hygienic reasons only. But we also know that ants help their living companions, even performing surgical operations on them.

In March 1973 the press reported that Russian entomologist Marekovsky, while projecting an enlargement of a documentary he had filmed over many months studying colonies of Amazonian ants, had noticed two ants which were cutting an excrescence from the body of a companion, and three ants which were extracting a splinter from another ant's side. The operations were performed on an area in front of the ant hill. While the surgeon ants were at work, other ants of the colony had formed a circle around the patient. All that isn't merely proof of intelligence, but of altruism as well, for it may be assumed that the surgeon ants didn't present a stiff bill to their patient afterwards, and much less in advance, as happens in human society.

Among the repetitive, usually cruel experiments on "behaviorism," today so much in vogue, some have "scientifically" proved the animals' humanity. As reported by London's *Daily Telegraph* (Sept. 9, 1970), Dr. S.J. Diamond of Cardiff University College, investigating animal behavior, found that one rat would press a lever to rescue another in danger of drowning. A monkey would renounce pressing levers which provided it with food if, at the same time, the use of that lever administered a shock to another animal. Thus the monkey preferred going without food rather than hurting a companion. Dr. Diamond, probably astonished, drew the conclusion that "experiments of this kind seem to point to a kind of altruism in animals other than man."

Any real knower of animals could have helped Dr. Diamond cut down on his electricity bill by letting him know that animals are endowed with a quality that is obviously entirely alien to vivisectionist researchers: compassion.

* * *

Birds are known for their territorial attachment to particular locations, which represent their vital space among the trees; to retain its exclusive use, bloody fighting can break out between them. But usually the wounded are not abandoned to die. Fractures are expertly plastered with mud. The woodcock and the wagtail have long been known for doing this. Now the robin may be added.

In fact the robin is fascinating ornithologists everywhere. As usual, a single intelligent human observer can enrich science more than all the vivisectors combined. Patient observations and drawn-out film sequences have shown, among other things, that a disabled robin may be attended at once, and usually by the very victor, which may feed its victim for months, even if that means missing the migratory flights at the risk of its survival. Can this be called instinct? Instinct would prompt the bird to think foremost of its own skin.

Zoologist Vittorio Menassé has reported an interesting item in the Italian monthly, *Animali e Natura*. In a study of motorists' behavior a fake accident was staged along a busy highway, with a seemingly blood-covered crash victim laid out on the roadside, next to a wrecked car. Hundreds of motorists went by, some accelerating to get away faster from the scene of the accident. But by now everybody knows that in our highly civilized society a person can die for want of assistance along a busy highway.

"This news item was called back to my mind by an incident witnessed at Legnago," wrote Menassé, referring to a region in Northern Italy where fledgling birds go into the making of one of the population's favorite dishes. "A wounded sparrow, lying helplessly in the middle of the street, was surrounded by other sparrows, which were trying to carry it to safety, heedless of the traffic. A motorist got out of his car and stopped traffic. Other motorists also alighted and surrounded the sparrows. Slowly, with great effort, the little birds managed to carry their companion to the side of the road, thence onto a nearby patch of grass, where they rested for a moment. Finally, with great collective effort they again got hold of their companion, and flew it over a nearby garden wall. This episode merits some thought," Menassé went on. "In these feathered little creatures there is something more than the couple of ounces of meat with which to season a plate of cornmeal. The incident reveals clearly that we may not consider them merely vegetative creatures incapable of real feelings. The little sparrows, hunted by man, were not deterred from helping their companion by the presence of so many people, of whose unusual benevolence in their regard they could not be aware."

Proofs of animals' mutual consideration or concern abound. When they discover poisoned food morsels, the rats cover them with their feces, to warn the less perceptive members of the community.

Most animals captured in the wild refuse to mate in the zoos, suppressing in themselves one of the strongest natural instincts, because they don't want their offspring to grow up in captivity. Some, having given birth, prefer seeing their young dead, and refuse to nurse them, or kill them. But in freedom they are model parents.

Human beings could in fact take as an example the wisdom and self-denial with which animals in their natural habitat rear and protect their young, without trying to domineer them, and then render them independent. As the young grow up, the parents pretend they are abandoning them, but keep watch over them from afar, and rush to their aid when they see them in real trouble. Tigers are known for this.

The German physician, Erwin Liek, relates in *Gedanken eines Arztes:* "In an aquarium, a big lobster tumbles on its back and can't right itself owing to its heavy dorsal shield. Its companions rush to the rescue and after numerous attempts succeed in putting it back on its legs . . . In South America some rabbit-like rodents, the *viscachas,* damage the crops. Periodically, the farmers plug the exits of their underground corridors, imprisoning them. As soon as the farmers are gone, other *viscachas* come in large numbers and free them. This is a clear case of altruism and neighbor's love. Many animals adopt little orphans." They even adopt the offspring of different species. Cats may nurse orphaned puppy dogs.

Erasmus Darwin, the naturalist doctor and poet who was Charles Darwin's grandfather, observed that when a lobster is vulnerable because it changes its shell, others keep constant watch over it. He had also seen pelicans regularly nourishing a blind companion, although it involved a flight of thirty miles to carry the fish from the sea.

A British miner once saw two large rats proceeding slowly along a roadside, each holding one end of a straw in its mouth. The miner clubbed one of them to death. To his surprise, the other rat didn't move, so the miner bent down to observe it more closely. It was blind.

The monkeys carry to safety, at the risk of their lives,

companions that have been wounded by hunters. Their grief over the death of a member of the group is so human, so touching, that many hunters never shoot a second monkey.

I have seen my children's three kittens leave their food bowl, and anxiously surround a very sick brother when it cried out in pain. My wife wanted to make an "experiment." Lying on her bed, she moaned as if in pain the next time the kittens were presented with their bowl—and sure enough they left it to jump on my wife's bed to console her.

When two wild animals are locked in mortal combat, the loser immobilizes itself, belly up, and spreads its paws in sign of surrender, as if imploring mercy: and usually obtains it.

But not in a laboratory.

CALVARY

As a rule, the experiment proper is but a stage in a long, terrible calvary.

A 1974 survey conducted in the South African Union revealed that during the two preceding years between 500 and 1,500 baboons destined for the local laboratories died before the start of the experiments, mostly of thirst or exposure during transportation. Often the mothers decapitate their sucklings during these trips.

In the German language the term *Affenliebe*—monkey love—defines an exaggerated maternal attachment. So one can imagine what a degree of despair and mental distress a monkey mother must reach before she decides to kill her own child. But she is evidently intelligent enough to realize that her offspring is better off dead than in the hands of the experimenters. One question remains unanswered: Who told her so?

The chief candidate for the laboratories is the chimpanzee, the primate that is the experimenters' favorite test animal, due to its closest resemblance to man. The highly intelligent baboons and sensitive rhesus monkeys are also much in demand. Already in 1955, *Times of India* (Sept. 16) reported that India was exporting yearly at least 250,000 monkeys, mainly the rhesus.

Even today the vast majority of monkeys supplied for research are caught in the wild, in big hunts in the forests of Africa, Asia and Latin America. So various species are now in danger of extinction, as a consequence of man's growing experimental folly. London's *Medical News* (Aug. 28, 1972) dedicated an extensive article to this problem.

Most monkeys are caught by shooting the nursing mothers. The suckling clings in terror to the dying parent and can then easily be captured. That's when their *via crucis* begins. Caging and transportation to the laboratories, often halfway across the globe, adds to the terror and misery of these timid, sensitive young creatures. Packed tightly in cages, they die in large numbers—of dysentery, pneumonia, exposure, suffocation, thirst, or just from fear or the stress and horror of the journey. In one case reported by London's *Daily Mirror* (Jan. 4, 1955), 394 rhesus monkeys, in transit from Delhi to New York, died of suffocation at London Airport because nobody had had time to look after them over the New Year revelries.

Conditions have hardly changed for the better since. On May 29, 1972, Miss Crystal Rogers, a welfare worker in India, wrote to the Deputy Commissioner of Lucknow District, U.P., India, a detailed account of what she had witnessed at Lucknow railway station:

". . . The cage stood in the burning sun and the monkeys showed signs of exhaustion . . . With some difficulty I obtained water which I found impossible to pour into the bone-dry container in the cage, due to the monkeys' fighting and scrambling to catch the drops . . . I removed two small monkeys that were unconscious, and found one already dead; the other revived somewhat with water, but was covered with cuts and other injuries and died shortly afterwards."

In average, for each monkey delivered to the laboratory, four more die, from wounds suffered during the hunts, or in the course of transportation. So the 85,283 primates sacrificed in American laboratories alone during 1971 involved the extermination of some 400,000 individuals.

Dr. Geoffrey Bourne, Director of the Yerkes Primate

Center, Atlanta, Georgia, has written in his recent book, *The Ape People:* "The great apes took 40 million years to develop from their mammalian stock; when they are gone they are gone forever, and their passing will make our lives poorer." Touching words, if we didn't know that they came from the director of a breeding center for laboratories, who, like many other vivisectors, would regret the extinction of the ape people mainly because they represent the researchers' favorite "material."

To forestall any such crisis, some 40,000 primates are currently being bred in the U.S., in various parks that simulate their natural habitat. But although in their natural state monkeys are very prolific, the ones bred for the laboratories provide only about 1 percent of the requirements, owing to their reluctance to mate.

In Europe, most dogs used by the "scientific" laboratories or the university professors are provided by the municipal dogcatchers and several private enterprisers, who also collect the stray kittens that are too weak to avoid capture—mainly in southern Europe, where the strays abound. In Rome the constant population of stray dogs has been estimated by the municipal authorities at between 100,000 and 150,000, the stray cats anywhere between one and two million. Many of them were house pets, abandoned by the owners when vacation time approached. In more "advanced" European countries—like Switzerland, Great Britain and the Scandinavian nations, where strays are rare—most laboratory animals come, as in the U.S., from special breeding centers: hapless creatures slated to be born, to grow and suffer without ever knowing anything of life except the wire mesh of their cages and the violence of man.

* * *

For the laboratory animal, death is the equivalent of mercy, of paradise. But most of them—except perhaps the apes—lack the concept of death, so they don't even have the consolation to know that an end of their suffering is sooner or later bound to come. Reports of suicide among animals are rare. One clear case was reported by the *St. Louis Post-Dispatch* of June 8, 1954, when the paper carried the picture and story of a little dog driven by its terror of the laboratory to leap to its death from a fifth floor window at the Washington University Medical School. Another dog died of a heart attack while being strapped to the operating board.

A happy dog can live up to about fourteen years and even longer. Caged, the dog dies of misery or impotent exasperation inside three or four years, even without being experimented upon. But it is rare that a laboratory expects a dog to live that long.

When Dr. Charles W. Mayo of the famed clinic in Rochester, in his tirade against the critics of vivisection, said that "the seasoned physiologist profoundly respects the integrity of biological systems," he added that "he knows better than anyone else that the validity of the results of his research involving animals ultimately depends upon even better care for them than for most house pets. And that is the quality of care the vast majority of research animals receive."

How sensible, logical do these words by the great professor sound—even though it seems a bit hard to applaud the intention of getting animals in as good a shape as possible before proceeding to destroy them body and soul. But let's compare these pretty words with some of the facts that broke through the smoke curtain with which vivisectionists so diligently try to cover up their trade.

Ironically, the first information was given to me in 1973 by a relative of this same Charles Mayo—Mrs. Pegeen Fitzgerald, President of the Vivisection Investigation League of New York, who also had a daily radio program on WOR. Mrs. Fitzgerald gave me an article to read, signed by Sonny Kleinfield, that had appeared in a New York student newspaper, the *Washington Square Journal,* and said in part:

"Since September, as part of a Washington Square College psychology department split-brain project, seven monkeys have been contained in neck braces. 'It's terrible and inhumane and completely unnecessary,' said Renee Wayburn, an NYU graduate now at

Columbia University, who had visited the laboratory located on the 10th floor of Brown building. Miss Wayburn's protest was directed at Dr. Michael Gazzaniga, associate professor of psychology, who is in charge of the project. 'I was even willing to try and get cages myself, yet he said it was unnecessary.' Three of the monkeys are kept in a sitting position with a Plexiglas neck brace which prevents neck movement. The other four are seated in small chairs and are secured both at the neck and waist and can only move their legs and arms. The monkeys have remained in these positions since the project's inception in September."

According to the article, Prof. Gazzaniga, who permitted this episode at NYU, presented the following alibi: "Animals in other universities are completely paralyzed, so that while they feel pain, they can do nothing about it; thus the care of monkeys here is mild, by comparison."

Showing what point of dehumanization man has reached in respect to laboratory animals, the newspaper report had gone unheeded and the monkeys remained in that neck vise until Pegeen Fitzgerald reported their plight in her radio broadcast of December 11. Then, and only then, did the ASPCA and the NYU health department act. Cages were provided for the unfortunate monkeys, who thus were at least able to move their necks while waiting for the "split-brain project" to start.

*   *   *

And now some excerpts from the testimony of Fred Myers, who represented the Humane Society of the United States in the Congressional hearings of 1962, which will be mentioned more extensively later:

"I indict Harvard University, Northwestern University, Chicago University, Creighton University, the University of Pittsburgh, the National Institutes of Health, Western Reserve University—every one of which I know to have been guilty of neglect and mistreatment of animals. I can and will supply details to any extent that this Committee desires . . . At Johns Hopkins University I have seen closely caged dogs suffering

from advanced bleeding mange, without treatment . . .
At Tulane University we found cats confined in cages
suspended from the ceiling, with the wire mesh of the
cage floor so widely spaced that they could not walk,
stand, or lie down in a normal manner. At New York
University I walked for hours, on a weekend, through
several floors of caged dogs, cats, monkeys, rats, rabbits, sheep and other animals, scores of them wearing
bandages of major surgery, and many of them obviously
desperately ill, without ever encountering any doctor,
veterinarian or caretaker . . . In the Children's Hospital in Cincinnati one of our investigators found small
rhesus monkeys chained by their necks inside steel
cages so small that the animals could barely move
. . . I have myself seen men with no academic degrees
and with no pretense at professional qualifications performing the work of a surgeon in a laboratory of the
National Institutes of Health. I have seen a fully
conscious dog, with an open incision into the thoracic
and abdominal cavity, lying on the concrete floor of a
corridor on that same laboratory, writhing desperately
but unable to rise, while men and women passed without so much as a sideways glance . . ."

MARTYRDOM

Let us see in what condition an animal wakes up
from a surgical operation, assuming that effective anesthesia was administered. Take one of the countless
cats subjected annually to the traditional brain operations that belong to the favorite laboratory exercises.

The animal is in the throes of the profound nausea
that follows anesthesia, often causing retching and
vomiting. The immobility to which it is condemned
by the tight ligatures is in the long run a torture in itself. The mandibular joints are bruised or broken from
the gag that according to instructions must keep the
mouth "as widely open as possible" throughout the
operation. The tongue is perforated: which causes
severe swelling of the tongue and more torture. The
palate has been split and the cranium trephined, causing added traumas and excruciating pains.

The victim finds itself in this condition if the vivisector has chosen "the most elegant method of decerebrating cats," so defined by J. Markowitz on page 335 of his vivisection manual—*Experimental Surgery* (Williams & Wilkins, Baltimore, 2nd ed., 1949)— adding that this "should be a standard technique in a physiological laboratory."

The author is presented as professor of physiology at the University of Toronto and former assistant in experimental surgery at the Mayo Foundation, Rochester, Minn. A summary of his description: "The animal is laid on its back. The tongue is retracted by a ligature inserted through the tip. The soft palate is incised in the midline from the posterior edge of the hard palate. The mucous membrane and muscles are separated from the base of the skull extending downward to the anterior border of the foramen magnum, and laterally to expose the tympanic bullae. The flap of mucous membrane and muscle thus made is retracted by ligatures. A motor-driven dental burr is now used to trephine through the base of the skull. When a thin membrane of bone remains this is carefully removed by means of a fine spatula. A dural hook or a needle is used to open the dura and allow the escape of the cerebrospinal fluid. The internal carotid arteries are now exposed in the neck and tied. This is a simple exercise in neurosurgery." So much for the exercise.

And the cat? Another "scientific" publication informs us about the fate of one of those creatures subjected to similar experience. *Pflügers Archiv für die gesamte Physiologie,* (Vol. 222, p. 598), the classic German periodical that has fascinated generations of physiologists, shows a photograph of a cat lying on its back, with its legs stretched up in the air, and this caption:

"Right after the operation on the brain, the cat had a tendency to turn to the right and topple on its flank . . . It clearly suffered from fits of hydrocephalia [abnormal formation or pressure of fluid in the cranial cavity]. On September 27, in the course of one such fit, the right cortex [outer layer of the brain] was removed. The animal remained alive, from the first operation on August 4, until March of the following year."

That these exercises, dating from the last century, are still in vogue today, emerges from an item in the *Philadelphia Sunday Bulletin* of August 26, 1973. It quoted Julie Mayo, a registered nurse of Brigantine, New Jersey:

"I would rather a butcher slaughter my dog than have him fall into the hands of research scientists. Researchers are disguised as civilized people, but have the heart and hands of barbarians. No matter what the means, no matter how grisly the experiment, they will claim the end result is justification. Their lives revolve around pithed frogs, scalded rabbits, decerebrated cats and dismembered dogs. But don't just shrug and turn your back—you could be next!"

* * *

Elia de Cyon is the man who was handed the vivisectionist ideals by his teacher Claude Bernard and, upon his return to his native Russia, where he became professor of physiology at St. Petersburg, passed them on to Ivan Pavlov. Cyon's voluminous manual, *Methodik der Experimente und Vivisectionen,* was written in German and published by Ricker, in Giessen, Germany, and St. Petersburg, in 1876—the same year when the world's first organized antivivisectionist movement was started in England. That manual has helped initiate in the joys of vivisection entire generations of physiologists, to the tune of such fascinating information as:

"Rabbits are preferable when one wishes to observe the immediate consequence of the cutting of the spinal cord and brain injuries. On the other hand dogs are preferable when it comes to studying in the surviving animal the consequences of heavy injuries, especially of the spine, because dogs, especially young ones, can stand this kind of operation better than rabbits. As far as the resistance to very serious injuries is concerned, cats are especially recommended, as I have gathered from my colleagues. I don't have personal experience with cats, because my aversion against them is such that I have never been able to experiment on them . . ." (p. 25)

Again Cyon: "The vivisected animals are kept alive if one wishes to use them for further observations, or else they die of a purposely inflicted injury. In the latter case, if the animal is to be killed in order to be sected, the choice of the type of killing will depend on the type of operation. If one can't cause the animal's death by suffocation through interruption of the artificial respiration, the best way to kill it—if one wishes to observe a region lying outside the thoracic cavity— is through bleeding, using the knife."

What is the correct way to use the knife? Cyon's instructions are very precise: "The knife is pushed between the ribs into the heart (that the blade has reached its proper location is revealed by the slight pulsations of the knife) and then by executing ample movements in various directions a large wound is procured; the animal then dies rather quickly evincing violent hemorrhagic cramps . . . if observations are to be made inside the thoracic cavity, the hemorrhage has to be obtained by cutting the ventral aorta or large peripheric arteries. But if one wants the blood-vessels to be as full as possible during dissection, one kills the animal through suffocation, or by a stab in the spine (*durch einen Stich ins verlängerte Mark*), or by blowing large amounts of air into the jugular vein, etc . . ." (pp. 44-45)

About anesthesia Cyon has this to say: "Anesthesia in physiological experiments is given mainly for two reasons: first to achieve certain general results, which facilitate the surgical intervention, and secondly to cause certain special effects that are useful for the purpose of the investigation." (p. 52)

That Cyon had well learned the Claude Bernard lessons about the arrow-poison, curare, is shown on page 57: "Animals immobilized by the administration of curare (but they need artificial respiration to be kept alive) are wonderful subjects for study, as curare practically doesn't influence circulation. The motor nerves are not affected by the poison, but retain their electro-motor and physiological capacities intact. The entire peripheral and central sphere of sensitivity is spared by the poison. The animals feel everything that goes on in them ..."

* * *

The cats of that time would have known how fortunate they were to inspire Cyon with such a repulsion that it made him incapable of experimenting on them if they had been able to read his description on pages 31-32:

"The most remarkable case of resistance that I have observed in a dog was the following: in a large, very strong dog I made first of all a transfusion from the femoral artery into the crural vein in order to test the Nussbaum tranfusion apparatus. Immediately after that I wanted to measure the animal's blood speed in the carotid artery by means of Ludwig's circulation gauge *(Stromuhr)*. The test, however, had to be interrupted, because some oil had mistakenly got into the peripheral end of the carotid. The animal, which was not anesthetized, became suddenly sleepy, probably as a result of emboli that had formed in the brain. Then I proceeded to test the irritability of the anterior cords *(Stränge)* of the spinal marrow. The opening of the spine resulted in a heavy hemorrhage, due to the strong muscles. This test succeeded fully, after I had first separated the spine at the height of the 7th neck vertebra, then lifted a whole section of the breastbone, of which I removed the rear cords together with the gray substance. Then I irritated the front cords, both electrically and mechanically. After this test was ended I separated the chest marrow also from the lumbar marrow and removed it completely from the vertebral cavity. Into the stomach of the animal, which was still in soporific condition, was poured a large amount of water. After a few hours the animal revived, tried to drag itself forward with its front paws, but didn't get far, drank water avidly, but wouldn't eat. It lived for another few days, revived somewhat, moved with great difficulty on its front legs, wagged its tail frequently. Four days after the operation it was killed by suffocation, in order to determine whether an accumulation of CO_2 would cause cramps in the lower limbs."

* * *

Wrote Dr. Stephen Smith, in *Scientific Research: A View from Within* (Elliot Stock, London, 1899):

"I spent considerable time at the Physiological Institute of Strasburg, the scientific home of Prof. Goltz, one of the most famous physiologists . . . Why so much time is devoted to verifying well-known facts is not clear . . . with frogs no anesthetic was used, and with dogs it was only a pretext . . . The animals were bound down in a rack, moaning piteously and trying to struggle, but all in vain . . . Then the operator would cut and slash to his heart's content, and all for no purpose . . . An attendant proudly pointed out pigeons that could not hold their heads up, and dogs that could move around and around only in circles . . .

"One vivisectionist announced that it does not hurt a frog to be thrown into boiling water, nor a cat to be baked alive. Can any statement be more ridiculous to the mind of a person of ordinary intelligence? . . . At Paris I worked for a time in the Pasteur Institute. It is a common practice there to perform laparotomy on rabbits, which means cutting open the abdomen. I saw that no anesthetic was given. I inquired of an assistant who had been there some years whether an anesthetic was ever given. He replied: 'No, never.' On one occasion two French medical men came in to pay the institution a visit. A rabbit was being cut open. They looked on with amused smiles . . .

"In some cases such cruelty was resorted to as the smashing of the eyeballs. Animals that survived the operation were kept in cages until they were strong enough to stand another torture. The results were pitiful. Some of them partly paralyzed, others with brains removed . . .

"It is nonsense to say that the animals do not suffer because they have a lower order of intelligence. Pain is conveyed by the nerves to the brain, but there are other nerves than those of intelligence, such as sight, smell, touch and hearing. In some animals these nerves are much more highly developed and sensitive than in man."

* * *

In fact there is reason to believe that animals are able to suffer more than man, and not only physically. Thanks to our power of speech and communication we have many compensations—apart from our attendants' efforts to make us comfortable—that the animals don't have. A laboratory animal can't understand why, while shaken by fever or in the throes of hepatic or biliar colics, it is locked up in that wire cage or bound so tightly to an operating table that the ligatures cut into its flesh. Or why those big surrounding monsters in white squeeze its belly and force-feed it again and again, pushing into its already seared gullet ever more of those powders and liquids that are destroying its liver and twisting its guts, that cause it again and again to vomit and defecate, whereafter it is submitted to the cold showers that get the cage clean. Or why its scrotum is submitted to still another electric shock, which causes its guts to twist, or its brain, causing one more convulsion.

Even the mere confinement is harder to bear for an animal than for a human being. Inmates in penal institutions can reach an advanced age and retain their mental balance—as several great books written in prisons testify— apart from the consideration that they are usually held there to atone for some crime. But imprisoned animals usually die young.

Let's listen to some of the vivisectors themselves inadvertently confirming the animals' sufferings. Wrote L. Hermann and B. Luchsinger of Zurich University in the classic *Pflüger's Archiv:* "When the cat is immobilized on the Czermak restraining table, the palms of its paws sweat profusely from fear and nervousness." (Vol. 17, p. 310)

In the same publication Prof. Luchsinger wrote some time later: "In long-lasting experiments, the reason why one often obtains negative results is certainly due to the fact that the animals are immobilized for too long a time with ligatures that are too tight."

How does one immobilize a cat dragged out of the cage? Here is expert advice: "The right hand grabs the cat by the neck and the left crushes the lower lumbar spine . . . A pressure applied with both arms immobilizes the animal . . . If the cat tries to free itself, one should squeeze the soft loins with the left hand, which is bearing down on the spine. This results in an extremely painful compression of the kidneys, and the cat surrenders at once." (From *Die operative Technik des Tierexperimentes,* by Prof. O. Haberland, Berlin, 1926).

More advice comes from one Charles Livon's *Manual* (p. 13): "To subdue a very recalcitrant cat, one resorts to partial suffocation by hanging, or to administration of curare. Since it is difficult to bind a cat's short mouth, the best way to muzzle it is by sewing the lips together (the Walther method)."

* * *

All this is ancient history. Scientific savagery has made noticeable progress since, as emerges from a quarterly magazine manual titled *Expérimentation Animale,* published up to 1975 by Vigot Frères, 23 Rue de l'Ecole de Médecine, Paris—a publisher who specializes in veterinarian literature.

I quote from a long article signed by a well-known Paris veterinarian, G. Marie Saint Germain, beginning on page 78 in Vol. 2, No. 1 of this magazine manual (1969), "Modalités de l'introduction en laboratoire de chiens et chats ne provenant pas d'élévages spécialisés," in which this veterinarian gives advice on how easiest to "examine" a dog's mouth after the animal has been solidly immobilized to the restraining board. "In many cases it is necessary to open the mouth by force and to insert a mouth-opener. When forcing a dog's mouth open, it is necessary to interpose between the dog's teeth and one's own fingers the dog's cheek. The dog will bite with less conviction if its teeth bite into its own mucous membrane. If the animal is too recalcitrant, one can bind a ribbon around each jawbone, facilitating the opening of the mouth by force."

On page 81 an item about cat-handling: "For opera-

tions of long duration, it is easy to perform on all four
paws the complete amputation of the last phalanxes,
thus removing the nails. One can protect oneself from
the jaws by applying a mouth-opener. Naturally, the
animal will cry very loudly, but the operator will be
safe."

* * *

Parabiosis is a widely performed, traditional operation that artificially creates Siamese twins by surgically
uniting two or more animals. This operation, besides
being utterly senseless in itself even if it were to succeed, has forever been doomed to failure owing to the
organism's well-known immunological reaction. Each
organism inevitably rejects the other to which it has
been united. In spite of the inbuilt failure of this kind
of "experiment," they rate high among the laboratory
exercises done with idiotic repetitiveness, regardless of
the predictable failures. Even Dr. Robert White of
monkey-head transplant fame has admitted having
done them.

What the animals subjected to this unnatural operation must go through may be gathered from the following instructions of Austrian Prof. H. Pfeiffer of
Graz: "As the animals that have been surgically united
have a tendency, especially in the first hours, to attack each other, inflicting sometimes mortal injuries,
this can be prevented by sewing the cheek of each animal to the corresponding front paw by means of a
strong silk thread, so tightly that the mouths of the two
animals can neither reach each other nor bite."
(From *Zeitschrift für die gesamte experimentelle Medizin,* Vol. 86, p. 293, 1929)

In the first experiments, after being sewn together
by the skin, the animals were tied to each other for
several days with twine. But the animals managed to
get free, tearing the skin. So they were sewn together
also by the muscles and the belly. The animals managed to tear themselves free just the same, lacerating
the tissues and the peritoneum and spilling the innards.
So the animals were totally immobilized with a plaster
cast. This didn't work either: "It was surprising to see

how quickly, even if a padding was used, the animals developed deformations of the chest, which probably in many cases were responsible for their death." So wrote a German experimenter, Dr. J. Froschbach (*Archiv für Experimentelle Pathologie und Pharmakologie*, Vol. 60, 1909).

Methods in Animal Experimentation, a modern three-volume book by William I. Gay (Academic Press, New York, 1965), gives some interesting insights on how one can prevent monkeys dying from decubitus wounds, meaning bedsores resulting from remaining imprisoned in restraining chairs for years. By changing the monkey's position, holding it even head down, one bedsore will heal while another is forming. Thus monkeys can be kept alive even for several years of uninterrupted torture, whereas in the past they died within a few months.

*   *   *

Not more enviable are the lives and deaths of the animals subjected to "simple" feeding experiments. Severe eye alterations are noted in diseased conditions produced by a diet deficient in Vitamin A. Actual ulceration and perforation of the cornea, (the front lens of the eye) was a condition "seen at different times in puppies eating linseed oil, oxidized butter," etc. These experiments were described by Prof. Mellanby, M.A., M.D., in the *Special Report*, No. 61, of the British Medical Research Council. Other symptoms included paralysis, tetany and convulsions.

In No. 167 of that Council's *Reports*, experimental scurvy induced in guinea pigs produced "tenderness and swelling of the joints, the animal frequently adopts a position in which it rests on its side while the affected member is held twitching in the air." In animals dying from scurvy "hemorrhages are most frequent in the limbs. In cases where they occur in the intestinal tract, blood is frequently passed in life, and death occurs suddenly."

The *British Medical Journal*, May 12, 1934 (p. 849) reported thus the effects of unnatural diet on rats: "The animals were hurled with great violence from side to side of their cages . . ."

The effect of excessive doses of Vitamin D. on 113 puppies was described in the *British Journal of Experimental Pathology,* Oct. 1932 (p. 403): "Pup No. 1 suffered from rapid loss of weight, vomiting, diarrhea, conjuctivitis which kept the lids almost completely closed, until death on the 11th day. At post mortem on pup No. 4 the bowel was found to be hemorrhagic and in part gangrenous."

The *British Medical Journal,* Jan. 21, 1928 (p. 91), described the following effect of "Experiments in Nutrition": "Sometimes the fits are delayed till about the 18th day when they are much more violent. The animal, in between the fits, walks on tiptoes, as though there were a permanent extensor spasm, and when the fits supervene dashes violently about the cage, screaming, or rolls over in convulsions with the jaws locked in an open position. Death is the usual sequel."

Ever since antiquity, man has known that an organism can live longer without food than without water. Only the experimental physiologists don't seem aware of it, if we are to judge by the thousands of experiments they constantly undertake to see how long it takes an animal to die of hunger or of thirst, as in the following case, reported by the *Medical Press,* Nov. 28, 1928, which is constantly being repeated by the new generations:

"Some curious experiments are reported on animals by de Boer, who observes that complete abstinence from food brings about death more quickly if fluids are withheld. Fasting pigeons die within 4 or 5 days of thirst, whereas if given water only they may live 12 days."

*   *   *

Vivisectionists like pointing out that for a great many experiments mice and rats are used, knowing that these animals have few friends among men. But this is so only because we have scarce familiarity with those species. Rats are particularly intelligent and sensitive animals, and the cruel "behaviorist" experiments keep proving that they don't behave much differently from us.

When one of those little rodents, having been poisoned, writhes in the laboratory cage, foaming at the mouth and defecating, seized by intestinal or gallbladder cramps and colics, it doesn't suffer less than a human being in the same condition, and the syringe that stabs its little body is the equivalent of a lance piercing a man. And can there be at this stage somebody still so naive as to assume that the cesarean sections to which the laboratories subject millions of mothers in order to obtain sterile rats are performed under anesthesia?

But of course the researchers' favorite animals have always been our cousin primates, being the most similar to man. They are used to test the effects of exposure to radioactive material, to poison gases, to blasts from high explosives, to various irradiations, to radon seeds implanted in the brain, to cosmic rays at a height of twenty miles above the earth (in plastic balloons). They are also used to determine brain areas localization, for the production of epileptic attacks (by multiple injections into the brain substance, the scarification of brain tissue, or the administration of electric shocks), for the study of the effects of leucomoty (a brain operation) after inducing severe neuroses, for the production of cancer, epidemic dropsy, trachoma of the eyes, gastric ulcer, guinea-worm infestation, pneumonia, poliomyelitis, rheumatism, severe shock from fatigue or from extreme cold or injury, to study the effects of sunstroke, or of the displacement of organs by various operations, and for the testing of toxic drugs. Moreover they get infected with anthrax, malaria, rabies, syphilis, and in fact with every possible disease, and are being used increasingly for the study of drug addiction and "behaviorism," preferably in response to electric shocks. And this list must not be taken as exhaustive by far.

Just one instance of what monkeys may go through is found in an extract from the *Lancet* of September 19, 1931, at a time when the scientists had not yet learned to disguise nauseating experiments in the smoke-screen language that is used today. It concerns monkeys that had been infected with rabies at the Lister Institute:

"December 10th: The monkey was found clinging to the bars of its cage uttering repeated and particularly piercing shrieks quite unlike the normal cry of the monkey . . . The animals appeared to be in a state of extreme terror . . .

"December 15th: The monkey had a staring gaze and seemed unaware of the presence of food, of its cage mate, or of the observer. It squealed continually. On interference [meaning provocation—Author's Note] it did not attempt to bite. The chin was abraded from constant picking with the fingers . . .

"After a short period, in which the animal was actively aggressive and in one case killed its cage mate, violent spasms, occasionally sufficient to throw the animal bodily across the cage, occurred. It gradually passed into a state of general weakness, ending in death . . ."

Three animals bit themselves severely, two chewing off the end of a finger, and one the whole skin of the forearm, exposing the muscles from the elbow to the wrist.

ANESTHESIA FOR THE PUBLIC

Some means had to be devised by the vivisectionists to insure perpetuation of their activities. Although man is by nature the most ruthless of all living beings —the only one that kills not only for nourishment but also for clothes, for ornament, for curiosity, for vanity, for gain, for sport—he is also a moral being. Hence, it may be assumed that once the public is fully informed of vivisection's inevitable cruelty, the majority will not stand for it, and ask for immediate abolition.

So to keep public interference at bay, the vivisectionists devised the anesthesia myth, designed to convince the public that animals don't suffer at all, that their sufferings are just fantastic inventions of a few hysterical cranks.

In Europe, the anesthesia myth has been achieved to a remarkable degree both through the secrecy in which all experiments take place, and by advertising the seemingly severe laws that "regulate" the vivisectionist practice. In most countries the state has been forced to admit that inflicting pain on defenseless animals is immoral. The laws that have been promulgated prove it. But in every country the purpose of the laws is regularly being circumvented, not only by the secrecy in which the experiments take place, but also by the addition of some clause that makes any torture legal.

Example: In Italy, legislation includes one paragraph that is more sweeping and reassuring than in most other countries: "Vivisection on dogs and cats is normally prohibited." And yet it is mainly dogs and cats that are subjected to vivisection in Italy. The catch is in the word "normally." For that proviso is nullified at once by a following clause, which adds, "except if it is considered indispensable for experiments of scientific research or if no other animals are available."

Another Italian law reads: "Vivisection may be done only under anesthesia, which must be effective throughout the entire operation." How humane—and how useful to the vivisectors, who can hold this law up to objectors. They don't hold up the clause that immediately follows: "Excepting the cases in which anesthesia is incompatible with the purpose of the experiment."

And further: "It is forbidden to resort, for further experiments, to an animal that has already been subjected to vivisection—unless it is absolutely necessary."

And who is to judge as to whether anything related to vivisection is necessary or not? The vivisectors, of course—in their capacity as "scientists." Which is the equivalent of the promulgation of a law that would say: "It is forbidden to kill, except when the killer considers it absolutely necessary."

* * *

In Great Britain a stipulation known as the "Pain Condition" has been imposed on experimenters. It reads. "If any animal at any time during any of the said experiments is found to be suffering pain which is either severe or is likely to endure, and if the main result of the experiment has been attained, the animal shall forthwith be painlessly killed."

There is more than one catch in this smoke-screen phrase. As usual, none other but the experimenter is left to decide whether "the main result of the experiment has been attained." And as there is no standard for measuring or assessing pain, what the victim may consider "severe" may be dismissed as trivial by the experimenter, especially as it is not he himself that is being subjected to it. The same goes for "likely to endure." Furthermore, vivisectionist indoctrination has produced a breed of pseudoscientists who think that the question of inflicting pain (on any creature except their own person) "is of no relevance today" —as Prof. Robert White from Cleveland has written in his "American Scholar" article which will come under closer scrutiny later in this work.

Furthermore, as the employ of anesthesia is incompatible with the post-operative observations, with all experiments on the nervous system, on pain, on behavior, on stress, on all experiments of long duration, on all those that induce any disease with the pretext of "studying" it, with the preventive efficacity and toxicity tests of all new drugs, it is clear that anesthesia is rarely applicable, even if there were among the experimenters a tenderhearted individual.

In practice, anesthesia is given to animals usually only at the inception of a serious surgical operation, and then mainly to keep them still. But since the animals, totally immobilized by the restraining devices, and solidly muzzled or surgically devocalized, have no means to voice any discomfort, nobody ever knows how effectively and for how long they are anesthetized.

The effect of anesthesia is anyway always short-lived, just as the post-operative pains are always atrocious and protracted. With animals they may last years.

Only Great Britain is obliged by law to reveal the number and type of experiments that the government has authorized. According to the figures published by

the Home Office, of the 5.8 million experiments performed on live animals in Great Britain during 1971,
more than 4.5 million were done without any anesthesia. Of the anesthetized animals, the great majority
recovered from the influence of the anesthetic and
suffered whatever pain followed. Less than 3 percent
of the millions of animals employed were put to death
in their sleep.

Vivisectionists dispute those official statistics, con-
tending that many experiments consist of a "mere
pinprick" and so naturally require no anesthesia. How
true. But the purpose of those pinpricks is usually to
infect the animal with cancer, with epidemic dropsy,
trachoma of the eyes, pneumonia, poliomyelitis, meningitis, rabies, syphilis, and other such niceties, then
watch the animal slowly waste away.

It was said earlier in this book that exaggeration
in the matter of vivisection is not only superfluous,
but impossible. In fact, even the official figures
obtained from the Home Office commit the sin of optimism. A true anesthetic causes loss of all consciousness, sensation or feeling: And this was undoubtedly
the sense in which the word was intended to be
interpreted by all lawmakers. But in the *Lancet,* in
the *British Medical Journal* and other such publications, operations are described for which the experimenters who were supposed to use anesthesia, used
other drugs instead that were no such thing.

As former Air Chief Marshal Lord Dowding reported to the House of Lords on July 18, 1957: "For
instance, dial anesthesia was used at Cambridge University during the tearing out of the eyes of cats."
Dial, as Lord Dowding pointed out, is not an anesthetic but a sedative and hypnotic for nervous insomnia.
Another sedative and hypnotic, Amytal, was used on
dogs that had their abdomen cut open, as Lord
Dowding revealed in the same address.

One of the rare tours of inspection that took place
in Italy recently revealed that the directors of some
vivisection laboratories weren't even aware of the existence of laws on anesthesia. The attitude of experi-

menters toward animal sufferings is the same everywhere, at all times.

Already a century ago, Dr. Emanuel Klein, a German physiologist who taught at London's St. Bartholomew Hospital, caused considerable embarrassment to his British colleagues with his too candid answers to the Royal Commission charged with investigating vivisection. All the vivisectors who had preceded him on the stand had assured the investigators that animals are either entirely insensitive to the extirpation of the eyes, of the liver, of the pancreas, of the gallbladder, to poisoning and burning, or else that they were always effectively anesthetized. Klein, recently arrived in England, was puzzled by all this hypocrisy, and declared in essence:

"Except for teaching purposes I never use anesthetics . . . A man who conducts special research has no time, so to speak, for thinking what the animal will feel or suffer." (*Royal Commission Report*, 1875, par. 3538-3540)

Where they exist, the laws on vivisection, designed to protect the animals, serve only to protect the vivisectors, since the prevailing secrecy makes the laws practically inoperative.

Some countries have not even bothered to introduce those smoke-screen laws with which to lull public opinion. The U.S., Canada, India, Pakistan, South Africa, Australia and New Zealand are among them. By Swedish law, control of laboratory animals is vested in the Swedish Veterinary Board, which is supposed to license experimenters and has power of inspection, but delegates this power to, of all people, the director of each laboratory.

In Switzerland, a member of the commission in charge of inspecting the university laboratories told me that inspections are made only by appointment, the vivisectors being given several days' notice. I committed a major faux-pas by asking why the commission didn't pay surprise visits. "We can't treat university professors like criminals!" was the indignant reply.

An interesting gambit is used in France, where most doctors simply deny that vivisection exists. They say it's a thing of the past. Of course France is not only the cradle of modern vivisection and the home of the Institut Pasteur, one of the most active vivisection laboratories in Europe, but it has even added a new kink to vivisection. In the forest land near Bordeaux, the French Education Ministry has founded a special laboratory called CEBAS—Center for Biological Studies of Wild Animals—in which at the expense of the unaware French taxpayer a Prof. R. Cavenc catches free animals of the forest for the purpose of vivisection.

In a 1974 letter of his, this professor assured me that he did it all "to alleviate human suffering." A letter of mine that pressed him for details has remained unanswered. In private, Prof. Cavenc confided that if he closed his laboratory a score of breadwinners would be out of work. And he couldn't be so cruel.

Another cute gimmick devised by the French is to replace the word vivisection in the school books with "dissection."

ANESTHESIA MADE IN U.S.A.

American vivisectors, seduced by the enormous research grants available, have so far successfully defeated all bills designed to curb vivisection in any way. This has been achieved through bribery in high political quarters, and by a systematic propaganda designed to convince the public and legislators that laboratory animals are already amply protected by the natural humaneness of the vivisectors themselves. Assurances of their unshakable humanitarian conscience were repeatedly given—by the interested parties themselves—in the course of the House of Representatives hearings which will be cited later in another connection.

Every American manual on animal experimentation contains elaborate instructions and recipes for anesthetizing every type of animal, including pigeons; although no one ever explains how one can be sure that a bird is effectively anesthetized. With human patients, the surgeon knows that the anesthesia becomes effective the instant the patient stops counting aloud. If in the course of an operation anesthesia wears off, the surgeon knows it because the patient starts shouting. It happened with me. The animal can neither be made to count, nor is it able to shout.

In fact one of the most effective "anesthesias for the public" that has been devised is the so-called "devocalization" of the laboratory animals. How does one prevent the cries of the victims from arousing the neighbors and the passers-by in the street? As a rule, by severing their vocal cords. This means added torture for the victim, especially while swallowing food; but what counts is not the avoidance of pain to the animals, but to the public sensitivity.

"Debarking" and "devocalizing" are two new terms with which the vivisectors have enriched the American language. In Europe, the severing of the vocal cords, although widespread, is illegal, so the vivisectors do it but can't admit to doing it. In the U.S., where nothing connected with "medical science" is illegal, the vivisectors freely admit that it is a routine procedure. They have developed new "sophisticated techniques" to achieve it. One of these techniques is the "electrocauterization," done mostly on dogs, which—perhaps because of their long association with man—are the most articulate and persistent complainers.

Dr. Gunther Kraus of Roswell Park Memorial Laboratories at Buffalo, New York, wrote in the *American Veterinary Medical Association Journal* (Vol. 143, No. 9, Nov. 1, 1963): "In our laboratory devocalizing dogs is necessary because of human patients in neighboring wards. We have used electrocautery for devocalization of more than 3000 dogs."

Electrocautery is a method of "debarking" where a hot cautery tip is used to burn the vocal cords. The animals, Dr. Kraus says, must be well under the anesthetic—not to spare the animal any suffering, but because "in lightly anesthetized dogs the hot cautery tip may stimulate jerking movements," so that the job would have to be done all over again, wasting the scientist's valuable time. The consequences of debarking may include chronic bronchitis, laryngitis, pneumonia, and severe hemorrhages.

Another still more "sophisticated" method of silencing dogs has been devised by burning, instead of the vocal cords, part of the brain with electricity, after the animal has been immobilized in a restraining device. This method was devised by Dr. Niles Skultety, associate professor in the division of neurosurgery at the University of Iowa College of Medicine.

According to *Archives of Neurology* (Vol. 6, Mar. 1962) before the operation the dogs were tested as to their reaction to pain and the amount and type of vocalization, produced by pinching the tail with a Kocher clamp. Most of the dogs were silent after the brain injury even when subjected to pain; but, after all, so are the dogs whose vocal cords are cut in the old-fashioned way. However, the new method involving electricity is fascinating American vivisectors, though some of its results might appear less than admirable to common mortals. The description of one dog so injured reads:

"It made no attempt to stand and did not eat or drink for the first 3 days after operation. By the 4th day it could right itself and crawl about the cage. The hind limbs assumed a position similar to that of a crouching animal, and the forelimbs were flexed. It never regained proper balance till the day it was killed (the 16th day), and it could easily be knocked down with a slight push. When pinched painfully it attempted to get at the source of stimulation, but its efficiency was impaired."

No matter what American textbook aimed at the general public you look up, you read about the "humane" treatment of laboratory animals. This, then, is the anesthesia to which the public is subjected. So the 1974 international edition of the Encyclopedia Americana includes under "Vivisection" this statement:

"Significant advances in anesthetic technique and in neurophysiology—chiefly the result of animal experiments—have enabled the scientists to develop laboratory animal methods as humane as those used in modern medical practice."

How can such statements be explained in the light of the various experiments revealed every day in the scientific papers, of which a cross-section will be presented in the next part? Very simply. The school texts on physiology are compiled by other physiologists, all trained in the vivisectionist mentality, most of them owing their "scientific" standing to their vivisectionist activity.

And as George Bernard Shaw put it in his various conferences on the subject: "Whoever doesn't hesitate to vivisect will hardly hesitate to lie about it."

Part Three

THE EVIDENCE

Readers are advised that they can skip without any loss, and in fact they should, this entire Part Three, which contains nothing but a small fraction of the experiments performed in the past or currently. Experience has taught that many people stop reading altogether when they come upon the descriptions of actual experiments, and my purpose is to have as many people as possible read this treatise. Why sacrifice time and paper on this part at all then? Because many a vivisector will simply deny that these things actually happen, and here is the proof that they do, and in fact all the time, day and night, in thousands of laboratories all over the world.

Digging up the evidence was no pleasant task, but at least it was not too hard to come by, for the vivisectors themselves are eager to report their experiments in specialized publications, carefully clad in anodyne terms. Keep in mind that currently more than two million reports of vivisection experiments are published each year. But the majority, of course, are never reported—those that the experimenters themselves consider useless, repetitive, or failures; or else those so obviously sadistic that no vivisector would dare to render them public, not even in a "scientific" paper. They mimeograph and circulate the reports among themselves.

*   *   *

When and how did it all begin? It began with Cain, of course. But we are interested mainly in what happens in our own time, when vivisection is tacitly accepted by the majority, being palmed off as a humanitarian undertaking of dedicated altruists.

First we must remember a few of the initiators of the so-called Modern Physiological School, for today's "official" medical science places them on a pedestal and presents them to the new generations as examples to follow. Many of their senseless experiments, performed already millions of times, keep being repeated today in private laboratories and medical colleges the world over.

The main feature of all those experiments is that the animals are never cured, but are made sick. The researchers' entire ingenuity focuses on this project: To get hold of healthy animals and to create in them experimental diseases and injuries. Which, being inflicted deliberately by arbitrary interferences, from the outside, are inevitably entirely different from any disease or injury that arises spontaneously or occurs by accident.

In 1825, twenty years before Claude Bernard converted the basement of his Paris home into a private vivisection laboratory, a book appeared in Copenhagen with the title *Physiological Results of Modern Vivisection*. It was written in German, which in northern and eastern Europe had replaced Latin as the scientific language. The Danish author, Peter Wilhelm Lund, had caught so well the mood of the period that he was awarded a prize for it by the Royal Academy of Copenhagen.

In his book, Lund passed in review the results of physiological experiments that he considered the most "interesting," involving many thousands of animals, done in laboratories all over Europe. The one refreshing part about Lund's book, in contrast with today's reports, is that the author never tries to justify the experiments as being helpful to mankind. Each served merely to satisfy somebody's "curiosity," to enable the person to publish papers that might gain a professorship for the author or at least some notoriety as a "scientist."

Sample experiments that Lund considered worthy

of his collection: How many quarts of water must be poured into a horse's lungs in order to kill it? On page 83, this example:

"Goodwyn already had observed that the animal can withstand extraordinary quantities of water without harm, and Schlöpfer had pointed out that the water had to be poured through a slit made in the windpipe, otherwise the larynx will contract, causing the animal to suffocate. These observations were confirmed at the French veterinary school of Lyon, where students poured water into a horse's windpipe in order to kill it. But to their great surprise the horse suffered no harm, until they poured all at once 30 quarts into his windpipe. Another horse, on which they wanted to repeat the experiment, died only after 40 quarts were poured into it all at once." The book goes on, citing similar experiments with numerous variations made elsewhere by other experimenters.

On page 149, in a chapter titled "Movements of the Brain": "Dorigny proceeded to scarify a dog's paw and discovered that every incision caused an acceleration of the brain movement. When the spinal marrow was cut just below the brain, the brain movements came to a stop, even if liquids were poured into the carotid arteries. When the cervical plexus was stimulated, the brain movements started anew. The same happened when the windpipe was ligatured and a nerve trunk was stimulated. After the carotid and vertebral arteries had been ligatured, the movements came to a stop, as Bichat and Richerand had already reported. But the movement started anew when the cervical plexus was violently stimulated."

On page 191, in the chapter "The Influence of the Magnet on the Heart": "From the spine of an 8 day old kitten, Weinhold drove out the marrow. After the heart had ceased beating, he filled the vertebral duct with iron filings and inserted a wire that he put in contact with the two poles of a magnet. After 5 minutes he felt evidence of pulsation and for about 40 minutes slight contractions of the heart. Without doubt we see here a collection of the most beautiful results for physiology and also for physics. They seem almost too beautiful! So I dare not yet believe they are true, before they are confirmed by other experiments."

Lund cites many more examples of the incredibly beautiful results obtained, as on page 332, in the chapter "Experiments on the Analogy of Nervous Power and Electricity":

"Of a cat that was giving no more signs of life, Weinhold filled the cranial and spinal cavities with an amalgam of mercury, tin and silver. After 20 seconds the cat showed such a vital tension that it raised its head, opened its eyes, stood staring, tried to crawl forward, toppled on its side, struggled back to its feet, then collapsed, exhausted. Meanwhile blood circulation and pulsation were lively, even when Weinhold cut open the animal's chest and stomach. In another cat Weinhold filled only the cranial cavity with the amalgam. He noticed that the pupil contracted and the cat evinced fright when approached by a flame, and it was startled and listened when the table was struck with a key."

Skipping the rest of the 344 pages of this prizewinning treatise, we come to the Appendix, which relates an experiment performed at Copenhagen's Royal Museum of Natural History on rabbits by author Lund himself, in the presence of his teacher, Prof. J. Reinhardt, to whom the book is gratefully dedicated. (Another vivisector dedicated a similar book to his mother.)

"First experiment: the rabbit's 7th pair of nerves was exposed on the left side. When the nerve was squeezed with tweezers, the animal evinced pain and contractions of the facial muscles. This happened also in all the following cases, so I won't mention it again. Other results could not be observed, owing to the copious hemorrhage caused by the operation.

"Second experiment: the skull was opened and the left hemisphere was extracted. The fifth pair of nerves, covered by the outer layer of the brain, was exposed and cut, while the animal was crying very loudly. Every sign of sensibility had disappeared from the left side of the face, the left eye appeared dead and opaque, but not the right eye. The 7th pair of nerves was exposed on the left side. When the nerves were squeezed, jerks of the body and movements of the head clearly indicated pain . . ."

The experiments continue with remarkable regularity. Only the fifth does not succeed, because after the skull had been opened, the left hemisphere removed and the 5th pair had been cut, the stupid animal let down the scientist and passed on.

DAWN OF A NEW WORLD

Claude Bernard, France's national hero and apostle of modern vivisection, had an oven built that left the head of the animal outside while the body was roasting inside. This enabled him to write one of his many pseudoscientific works: *Leçons sur la chaleur animale, sur les effets de la chaleur et sur la fièvre* (1876), meaning "Lessons on animal heat, on the effect of heat and on fever." The founder of today's vivisectionist method actually hoped to discover through that oven "the secret of the fever": as if body heat caused by baking were the same thing as a fever caused by an infection. Neither Bernard nor his disciples ever realized that he was confusing cause and consequence—that in a patient the high temperature is the consequence of the ailment, not the cause. Bernard described in detail the slow death of dogs and rabbits roasted alive, his oven's only contribution to science being the information that a dog with the head outside the oven takes more time to die than one that is entirely locked in.

*   *   *

One of Bernard's German contemporaries, Prof. Emanuel Klein, infected with the virus of diphtheria the eyes of several cats. He reported that the infection lead to the perforation of the eyes and the death of the cats after a fortnight of intense suffering.

*   *   *

Claude Bernard, with whom we shall get better acquainted later, spawned whole generations of vivisectors who helped spread and popularize the practice throughout Europe.

One of them was his close friend Paul Bert, also Minister of Public Education, who described one of his own experiments in the *Revue des Deux Mondes* of September 1, 1864. Having immobilized a dog with a massive dose of curare (which paralyzes the nerves so totally that artificial respiration must be applied to keep the subject alive, but leaves sensitivity intact and even increases it), Bert proceeded to cut up the animal. First he removed all the flesh from one side, from the head to the hip, exposing the visceral, median, pneumogastric, sympathetic and infra-orbital nerves. For 10 consecutive hours these exposed nerves were then submitted to electric stimulations, the helplessly curarized animal being unable to vent his sufferance with a single cry. The experiment was crowned by a discovery which was duly reported: Whenever the pain reached a climax, the dog urinated! . . . Then the experimenters went calmly home leaving the dog in care of the machine that had to keep its lungs pumping until the next day, when they intended to continue their "observations." But the stupid dog let them down and passed on during the night.

* * *

Prof. John Reid, who popularized vivisection at Scotland's St. Andrew University, is mainly remembered for his experiments on dogs' cranial nerves, involving excruciating suffering, as he, too, worked without any anesthesia. He also made a "study" of the effects of fear on the heartbeat, for which he used dogs that had already experienced painful vivisections. An abstract of one of his reports reads:

"At a longer or shorter period after the operation, the pulsations of the heart were reckoned . . . after the dog had been caressed for some time to calm its fears. It was then lifted up on the table on which it had been previously tied and operated upon, and after having been spoken to harshly, the pulsations were again reckoned . . . In the seventh dog the pulsations, 8½ hours after the operation, were 130; when placed on the table and made to struggle, the pulsations, as far as could be made out, were about 220; when he had been subjected to pain, and had struggled more violently, they became so frequent that they could not be accurately reckoned, but were at least 260 in a minute."

These sordid statistics, that Reid recorded in detail, would not be published today, when the importance of secrecy has been realized, but in Reid's day they were thought worthy to be published at least three times: first, in *The Edinburgh Medical and Surgical Journal,* then in an address to the British Scientific Association, and in Reid's own book, *Physiological Researches.*

*   *   *

Paolo Mantegazza, the intrepid professor of pathology at the University of Pavia, and known in his native Italy also as a novelist, invented a new torture instrument in order to write *The Physiology of Pain:* a triple-action tweezer that he named the Torturer, through which he wanted "to study the mechanics of respiration under the influence of pain." A rabbit that had been tortured with this instrument for five minutes was still so agitated and shaky forty minutes later that Mantegazza wasn't able to count its breathing rate, which was the purpose of the experiment. Another rabbit was tortured in the instrument for two solid hours, whereafter Mantegazza in addition hammered two long nails into the legs through the palms of the paws. He wrote that he thus caused the rabbit a more intense pain than through any previous torture. He also reported that two albino rats, after having been tortured for hours, finally attacked each other, and when they had no more strength left to bite, they remained tightly embraced, panting and whining. (Very similar experiments involving thousands of dogs and cats are being made in U.S. universities today.)

Mantegazza's conclusions, as regularly happens in

the small world of vivisection, were questioned by some of his colleagues: in this case by Ugolino Musso and Haidenheim, who repeated his experiments, without coming to any final conclusions either.

Mantegazza accused one of his rivals, Moritz Schiff, of being incapable of serious research on pain, because he was "too tender-hearted toward animals." Everything is relative. Schiff, a German who lived in Florence, had just become a member of the newly founded Animal Protection League when he was driven out of town by outraged citizens who had discovered what went on in his laboratory. In fact, Schiff ranked high among the vivisectors of his period, even though his exaggerated "sensibility" that Mantegazza had deplored prompted him to cut the vocal cords of his victims in order to prevent, as he said, "nocturnal concerts which might discredit physiological research." His "research" included filling with sand and pebbles the stomach of dogs after sewing up their intestine, and in pouring boiling water into them to see how long it would take them to die.

All these reports don't come from some madman's diary, but are typical examples of what can be found in the best known textbooks of their time, and have been reported by the very experimenters who performed them. To Paolo Mantegazza, who in 1870 was nominated senator, the Italian Encyclopedia dedicates an entire column. The biographer—presumably himself a physiologist—defines Mantegazza as an *anthropologist, hygienist, pathologist and writer*.

* * *

French Prof. Brachet reported the following "moral" experiment, as the psychological experiments were called at the time:

"I inspired a dog with as much hatred against myself as I could, tormenting it in every possible way. After I tore out its eyes I could approach it without frightening it. But when I talked, its anger was again aroused. Then I perforated its eardrums and poured hot wax into its ears. Once the dog was

unable to hear me, I could approach and caress it . . .
The dog seemed to take pleasure in my caresses."

*   *   *

One of the countless monuments to vivisectionist
futility is a "study" on shock by an American doctor,
George W. Crile, who sacrificed 148 dogs for the
purpose. Here is a summary of his book, *Surgical
Shock* (Lippincott, New York, 1899):

"I tarred some of the dogs and set fire to them. I
disembowelled others and poured boiling water into
the cavity. I held their paws over a blowtorch. I
crushed the testicles of some male dogs. I broke
all the bones of their limbs. I gouged out the eyes of
some dogs and scraped the orbits. In others I manipulated the intestines. I poured ether into the windpipe. I shot one with a .38 pistol, another with a .32
pistol. I manipulated the kidneys of one dog, then its
liver, then I inflicted a serious injury to one of its
kidneys, then I shot it with a .32 pistol."

However, 55 years and hundreds of thousands of
equally stupid and cruel "experiments on shock" later,
the experimental physiologists knew just as much about
shock as Crile had known when he started his experiments, namely nothing; to wit:

"We finished the First World War with several
rival theories about shock, all which we now know
to be wrong—or shall we say 'now believe to be
wrong,' for in medicine truth and error are transient terms." So wrote Sir Henage Ogilvie, Master of
Surgery, in Britain's *Medical Press,* Oct. 20, 1954,
page 354. And after more hundreds of thousands of
similar experiments, today's experimental physiologists have multiplied the confusions, but are as unable
as ever to answer the simple question: "What is
shock?"

*   *   *

The Crile book, a worthy conclusion to the vivisectionists' efforts of the last century, fascinated experimental physiologists as much as Claude Bernard's
pseudoscientific works. And while the countless ex-

periments on living animals had achieved nothing but to assemble a mass of sterile data, of useless facts and figures, medical art and surgical technology had taken giant steps forward without using animals—through the sheer exercise of human intellect and clinical observation.

Chloroform, ether, laughing gas, iodine, digitalis, quinine, aspirin, belladonna, strophantin, had all been found without resorting to animals. Fever thermometer, pulse count, stethoscope, auscultation, percussion had been devised without animal tests. Pasteur had announced the germ theory based on various studies on the fermentation of wine and beer. There had been the discovery of X rays by Roentgen, which—like that of radium a few years later—was not due to animal experimentation any more than the rediscovery of the importance of hygiene and of asepsis in surgery in general. If we took all these discoveries away, modern medicine would have practically nothing left. And they lifted surgery out of the medieval doldrums, thanks to the great British innovators like Bell, Clay, Keith, Fergusson, Tait, Treves, who all had explicitly declared that vivisection could only lead medical art astray.

The surgical progress will be examined in Part Four. First we must see how the physiologists of the last century, after deceiving themselves, went on deceiving others, making the new generations believe that what they were doing was by no means corrupt and obtuse, but useful and admirable.

THE 20TH CENTURY

The famed Russian Ivan Pavlov was the pupil of Cyon, who had been the pupil of Claude Bernard. Working with up to 70 assistants in his Moscow laboratory, he "discovered" what the Greeks already knew —that the mere idea of food could produce salivation and hence secretion of gastric juices in a dog, no less than in man. His published works represent one of the most remarkable monuments to vivisectionist futility, and in this sense they are recommended reading.

They are also a monument to man's blind cruelty, which we may just as well call sadism, though vivisectors would rather call it "scientific curiosity."

Pavlov showed great ingenuity devising always new ways in which to cause mental agony. In one case he employed dogs that had suffered from a severe flood in Leningrad. They had been shut up in a kennel when the water had poured in, and many of them had stood for days with their heads barely above water. Pavlov put these animals in cages and ran water under them, making them believe the floods were coming back. This experiment was repeated many times with the same dogs, in each instance reducing them to an agony of cringing terror.

Another animal had been taught to associate fear with a difference in the beats of two metronomes. At the beat, the dog began to tremble, its eyes widened, saliva dripped from its mouth, there was a deep, gasping breathing, now and then a moan, and abruptly the dog sank in a heap on the top of the desk. The same dog had been trained to fear falling down stairs, and stood at the top of the stairs in an agony of terror.

After operating twice on the brains of numerous dogs, Pavlov described their manifestations of pain, their nervousness, their extreme sensitivity and convulsive state, accompanied—evidently to Pavlov's surprise—by fits of hostility toward their torturer. In his report, the 1904 Nobel laureate wrote: "The seriousness of their convulsions keeps rising up to their death, which usually comes 2 years after the operation." Two years . . . But there is one dog that Pavlov remembered with particular fondness: a mongrel which in the course of two years withstood no less than 128 surgical operations before passing on to a better life.

(After Pavlov's time, another dog was kept alive for nine years with an open stomach, to observe its digestive process; practically for all its life time. "A dog's life," commented the experimenter, who besides everything else had the gift of humor.)

* * *

Most human beings can't tolerate for 10 seconds a grain of pollen in the eye. Cat and rabbit eyes are far more sensitive than man's. No sooner had the United States outgrown its scientific backwardness and become "civilized" than American physiologists made it a point of honor to outshine their European colleagues. In 1904, *American Journal of Physiology* reported one of the many experiments in which the eyes of cats were burned with various substances, after the eyelids had been cut off, to make the burning more effective. This was merely a preview of the long list of horrors that were invented in the New World, and from there rebounded to the Old.

Actually, Europe didn't have to copycat America yet. We read in a German textbook on medicine: "Sonnenberg has made a series of experiments on dogs. He put their paws into boiling water. On some dogs the spine had previously been severed. The sixth animal, a big German shepherd, died after 6 hours and three immersions into boiling water." (*Handbuch der allgemeinen Pathologie*, Prof. Krehö, Heidelberg, 1908)

* * *

Prof. Monakow and Dr. Minkowsky of Zurich University performed many brain experiments in which they also extirpated the eyes of cats and dogs. They reported that "it wasn't possible to keep the animals alive for more than 3-4 months after the operation." (From the Institute of Brain Anatomy, University of Zurich, treatise of Dr. Minkowsky, 1913)

Prof. Walter R. Hess of the University of Zurich, who was to become a Nobel laureate, experimented extensively on monkeys, cats, and frogs. Of one experiment, in which he used 50 frogs, he wrote: "Through primary movements of the animals, which are pinned with needles, one doubtlessly causes extreme pain, which subsequently is transmitted to the vagus nerve." (*Pflügers Archiv*, 1922, p. 197)

* * *

The *American Journal of Physiology*, Mar. 1923, described experiments on the reflex of the pupils of over 200 cats, after their ciliary nerve (that moves the eyelash) had been extirpated together with the entire nervous nodule. From the report:

1. The cat, sewn into a bag with only its head poking out, is placed against a crate containing a dog. By causing the dog to bark furiously, one notes: after 3½ minutes, sweat on the palms of the cat's paws; after 4 minutes, the hair bristles; after 5 minutes, dilatation of the pupils. After which the cat's suprarenal glands are extirpated and the experiment is repeated.

2. The cat is immersed several times in cold water and is then exposed in wet condition to a blowing ventilator.

3. The cat is placed in icy water. After 3 minutes it starts trembling; after 10 minutes its pupils get dilated. Then its suprarenal glands are extirpated and the experiment is repeated.

4. The cat's mouth and nose are hermetically taped shut. Death by suffocation occurs in 40 seconds.

Other bright ideas, anyone?

* * *

"Blum noticed that animals deprived of their parathyroid gland gave clear signs of psychic changes. They had hallucinations, became violent against themselves, scratched themselves inflicting deep wounds upon their noses and eyes . . . Others appeared dazed, remained motionless, head down, eyes dead, tottered and collapsed." (*Schweizerische Medizinische Wochenschrift*, 1925, Vol. 28, p. 657)

* * *

Time passes, and for all the protests of many eminent medical men, vivisection keeps spreading behind the locked doors of the laboratories, ignored by the public at large, who hope that *some* good may come from it. Germany, France, the U.S., Switzerland, Great Britain—technologically the world's most developed nations—are way up in front, tacitly protected by the big news media.

Berlin, 1927: Wanting to find out whether cats eat human flesh, Prof. Strauch resorts to what he considers the most apt material: stillborn children, obtained from a state agency. The little bodies were taken to a basement together with a cat that was not being fed, only watered. After several days, the cat hadn't touched any of the bodies yet. To whet its appetite, the professor presented it with a morsel of meat from the section of another body. The cat gobbled it, whereafter it overcame its initial misgivings about human flesh and nibbled an ear and an arm. This experiment was then repeated with various cats. Prof. Strauch crowned his "investigation" publishing the pictures of the maimed bodies. (*Deutsche Zeitschrift für die gesamte gerichtliche Medizin,* Vol. 10, Fol. 4-5)

* * *

Prof. J. Barcroft of the Physiological Laboratory of Cambridge describes in two articles in *Journal of Physiology* a whole series of experiments he started in 1927. For instance, he forced a dog to swim in deep water after excising its spleen; another dog, equally deprived of the spleen, was forced to run for 4 miles behind a bicycle at a speed of 12 m.p.h.

American Journal of Physiology (Jan. 1927) described experiments performed on 30 pregnant dogs at Western Reserve University by Drs. Rogoff and Stewart of Ohio. The report states that some of the dogs died in agony, "yelling as if crazy."

An article in the same journal was titled "The Interruption of Pregnancy by Ovariectomy in the Aplacental Opossum—A Study in the Physiology of Implantation—From the Department of Zoology, University of Texas, Austin." Here we find experiments upon opossums that ran into the hundreds. Their reproductive organs were cut, or removed, or partially dissected, or cauterized, both in pregnant and non-pregnant females, and the period of their survival varied from two days to a month, while they were subjected to continuous examinations and probings. These experiments are extremely popular, as shown by the unusually long bibliographical list, which includes work done on cows, dogs, rabbits, guinea pigs and monkeys.

*   *   *

How and why did one test a remedy on animals in the twenties? A Zurich professor, Siegwart Hermann, explained it. Having discovered that a popular medicine named "Kombucha" was very beneficial, he proceeded to produce it industrially. But doctors refused to prescribe it because it was considered a "popular medicine", i.e. "unscientific." Now we give the word to the professor:

"I was sure my colleagues' reticence would cease as soon as I published the results of animal experiments. I got a large number of dogs, cats, rabbits and white mice, made them sick through Vigantol, which causes serious calcification of the blood vessels and of several organs, and their condition improved through administration of Kombucha." (*Die Umschau,* Vol. 42, 1929)

A description by Prof. Hermann: "The cat falls sick inside 8-12 days, vomits and won't eat. After force-feeding it with more Vigantol, the cat develops unquenchable thirst, loss of 50% of body weight, blood appears in the urine, the cat is unable to stand upright, dies at the end of 3 weeks. Administration of Kombucha cures the malady."

*   *   *

The *Lancet,* considered the most authoritative medical magazine, reported in its May issue of 1930 an experiment on a group of dogs in which the end of the intestine had been sewn up making it impossible for them to defecate. Death came following terrible agony between the 5th and 11th day. The experiment was repeated on another group of dogs, which survived from 8 to 34 days. The identical experiment had already been done by Claude Bernard and Company, it has been done ever since continuously on thousands of animals, and is still being done today, mainly in the U.S.

* * *

It is 1931. Cancer has begun its worrisome increase, and so have the psychoses, neuroses, epilepsy, diabetes, the arthritic and rheumatic diseases, the cardiovascular troubles—all maladies that the experimenters had tried to cure through animal experimentation. Meanwhile, hygiene, homeopathy, osteopathy, chiropractic, which have nothing to do with animal experimentation, are raising medical art gradually up to the Hippocratic level again. Nevertheless, the experimental fury runs wild in the university laboratories, swallows constantly growing slices of the national wealth, with the complicity or apathy of the national leaders, who declare that only the "specialists" can judge merits or demerits of medical research. Meanwhile, these specialists find it impossible to get subsidies without presenting some experimental "project," and since experimenting on people is not yet officially allowed, animals must be used.

Not only Claude Bernard's experiments are being repeated everywhere, but also those that Galen made 17 centuries earlier. And there are ingenious innovations. In Germany, at the University of Cologne, female baboons are tied to the restraining table with their legs stretched up in the air at a right angle, and a catheter and a cystoscope is introduced in their gallbladders and kidneys. None of them survives for more than two investigations, because the instruments, too large for monkeys, tear up the ureter. Furthermore, those stupid baboons didn't collaborate with the bright scientists—they kept squirming while their ureter was torn, as we can presume from "it wasn't possible to immobilize completely the animals, which were not anesthetized." So reports *Deutsches Archiv für Klinische Medizin,* Vol. 170, Mar. 25, 1931.

Journal of Clinical Investigations (Vol. 24, No. 2, Mar. 1945, p. 127) reports a whole series of experiments involving the slow deaths of many hundreds of animals—mainly dogs and rabbits—at the Department of Radiology, University of Rochester School of Medicine and Dentistry, Rochester, New York. The dogs' paws were crushed in the Blalock Press, as vivisectors Renato A. Ricca, K. Fink, Leonard I. Katzin and Stafford L. Warren wanted to prove that others had not performed previous crushings with scientific thoroughness. They declared that "despite the great number of shock reports, there is sufficient lack of standardization to introduce a large element of confusion and controversy."

Those university "scientists" were intent on one point—that room temperature changes the time at which animals die of torture and shock. They were not concerned with any other point. In one case, 300 dogs were used; many more in other, identical experiments. The "scientists" concluded that an animal in shock is better off in an atmosphere that enables it to keep its own inner temperature as nearly normal as possible. Apparently they had been unable to arrive at this conclusion by means of the strenuous exercise of common sense.

Looking up former similar experiments, one discovers that famous vivisectors had used different means to mash dogs' legs, for instance a rawhide mallet instead of the Blalock Press, and that, as a Chicago doctor pointed out, the conclusions that science can draw from these experiments are two: 1) an animal won't die so quickly if he is treated a little less savagely, and 2) when it comes to mashing dogs' legs, every vivisector has a great deal of company.

FOR HUMANITY'S SAKE

In vivisectionist savagery, scope and sheer stupidity the New World has long surpassed its master, the Old. This happened under the impulse of the huge subsidies that the U.S. government, as well as private individuals, give to "medical science"—the word "science" having become the equivalent of "research" in the U.S. The private subsidies come from people such as the Rockefellers—who for reasons best known to themselves always seemed to have a severe guilt complex about their huge fortune—all the way down to the child in the street who drops a nickel in a box marked "Help Defeat Cancer," not knowing that anti-cancer associations deal almost exclusively with vivisection, and that research has never lacked money to fight cancer, but only lacked brains.

When John D. Rockefeller, founder of the dynasty, died in May 1937, aged 98, it was announced that he had given more than $530 million to his philanthropic foundation. In 1901 he had founded the Rockefeller Institute of Medical Research, which years later was transformed by a special act of the legislature into a university devoted to research in the biological and medical sciences. Thus was laid—with the best of intentions—the basis for the greatest enterprise of scientific barbarism and savagery the world has ever known. Rockefeller intended it in memory of his wife who had died in 1918. Would she have appreciated it, knowing that most of the money spent in her honor went into useless tortures of animals, which in time were to spell untold suffering for mankind? It is likely that Rockefeller himself didn't know that he had been brainwashed, like most of the public, into believing that vivisection was useful to mankind and harmless for animals.

Ironically, both the founder of the dynasty and his son, John D. Jr., who died in 1960 at the age of 86, attributed their own excellent health to the avoidance of drugs, and followed no other miracle cure than a frugal diet of natural foods. And Junior's personal physician, Dr. Hamilton Fiske Biggar, was a homeopathic doctor and a fierce antivivisectionist, but he never succeeded in curing his illustrious patient of the delusion that contributing to vivisection was the best way of atoning for his wealth.

Let us examine some experiments that took place during the Rockefeller dynasty, many of them with Rockefeller money:

Arthur A. Ward, Jr., of the Department of Psychiatry, University of Illinois, reported in *Journal of Neurophysiology*, (Mar. 1947, pp. 105-112) that he wanted to measure "brain waves" in cats and dogs. Such waves come from minute electrical activity of the brain of a creature suffering deadly convulsions. Ward supplied numerous charts of the brain waves in question, but didn't suggest how they could be put to any particular use. He must have been just as baffled about it as we are. But he was greatly successful in producing convulsions by injecting a chemical substance (sodium fluoroacetate) in each animal. He described only the reactions of the cats.

One hour after the injection, the cat began to retch and drool, showed "appearances of fright," began looking for a hiding place and emitted what Ward called a "distressed crying." Then the animal had violent fits of an epileptic nature. Its back bent involuntarily, its legs stiffened, and often it was thrown to the ground. At first the seizures came only once every 10 minutes. They became more frequent and severe, until the animal passed into a state of continual seizure, up to its death, after a total elapsed time of from 3 to 5 hours.

A similar experiment was made at the Laboratory for Neuro-Psychiatric Research, Sinai Hospital, Baltimore. The report was by experimenters Albert A. Kurland and H. S. Rubinstein themselves and bears No. 15957 in the *Proceedings of the Society for Experimental Biology and Medicine*, Vol. 65, June 1947, pp. 348-351.

The two "scientists" lead off by remarking that cats can withstand terrific convulsive shocks of electricity without dying, but that there are few graphic reports of the exact types and kinds of a cat's brain waves during convulsive shock. So they decided something ought to be done about it, without attempting to explain to what use.

Twelve cats were used. Each had electrodes attached to its skull to record the brain waves. Other electrodes were attached elsewhere to shock the animal. After the cat, not anesthetized, had been locked in a small box, the shattering bolts of electricity began.

Each shock was strong enough to inflict a marked

convulsion. Shocks were delivered 5 minutes apart. If the cat survived a good many of these, it was removed from the box, to be shocked again some other day. Some of the cats were thrown into as many as 95 separate convulsions within a period of 3 weeks. Some died before that time. Of the 12 cats, 7 died, 5 lived. The experimenters' "conclusions": cats show a "surprising" ability to recover from shock treatment. No attempt was made to explain what connection there might be between the shocks given to those cats, far stronger than any shock ever given to human patients by physicians who are earnestly attempting to relieve illness.

So at the National Institute for Medical Research, Mill Hill, London, W. Feldberg and S. L. Sherwood injected a number of widely different chemicals into the brains of cats. They reported that one substance either "produces a peculiar high-pitched cry or the cat retches or does both." Another substance causes "profound motor impairment." The injection into the brain of a large dose of Tubocurarine caused the cat to jump "from the table to the floor and then straight into its cage, where it started calling more and more noisily whilst moving about jerkily . . . During the next minutes, the movements became wilder . . . Finally the cat fell with legs and neck flexed, jerking in rapid clonic movements, the condition being that of a major (epileptic) convulsion . . . Within a few seconds the cat got up, ran for a few yards at high speed and fell in another fit. The whole process was repeated several times within the next 10 minutes, during which the cat lost faeces and foamed at the mouth." The animal died 35 minutes after the brain injection. *Journal of Physiology*, 1954, recorded this scientific exploit for posterity.

But of course similar experiments had already been done long before that. The *Journal of Physiology* of May 15, 1949, contains a report on cats in the Royal Naval Laboratory at Alverstoke. They were exposed to 100 percent oxygen until they convulsed or died. The lucky ones convulsed and died after 3 days of continuous exposure. One was removed after

67 hours, suffered convulsions 15 times at short
intervals and was then killed. An unlucky cat was inter-
mittently exposed for 45 days, then it was given another 45 days to recover, was then put back into the
chamber where it took a week to die. The same journal
describes experiments on pregnant cats after mutilation and other revolting experiments on their eyes.
There is also a description of the making of a window
in the chest wall of a cat and the insertion of a light
bulb so that observations might be made during experiments.

*   *   *

It may be mere coincidence that cats are the most
widely hated animals, and at the same time the ones
most used for the kind of particularly cruel, painful
and senseless experiments, under the pretext that their
nervous system is the most similar to man's—although
in actual fact it would be hard to find a species with
a more different nervous system. Even a frog's nervous
system is closer to man's than a cat's.

Dr. Richard Ryder, the British clinical psychologist
who performed many animal experiments but later
recanted, reports in his excellent book *Victims of
Science* (Davis-Poynter, London, 1975) that in British
universities, cats' brains have been isolated and maintained alive, still attached to the animal's body. These
unanesthetised and apparently fully conscious brains
were then observed for their reactions to the injection
of various drugs.

The Winnipeg *Tribune* of October 8, 1975, quoted
this same Dr. Ryder as telling an audience at a conference in Toronto of an experiment where "cats had
their tails cut off and were blinded, then they were
put into a revolving drum to see how long they
could stay awake before they died."

*   *   *

But for all their great interest in cats, the researchers don't neglect man's best friend. Dogs are
being sacrificed everywhere in even larger numbers

than cats, but usually for a different type of experiment.

According to an estimate of Rutger's University, published by *Christian Science Monitor,* (July 18, 1973) in 1972 some 500,000 dogs were sacrificed in the U.S. against 200,000 cats. Of course, the experiments done on dogs are no restful vacation either. There is the constant experiment that has merely the purpose of making dogs die from peritonitis—the same extremely painful ailment from which a human being suffers as the aftermath of a ruptured appendix. One such experiment was reported in *Surgery,* Sept. 1947, pages 550-551, and was carried out by Drs. Sanford Rothenberg, Henry Silvani and H.J. McCorkle, all of the Division of Experimental Surgery of the University of California Medical School. In their article the doctors refer to the fact that there existed already a method of producing peritonitis in dogs, by tying off surgically the base of the appendix and then giving the victim a quarter-glassful of castor oil. But, they explained, they wanted to "improve" this method, which was done by devising an even more agonizing procedure.

With each dog strapped down and his belly laid open, the "surgeons"—subsidized by the American taxpayers who of course had never been asked for their consent—tied off and crushed the appendix, then cut out part of the intestinal tract and the spleen. With the intestinal system thus mutilated and unable to function normally, the dog was made to swallow a large dose of castor oil. The authors stated that thus "a fatal, fulminating, diffuse peritonitis of appendical origin may be uniformly produced in dogs."

In the experiment 56 dogs were used, but no effort was made to find a cure. Admittedly, the only purpose was to cause peritonitis, to publish an article that qualified its authors as "modern scientists," and from which the reader can gather that all dogs died, under excruciating pain, after an "average" survival time of 39 hours.

Other adventures into science include one by Drs. Hans O. Haterius and George L. Maison of the

Dept. of Physiology, Boston University School of Medicine, who reported this other pointless exercise in *Journal of Physics* (Feb. 1948): They immersed 21 dogs in a tub of iced water to observe how long it would take the dogs to "collapse." Having caused an animal to collapse, Haterius and Maison then proceeded to rewarm it in a tub of warm water. If the dog managed to survive they put it back in the ice water. One of them collapsed in as little as 67 minutes, another took as many as 193 minutes. The "scientists" thus learned what the best treatment is for an animal suffering from super-cooling: to warm the animal up. They said so in their article, and that was their total scientific contribution.

Of the 21 dogs, 13 survived—presumably to be subjected to other vivisectional whimsies later on.

* * *

According to a procedure described in the *Yale Journal of Biology and Medicine* (May 1949) E. Lempke and Harris B. Shumacher, Jr., of the Schools of Medicine of Yale and Indiana Universities, wanted to apply to dogs what they already knew from human experience: that the effects of frostbite are less severe in a foot or leg whose nerves have been cut by surgery. "On the basis of what we know . . . it could be anticipated that sympathectomy would afford some protection against frostbite," they wrote. This is of academic interest to the extent that not even the vivisectors who performed the experiment ventured to suggest that people should have their nervous systems surgically ruined in order to be protected against the possibility of frostbite. Using 10 dogs, they "disconnected" the nerves of one hind leg from the nervous system. They gave the dogs 8 days to recover, then removed all the hair from their hind legs and placed them up to the hocks in a freezing mixture of ether chilled by solid carbon dioxide.

With both hind legs frozen solid, each dog was returned to its cage, to wake up from what the experimenters called a "light" (i.e., non-existent) anaesthesia, and to experience how it feels to have the frozen legs begin to thaw out and swell. In some dogs the swelling tore the skin apart. The "scientists'" observations continued until gangrene developed in the maimed members, or until a particular dog somehow managed to recover. All the legs were badly injured. Some of them actually fell off.

An experiment described in the *American Journal of Physiology* (Oct. 1949, pp. 143-148) by Henry D. Janowitz and M.I. Grossman, of the Department of Clinical Science, University of Illinois, was made to answer this profound point: Why does a creature feel like not eating any more once its stomach is full?

If the reader wonders how on earth two sane, grown-up human beings could even just have thought of such an experiment, let alone suppose that it could have an actual purpose, we might venture to answer that those university "scientists" were neither sane nor really grown-up by any normal standards. Nor are today's faculty directors who keep authorizing such utter nonsense and disburse money to make it possible. And what about the so-called "scientific" publications which report them with a straight face?

By means of a tube installed in the stomach of each dog, the scientists proceeded to place food or indigestible bulk in it, to give the dog the impression of a full stomach. This led to a notable discovery: if 40 percent of food or bulk was placed in the dog's stomach before mealtimes, the dog ate less than usual. This was just a foreplay. Next the dogs' throats were cut so that whatever they ate fell on the floor through the slit in the foodpipe. This also led to interesting results: Whereas the average normal dog will eat for 2.5 minutes, a dog with a severed foodpipe will go on eating for an average of 14.1 minutes. Even more amazing to the scientists, the dog will still prove to be hungry one hour later—possibly as a result of the fact that his stomach is empty.

* * *

Before reporting the next experiment, it may be well to ask the reader this question: "In order for your doctor to treat effectively any illness you have, do you think it is vital for him to know precisely how long a pigeon can live without food at a below-zero temperature?" If your answer is yes, then the following experiment was important. To you, that is. It was reported by Eugene Streicher, Donald B. Hackel and Walter Fleischmann of the Medical Division, Army Chemical Center, Maryland, in the *American Journal of Physics,* May 1950, pages 300-306.

Each of a good many pigeons was placed in a sealed jar in a cold chamber at 40° minus F. At intervals of 24 to 48 hours, some pigeons were removed from the cold to be killed and studied. Others continued to freeze and starve in the cold chamber. In the end, the scientists learned that husky pigeons could live under these circumstances for as long as 144 hours—6 full days—before succumbing to cold and starvation.

* * *

We know little about how pigeons feel, except that they also must submit to the universal law that causes every organism dying by unnatural means to suffer greatly before the final release comes. We know more about how monkeys feel—much like man himself. So they are being used to an increasing extent in the laboratories, largely on account of the growing, though seldom publicized, conviction among research workers that the result of experiments with other animals are untrustworthy, contradictory and all too often dangerously misleading.

One experiment on female rhesus monkeys involved a transplant operation to cause the menstrual flow to issue by other channels than the normal. The procedure in all cases was to open the abdomen, cut across the neck of the womb (cervix) and, leaving the lower portion of the cervix in its normal position, shift the uterus and upper portion of the cervix to another site so that menstrual flow through the cut end would take place in its new position. Many of these monkeys suffered for years before dying. Examples:

In monkey No. 872 transplantation was into the peritoneal cavity. She developed intestinal obstruction and died from perforation of the colon and peritonitis 3 years and 35 days after operation, having meanwhile menstruated into the peritoneal cavity each month. Monkey No. 889 suffered a fatal hemorrhage caused by gangrene of the vagina. Monkey No. 874, having survived complications of obstruction of the ureter with consequent distension of the kidney, hemorrhage into the cervix and a fistula, was killed 4 years and 7 months after the initial operation, when extensive damage to the internal organs was revealed. In monkey 884 the cut cervix was attached to the anterior abdominal wall, whereafter menstrual blood was discharged through the fistula thus established. At the end of two years the uterus was again shifted so that menstrual discharge took place through the lower rectus muscle area. In this miserable condition the monkey was observed for a further 343 days.

And the end result? An article in the *American Journal of Obstetrics and Gynecology* (Vol. 66, Nov. 1953, p. 1082) which gave an aura of "scientists" to the team of individuals who had been able to conceive and perpetrate this idiocy, by which they seemed thrilled to the point of describing it as "epoch-making." Their conclusion was: "This experimental method seems to have great promise," leading to the usual "further investigations are necessary," which has become a regular refrain meaning "give us more funds."

Some quarter of a century has elapsed since that article appeared. Have the further investigations been done? Have the promises been realized? Nobody asks. The public can't even keep up with the razzle-dazzle of other experiments science is making daily, usually repetitive ones.

Here's another one to see once more what happens if the kidneys are removed. W.F. Hamilton Etal, of the Medical College of Georgia in Augusta, used 17 dogs for this purpose, and published his findings in the *American Journal of Physiology* (Vol. 194, No. 2, Aug. 1958, p. 268). After removal of both kidneys, while the dogs were "in good clinical condition," approximately 50 percent of them had to be discarded "because they vomited and were in bad condition."

They were force-fed by stomach tube, which meant, of course, an added torture, although allegedly anesthesia was used "for some of the tests"—though we never know how effective the anesthesia was since the devocalized dog can't tell, and the experiment usually lasts much longer than the anesthesial effect. The author concluded that dogs without kidneys were *different* in their reactions from dogs *with* kidneys! This momentous discovery was financed by Grant H 240 for $20,700 in 1958, and Grant H 240 for $24,491 in 1959.

While injection into the brain, or exposure to different substances, or extirpations of various organs keep being done to this day, the administration of electric shocks has become one of the most popular exercises in medical schools, as they don't even require any manual skill, let alone any strenuous work or intellectual activity. Most experiments done are never reported, of course. But *Scientific American* found worthwhile reporting in 1958 that one J. V. Brady placed monkeys in restraining devices and gave them electric shocks every 20 seconds during 6-hour experimental periods. After 23 days the monkeys began to die suddenly of stomach ulcers in agonizing pain. Interesting, isn't it?

THE STRESS FACTORIES

Hans Selye, a Canadian born in Prague, Czechoslovakia, inaugurated at Montreal University mass torture of small animals, to announce a discovery that seemed of great importance to him and his associates: that animals answer in a constant, typical way to various types of brutal treatment.

It was to further this kind of "work" that R.L. Noble and J.B. Collip of the same university built in 1942 the drum named for them, designed to slam the enclosed animals up and down, back and forth, against the iron bumps of the revolving device, which is being used to this day in physiological laboratories. After this treatment, the animals have scrambled intestines, crushed tissues, broken teeth and bones, ruptured livers and spleens, internal hemorrhages of the brain and stomach. So, 20 years after introduction of this drum, one could read that at the Illinois College of Medicine, Chicago, hundreds of rats were rotated ". . . approximately 2,400 times," according to a report in *Proceedings of the Society for Experimental Medicine and Biology,* Mar. 1962, pages 674-675.

To enable Hans Selye to compile his monumental, allegedly scientific volume entitled *Stress* (1950), not hundreds, not thousands, but millions of animals—mainly mice, rats, rabbits, cats—were submitted in countless laboratories to poisoning, burning, traumatic and electric shocks, various frustrations, crushing of bones and muscles, swimming to the point of exhaustion, exposure to freezing cold, screeching sirens, extirpation of various glands and organs including the whole stomach and bowels (evisceration), often before they were spun in the Noble-Collip drum. And all this keeps being done today.

Selye coined the medical term internationally known as "stress," but he and his colleagues are to this day busy trying to explain what it means. Of his book, a leading article in the *British Medical Journal* (May 22, 1954, p. 1195) said with characteristic British understatement: "Some of Selye's ideas are hard to accept, and his terminology does not make the understanding of them easier. Other investigators have not always been able to reproduce his experimental findings, and the interpretation and significance of the results, particularly when applied to man, are not clear . . . It is doubtful whether the experimentally induced pathological lesions in rats previously conditioned by the removal of one kidney and fed on a high-salt diet, are the same as those occurring in the human connective tissue diseases."

In 1956 Selye republished his volume retitling it *The Stress of Life,* (McGraw-Hill, New York) cutting out various confusing parts and trying to make the rest clearer, but without much success, it seems to me. On page 46 he says that for scientific purposes, stress is defined as the state which manifests itself by the General Adaptation Syndrome (which is generally abbreviated as GAS). "The latter comprises: adrenal stimulation, shrinkage of lymphatic organs, gastrointestinal ulcers, the chemical composition of the body, and so forth. All these changes form a syndrome, a set of manifestations which appear together."

He gets more and more involved explaining what he means, and after spending much space enumerating everything that stress is not, he tries once more to define what stress *is* (p. 54): "Stress is the state manifested by a specific syndrome which consists of all the nonspecifically induced changes within a biological system. Thus stress has its own characteristic form and composition but no particular cause."

My layman's comment to this last statement—Selye's book is in fact aimed at laymen—is that the stressed condition in millions of small animals had a particular cause indeed: mainly Hans Selye, M.D., and the Noble-Collip drum.

In fact Hans Selye was extremely successful provoking stomach ulcers in mice and rats. Naturally, those ulcers caused by rotating drums and electric shocks in animals or other brutal interferences have very little in common with the ulcers that man develops: first, because a man is not a mouse, and secondly because he has not been tortured as the mouse has been, so that his ulcers have an entirely different origin: and consequently neither a cure nor prevention can be found through this kind of "research." But probably only people who have not been brainwashed in modern medical schools are able to grasp this simple truth.

Hans Selye goes a longer way than most other vivisectors trying to convince the layman that vivisectors are humanitarian: "I have never met a professional investigator," says he on page 69, "who was not concerned about the question of cruelty to animals and did not attempt to avoid it . . . Even if an experimental surgeon were a degenerate sadist he would have to anesthetize his animal for major surgery because delicate operations cannot be performed if the animal struggles." So what? It's when the animal wakes up from anesthesia that his hell begins, and usually ends only with death, which usually takes much too much time coming. And it isn't necessary to be a sadist to make others suffer—it is enough to be indifferent, unfeeling.

His efforts to minimize the horror of vivisection become even more evident on the following page: "In our Institute last year, we used about 400 rats a week for research." Four hundred a week sounds considerably less than some 21,000 in a year, assuming his figures are accurate: And what about the thousands of other "institutes" that have been duplicating Selye's exercises since the early forties?

And then again (p. 70) the anesthesia myth: "In a standard experiment a rat is anesthetized with ether, or some other anesthetic, until it is completely unconscious and unable to move or feel pain. Then the experimenter can expose a gland and remove it to learn how the rat will react to stress without this organ . . ." The truth of the matter is that right after one of these operations, while in the terrible throes of postoperative effect, as soon as the animal is fully conscious again, it will be thrown in a tank or exposed to burns or freezing, etc. etc. to see how it reacts to Hans Selye's stress in its maimed condition . . .

In sum, Selye and Companions have allegedly identified a hormone excreted by the animals submitted to laboratory brutalities, and have reproduced it chemically. As a consequence, when a doctor today diagnoses in a patient a "nervous stomach" or a "stressed condition" or "psychosomatic perturbations" (every smart doctor can make up his own definition), this patient runs the risk of being administered some synthetic "compensation hormone"—ACTH, or some Cortisone combination, or some other equally noxious chemical—representing the worst possible treatment, bound to aggravate through the addition of new poisons the patient's already impaired organic and psychic condition. (Cortisone has even created a new type of insanity: "Cortisone-induced madness.")

* * *

On page 205 of his book, Selye in fact claims that "some of the resulting diseases of adaptation can be corrected . . . for instance, by the administration of hormones, the removal of endocrine glands, or by treatment with drugs which suppress endocrine or nervous activity."

But there are more and more doctors who claim that the remedies recommended by Selye are incomparably more damaging than the maladies they are supposed to cure. In fact the advent of Selye does not seem to have clarified matters much. Says he on page 73: "In 1950, when I published *Stress,* the first technical treatise on this subject, I had to discuss more than 5,500 original articles and books which dealt with various related topics. Since that time, every year, my coworkers and I published a volume entitled *Annual Report on Stress.* In each of these books, we had to report on between 2,500 and 5,700 publications."

Questions, anyone?

*   *   *

P.S. For his divertissements on stress Hans Selye has reaped not less than 16 university degrees *ad honorem* and some 50 different medals, prizes, awards, and honorary citizenships, while alone the U.S. National Institutes of Health grants (American taxpayers money) to help finance his mass carnages between 1950 and 1963 amounted to at least $728,926.

TODAY

In the course of time, the experiments have expanded in number and scope, new tortures have been devised, especially with the help of electric shocks or psychological torments. But at the same time the smoke screen of secrecy or deception that envelops the experiments has been thickening.

In Europe, the laboratory secrecy protects the experiments forbidden by the laws that have been introduced in most countries to appease the abolitionists. But it is almost impossible to inform the public about the experiments, because the mass media refuse to report them and, when they do, the vivisectionists always get the last word.

In the U.S. there are no legal restrictions. The vivisectionists have demanded—and obtained—complete "freedom of vivisection," as if they were asking for freedom of thought and expression, and the researchers continue to publish some of their exploits, but in the specialized press only; and they are careful to clad their reports in anodyne, benign language, which includes the continual mention of "anesthesia" or at least "light anesthesia." When it comes to papers relating particularly revolting experiments, which not even the most careful wording can disguise, the experimenters mimeograph and circulate them among themselves, marked "Confidential," rather than going on record by publishing them in the specialized magazines.

Also, the public attitude seems to be more callous in the U.S. than in Europe. The American public has been trained to accept meekly anything that sails under the flag of Science.

First, the growing number of medicinal and cosmetic products mean suffrances and death for millions of animals. Face-powder ingredients are being pumped into beagles' stomachs until they burst. Most of those ingredients are non-poisonous, so it's just a matter of the massive doses rupturing the dogs. Manufacturers are only carrying out such tests to protect themselves in case they are involved in a court case. Then they can claim that they were blameless, having carried out extensive tests. Rabbits are immobilized for weeks in restraining devices, the fur is shaved and skin irritants are applied to the exposed skin for weeks, causing severe burns, or to the rabbit's eyes, which are held open with metal clamps.

Toxicity tests, allegedly made to determine to what degree a new substance is poisonous, are being conducted with the so-called "LD-50" test, meaning "lethal dosage for 50% of the animals employed." It is a crude hit-and-miss procedure, and scientists everywhere have expressed doubts about its validity. But in most countries the health authorities make these tests compulsory, even for the commonest drugs, like tranquilizers, laxatives, sleeping tablets, medicines to cure colds, and so on.

The standard LD-50 test consists in forcing massive doses of the test substance down the throat of a large number of animals to discover at what dosage level about half of them die—always wretchedly—within 14 days, while the other half just manage to recover after teetering for days between life and death. Often such large quantities of the new substances are required to kill the animals that they have to be force-fed, which is a torture in itself, and usually injures the gullet. The test is then repeated with lower doses until the so-called researchers assume they have discovered the "safe" dose—although the safety actually always applies only to that particular animal. But modern "scientists" refuse to be held up by such trivialities. They calmly multiply the body weight of that particular animal species—usually rats and mice —proportionately to the weight of a human being, and hope for the best. The LD-50 test is used even for testing lipstick ingredients, which are force-fed, mainly to rats and mice, until half of them die; or else the new lipstick is applied in massive concentration to the anus of rabbits, which according to the scientists has a close physiological relationship to women's lips. Johnson and Johnson, Mary Quant, and many other world-renowned firms use animals for their "safety" tests.

Although clumsy to the point of being grotesque, it is the only system the scientists have been able to devise for establishing toxicity and irritability, and is recommended by the World Health Organization in Geneva, in its Technical Report No. 482 (1971). It demonstrates the low-water mark reached by the "official" medical authorities, who are either employed or misled by the pharmaceutical and cosmetic giants. The manufacturers can always claim that they "did the required tests" when something goes wrong, as it usually will, sooner or later.

WHO's report, titled *Evaluation and Testing of Drugs for Mutagenicity: Principles and Problems,* and subtitled *Report of a WHO Scientific Group,* includes a small print on the title page, suggesting that deep down the Powers that Be of WHO have no blind trust in the "Scientific Group" charged with compiling that report. The small print reads: "This report contains the collective views of an international group of experts and does not necessarily represent the decisions or the stated policy of the World Health Organization."

*   *   *

Just as cruel and fallacious as the toxicity and irritability tests are the experiments designed to assay the value of new tranquilizers, which are being turned out in ever new combinations ("a drug on the market"), either because the public has discovered the uselessness of the existing ones, or because it has become impossible to hide their noxiousness.

Psychopharmacology Abstracts, subtitled *The National Clearing House for Mental Health Information,* is a magazine published by the U.S. Department of Health, Education and Welfare with the money of the American taxpayer. Each issue contains a long list of "abstracts" or summaries, each of which reflects the results of experiments involving many hundreds or thousands of animals.

Those abstracts teem with chemical symbols and specialized definitions, so the layman reader assumes that the men behind them can't help being geniuses, who do vital, intelligent work. On closer examination, the work turns out to be somewhat less than intelligent.

Item: "In rats that would not ordinarily kill mice, lateral hypothalamicin injection of crystaline carbacol elicited killing . . . Carbacol was ineffective when injected into the medial, dorsal or ventral hypothalamus . . . 10 references." (Feb. 1971, p. 81)

The above simply means that some new drug combination was injected in various parts of the hapless animals' brains and then their reactions were reported. Now it so happens that even a sudden injection of regular tap water would substantially alter the be-

havior of any individual rat—animal or human. "10
references" means that the results or the communica-
tions of 10 different researchers or institutions have
gone into the making of the abstract.

From page 80 of the same issue: "Observations of
the behavior of 26 male cats before, during and after
daily administration of the tryptophan ̄ hydroxylase
inhibitor, para-chlorophenylalaline, revealed that
hypersexuality, increased aggression and perceptual
disorientation are sequelae of chronic administration
of the drug . . . 26 references."

Page 83: "Adult cats were used to study the effect of L-dopa on brain norepinephrine levels . . .
within 45 minutes of administration, L-dopa produced
a striking state of excitement . . . The evoked behavior was similar to sham rage in which features of
flight predominated . . . 62 references." (!)

And from the Oct. 1973 issue, page 137: "Chemical stimulation of the caudate [they mean "tail"—
Author's Note] in cats by means of NMA, an excitatory agent, was studied to discover the extent
of participation of the caudate in modulating behavioral and electrocortical activities. In chronic cats,
unanesthetized and anesthetized, intracaudate microin-
jections of NMA produced a broad spectrum of
excitatory responses which included: rage (only unanesthetized preparations), tremors and gross body
movements, mydriasis and salivation. In the anesthetized preparations, intracaudate NMA also exerted an
analeptic action in that it activated the cortex (abolished spindling activity), roused the animal with opening of eyelids, involuntary movements, vocalization,
increased respiration and accelerated heart rate . . . It
is concluded that the caudate participates directly in
modulating motor, behavioral and electrocortical activities, and that the depolarizing action of local NMA
disrupts inhibitory control in the caudate to produce
extensive excitation of the CNS. 19 references."

*   *   *

The following experiment, made at the Veterans
Administration Hospital at Northport, New York,

was reported by one *Journal of Genetic Psychology* (Vol. 102, 1963).

The purpose of the experiment was to induce insanity in kittens, of which two litters were used by a team of "scientists" under the direction of one Emanuel Storer. Beginning 7 days after birth and for the next 35 days, the kittens were given a total of 5000 electric shocks to the hind legs. These shocks were introduced gradually, with finally as many as 700 per day being given. The observers made the startling discovery that "the kittens at times retreated to the far side of the cage."

The shocks were given during the nursing period. The experimenters wrote that "the behavior of the mother cat merits attention. When she eventually discovered that the experimental kittens were being given electric shocks during the feeding process or whenever it was close to her body, she would do everything possible to thwart the experimenter with her claws, then trying to bite the electric wire, and finally actually leaving the experimental kitten and running away as far as possible whenever the electrodes were on the kittens' legs. Her attitude toward the experimental kitten when the electrodes were removed was one of deep mother love. She would run over to the kitten, try to feed it or else comfort it as much as possible."

During a follow-up experiment, after the kittens had been given time to recover somewhat, they were again given shocks to the rear legs, and the "scientists" reported that the kittens "tended to resume their previous schizophrenic behavior." It doesn't take a professor of psychiatry to realize that the only thing those experimenters were looking for was scapegoats for their own mental condition.

* * *

Dr. Colin Blakemore, a 28-year-old Cambridge physiologist, told the British Association for the Advancement of Science in Leicester how he sewed up the eyes of 35 kittens, allegedly to find a way to cure squints. He found out that cats with one eye sewn up shortly after birth could not see out of it when the stitches were removed. Neither could cats which had both eyes sewn up. In an interview to the London *Daily Mirror* (Sept. 6, 1972), Dr. Blakemore defended his experiments as "ethical" because "kittens like living in the dark."

He said that he was an animal lover, "like most scientists who work with animals," and added: "Cats make ideal subjects, because their eyes are more like humans' than those of other animals."

Utter nonsense, of course. Cats' eyes differ radically from ours, both in structure and reactions: They see in the dark and we don't, theirs remain closed long after birth and ours open up, their pupil is vertical and ours horizontal, theirs must focus on a particular object at a distance while ours have a wide-angle view, they have even been recently discovered to have cells which in all other animals occur in the ear only, etc. There couldn't be, in fact, a more different eye from ours than the cat's. But with the pretext of the greatest similarity with man, every kind of animal has been used—from the mouse to the pig to the elephant.

The kittens used in Blakemore's experiments were "humanely" destroyed after 16 weeks. "I would have liked to keep them alive for further study, as they do in America," Dr. Blakemore added ruefully. "But they had to be destroyed under a Home Office ruling."

* * *

If the British experimenters try to justify their experiments on ethical grounds and claim, like Blakemore, that they are driven by a deep love of humanity, the Americans waste no time on such niceties. In the U.S.A., the "originality" of an experiment is in itself a merit. So when at the University of Oregon somebody recently proceeded to put a new shift into practice, the weekly *Science* (Feb. 16, 1973) was proud to report and illustrate it, for the benefit of its worldwide "scientific-minded" readership:

Six litters of mice were used for that experiment, with 7 to 9 mice per litter. One or both forelimbs were amputated on the infant mice, which were then "observed for the effect of amputation on the grooming behavior" over a period of 5 months. The experimenter announced that normal mice groom themselves by licking their forepaws and then rubbing them along their snouts or over the tops of their heads. He reported that the limbless animals attempted to groom themselves even though the limb stubs were "moving away from the tongue" when the mice tried to lick. He stated that these animals "deprived of normal contact between the forepaws and the tongue" would lick the cage floor, the cage sides, or "even another mouse," as if they expected some kind of contact sensation from the extended tongue. He concluded that genetic factors are of "major importance" in the performance of grooming by mice.

THE BRAIN

The study of the brain, which as a rule exerts the greatest fascination on people who are preoccupied with their own mental balance, is today conducted with ever increasing means and more complicated implements. Time was when a lonely scientist like Weinhold would pour an amalgam of metals into the emptied cranial cavity of some stray kitten. Today, complex and expensive electronic apparatuses are employed to investigate the brains of tens of thousands of cats and, whenever the brain experimenters can afford the higher cost involved, the brains of primates, meaning monkeys that are most similar to us.

It has always been clear to real medical men, and they have been saying so for over half a century, that such experiments can never lead to anything, except to confusions that are comparable to those that reign in the brains of the experimenters themselves. The reason is easy to understand.

A primate's brain, like man's, is an electronic laboratory of incalculable complexity. Its balance rests on the harmonious interdependence of far more than 10 billion nerve cells and a hundred billion "glia" cells. Any interference from the outside—let alone the brutal insertion of cannulae and wires—is bound to upset this delicate balance. Moreover, the gray matter being humid and the electrodes being electrodes, countless and unforeseeable contacts between them get established, falsifying any result. Furthermore, the "experimental material" consists of animals that are severely traumatized and frightened by the violence they have inevitably been subjected to by the time they are immobilized in their restraining devices, so that their mental state is almost as unbalanced as that of their torturers to start with.

Again and again leading medical men have pointed out the futility of vivisection for studying the brain of man, but to no avail. Dr. Bernard Hollander wrote in the English magazine *Medical Press* as far back as 1931 (May 20, p. 411):

"Sixty years ago it was confidently anticipated that experiments on the exposed brains of living animals would speedily disclose the inner working of the brain and make mental disorders disappear forever. These extravagant hopes have not been fulfilled. It was fantastic to expect a solution of the working of the human brain, or to get any light thrown on the origin of mental disorders, from the stimulation or destruction of bits of the cerebral tissues of monkeys, dogs or cats."

Hecatombs of cats slowly tortured to death (some of them survived several brain operations over a period of months) by Zurich University professor and Nobel laureate Walter R. Hess have served no medical purpose, but allowed him to claim that he had been doing "research on brain control of the body" and that he had localized no less than 3,500 different responsive spots (*Reizstellen*) in a cat's brain. Like all vivisectionist claims, this also has meantime been debunked. The Portuguese "scientist" who shared the Nobel prize with him, Antonio Egas Moniz, had incorrectly been advertised as being able to cure mental trouble by surgical operations. Both had been so skillful in making their colleagues believe that they had shed new light on man's brain that they were considered worthy recipients of the 1949 Nobel Prize in Biology. But further experiments on cats and monkeys have meanwhile totally debunked those alleged discoveries. Unfortunately, neither Hess nor any of his colleagues who to this day delight in experimenting on cats' and monkeys' brains have added even just one comma to what the British brain specialist Hughlings Jackson (1834–1911) had discovered and described by observing patients suffering from head injuries and from dissecting human cadavers.

Peter Hays, professor at the University of Alberta and senior lecturer in psychiatry at London's St. George's Hospital, who has covered the subject most comprehensively in *New Horizons in Psychiatry* (Pelican Books, 2nd Ed., London, 1971) has written, for example:

"With the lost hopes of cerebral localization went the hopes that neurosurgery could ever be of great importance in the treatment of psychiatric patients as a whole: for if a certain functional unit is overacting in the brain and thereby producing symptoms, its destruction by surgery is liable to be, and in practice is, associated with damage to other units at the same time."

And in *Science Digest* (Nov. 1972), a scientist, W. H. Wheeler, has written: "Most of the work on brain research has been done on cats and monkeys. It is risky to extrapolate such data to the human brain. . . . The electrodes may be simply picking up signals in transit to some other part of the brain—like tapping a telephone line. Listening to a conversation doesn't necessarily indicate where the speakers are. The same holds true for electrodes implanted to control behavior . . . The control of behavior by means of electrodes does not provide any certain data on how the brain's functional areas are organized. The very existence of functional areas as such has been widely debated and solid evidence is still elusive."

But our medical investigators never allow themselves to be discouraged by uninterrupted failures, and brain experiments march happily on, to wit:

Under the title *"Mysteries of Bird Flight,"* Zurich's revered *Neue Zürcher Zeitung* (Nov. 12, 1972) reported, without laughing, that a team of "young zoologist scientists" of Saarbrücken University had decided to investigate the "biophysics" of bird flight. They inserted the usual electrodes into the brains of numerous migratory birds they had captured, in the hope of registering minutely their physiological reactions by means of complicated electronic apparatuses. The article didn't forget to tranquilize its readers by assuring them that the electrodes had been implanted into the birds' brains "under anesthesia," neglecting to point out that mention of anesthesia was principally meant for the reader's benefit, of course, since no bird has ever told us how effectively it was anesthetized.

The insertion of an electrode into the brain involves the perforation of the cranium—a highly traumatic experience that upsets the entire organic balance and natural reactions, not to mention what the insertion of the electrode does to the victim's mental balance. And in this miserable state, the birds, set free again, were supposed to fly to their customary nesting places —usually so far away that even healthy birds may fall by the wayside—and furthermore to reveal "the mysteries of flight" to a confused team of mechanistic investigators.

But it is most unlikely that the readers of that article will some day remember to ask what ever became of that study on bird flight, busy as they are reading about all the new wonders with which medical science is always just about to surprise mankind.

My written inquiry with the Saarbrücken University got me in reply a lengthy paper, dated 1975, filled with graphs, flow charts and algebraic formulae about the aerodynamics of bird flights and bird wings, but not a word of revelation about the mysteries of the bird flight's "biophysics" that those electrodes implanted in the migratory birds' cranial cavity were supposed to reveal to the team of "young zoologist scientists."

"PROFOUND RESPECT"

"The seasoned physiologist profoundly respects the integrity of biological systems." (From the President's Address read before the 71st Annual Session of the Western Surgical Association, Galveston, Tex., Nov. 21–23, 1963, as reported by *Archives of Surgery,* Apr. 1964. The president was famed Charles W. Mayo, M.D., of Rochester, Minnesota.)

The experiments reported so far, and the ones following in this final part—representing only a tiny percentage of the experiments that are being performed the year round—have not been selected for their originality but, on the contrary, have been chosen at random and represent a typical cross-section. And they don't seem to tally at all with the noble words Dr. Mayo delivered in Galveston, before launching into a tirade against anti-vivisectionism. Some of the experiments that follow were *required* for the students to obtain their advanced degrees, and were conducted under the supervision and guidance of senior researchers—faculty members who were pursuing their own animal experiments—not unlike "supervised" experiments by students in American secondary schools in which both students and teachers team up to conduct educational torture on every kind of helpless, guiltless animal. Thus Dr. Charles Mayo made a deliberately misleading declaration.

*   *   *

In *Animals, Men and Morals* (Gollancz, London, 1971), Prof. Richard Ryder described how researchers for Technology, Inc., of San Antonio, Texas, constructed a pneumatically driven piston to impact an anvil attached to a special helmet called HAD I, which they used on several monkeys. As the blows were insufficient to cause concussion, they made a more powerful device called HAD II, which they used on the same monkeys, and found that it caused cardiac damage, hemorrhages and brain damage from protrusion of plastic rings which they had implanted under the monkeys' skulls. Monkey No. 49-2 was again subjected to HAD II six days later, then 38 days later was struck multiple blows until she died. Some of the animals who temporarily survived suffered subsequent fits, and the researchers were "impressed" to find that after the experiments the monkeys' behavior "was distinctly abnormal. The usual post-acceleration behavior in the cage was that of hanging upside down cowering in a corner."

* * *

The *Journal of Surgery, Gynecology and Obstetrics* reported in its March, 1963, issue that the doctors C. Andrew, L. Bassett and Daniel K. Creighton, Jr., removed the flesh of the bone from the legs of 16 dogs and replaced it with other flesh. Four animals were killed after 30 days in agony, the others after 6 months in agony.

Peritonitis, already mentioned in this treatise, once a very dangerous infection of the abdominal cavity caused by feces from a ruptured intestine or appendix, was brought largely under control many years ago by antibiotics (which in turn had not been discovered by animal experimentation). Nevertheless, three medical experimenters at the University of Mississippi once more reported provoking peritonitis in 923 dogs by injecting feces into the abdominal cavity. Peritonitis causes excruciating pains accompanied by retching and vomiting, and entails death if untreated. These well-known facts were confirmed when hundreds of those dogs were allowed to die untreated, while others were treated and recovered after long suffering. The only "fact" added to the existing knowledge was an article in *Annals of Surgery* (May 1962, pp. 756-767) identifying the experimenters as Dr. Curtis P. Artz, Dr. William O. Barnett, and J. B. Grogan, M.S. Grant to Dr. Barnett was $22,750 in 1961 and $20,-450 in 1962.

* * *

To the monotonously repetitious experiments on smoking, Dr. Samuel W. Hunter, Dr. Dom-Bernardez and Victorine Long, M.S., at St. Joseph's Hospital, St. Paul, Minnesota, added a new kink when they mutilated dogs by extending a graft to the bronchial tube through the chest wall to the outside of the body. With every breath, the dogs were forced to take smoke into their lungs, until they died of collapsed lungs, infections and pneumonia, as reported in *Diseases of the Chest,* Vol. 38, No. 2, Aug. 1960.

* * *

At Harvard, the university that is expected to prepare the finest American scientists and future leaders of the American nation, 30 stray mongrel dogs were used to test effects of "highest possible" electric shock on barrier jumping. Experimenters stated that if given a high-voltage electric shock just below the intensity that will paralyze his muscles, the dog will "scramble vigorously around the compartment, slamming into walls, or leaping up against them; he will simultaneously emit a high-pitched screech, will salivate profusely, will urinate and defecate, and will roll his eyes rapidly and jerkily." They said that the hair of the dog will stand on end, his muscles tremble, his breathing will be short and irregular, and that sooner or later the dog's "vigorous scrambling" will result in his getting over the barrier to safety. They stated that they would like to define anything the dog learned from the experience as "traumatic learning." They said that they were unable to observe visceral changes in dogs without instrumentation, but reported a "primitive perceptual defense" of one dog who hid his head so that he could not see the raising of the gate which signaled a coming shock. Experimenters concluded that when they tried to explain their results, several "inadequacies in current learning theories were revealed." (Harvard University, experiment paid for by Laboratory of Social Relations, Rockefeller Foundation, and reported in *Psychological Monographs,* 67, 4; the whole of No. 354, 1953)

* * *

At least 40 dogs were used to test "effects of electric shock on jumping." The animals were placed in a "shuttlebox" divided into two compartments by a movable barrier set at the height of each dog's back. "Intense" electric shocks were delivered hundreds of times to the dogs' feet through an electrical grid floor of the test chamber. Experimenters said that dogs trained to associate a buzzer with the footshock jumped over the barrier when the buzzer sounded even though no shock was delivered. In an attempt to "discourage" one dog from jumping, experimenters forced the animal to jump into shock one hundred times. They said that as the dog jumped he gave "a sharp anticipatory yip which turned into a yelp when he landed on the electrified grid." Experimenters then blocked the jumping passage with a piece of plate glass and tested the same dog again. They reported that when the buzzer sounded the animal "jumped forward and smashed his head against the glass" and that after 10 or 12 days of this the dog "no longer resisted being placed in the apparatus." They stated that the "picture is surprisingly akin to the clinical picture in compulsive neurosis." Experimenters concluded that a combination of the plate glass barrier and foot shock were "very effective" in eliminating jumping by dogs. (Paid for by Rockefeller Foundation; "facilitated" by Laboratory of Social Relations, Harvard University; *Journal of Abnormal and Social Psychology,* Apr. 1953)

* * *

How much of your hard-earned cash would you spend to find out about the "sexualization of the rat," a favorite subject with experimenters? On this momentous question a research project was based. "Does a romantic rat keep his interest longer when he has a change of females?" That question so intrigued the federal bureaucrats who hand out the enormous sums voted by Congress for health and medical research that they gave Grant No. 1951 (in 1962) of $22,-885 to experimenter Alan E. Fisher of the University of Pittsburgh, so that he could devote his time trying to find the answer. He carried on elaborate tests, and his report, covering 7 full pages, published at the expense of the taxpayers, can be found in *Journal of Comparative and Physiological Psychology,* Vol. 55, No. 4, Aug. 1962.

* * *

This was by no means the end of such exercises. After detailing similar experiments of his own during 1962, in the final conclusions one Dr. Beach agreed with Fisher that male rats are stimulated by a change of females. He also reported that bulls, male monkeys, male water buffaloes and men can be compared to rats so far as their sex life is concerned. "Many husbands," he reported, "would like to engage in extramarital affairs." But he indicated that it isn't easy to collect data on this because "human sexual activities are so channeled and restricted by social conventions and moral codes . . ." Dr. Beach has also always been generously supported by federal grants. For his 1962 investigations into the sex life of rats he was given $32,085 of taxpayers' money under Grant No. 4000 03." (*Journal of Comparative and Physiological Psychology,* Vol. 56, No. 3, June 1963, pp. 636-644)

* * *

Small rhesus monkeys, caged singly, were taught to jump up on a shelf, which was the only possible spot for them to escape painful electric shocks. After the monkeys had learned to do this, the experimenters then placed two monkeys in the cage. The current would be turned on and both monkeys would instantly leap for the safety of the shelf. This is where the fun began, for there was room for only one monkey on the shelf. The pitiful reactions of the monkey that "lost" and had to take the very painful punishment are recounted in detail by the experimenters in their published report. They tell of the whining, crying, cringing, and the pathetic efforts to escape the shock. "Losers" made appealing overtures, begging the "victors" to share the shelf. There were a great many fights "resulting in deep lacerations and other severe injuries to the combatants," as the experimenters reported. (Experimenters: J. Banks and Robert Miller, University of Pittsburgh, Grant No. 487 C 8 used for experiment, $18,000. *Journal of Comparative and Physiological Psychology*, Vol. 55, No. 1, Feb. 1962, pp. 137-141).

*   *   *

Experimenters at St. Joseph's Hospital in Burbank, California—financed, of course, with taxpayers' money in the name of "medical science"—obtained old dogs from an animal shelter operated by the City of Los Angeles Department of Animal Regulation and used them in experiments to induce heart attacks (coronary occlusion, or myocardial infarction).

First, the old dogs were fasted for four days, then subjected to irradiation; "Three dogs died within two weeks following severe hemorrhagic gastroenteritis probably due to radiation damage."

Survivors were fed a diet abnormally high in fat and cholesterol and were given drugs to suppress thyroid action. (Some dogs died in their runs before the actual experiments got underway.) To the survivors, "stress" next was applied in the form of pitressin injections and electric shock. (Pitressin is a hormone that raises pressure in the arteries.)

Two dogs died in ataxia and collapsed after the first injection of pitressin. Eight dogs lived to endure, although already sick, a different type of "stress": they were put into a "Pavlov Stock," the torture rack so named in honor of the Russian vivisector who devised it.

The dogs put through this experiment were held with heads rigidly immobilized in the stock, and fastened with thongs drawn around the legs. Straps were placed around the body between the fore and hind limbs to restrict movement further. Heartbeat, movement and respiration were monitored by machines to which the dogs were connected. For 9 hours these sick, old dogs were maintained in the rig while being shocked with electricity.

Two dogs died right after the stressing. One only after 37 weeks of experimentation: of "suffocation" when he ". . . struggled in the Pavlov stock . . " In other words, the old dog strangled himself in his harness as he struggled to escape.

Dog "K" died after 77 weeks of experimenting—60 ordeals of shock treatment. When he first began to have symptoms of a damaged heart, which was what the experimenters wanted, he was subjected to stress in the stock every few days. Finally, his right eye showed signs of a stroke or cerebral accident.

Thus encouraged, the experimenters gave the old dog the "maximum stresser" treatment—90 shocks a minute. "One hour and 15 minutes after his last shock" (a possibility of 6,750 electric shocks later) "the animal expired," the experimenters recorded in their report.

Dog "A" also died after receiving the maximum shock treatment (40 weeks of experimenting). After he had endured 30 consecutive shocks, this Dog "A" didn't show enough heart damage to meet the requirements of the experimenters so ". . . the shocks were continued. The animal soon appeared to be in temporary respiratory distress," the experimenters reported, "Presumably as a consequence of active struggling against the stock." He was then given artificial respiration and the shocks were continued until his old heart gave out and he died in the torture rack.

Nine dogs out of 23 died under experimentation. The others were killed for autopsy during various stages of their distress. The experimenters were Harry Sobel, Ph.D., Carl E. Mondon, M.S., Reuben Straus, M.D. Federal Grant H 006858 in 1962 to Dr. Sobel for this experiment purporting "study of artery disease" was $21,646. (*Circulation Research*, Vol. XI, Dec. 1962, pp. 971-981)

* * *

Another investigator found that dogs shut up in a box in complete isolation for the first eight months of life do not react to pain as do dogs raised normally. When such abnormally raised dogs are finally released

into a normal environment they fear almost everything. They have "whirling fits" and react to strange
objects with intense excitement and emotionality. Of
course, every object presented to them is strange, since
they have never seen anything but the inside of a
small box. When these dogs are given a painful
electric shock, they sometimes "freeze" on the grid
and make no effort to escape.

This failure to try to escape from pain fascinated
the experimenter. He tested this reaction time after
time by holding flaming matches under the dogs' noses
and he ". . . jabbed them with dissecting needles."
The emotionally disturbed dogs did not seem to realize
that the experimenter was the source of their pain.
This pseudoscientist also "pursued" the terror-stricken
animals with an electrically charged toy car, trying to
hit them with it. On contact with a dog's body the car
delivered a shock of 1,500 volts.

No, this was not a mentally retarded person playing
a cruel game. This was done officially in the name of
"science" at McGill University. (Experimenter: Ronald Melzack, formerly of McGill University and the
University of Oregon, then at Massachusetts Institute
of Technology at Cambridge. He received a federal
grant of $22,370 in 1962, and one of $34,251 in
1961. Reports of these experiments and those in the
past were reported in *Science*, Sept. 21, 1962, *Journal
of Comparative and Physiological Psychology*, Vol. 47,
1944, pp. 166-168, and *Ibid.*, Vol. 50, No. 2, 1957,
p. 155.)

*   *   *

Surgery, Gynecology and Obstetrics (Mar. 1968)
reported an experiment that consisted of making in-
cisions 1.7 millimeters in length in the eyes of 45
dogs and 47 rabbits in order to watch the repair process over a 7-day period. Whether it is valid to assume
that the same processes are identical in animals as
they are in man is beside the point, because of the
multitude of eye injuries in men and women which
have been studied and minutely recorded over the
years.

*   *   *

O. S. Ray and R. J. Barrett of Pittsburgh gave electric shocks to the feet of 1,042 mice. They then caused convulsions by giving more intense shocks through cup-shaped electrodes applied to the animals' eyes or through pressure spring clips attached to their ears. Unfortunately some of the mice who "successfully completed Day One training were found sick or dead prior to testing on Day Two." (*Journal of Comparative and Physiological Psychology*, 1969, Vol. 67, pp. 110-116)

* * *

In 1969 the *British Journal of Ophthalmology* reported experiments by H. Zauberman, which measured the actual grams of force needed to strip the retina from cats' eyes. Dr. Zauberman didn't even remotely try to explain to anybody how this, or similar previous and subsequent experiments, could possibly aid in treatment of detached retinas in humans.

* * *

At the Department of Psychology, University of Aberdeen, Scotland, an experiment was done to see whether taking vaginal smears from rats tended to make their subsequent behavior more venturesome or less venturesome, i.e., whether it affected their "exploratory behavior."

The experimenter divided 24 female albino rats into 3 groups. One group of 8 had vaginal smears taken and were then laid on their backs while the experimenter stimulated their vagina with a glass rod. Another group received the same treatment, except that the rectum instead of the vagina was stimulated. The third group were stroked by the experimenter on their bellies, instead of having rods inserted in them. Four animals from each group were stimulated as described immediately before each trial in the enclosure, and four immediately after. The enclosure had Perspex sides and roof, the floor was marked out in squares. The number of squares entered by the rat during a two-minute period was recorded, and was intended to be a measure of the rat's degree of venturesomeness.

134 Slaughter of the Innocent

The rats were placed in the enclosure and watched once a day for two hours a day, for a period of 16 days. In conclusion, the experimenter said that vaginal smear-taking had "no effect on the exploratory behavior of the rats in this study," even though the E.E.C.s (brain activity recording tests) on the animals "were abnormal for a time." (*Animal Behavior*, Vol. 16, 1968, pp. 534–537)

What about the experimenter's own brain activity? Somebody overlooked the possibility of an interesting test there.

* * *

105 guinea pigs were used to test "influences of sight upon shock-avoidance." The eyes were cut from some of the animals and their eye sockets were sewn shut. Other guinea pigs were subjected to cortical damage in the rear of the brain. Some were subjected to both removal of the eyes and brain damage. One group of normal animals was tested in total darkness as an imitation of blindness. All guinea pigs were trained to associate buzzing noise with foot shock delivered in an experimental "shuttle" box, and then observed for escape responses. Experimenter said that the blind animals learned to follow the wall of the box in escaping and behaved "more efficiently than intact animals, except when a door or other obstacle barred the escape path. (Ph.D dissertation; State Univ. of New York at Buffalo; paid for by the National Institutes of Health; *Journal of Comparative and Physiological Psychology*, Sept. 1971)

* * *

To test the effects of starvation on eating, 24 pigeons were used. Some birds were starved to 70 percent of normal body weight. Experimenters reported that the pigeons ate more food more often when they were hungry than when they were not . . . They stated that the relationship between food deprivation and eating is an "exceedingly complex" problem. (Research Career Development Award; City College of the City Univ. of New York; paid for by the National Institute of Mental Health; *Journal of Comparative and Physiological Psychology,* Sept. 1971)

*   *   *

Brain damage was inflicted by surgery on 38 cats, and electrodes were implanted in their heads. Then the cats were electric-shocked in mouth and brain. Experimenters said that brain shock caused the cats to forget mouth shock and that the electric current seems to act as a lesion by "scrambling" patterns of brain cell impulses. (Univ. of Utah; paid for by the National Institute of Mental Health; *Journal of Comparative and Physiological Psychology,* Oct. 1971)

*   *   *

12 monkeys were used in three experiments; 6 of them were used twice. The animals were placed in restraining chairs and electric shocks were delivered to the tail. The shocks, which ranged in intensity from 160 to 300 volts, were adminstered every 30 to 60 seconds for 3 or 6 minutes. Shocks could not be modified in any way by the monkeys' behavior. Experiments tested the effects of shock on bar-pressing, key-pressing, and tube-biting responses of the monkeys. In one experiment, five monkeys were subjected to a hinged neck yoke that "insured proximity of the monkey's head to the bite tube." Experimenters said that the monkeys increased their biting "as the time for the next shock approached" and, when the tube was withdrawn, the monkeys expressed their aggression by pressing a key more often. They said that biting was the "preferred response" of the monkeys and that examination of the response bar "frequently revealed evidence of bar biting." 6 of the 12 monkeys were not used in the third experiment because they had been used in some other experiments "or had deceased." (Anna State Hospital and Southern Ill. Univ.; paid for by Illinois Dept. of Mental Health; *Journal of the Experimental Analysis of Behavior,* May 1972)

*   *   *

7 rhesus monkeys 3 to 5 years of age were used; their sense of smell was destroyed by surgery, and the

eyes of two monkeys were cut out. X-radiation directed
into faces. Experimenter said that the monkeys in his
experiment could see the X rays. (Ph.D. dissertation;
Fla. State Univ.; paid for by the U.S. Atomic Energy
Commission, U.S. Air Force; *Journal of Comparative
and Physiological Psychology,* Feb. 1972)

* * *

8 monkeys were asphyxiated at birth for 7-10 minutes, and were tested for visual responses at 8-18
months of age. Experimenters concluded that monkeys
asphyxiated at birth are more sensitive to visual stimulation than unasphyxiated monkeys. (MA thesis;
Jewish Hosp. & Med. Cent. of Brooklyn; paid for by
the National Institute of Child Health and Human
Development; *Journal of Comparative and Physiological Psychology,* Mar. 1972)

* * *

The ovaries were removed from 48 rats, vaginal
opening was covered with masking tape, then the females were exposed to male rats. Experimenters recorded avoidance of males by the females. They said
that females permitted full coital stimulation were less
receptive to subsequent male approaches and that this
"may be related to the tissue insult of multiple penile
insertions." They concluded that coital stimulation "has
been overrated" in the female rat. (San Fernando
Valley State Coll., *Journal of Comparative and Physiological Psychology,* Mar. 1972)

* * *

31 rats were starved for 7 days. Experimenter then
offered them live mice, two-week-old rat pups, and
young weanling rats. The hungry rats killed and ate
the rat pups as often as they did mice. Experimenters
concluded that hunger was a powerful determinant in
causing rats to kill. (Temple Univ.; *Journal of Comparative and Physiological Psychology,* Jan. 1972)

* * *

Electrodes were implanted in ear tips and outer
corners of the eyes of 27 rabbits. The loop of suturing

thread was tied to inner movable membrane of right eye and coupled to a photoelectric monitoring device. Upper and lower eyelids were held apart by hooks slipped over their edges and attached to head strap. Rabbits were then placed in restraining box in darkness. Electric current was applied and movement of the eye was membrane-recorded. Conclusion: Membrane movement is directly related to pain stimulus of the eye orbit. (Univ. of Montana; paid for by the National Institute of Mental Health; *Journal of Comparative and Physiological Psychology*, May 1972)

* * *

Lesion-producing electrodes were inserted into the brains of 44 cats. They were also subjected to stimulating electrodes implanted in the brain base. The lesions and shocking of the brain produced biting attacks upon presented rats, hissing, growling, ear flattening, hair erection, and dilatation of eye pupils. Additional shock to feet caused the cats to lift their paws and attempt to move away. (Ph.D dissertation; Univ. of Minn.; paid for by the National Science Foundation; *Journal of Comparative and Physiological Psychology*, Dec. 1972)

* * *

The number of bone fractures that doctors have seen, studied and treated over the centuries certainly must have run into millions, yet from the experiments being performed on animals you would think they had just discovered what a fracture was. Still another fracture experiment, reported in the November issue of *Surgery, Gynecology and Obstetrics,* runs the gamut with 27 adult rabbits. Eighteen of the rabbits were used as a series wherein a limb of each was fractured with a saw, and then surgical division of some of the tendons was performed. Nine others were used as a control group, only the limb being fractured.

Two rabbits from the first group and one from the control group were sacrificed at one day, three days, one week, and thereafter at weekly intervals up to six weeks. Three were sacrificed at nine weeks. At the time of sacrifice the rabbits were perfused, via a tube in their hearts, with a dye that circulated through their bodies. Other techniques followed, at the end of which the bone became transparent and a three-dimensional view of the vascular tree could be observed, the purpose being to note the response of blood vessels to bone fracture as healing proceeds, until finally the rabbits are gone and only the bones are left.

So by this time we probably know as much about bone fractures as the ancient Egyptians, or maybe the Chicago Bears football team.

*   *   *

Another experiment that has become increasingly popular is to train a group of rats to respond to certain conditions, then kill them, grind up their brains and feed them to a new group to observe if the "acquired learning" has been transmitted by eating the "trained brains."

This has been going on also at the Georgia Institute of Technology, at Atlanta. They take a batch of hundreds of rats at a time and put them in glass cages with a water fountain continually running next to an electric light. When the light is not on, an electric current is passed through the water; then, if a rat tries to drink, he receives a shock. A small computer is used to determine the ratio of "good attempts." When the ratio nears unity, the rat is qualified as "trained"— receives his B.A., as it were. He is then sacrificed and his brain is fed to a new recruit. (This series of experiments was reported in the Jan. 17, 1973 issue of *Computer World*.)

*   *   *

In case there is still someone not yet fully convinced that the experimenters and those who assign them grants are either in need of intensive psychiatric treatment or else should be brought to court for misuse of public funds, these final items: By controlled feeding, a batch of pigeons were starved to 80 percent of normal body weight, then electrodes were implanted around their pubis bone (near genitals) for delivery of electric shocks. The birds were trained to peck a key to obtain food and then were "punished" with shock for pecking. Drugs, including morphine, pentobarbital, amphetamine, mescaline, and chlorpromazine, were injected into the breast muscle of birds to test effects of drugs on the number of pecks the birds made while being punished. (One bird died from a concentrated dose of a drug solvent and was replaced by a bird of similar weight.) Experimenter said that most of the drugs tested increased low rates of both punished and unpunished pecking, but he warned that "because so many factors may influence the effects of drugs on punished behavior, any simple description of the effects of a drug on punished behavior is probably an oversimplification." (Univ. of North Carolina at Chapel Hill; paid for by Hoffman La Roche, Inc., and U.S. Public Health Service; *Journal of the Experimental Analysis of Behavior,* Jan. 1973)

* * *

Curious to see how "intense" electric shocks would affect chickens, experimenters at Tulane University, New Orleans, used 36 chickens, 3-weeks old, which remained immobilized by the shocks for 27 minutes. Experimenters concluded that there is "an essential fear component in the immobility reaction of domestic chickens." (*Journal of Comparative and Physiological Psychology,* Jan. 22, 1972.)

* * *

Scientists at the University of California decided that goldfish were an "ideal species" for experiments in fear because, unlike other animals, they do not "freeze" when frightened, and obtained financing by the National Institute of Mental Health for the following exploit. Test boxes were divided into two compartments by a 3-inch-high barrier and placed in an aquarium containing 4 inches of water, thus allowing 1 inch above the barrier for the 156 goldfish to use in escaping electric current applied between side walls. Shock intensities of between 6-18 volts were delivered. Experimenters said that 18 volts was "sufficient" to kill some of the fish. Best escapes were made at 9 volts, but swimming dropped off at high levels of shock intensity because strong shock "produces some type of suppression." Experimenters added that 12-volt shock compared to 6 volts is "psychologically intense" to a fish, but the same fish would find the 12-volt shock "psychologically weak" if he were also to receive 18 volts. (*Journal of Comparative and Physiological Psychology*, Apr. 1971)

*　　*　　*

Then I came across experiments made on ants. But I suppose the reader has got the general idea by now.

Part Four

FACTS AND FANTASIES

In ancient times the bearers of bad news were decapitated. Today they are simply ignored.

Since the vast majority of people who choose to ignore the bad news from the vivisection front feel guilty at heart, they take recourse to a well-known psychological foil: They persuade themselves that vivisection is immensely beneficial to mankind, and by no means cruel to the animals; and that vivisectionists are noble, saintly individuals, dedicated entirely to the well-being of mankind. So they even refuse to challenge their most blatant absurdities or to examine any evidence against them.

When a vivisector speaks, he will always find many people willing and eager to believe him, because "he is a scientist"—endowed with some magical, divine knowledge, denied to common mortals.

In the modern world, Science has become a form of established religion, and scientists its priests and ministers, to whom you had better listen—or else. Thus the Encyclopedia Americana can nonchalantly affirm under "Animal Experimentation" that "there is not a single important knowledge of medicine that doesn't owe something to animal experimentation." And this statement is echoed by the Britannica (directed since 1961 by an editorial board of the University of Chicago, in whose medical college some of the worst vivisectionist abuses are being committed as a matter of general practice): "There is not a single modern and substantial item of medical knowledge that does not owe something to the animal experiment."

That the history of medicine proves the utter falsity of such claims does not seem to disturb the medical faculties and the news media, which prefer to make believe that all is well with present-day research.

LINES OF DEFENSE

A revealing statement was once carelessly made by one of America's top "scientists," Dr. Andrew C. Ivy of Chicago's Northwestern University Medical School. He was the "researcher" who introduced rubber balloons into the stomachs of dogs and then distended them with water until the dogs died after long hours of agony, as reported in *Archives of Internal Medicine* (Mar. 1932, p. 439). Dr. Ivy was also the godfather of Krebiozen, the drug that was hailed as the final solution to the cancer problem a few decades ago, but meanwhile turned out to be an out-and-out fraud. Nevertheless, his reputation loomed so large in the American medical world that he acted as the "vivisection expert" at the Nuremberg trials against the German doctors who had experimented on the concentration-camp inmates.

In a three-page editorial in *Clinical Medicine* (Aug. 1946, Vol. 53, p. 231), excoriating antivivisectionists, this Dr. Ivy lamented that it cost more than $25,000 to defeat an antivivisection bill in New York State, and at least as much to defeat a similar bill in California several years earlier. Considering what has happened to the U.S. dollar since, that would be the equivalent of spending $100,000 today—a sum any antivivisectionist society would be glad to have at its disposal to advertise the truth.

Another insight is in *Experimental Surgery,* the already cited vivisection manual by J. Markowitz: "There must be many people opposed, for instance, to the use of automobiles, who must wish to unite to bring about legislation to banish motor-cars from our streets; but their position at the outset is hopeless, *for* they could not possibly succeed against an industry with billions of dollars at stake."

Apart from the consideration that vivisector Markowitz characteristically doesn't seem to see any difference between a mechanical product and sentient creatures systematically tortured, both statements reveal that vivisection has a lot of money at its disposal and is ready to spend it in order to perpetuate itself.

The United States, banking on its technological preeminence, sets the trend in matters of medical research for the rest of the so-called civilized world, which unquestioningly has accepted the Cartesian and Bernardian myth that living organisms react like inanimate matter, and that health and disease can be computerized like airplanes and spaceships.

In the nation's Capitol, well-paid lobbyists of the drug industry are constantly at work persuading congressmen and senators that any interference with vivisection would be disastrous for the nation, while PR men from coast to coast hire or otherwise influence members of the mass media to help convince public opinion and government that the salvation of mankind depends on the vivisectors, be they employed by the industry or members of the medical schools.

Some intelligent individuals in highly responsible and influential positions are sincerely convinced that vivisectors, whom they prefer to dub "scientists," are philanthropists, good Samaritans, opposed only by those who would much rather see a child die than a dog.

In fact the vivisectors' favorite foil in conversation is: "Which shall it be—a dog or your baby?"

The vivisector who piously utters these words can usually rest comfortably in their protective shade. "Dogs or babies" conveys the impression that if vivisectors couldn't use animals they would have to use babies—and that antivivisectionists want them to do just that.

But all the existing evidence indicates that most of those medical men who are bitten by the experimental bug, experiment on animals *and* on babies—preferably on babies, whenever they can get away with it. A later chapter, "Human Guinea Pigs," will deal with that aspect of today's medical "research."

The charges of inhumanity that the vivisectors usually bring against their critics can assume comic aspects. In the introduction to his *Experimental Surgery*, whose 546 pages are crammed with instructions on how to perform every known vivisectionist operation, Markowitz uses up six full pages accusing antivivisectionists of every imaginable moral turpitude, including . . . sadism.

There is not one argument the vivisectors haven't thought of to justify their practice—to the point of invoking self-defense and religion. So in a debate at the Institute of Physiology at Basel, Switzerland, (Jan. 31, 1903) Prof. Leon Asher of that university said:

"Since you antivivisectionists always speak of ethics, one might ask oneself whether it isn't a sacred case of conscience to follow the call toward the solution of the mysteries of life, and whether man shouldn't consider it a *religious duty* to satisfy the desire for exploration that Providence has placed in our hearts, without asking whether our research on life has any value for medical science or any other practical value. And if the physiologist, to achieve this, has to inflict pain to the animals, he suffers more than the antivivisectionists, for he knows the life of the animal, and the layman doesn't."

This probably represents the acme of vivisectionist hypocrisy. And by branding all adversaries as "laymen," this professor deliberately ignored that they included some of the top names of medical science.

And I have heard one vivisector, whose name I fortunately do not remember, exclaim that "it is incredible how *stupid* antivivisectionists are—they go against their own best interests!"

*   *   *

A heinous crime by an uneducated person, or by one who is plainly mentally deranged, doesn't endanger public morals, for everybody is agreed that such a person should be either imprisoned or submitted to psychiatric treatment. But vivisection is advertised as a noble, humanitarian activity. Who says so? Directors of reputable clinics and laboratories, famous "scientists," people of consequence, university bigwigs. And that's what prompted Hamilton Fiske Biggar, John D. Rockefeller's personal physician, to say: "It is because these savageries are committed by men who are respected and admired that they are so utterly dangerous to our national morality. It is evident that this hardening of the sympathetic nature of the physician is liable to react upon the sick under his charge in careless and unfeeling treatment. The same mental temperament and condition that delights in experiments on subhuman animals would permit the practitioner to experiment on a patient."

* * *

To make the idea accepted and gain the support of governments and media, the vivisectionists have spread the following credo:

Vivisection is indispensable to the development of biology and medicine. To vivisection we owe the greatest discoveries of the past, starting with the circulation of the blood, the discoveries of Spallanzani, Galvani, Volta, Claude Bernard, Pasteur, Koch, up to the latest drugs, vaccines, vitamins, the development of surgery, the investigation of cancer, etc. Thanks to vivisection, life expectancy has increased and is going to increase still further—practically the sky's the limit. With the help of vivisection we could have avoided the Thalidomide tragedy. Through vivisection we are going to abolish cancer, arthritic, rheumatic, circulatory, heart, mental and venereal diseases. Vivisection will give sight to the blind, hearing to the deaf, fertility to the barren, youth to the old. We vivisectors are all animal lovers, more than our critics. Our work is beneficial not only to humanity, but to the animals as well. Our opponents are just a small bunch of hysterical spinsters, sexual deviates and befuddled old fogies. The medical men who disagree with us are ignoramuses. Besides, the animals don't suffer—either because they aren't able to feel pain, or because we treat them with as much love and kindness as we treat our human patients.

I know that I haven't added a single word of my

own to this vivisectionist credo, and I hope I haven't
forgotten any.

* * *

The first objection is a moral one. If vivisection
were useful instead of damaging, that would be an
aggravating rather than an extenuating circumstance,
for it would sanction the principle that the end justifies the means—that well-worn picklock which has
always opened all doors to wickedness, including those
to Auschwitz and Buchenwald. If man accepts this
principle, he can no longer consider himself a morally
superior being.

As to "the small bunch of regressive, misguided
fools" who have rejected vivisection on all counts,
they happen to include Leonardo da Vinci, Voltaire,
Goethe, Schiller, Schopenhauer, Victor Hugo, Ibsen,
Wagner, Tennyson, Ruskin, Tolstoy, Cardinals Manning and Newman, Mark Twain, G. B. Shaw, Ma-
hatma Ghandi, C. G. Jung, Clare Booth Luce, Nobel
laureates Albert Schweitzer and Hermann Hesse—to
name but a few of the deceased ones, and known in
the English speaking world. If human culture has a
voice, it is theirs. If there is any justification for the
existence of the human species on earth, it is to have
brought forth a few individuals like these; and not
the hominids of the lab subculture.

The antivivisectionists included also outstanding men
of action, like Garibaldi, Bismarck, Lord Dowding.
And all had their feet firmly planted in the reality of
their time, several of them having also contributed
to the advancement of science.

Leonardo, the universal genius, was not only one of
the greatest artists and technological innovators of all
times, but also one of the world's topmost experts on
anatomy. Schiller's graduation thesis, "The Philosophy
of Physiology," is the first known study of psychosomatic medicine. Physiology was also among the many
interests of that other universal genius, Goethe, whose
observations shed new light on the structure of the
human skull. Albert Schweitzer, the great humanitarian, philanthropist, philosopher and musician of world

renown—the foremost interpreter of Bach's music on the organ—was also a practicing physician who dedicated most of his life to caring for the blacks in his jungle hospital. Air Chief Marshal Lord Dowding, who carried his antivivisection fight to the House of Lords, led the Royal Air Force in the Battle of London. These names, then, are part of "the small bunch of hysterical cranks," etc.

As for medical men who denounced vivisection as senseless and misleading, their names could fill a whole book, and in fact they do: More than four decades ago Ludwig Fliegel, a Zurich dentist, cited a thousand of them in a volume titled *1000 Aerzte gegen die Vivisektion*, which means just that: "A Thousand Doctors against Vivisection."

Now let us briefly examine, in the light of history, the vivisectionists' claim that animal experimentation in the past, present and future has been or could ever be essential to medical science. Luckily, even the briefest perusal of the available evidence proves the falsity of these assertions and provides historical proof that clinical observation is the only road to medical science, and that some of the most influential mass media have been systematically spreading untrue information—whether with the deliberate intent of deceiving or in good faith is quite irrelevant at this point.

HISTORY

Hippocrates is considered the greatest physician of antiquity, and many consider him the greatest of modern times as well. Ever stronger currents today point toward a return to Hippocratic principles and wisdom, which Greece had probably adopted from Persia and India, where medical art and surgical science had always been very advanced.

Hippocrates lived in the Fifth Century B.C., and all historians concur that he taught more validly about epidemics, fever, epilepsy, fractures, the difference between malignant and benign tumors, health in general, and most of all the importance of hygiene and the ethical values in medicine. A great clinician, he would observe the patient attentively and then help him to be cured by *vis suprema guaritrix:* Nature, the supreme healer. He laid utmost stress on hygiene and diet, but used herbal medicines and surgery when necessary.

Actually, the only sure knowledge we have of him is that he lived, for he is mentioned in Plato's writings. His own writings have not been preserved. Nevertheless, various publishers have in recent years published *Hippocrates' Works*, all apocryphal.

Henry E. Sigerist, the Swiss who held the Chair of History of Medicine at the Universities of Leipzig and Johns Hopkins, and whom many consider the outstanding historian of our time, describes Hippocrates' medical philosophy thus:

"Nature heals. The doctor's task consists in strengthening the natural healing powers, to direct them, and especially not to interfere with them. The dietetic treatment is the best. Through the food the power regenerates itself. Hippocratic dietetics reached a level that to our day merit our great admiration." (*Grosse Aerzte,* 6th ed., Lehmann, Munich, 1969, p. 28).

In another of his medical works, *Krankheit und Zivilisation* (A. Metzner, Frankfurt, 1952, p. 237) Sigerist stated: "The dietetical prescriptions which the Hippocratic doctors had elaborated for their patients are the same that are being prescribed today."

Not much reasoning is required to understand that the same diet that helps to restore a patient's health will also keep a healthy person physically sound—today no less than in Hippocrates' day.

But only today do we fully realize how valuable Hippocrates' teachings were, based solely on his clinical observation and true medical intuition. So we know from operations and autopsies that a liver which has been ruined and scarified by wrong alimentary habits can regenerate itself completely—provided the damage is not too great—in a comparatively short time (1–2 years) of proper diet, whereas the intake of "little liver pills" is bound to worsen the condition, poisoning the organ still further. When today a drug-swallowing hepatic patient recovers, it is in spite of the drugs, if luckily they are ineffective, and not because of them.

Historian Sigerist, having been formed at the conventional medical schools of France, Switzerland and the U.S., was not antivivisectionist, so he can hardly be suspected of antivivisectionist bias when he wrote of the man he regarded as the greatest doctor of our time, Germany's August Bier, the inventor of lumbar anesthesia:

"After 1920, Bier turned his back entirely on individual experimentation. To his mind it is a mistake to believe that today's medical art has reached a higher level than ever before, and he called for the establishment of a completely new medical system. The true medical art has declined, having been overshadowed by laboratory research. The sense and understanding of the whole has been lost, the result of experiments is being extrapolated to man without any critical sense . . . Frog and rabbit say nothing . . . Medicine is lucky to have in Hippocrates a great paradigm. We must return to a true medical concept, to the 'clinical outlook'" (*Grosse Aerzte,* p. 436)

The March 20, 1904, Paris edition of the *New York Herald Tribune* brought opinions of dozens of well-known doctors, all antivivisectionists, including the following of a Dr. Salivas: "The immortal Hippocrates never vivisected and yet he raised medical art to a level from which we are very far today, in spite of the alleged great modern discoveries."

All historians have attributed to Hippocrates a very high ethical sense, which is irreconcilable with vivisectionist practices. It is not by coincidence that the physicians' oath bears Hippocrates' name and not Galen's.

* * *

Galen (130–200) was a passionate vivisector and the first physician on record who demonstrated the danger of animal experimentation for medical science. His vivisections of animals did not merely fail to teach him

anything about man, but became the source of grievous mistakes that were to wreak havoc on mankind for
15 centuries. All his valid knowledge came from his
clinical experience, how to set broken bones, for instance, and the therapeutic value of certain herbs.

Galen was 30 years old when he came to Rome
from his native Pergamon in Greece, where he had already gained a reputation as the doctor to the gladia-
tors, and in the next 30 years he was to become the
personal physician to five emperors.

He was also a prolific writer on medical art, and his
monotheistic ideals, his belief in one supreme being,
led the Catholic Church later on to decree his scientific doctrine as the only "correct" one. For various
centuries, whoever dared raise doubts about a Galenic
teaching was made to recant on the rack of the Holy
Inquisition. As a consequence, humanity had to suffer
for 15 centuries from many fatal mistakes.

In 192 a fire destroyed most of Galen's personal
library, which included 400 of his medical treatises.
Had the fire destroyed them all, we would have to believe meekly the traditional teachings that describe
Galen as the greatest medical man of antiquity. But
the fire spared 98 of his works; and from them it
emerges that all his valid knowledge came from his
clinical experiences, from his contact with patients—
like his belief that organic reactions are influenced by
the mind; whereas all his major errors derived from his
experiences with animals. He had a vast knowledge of
curative herbs, like all Greek doctors who had imported this knowledge from Asia.

In the course of time, the humane and hygienic precepts of Hippocrates were scorned. Plinius tells us
that up to the First Empire the Romans had been a
healthy people, thanks to the prevalent hygiene and
sanitary services, exemplified by the aqueducts and
public thermae. But by and by, the reasonable Hippocratic precepts like a frugal, simple diet and rigor-
ous cleanliness, which could be had for nothing, lost
their fascination as a new breed of medical men discovered that there was more money in preaching the
importance of magic, amulets and astrology.

Not only in the Orient and ancient Egypt, but also in the Rome of the First Empire, surgery had been highly developed. Operations performed in antiquity included tonsillectomies, removal of cataracts and goiters, the trepanation of the cranium, the excision of tumors, the removal of gall and kidney stones, even plastic surgery. Celsus, the antivivisectionist Roman best qualified for the title of original scientist, and a follower of the Hippocratic school, had described many of these operations in a First Century A.D. manual on surgery. But in the following centuries the gradual abandonment of Hippocratic hygiene, not yet known as asepsis, started increasing the danger of surgical operations to such an extent that little by little they were reduced to a minimum.

In the Middle Ages, they were mostly confined to amputations, which were performed only in extreme cases, owing to the almost inevitable danger of infection and the difficulty of checking hemorrhages. The technique employed by the Greeks to ligature the vessels had gone the way of all ancient surgical science, and the stumps were cauterized with red-hot irons or boiling oil.

Many of Galen's teachings were disastrous for mankind—such as his belief that pus is beneficial and essential to healing, or that fruit is harmful. Galen had noticed that dogs and cats shunned fruits, and it was to be medieval man's misfortune that Galen's father, who never touched fruits, reached an advanced age, so Galen saw in this a confirmation that the avoidance of fruit insures old age.

These and other Galenic misteachings made themselves tragically felt throughout the Middle Ages. The teachers of anatomy knew no other texts than Galen's: woman has two wombs, one for the male children, the other for females. Urine is secreted directly from the vena cava. The blood passes from the right ventricle of the heart into the left ventricle through invisible pores. Galen had acquired all these and many other wrong notions either through his experiments on live animals, or in spite of them.

And his many vivisections had failed to reveal to

Galen that the blood circulates, although he investigated the problem. In fact he is credited with the discovery that the veins do not contain air, as his contemporaries believed, but blood.

The abandonment of hygiene as an old-fashioned, pagan superstition was welcomed by the Church, owing to her horror of sex and nudity, and was fostered by her with dire consequences for mankind. Not only were the classic Greek statues and images of nudes destroyed, clad or painted over in most of Europe, but the public thermae, which had done so much to keep the Greek and Roman people healthy, were closed down. Body washing and even just looking at one's own nudity were considered evidence of sinfulness and depravity, and the few people who were sometimes ordered by their doctor to take a bath were lowered into the tub fully clad. To this day, for the rare baths in some Italian parochial boarding schools, a chaste bathing suit must be worn in the tub, and mirrors are absent.

All the medical historians (Sigerist, Dubos, Inglis), concur that the disappearance of the great medieval epidemics, including the bubonic plague which wiped out almost half of Europe's population, was not due to a specific therapy, but to the introduction of hygiene, of the sewer system and clean water in the cities, and that the startling betterment these institutions brought, raising life expectancy dramatically, started half a century before large-scale vaccination was adopted. Oddly enough, it did not seem to occur to any of those historians that what they defined as the "mysterious" insurgence of those epidemics, was not mysterious at all but the inevitable consequence of Church-supported Galenism, *i.e.* the abandonment of Hippocratic hygiene. The disastrous plagues of the Middle Ages were the legitimate offsprings of the sad, long-lasting union between the sexuophobia of the Church and the extrapolation to man of observations made on animals, which, for instance, need no washing with lots of hot water and soap after bringing forth, because the antiseptic effect of their own saliva is sufficient to prevent puerperal fever. Today, pestilences keep turning up wherever populations are crowded and cleanliness is absent. In unhygienic southern Italy, puerperal fever causes as many deaths as a century ago.

The ancient Greek and Romans, who considered it normal to blind the rebels, impale the enemy soldiers and put to the sword the vanquished populations, had forbidden on pain of death the section of human cadavers—but not of living animals; and later on the Church retained that attitude. This explains why in the western world the medical men who were trying, like today's vivisectors, "to discover the secrets of human life" by cutting up live animals, moved backward instead of forward, forgetting Hippocrates' teachings and getting morassed deeper and deeper in a Galenism seasoned with magic, astrology and religion. And then, as now, the majority went along, unthinkingly.

* * *

Some of the Greek culture and medical science that Europe had mislaid during the Dark Ages lived on and evolved in the East, as the Greek texts were translated into Syriac and from Syriac into Arabic. A few Oriental lights shone in the medieval fog—in the 10th Century, Al-Buruni, who came from central Asia, and has been overlooked by the western historians, and in the following century Persia's Razes and the Arab Avicenna. But the great change was not to come until Martin Luther helped lift the veils of obscurantism.

The first step out of the medical darkness was taken by Andreas Vesalius, a Belgian who since childhood had been cutting up live mice, cats, dogs, and had declared that his favorite animal was the pig, for it never stopped grunting under the knife, while the other animals after a certain point stopped complaining.

His vivisections taught Vesalius nothing. It was only when he started dissecting the bodies of the hanged he had stolen outside the walls of Lüttich that he discovered Galen's errors, and published his findings in a treatise which is still considered a masterpiece of descriptive anatomy: *De humani corporis fabrica,* illustrated in Titian's laboratory and published in Basel in 1543.

But it was still dangerous to hint that Galen had erred. A few years earlier, Paracelsus had lost his teaching position at the University of Basel for having publicly burnt Galen's works; and his dismissal had been requested by the students themselves, who worried about such disrespect of accepted standards. And as late as 1560 an Englishman who wanted to be a doctor was asked first to recant the doubts he had expressed about Galen's teachings.

In fact Vesalius, who was teaching anatomy in Italy, at Padua University, could well have paid the penalty of heresy and been burnt at the stake, as was to happen ten years later to Miguel Servetus, the Spanish doctor-priest who had sectioned a cadaver; but he explained that he didn't want to contradict Galen, but rather to demonstrate how accurate his descriptions had been, except for that venial little sin of assuming that what was true for a quadruped was equally true for man. However, the majority of the university brains, including his teacher Jakobus Sylvius, took their distances, accusing Vesalius of "heresy and folly." And Vesalius preferred to repair to Spain.

Truth had nevertheless started coming into light; but Galenism proved thick-skinned. Ignorance, especially the ignorance of the learned, has always been slow to die. For example, based on his observation of quadrupeds, Galen had described the human hipbone as being flared, like that of an ox. When Vesalius' book brought out the truth, the university teachers would not admit that they had perpetuated a millenarian error, and explained that since Galen's day the human hipbone had changed shape owing to the habit of wearing pants instead of the toga.

It took almost two centuries after the publication of Versalius' work to dissipate the last remnants of Galenic fog—but only to make room for another doctrine that was equally wrong and tyrannical, but far more harmful.

*   *   *

In 1628, less than a century after Vesalius' book, another famous work came out: the treatise on the circulation of the blood by William Harvey, an Englishman who had studied at Padua. The medical historians called him the "discoverer" of circulation, setting the blueprint for all the following historians, whose research usually consists in copying each other. And Harvey's alleged discovery was to become one of the battle horses of vivisectionists.

That the blood circulates had been known for thousands of years. Even if Galen never knew it, the Orientals did. So already *Nei Cing,* ("The Book of Medicine"), which forms the basis of Chinese medical literature, compiled in 2650 B.C. by scientist Emperor Hwang Ti, included these words: "All the blood in the body is under the control of the heart . . . The blood current flows continuously in a circle and never stops."

Not even today has all Oriental knowledge penetrated the West. Much less so in the Middle Ages. Suffice it to remember that Marco Polo, who introduced spaghetti from China to his native Italy, forgot to mention paper and printing, which the Chinese had been using for centuries. Nevertheless, that the blood circulates wasn't a secret for the medieval scholars. Too many had already spoken about it. In the 13th Century the Arab Ibn an Nafis had written that the blood passes from the right side of the heart, through the lungs, to the left side. (His work was reexhumed from oblivion just before the Second World War.)

Another who knew about circulation was Leonardo da Vinci, who for the sake of his art had studied the usual corpses of the hanged and discovered the function of many internal organs. In fact Leonardo rather than Vesalius would be considered the father of modern anatomical knowlege if the assistant who was to reproduce his drawings for the book he was preparing hadn't died. Leonardo's original drawings are now scattered in many lands. Leonardo had already recognized that the basis of the two great arteries through which the blood issues from the heart are provided with valves that prevent the blood inverting its course and returning to the heart.

The question of the circulation of the blood evolved very slowly in the western world because it was at odds with the "official" science of the day—with the opinion of Galen, according to which the blood was in a state of continual flux and reflux, like the ocean's tide. Also the heretic Servetus had explained in his *Restitutio Christianismi* that the blood passes from the right to the left side of the heart, going through the lungs, and that in the course of this passage it got "refreshed" by something taken from the air: which is a quite accurate description of what actually happens. No wonder Harvey's claim to have discovered the circulation caused an immediate controversy.

It is clear that experiments on animals did not originate the theory that he propounded in his treatise, but experiments he made on corpses, and on himself. He made beautifully simple experiments on the living body by ligaturing his own arm and noticing on which side the blood accumulated. Thus he "discovered" what was amply known, without the necessity of vivisecting animals. Then on the corpse of a man who had been hanged he forced water into first the right side of the heart and then the left, watching the direction and course of the fluid in each case. (*Life and Works of William Harvey*, Sydenham Society, Ed. by Willis, p. 507)

In his treatise, dedicated to the King of England, he couldn't admit that he had broken the law by experimenting on a human corpse, so he claimed to have come to his conclusions by vivisecting 80 different kinds of animals, a plainly ridiculous affirmation. Once the principle was established, there would not have been much sense in going through the same motions with 80 different species. But it helped establish his reputation as an earnest, thorough "scientist." Galen had kept vivisecting animals to "discover the truth" about the blood, and had come to wrong conclusions.

Lawson Tait, the greatest surgical innovator of modern times and foremost expert on medical science, went on record with a paper read on April 20, 1882, before the Birmingham Philosophical Society, and had this to say about the question of Harvey's merits:

"Take the case of the alleged discovery of the circulation of the blood by Harvey, and it can be clearly shown that quite as much as Harvey knew was known before his time. That he made any solid contribution to the facts of the case by vivisection is conclusively disproved, and this was practically admitted before the Commission by such good authorities as Dr. Acland and Dr. Lauder Brunton. The circulation was not proved till Malpighi used the microscope, and though in that observation he used a vivisectional experiment, his proceeding was wholly unnecessary, for he could have better and more easily used the web of the frog's foot than its lung. It is, moreover, perfectly clear that were it encumbent on anyone to prove the circulation of the blood now as a new theme, it could not be done by any vivisectional process but could, at once, be satisfactorily established by a dead body and an injecting syringe. In fact, I think I might almost say that the systemic circulation remained incompletely proved until the examination of injected tissues by the microscope had been made."

* * *

Of true value to science was the invention of the microscope by Anthony Leeuwenhoek (1632–1723), a Dutch dry-goods store owner who liked to grind ever more powerful lenses in his spare time, until he became the first person who saw a unicellular organism, today named microbe, by means of an instrument that today we call microscope.

The Dutchman hadn't been dead long when in Italy Lazzaro Spallanzani was born (1729), who became a university professor at Reggio and Pavia. Although he was a priest, he was an indefatigable experimenter in every field, including vivisection. To "discover the secret of life" he started shearing off the legs of toads during copulation. But his contributions to science came from other fields.

The majority of the so-called "natural philosophers"

of the time,* including the great French naturalist Buffon, believed that all small animals such as insects, frogs and mice were born spontaneously, springing from cow dung or mud. Spallanzani was the first to prove that not even a microbe comes from nothing. Observing a single germ under the microscope, he saw it narrow in the middle, then divide, and multiply. Through a long series of experiments he demonstrated that by heating a liquid all the germs in it die and no new germs can generate so long as the container remains sealed. (To achieve this he fused the neck of his bottles over a flame.)

The implications of this discovery were far too momentous to be realized at once by anyone, including Spallanzani himself—let alone to be put forthwith to any practical use. In fact they contained all the notions for the future works of Pasteur and Koch, and for the canning of food for conservation, which could have enabled Napoleon to win his Russian campaign and change the course of history.

With the death of Spallanzani in 1799 we reach the threshold of another century, of a new period for mankind. The world had rid itself of the superstitions of Galenism, except one—which, like the germ observed by Spallanzani, had already started dividing and multiplying, taking up ever more monstrous forms.

But as yet nobody seemed to have noticed.

THE ADVANCES

Before leaving definitely the moribund 18th Century, let us briefly see what other important advances were made inside that span, beyond those of Leeuwenhoek and Spallanzani.

In 1757, when scurvy was decimating the crews of the British Navy to the point of endangering the ef-

---

* The term "scientists" hadn't been coined yet. It is supposed to have been invented in 1840 by the British philosopher William Whewell, who was interested in the physical sciences. At the beginning of the 19th Century, what we today call "scientists" were called "philosophers," and their tools "philosophical instruments." The earliest evidence in the Oxford English Dictionary of the word "science" being used in its modern sense is from 1867.

ficiency of the Home Fleet, James Lind, a doctor of the naval hospital at Portsmouth, advised the Admiralty to add lime juice to the diet of the crews that had to spend many months at sea. Ever since the 16th Century lime juice had been regularly supplied to the Dutch trading ships sailing to the East Indies, and their crews were free of scurvy, and later on the British Merchant ships had also employed lime juice with success. But the Admiralty brains didn't believe that such a simple and inexpensive remedy could cure or prevent such a deadly malady. And yet Captain Cook had followed Lind's advice and remained at sea 3 years without a single case of scurvy developing on board his ship. But it was only after Sir Gilbert Blane cured an outbreak of scurvy in 1784 that the Admiralty gave serious thought to the matter, and in 1795 an order was at last promulgated providing for the issue of lime juice to the crews of the Royal Navy; that is why the English sailors, and later all the Britishers, were called limeys.

Lime juice contains Vitamin C, a potent antidote against scurvy, and this had not been discovered through animals, for a great many of which lime juice is fatal. Vivisectors later on caused mortal scurvy in innumerable animals by feeding them unnatural diets, and continue doing so today just to prove and reprove what the Dutch of the 16th Century already knew. But exactly how our modern medicine men have managed the hat trick of *creating scurvy in man through administration of Vitamin C* shall be explained in the chapter "The Devil's Miracles." In this one we shall see the major advances made.

Viennese clinician Leopold Auenbrugger had introduced in 1791 the diagnostic method of percussion, consisting of tapping the surface of the patient's chest and abdomen to find out the condition of the parts beneath by the sound emitted. It can reveal the enlargement of the liver or the heart, or an edema of the lung, and it was the forerunner of auscultation, equally important today in diagnostics.

The first great step toward the cure of heart disease —and so far also the last—was the discovery of digitalis in 1785 by William Withering, an English physician and botanist. He tested an infusion made of the dried leaves of the foxglove flower—which had been used among country folk as a remedy for dropsy or edema—on his heart patients, and with such success that it was soon included in the Edinburgh Pharmacopeia. It was named digitalis because the petal of the foxglove flower is shaped like a finger.

Digitalis is among the few drugs in the world's pharmacopeia that has proved of lasting value, and it was discovered, like all the other fundamental drugs, without animal experimentation. There is no more valuable remedy today for lowering ventricular rate in cases of a heart disorder now called auricular fibrillation.

Iodine, another fundamental medicament of lasting value, has been in use as a dressing for some 150 years. That means before the enunciation of the germ theory, and therefore before the nature of infection was repropounded by medical science, which during the centuries of Galenism had derided the hygienic precepts of antiquity, confirming that by dint of new wisdom man forgets the old.

In Watson Cheyne's classical *Antiseptic Surgery* (1882), the first standard work in English on the use of antiseptics, it is recorded that the application of iodine as a dressing for wounds was well known in 1859. The authority quoted is French surgeon Louis Velpeau, (1795–1867), who claimed in that year that the practice had already been well established for at least 30 years. This takes us back to 1829, 18 years after the element itself had first been isolated in a pure state by Bernard Courtois.

In South America the natives used quinine against "swamp fever" (malaria), and with the help of that natural remedy the disease was controlled in Europe, too. Long before that, some thinking individuals had observed that malaria occurs most frequently in the vicinity of swamps, and for that reason many swamps were ordered drained; that was long before anyone had discovered that malaria is transmitted by mosquitoes, and that mosquitoes breed in swamps.

The first "modern" type of vaccination was due to Edward Jenner, who in 1796 inoculated a boy with a smallpox vaccine he had developed. This case is among the best known in medical history, so we need not dwell on it except to recall that Jenner reached his conclusion after 21 years of patient observations and reflection, in what we would call today "clinical observation."

Although Jenner had anticipated Pasteur by 80 years, his vaccination was by no means the first in history. Vaccination had been practiced in the Orient ever since ancient times, and the Oriental smallpox vaccination had been practiced in England for the first time in 1717, when it was introduced by Lady Mary Wortley Montagu, the wife of the British ambassador at Constantinople.

The Turkish method consisted of taking from the pustule of an infected individual as much liquid as had place on a pinpoint and scratching with it the skin of the person to be vaccinated. Sometimes this vaccination ended, like today, in death, so various methods had been devised to decrease the virulence of the liquid: it was left to macerate in water for several days, or else a crust was left in water before it was used. The Chinese blew pulverized crusts into the nose of the people to be vaccinated.

The social position of Lady Mary brought the Turkish method to the British Royal Family, who had a dread fear of smallpox after the young and beautiful Queen Mary had died of it at the end of the previous century. But to play it safe, the king first had the vaccine tried out on six prisoners who were waiting for execution in the Newgate prison.

Thus animal experimentation had nothing to do with the discovery and development of vaccination either, nor could it have had, since the gravest human infections are not transmittable to animals, or take up different forms in them. Later on, to produce vaccines on a large and lucrative scale, the industry took recourse to animals, because medical thought had already been channeled into the one-way direction of animal use; and with what dire results, we shall see

in another chapter. When later it became necessary
to develop safer means than animals in order to prepare vaccines, the means were found. Thus once more
the use of animals had only retarded medical science
and caused untold havoc among mankind.

But before going into this we must see how surgery
was freed of the two main shackles that had not
only caused it to stagnate in a Galenic condition, but
had thrown it back to a prehistoric level.

SURGERY

While in most other fields of science and technology
the western world was rapidly making important discoveries, in one field all knowledge was morassed:
surgery. Worse, the kind of surgery practiced in the
Middle Ages and up to the first half of the 19th
Century represented a gigantic step backward compared to the large variety of delicate operations that
had been performed thousands of years earlier in India, Egypt and Babylon, then also in Greece and Imperial Rome.

The surgeons of antiquity must have known highly
sophisticated techniques, but they had been lost, like
the architectural techniques of the ancient Egyptian,
Roman, and South American cultures. We don't know
how some of the ancient surgical instruments that have
been preserved were used. But we know that already
before Hippocrates' time, hygiene played a basic role
in surgical technology no less than in medical art. The
Hindu surgeons were instructed to wash their hands
and nails very carefully, and never to open their
mouths during an operation, lest the wound get infected.

It was probably the Hindu medical schools of the
two physicians, Atreya and Sursuta, at some time of
the 6th Century B. C., that influenced Greek anatomy
and medicine. Sursuta's work, one of the greatest of
its kind in Sanskrit literature, was especially important
for surgery. He described operations, advocated dissection of cadavers for surgical training, and steriliz-
ing wounds by fumigation. One can truly say that

modern surgical *progress* has consisted in *regressing* —in finding its way back at last to what was well-known thousands of years ago, but had meanwhile been forgotten.

The historians have declared themselves unable to explain why the surgical art of antiquity fell into oblivion, but the reason is clear. The reason was the same that brought about the medieval pestilences: As hygiene was derided as superstition, fatal postoperative infections became so frequent that all major surgery was gradually abandoned, except the inevitable cases of accidents or battle. Also the art of ligaturing the blood vessels was lost, to be replaced with the easier and speedier cauterization by means of hot oil or iron. This probably happened during the great wars of the Middle Ages.

What we know for sure is that up to the middle of the past century any advance in the field of surgery was impeded by 1) the fear of pain, and 2) the fear of postoperative mortality from infection, which was very high even in simple operations.

* * *

In the surgeons' hands the patients had to go through such tortures that some preferred committing suicide rather than submitting to an operation. The few who were brave or foolish enough to accept, cried and struggled on the operating table, some to the point of insanity, or collapse and death. So the surgeons were valued according to their speed. The record for an excision of a gallstone was supposed to have been 54 seconds. Guillaume Dupuytren, who operated up to 1835 and was France's highest paid surgeon because he was the quickest, used to say that pain can kill like a hemorrhage.

Since human beings, however indifferent to the sufferings of others, are unwilling to face their own, much less to pass on to a better life, the surgeons of the last century had plenty of free time. Most surgery was practiced by barbers, and was usually limited to setting fractured bones, excising external tumors, and performing only inevitable amputations,

which often ended in death due to infection. The rediscovery in France of the ligaturing of the vessels by
Ambroise Paré—not a medical man, as is generally
reported, but a barber—had reduced fatal hemorrhages, but deaths caused by "blood poisoning" or
infection had increased correspondingly. Today we
know why.

Cauterization, which in the Middle Ages had replaced ligatures, had had the power to disinfect the
wound. But the surgeons didn't realize that, as the
germ theory had not yet been announced, nor had
the importance of cleanliness been rediscovered as yet.
To protect their long frocks, the surgeons of the time
wore over them old overcoats which were never
cleaned, for the crusts of blood and pus on them testified to the wearer's experience: the thicker the crust
the higher the fee.

The two big barriers of pain and infection started
coming down almost simultaneously toward the middle
of the last century.

*   *   *

Why it took so long for anesthesia to come into
general use in the western world is inexplainable, since
the pain-killing power of certain plants, like opium
and hashish, was already known in ancient times and
among many primitive peoples. The oriental doctors
of antiquity must have used some sort of anesthesia
for their various operations of high surgery. Only Chinese acupuncture has been preserved to our day, and
in expert hands its great utility for anesthesia has been
proved beyond doubt even to modern science.

In the 13th Century, Michael Scot, the Scottish
astrologer and alchemist who translated medical works
from the Arabic, wrote for the surgeons a recipe for
an analgesic composed of mandrake, opium and henbane; but perhaps no one dared use it because Scot
was also considered a magician, which is why Dante
assigned him a place in Hell: *"Michele Scotto fu, che
veramente delle magiche frodi seppe il gioco."* (*In-
ferno*, XX, 116-117)

Three centuries later, Paracelsus imported from the

East another opiate, laudanum, and among his recipes
found after his death there was one he had called
"sweet vitriol," which on examination turns out to be
today's ether. In fact the Middle Ages was the period
of various sleeping potions; the literary works, including Shakespeare's, are full of reference to drugs that
induced deep, death-like sleep.

The first modern anesthetics were found by chance
—it couldn't have been otherwise—and by personal
experience. As early as 1800 Sir Humphry Davy suggested that nitrous oxide might serve the purpose, and
in 1803 the German pharmacist Friedrich Serturner
had derived morphine from opium; but probably because he had tried it on dogs, in which morphine can
cause maniacal excitement, its value as an anesthetic
was not recognized for several decades.

Horace Wills, an American dentist, finally used
Humphry Davy's nitrous oxide to extract the tooth of
a colleague, and thus the so-called laughing gas found
its way into practice. Then in 1846 Dr. William Mor-
ton, an American dentist functioning as the first
anesthetist, enabled John Collins Warren to perform
the first surgical operation under ether anesthesia at
the Massachusetts General Hospital, in front of numerous students and doctors. It was a complete success. The fight against pain was won.

The next year James Simpson—after tests made on
himself and on friends—used chloroform (known
since 1828) for the first time in a surgical operation.
But scientific information being less fluent and widespread in the last century than today, in France Flourens decided some years later to experiment with
chloroform on animals, and the results led him to dis-
card it as an anesthetic altogether, while in England
Sir Lauder Brunton's experiments on 490 dogs, horses,
monkeys, goats, cats and rabbits, under the auspices
of the Hyderabad Commission, gave results which
were ridiculed by all the leading British anesthetists.
(*Lancet,* Feb. 8th, 15th, 22nd, 1890)

So once more, animal experiments retarded the
adoption of one of the most useful drugs of all times.

The inventor of lumbar anesthesia was German Dr.

August Bier, who had himself injected with a 1 percent solution of cocaine into his spine in order to observe its effect. Sigerist, the historian, states in his already mentioned work: "Bier in 1899 announces the immortal lumbar anesthesia, the invention that brings his name into the history of medicine." ·

As the second British Royal Commission Report on Vivisection was officially to establish: "The discovery of anesthetics owes nothing to experiments on animals." (p. 26)

*   *   *

But meanwhile medical art had already effected the greatest progress of all by starting to return to the long-forgotten hygienic principles. The year 1847 had marked the beginning of the war on infection, thanks to Philip Ignaz Semmelweis, a Hungarian who was director of Vienna's *Allgemeines Krankenhaus*. In that city hospital, puerperal fever was killing one child-bearing woman out of four—the same rate of mortality as occurred at the Massachusetts General Hospital in cases of amputation. In Paris the situation was even worse: 59 percent of the amputees used to die. Abdominal operations were rarely tried before the discovery of anesthesia, and if they were tried, the results were even worse. In England 86 percent of the women subjected to Cesarean section died.

Semmelweis hadn't seen a germ any more than Hippocrates ever had, nor had he heard anything about a germ theory, which was still to be announced: but both physicians had reached the identical conclusion thanks to true medical intuition and the sheer exercise of their intellectual powers—the intelligent clinical observation that has solved so many great medical problems.

Others before Semmelweis had suggested that puerperal fever might be a contagious disease, and that hygiene could prevent it; but they had been laughed at. Animals didn't get sick and die of fever when they gave birth; so why should people? In 1795 Scotsman Alexander Gordon gave ample proof that the disease was contagious, in a paper titled *Treatise of the Epidemic Puerperal Fever of Aberdeen,* in which he stressed the need of disinfection by nurses and physicians attending lying-in women. Although the evidence he offered was indisputable, it went under amid the general hilarity of the medical giants of the time.

In 1843 Oliver Wendell Holmes, professor of anatomy and physiology at Harvard, and father of the namesake jurist, wrote *The Contagiousness of Puerperal Fever*. It also met vigorous opposition from the leading obstetricians, and its facts began being acknowledged only after it had been enlarged and reprinted in 1855. The late English historian, Lord Moynihan, called it "one of the greatest essays ever written in the history of medicine." Semmelweis had not heard of the English works when he came to the same conclusion and put them into practice.

It happened the day Semmelweis interrogated a lying-in patient who was in despair because she had been assigned to the ward of the obstetric students rather than to the midwives. From her, Semmelweis learned that the women of Vienna were convinced that with the students they risked death much more than with the midwives. At that moment Semmelweis had his flash of intuition that started modern medicine toward its most important conquest—the restoration of pre-Galenic hygiene, long before Pasteur came along.

A few days earlier Semmelweis had seen a colleague die, who had cut and infected himself while performing an autopsy on a victim of puerperal fever, and had shown the same symptoms as the women who died of puerperal fever. The students also performed autopsies; not the midwives. So Semmelweis concluded that puerperal fever must be of infectious nature. For this reason, and not because they were less able, more students than midwives infected the lying-in patients.

That very day Semmelweis began his war against contagion: He demanded absolute cleanliness, and disinfection by chlorination, of everybody connected with the maternity ward. But the doctors didn't like this innovation, which they considered humiliating and ridiculous. However, within a couple of years, Semmelweis reduced mortality in the maternity ward by 90 percent. But he got no credit for it, because he couldn't *demonstrate* his theory through animal experiments, which were already the great vogue. And when he started calling assassins the obstetricians who still refused to wash their hands, the Austrian doctors banded together and had him ousted.

Semmelweis returned to his native Budapest and published a book about his findings. But as his countrymen, too, derided him, he became insane, and he died without witnessing the triumph of his ideas.

*　*　*

Semmelweis and the few of a like mind obtained recognition a quarter of a century later, when the germ theory was announced—another fundamental step that owed nothing to animal experimentation. Thus the other great danger of surgery was eliminated: postoperative infection.

As soon as the two great barriers that had been in the way of surgical progress were removed—the fear of pain and infection—surgery developed rapidly, as operations became possible that had never been tried in modern times, and the surgeons, first exploring dead bodies, then operating on the living, perfected within a few years the techniques that are fundamentally still in use today.

For over a century the vivisectors had done surgical exercises on animals, without having to worry about the pains they were inflicting or the danger of infection, but surgery had been unable to rise above the medieval morass. It was only when it became possible, thanks to anesthesia and asepsis, to operate directly on man that surgery recouped in a few decades practically everything that had been lost in the Dark Ages.

And soon another discovery that had nothing to do with animal experimentation came to the surgeons' aid, revealing to them beforehand exactly where to cut: Roentgen's X rays.

SURGICAL TRAINING

"Practice on dogs probably does make a good veterinarian, if that's the kind of practitioner you want for your family." So wrote Dr. William Held, internationally famous Chicago physician—one of the many great medical men who regarded the practice of vivisection as dangerously misleading for medical art.

It is not hard to understand why exercises on dogs —the favorite animal of the surgical experimenter— can't develop surgical skill in respect to human patients. In the dog's narrow, peaked chest the operational field is so different from man's that operations require in part specially built instruments. Also the shape and disposition of all organs differ markedly. So the surgeon who has learned to locate, say, the femoral artery in the dog will find it hard afterwards to locate it in a human patient. And the skin, tissues, tendons, in sum all parts of the dog, react differently under the knife, being either more elastic or tougher or less so than in man. The postoperative reactions also differ. So all animals are much less subject to infections, and the surgeon who has succeeded in cutting up a dog without killing it credits his own skill for his success rather than the animal's superior resistance: a dangerous illusion.

Likewise the vivisectionists' claim that our knowledge of human heart surgery derives from exercises on dogs is plainly absurd; since the dog has a highly irregular, intermittent pulsation, there couldn't be an unsafer guide to man's heart. All our knowledge of the human heart derives from the section of cadavers, from accidents in which the doctor had to intervene directly on man to save his life—as in the countless cases of battle injuries and traffic accidents—and through radiological observations. Obviously, those practicing surgeons who happen to be fond of vivisection will claim that they derive their skill through working on animals. My advice to those who need surgery is to keep away from such people, for they are dangerous surgeons, and pitiless men.

The same holds true for brain surgery. The millions of animal experiments that purported to ascertain the localization of the cerebral functions have merely created confusion, adding nothing useful to the teachings of Hughling Jackson, who had never experimented on an animal. And this had been clearly predicted by Jean-Martin Charcot (1825–1893), the father of modern neurology: "Experiments on animals designed to establish the localization of cerebral functions can teach us at best the topography of that particular species—never the topography of man," said Charcot. Even Claude Bernard had realized that.

Now let us take an X-ray look at the vivisectionists' battle horse: the blue babies case.

* * *

"Blue babies" defines newborns suffering from a defect of the valves leading to the pulmonary artery that carries veinous blood to the lungs. Because the oxygenation of the blood is insufficient in such children, their skin appears bluish, and they develop shortness of breath. They seldom survive to maturity if left untreated.

To remedy that condition, American surgeon Alfred Blalock had introduced in 1944 an operative technique based on clinical observations made by heart specialist Helen B. Taussig, a German refugee. Blalock claimed to have developed his technique through numerous exercises on dogs—however puzzling such a statement may sound to anyone who is aware of the anatomical, organic and functional differences between the heart of man and dog.

Then the London surgeon R. C. Brock of Guy's Hospital developed an entirely different technique by careful postmortem observation correlated with symptoms evinced during life, and the application of sound reasoning. The report in the *British Medical Journal* (June 12, 1948) makes it quite clear that the whole procedure was evolved without experiments on animals at any stage.

A third technique, not involving animals either, was developed by two English surgeons, N. R. Barrett and Raymond Daley of St. Thomas Hospital, London. This technique was developed along the lines of logical deduction, as described in the *British Medical Journal* (Apr. 23, 1949).

The survival rate in all these cases is the same, proving once again—if further proof were needed—that those who try out something on animals first, do so not because they have to, but because they want to —like that enthusiastic vivisector Alfred Blalock, inventor of the "Blalock Press" designed to crush without effort the extremities of dogs.

The British surgeon-historian M. Beddow Bayly had this comment in his *Clinical Medical Discoveries* (1961): "It is significant that both of the latter methods have proved of value in cases that are unsuitable for the treatment by Blalock's method . . . Finally, there is no reason to believe that Blalock's operation, based as it was on logical reasoning, just like Brock's, could not have been applied with as much success to human patients without the preliminary recourse to practice upon dogs. If this was unnecessary to Brock's success in this country, it is surely logical to conclude that it was equally unnecessary in the United States."

In Great Britain surgeons have had for a century experience with human patients only, for under the Cruelty to Animals Act of 1876 it is provided that no experiment shall be performed on animals for the purpose of attaining manual skill. And it would be very difficult for anyone even today to disclaim Sir W. Heneage Ogilvie, medical doctor and Consulting Surgeon to Guy's Hospital and Royal Masonic Hospital, who declared in the *British Medical Journal* (Dec. 18, 1954, p. 1438):

"British surgery has always stood high because it can be claimed, and not without reason, that every surgical advance of major importance has come from this country."

*   *   *

But even more revealing is what the vivisectors themselves say in their unguarded moments about the uselessness of vivisection for medical science.

In *Experimental Surgery,* the monumental vivisection manual, J. Markowitz gives fair warning in his introduction that "The operative technique described in these pages is suitable for animals, usually dogs. However, it does not follow that it is equally and always suited for human beings. We refuse to allow the student the pretense that what he is doing is operating on a patient for the cure of an ailment."

So this top expert states explicitly that vivisection doesn't really help train the surgeon; he even says it can be misleading, and furnishes a memorable example: "In our student days intrathoracic surgery sounded very mysterious and formidable. We know today that it need not be so. What caused the difficulties was that the surgeons assumed the nature of pneumothorax as encountered in the dog to be similar to what will occur in man. This is only true for the side that is opened, for a man has two separate chests, each harboring a lung, and each capable of sustaining life . . . In the dog, even a small puncture of one pleural cavity will cause fatal collapse of both lungs."

Thus also pneumothorax, which for many years has saved so many human lives, would never have been attempted if the surgeons had used animal experimentation as a guideline.

Markowitz gives repeated evidence that with him also experimentation has become just a paranoid fixation, as when he comes up with this bright idea (p. 446): "It would be an interesting exercise to remove both kidneys of a dog, and 3 days later, when he is at the point of death, to transplant a kidney from another dog into his neck."

That he doesn't expect anything beneficial to come out of all the "exercises" emerges from page 440: "In general, surgery has accomplished as much as is possible by means of asepsis, dexterity, and careful preoperative and postoperative care. Unless some new physiological principle is evolved, it would appear that surgery has reached its limits."

Then what *is* the sense of continuing all these surgical "experiments" on animals? The author solves the puzzle only on page 532, at the very end of the book, in the best tradition of the mystery thrillers, when he writes:

"No study could prove more enthralling and gratifying, and simultaneously lucrative."

MAJOR SURGEONS SPEAKING

Sir Charles Bell (1774–1842), Scottish anatomist, doctor, and surgeon, is famous for his contributions to the study of the brain and the nervous system. He was a practicing physician and surgeon, and also professor of anatomy, physiology and surgery at the University of London and of Edinburgh. In 1807 he announced his discovery that the anterior spinal nerve roots are motor in function, while the posterior spinal nerve roots are sensory ("Bell's law"). The Britannica's comment: "These discoveries are regarded as the greatest in physiology since that by William Harvey of the circulation of the blood."

In his fundamental book, representing "a republication of the papers delivered to the Royal Society on the subject of the nerves," Bell wrote:

"Experiments have never been the means for discovery; and a survey of what has been attempted of late years in physiology will prove that the opening of living animals has done more to perpetuate error than to confirm the just views taken from the study of anatomy and natural motions." (*An Exposition of The Natural System of the Nerves of the Human Body*, London, 1824, p. 337)

*   *   *

Charles Clay, M. D., according to the (British) *Dictionary of National Biography* (Supplement II, p. 30) "may fairly be described as the father of ovari-

otomy as far as Europe is concerned . . . He was also
the first (1843) to employ drainage in abdominal surgery, and he brought into use the term 'ovariotomy'
. . . President of the Manchester Medical Society and
original member of the Obstetrical Society of London,
he declared, as reported by the London *Times* (July
31, 1880):

"As surgeon, I have performed a very large number
of operations, but I do not owe a particle of my
knowledge or skill to vivisection. I defy any member
of my profession to prove that vivisection has been
of the slightest use to the progress of medical science
and therapeutics."

*   *   *

The name of Lawson Tait, the gynecologist from
Birmingham who performed more than 2,000 laparot-
omies at a time when such an operation was still rare,
looms larger than any other in the period which is considered the age of giants in surgical progress. Many
of surgery's present-day techniques originate from
him. He performed his first ovariotomy in 1868, when
he was only 21, and by 1872 his name had gone
into medical history with what became known in England and America as "Tait's operation"—the removal
of the uterine appendages for chronic ovaritis. In
1877 he began to remove diseased Fallopian tubes, and
in 1878 he described a new method of treating chronic
inversion of the uterus. All this, before he reached the
age of 35. He performed the first chole-cystotomy, a
gall-bladder operation, in 1879. In 1880 he was the first
one who successfully removed the vermiform appendix
for the relief of appendicitis (in Germany credit for
this "first" operation is usually given to Swiss surgeon Rudolf Ulrich Krönlein, who first performed it
some 5 years later.) In 1883, Tait performed the first
successful operation in a case of ruptured tubal pregnancy. He challenged Lister's method of antisepsis by
carbolic acid spray because of its damaging effect and
was the first exponent of today's aseptic surgery. In
1887 he was elected President of the newly formed
British Gynaecological Society. He won the Cullen

Prize "for the great benefits brought to practical medicine by surgical means," and the Lister Prize for the whole 1888–1890 period.

So if anyone who ever spoke about surgery knew what he was speaking about, it was Lawson Tait. And everything he said and wrote about vivisection, which he had practiced, is a merciless indictment against it, for he considered it deleterious not only for medical practice in general but also for the medical mind. Tait's opinions can't be dismissed as irrelevant today merely because they stem from many years ago. On the contrary. They are important because he spoke in, and of, the period of modern times' greatest surgical progress: a progress which, so the vivisectors tell us, was due to them. And their deliberate falsehoods must be exposed without reprieve, once and for all.

The Birmingham Philosophical Society's Basic Transactions include the very long paper that Lawson Tait read to his colleagues on April 20, 1882, and irrefutably denounce vivisection on every count. The paper comprises many pages. Here are a few excerpts, by the way of example.

"I dismiss at once the employment of experiments on living animals for the purpose of mere instruction as absolutely unnecessary, and to be put an end to by legislation without any kind of reserve whatever . . ."

And further on:

"It must be perfectly clear that to answer all these questions specific instances must be given, and that they must be analysed historically with great care. This has already been done in many instances, and I am bound to say, in every case known to me, to the utter disestablishment of the claims of vivisection . . . As a method of research it has constantly led those who have employed it into altogether erroneous conclusions, and the records teem with instances in which not only have animals fruitlessly been sacrificed, but human lives have been added to the list of victims by reason of its false light."

In the *Birmingham Daily Post* (Oct. 4, 1892), Tait wrote:

"Some few years ago I began to deal with one of

the most dreadful calamities to which humanity is subject by means of an operation which had been scientifically proposed nearly 200 years ago. I mean ectopic gestation [extrauterine gestation]. The rationale of the proposed operation was fully explained about 50 years ago, but the whole physiology of the normal process, and the pathology of the perverted one, were obscured and misrepresented by a French physiologist's experiments on rabbits and dogs. I went outside the experimentalists' conclusions, went back to the true science of the old pathologist and of the surgeons, and performed the operation in scores of cases with almost uniform success. My example was immediately followed throughout the world, and during the last five or six years hundreds, if not thousands of women's lives have been saved, whilst for nearly forty years the simple road to this gigantic success was closed by the folly of a vivisector."

Tait adds some information that gives a revealing insight on the twistings of vivisectors' minds in general:

"One of the conclusions of my operation was a physiological one, as simple as possible, and following from my facts as certainly as night follows day. It was that the peritoneal cavity was capable of digesting the soft gelatinous tissue of an early foetus. But this did not satisfy our German men of science, one of whom immediately set out to work, and, removing the immature babies from the wombs of a number of animals, he planted them in the cavity of the peritoneum of the same animal. Thus he assumed that he 'confirmed' my statements. I shall not harrow your readers by a description of what the sufferings of these poor little animals must have been, because I do not take up what is called the mere sentiment of this question; but I proclaim that the whole of this objectionable proceeding was useless and ridiculous . . ."

*   *   *

Sir Frederick Treves, Director of London Hospital, surgeon to the Royal Family and world-renowned authority on abdominal surgery, wrote in the *British Medical Journal* (Nov. 5, 1898, p. 1389):

"Many years ago I carried out on the Continent sundry operations upon the intestines of dogs, but such are the differences between the human and the canine bowel, that when I came to operate on man I found I was much hampered by my new experience, that I had everything to unlearn, and that my experiments had done little but unfit me to deal with the human intestine."

* * *

Dr. Stephen Smith, a surgeon who had worked at the Pasteur Institute and at the Physiological Institute of Strasburg, wrote in his book *Scientific Research: A View from Within* (Elliot Stock, London, 1899): "I agree with the eminent English surgeons who have gone on record as asserting that vivisection is of no value to humanity."

Now let us jump half a century.

* * *

Dr. Salvador Gonzalez Herrejon, Director of the Mexican National School of Medicine, published a long article condemning vivisection in the *New York Journal American* (July 13, 1947), including:

"Anything the students might learn of anatomy by working on dogs is unimportant in relation to humans, for the location of the viscera, spleen, nerves etc., of the animal, although somewhat similar, is different. We see clearly that in vivisection students perform high surgery with results which are gained only by the high physical tolerance of the animal, and they operate with the irresponsibility which this high tolerance induces. Is it prudent to teach the student that he can open the stomach of a human with such facility? And is it not unjustifiable cruelty to permit students to make an unnecessary and mutilating operation on a dog today, make another tomorrow, and again another, and so on until the dog dies? Is it not an immoral method of teaching, destroying respect for life, proper sentiment and piety? Obviously it is."

And still many years later, in the course of a round table on vivisection at the Press Club of Naples, the chief surgeon of Naples' prestigious Ospedale Pellegrini and Professor of Surgery at Naples University, Dr. Fernando De Leo, condemned vivisection without reticence, defining it "a shameless and useless practice."

Now how can one explain the contradiction between the aforementioned statements of some of the great medical authorities of modern times, that have condemned vivisection on every ground, and those vivisectors who claim that it is an indispensable tool for medical progress? Again the only explanation I am able to offer is George Bernard Shaw's:

"Whoever doesn't hesitate to vivisect will hardly hesitate to lie about it."

*   *   *

How then is the good surgeon formed? It has been most sensibly explained, among others, by Abel Desjardins, President of the French Society of Surgeons, professor of surgery at the *Ecole Normale Supérieure,* France's most prestigious seat of surgical teaching, and chief surgeon at the College of Surgery of the Faculty of Paris. Here a summary of his speech at the Congress Against Vivisection, Geneva, on March 19, 1932:

"The basis of surgery is the anatomy. That's why surgery must first be learned from anatomical treatises and atlases, and then by secting a very great number of cadavers. Thus you not only learn the anatomy, but also acquire the indispensable manual dexterity. From there you go on to learn the practice of surgery. This can only be acquired in the hospital and through daily contact with the patients. You must have been an assistant before becoming a surgeon . . . At the end let's examine how one comes to the actual surgical operation. First you watch, then you assist a surgeon. You do this a great many times. After you have understood the various phases of an operation and the difficulties that may arise, and have learned how to overcome them, then, and only then, may you begin to operate. First, easy cases, under the supervision of an experienced surgeon, who can warn you of any wrong step or advise you if you have any doubts on how to proceed . . . This is the real school of surgery, and I proclaim that there is no other . . . After I have explained to you the real school of surgery, it is easy to understand why all the courses of surgery based on operations on dogs have been miserable failures. The surgeon who knows his art can learn nothing from those courses, and the beginner doesn't learn from them the true surgical technique, but becomes a dangerous surgeon . . . Furthermore, vivisection corrupts the character, because it teaches you to attach no importance to the pain you inflict."

* * *

Nothing illustrated the uselessness, or the danger, of trying to acquire surgical skill by exercises on animals, as is being done in the U.S., than an essay in *Time* (Dec. 17, 1973). As a heading, *Time* recalled an opinion of the Supreme Court of the U.S. in 1898: "Character is as important a qualification as knowledge." As to the character *and* knowledge of the average American practicing physicians, practically each one of them trained on vivisection, the *Time* essay had this to say, among many other uncomplimentary things:

"Each year in the U.S. thousands of patients die needlessly, or needlessly soon, or have the quality of their remaining life irreparably damaged, because they have received incompetent medical care . . . Malpractice suits now jam the courts . . . Much of the science part of medicine remains largely hit or miss . . . There is a broad spectrum of incompetent and unwarranted surgery. One reason for the spate of sterilyzing hysterectomies and other dubious operations may be simply that there are too many surgeons. The U.S. has twice as many in proportion to population as Great Britain—and Americans undergo twice as many operations as Britons. Yet, on the average, they die younger."

The medical organization, as usual, refused to be

impressed, much less to change its ways. In 1975, according to Zurich's *Tages-Anzeiger* (DDP, July 17, 1975), American Dr. Sidney Wolfe revealed to a Congressional Committee that Americans spend yearly $5 billion for entirely unnecessary surgical operations, which every year cause about 16,000 unnecessary deaths. Instance: One Dorothy O'Grady from Ft. Lauderdale, Fla., complained about back pains to her doctor, who right away subjected her to a hysterectomy. The complications that developed kept the patient in the hospital for a year. A visit by another doctor then revealed that all she needed to get rid of her back ache was a half inch lift on her left heel.

VACCINES AND OTHER CONFUSIONS

Only to leave none of the vivisectionist claims unanswered: For the experiments of Galvani and Volta —which didn't concern medicine in the first place, but electricity—no living frog was used, but a dead one. "The metallic couple excites in the dead frog the nerve that directs muscular contraction." (Enciclopedia Italiana: "Galvani") Volta soon renounced working on dead frogs, having found more suitable experimental material in inorganic matters. (*Op. cit.* "Volta")

The incredible confusion reigning today in medicine extends to the historical and school texts. So the Encyclopedia Americana (ed. 1972) states that Sir Charles Bell discovered in 1807 that the anterior spinal nerve roots are sensory (Bell's law), and under Magendie: ". . . demonstrated what is known as Magendie's law: that the anterior spinal nerve roots are motor in function and the posterior are sensory." A historical examination of the two men's recorded conferences and writings proves that Magendie tried to usurp the Scotsman's discovery, having brought no contribution whatever to physiology, in spite of his innumerable vivisections.

Compounding the confusion, the Britannica claims that Galen already discovered practically as much almost 2,000 years ago: "He performed sections of the spinal cord at various levels and observed the resulting sensory and motor disturbances and incontinence."

But in the column "Science" of that very same encyclopedia, one is surprised to learn that some other scholar attributed that same discovery to a whole school: "At Alexandria the teachers' experiments on animals led them to distinguish between the posterior nerve roots of the spinal cord, which convey sensation, and the anterior, which convey the motor impulses."

As for Pasteur, most encyclopedias, including the Britannica and the Americana, credit him with the discovery that germs don't spring into life spontaneously, but originate from other germs, and that heat kills them. It was in fact Spallanzani who demonstrated this a whole century earlier.

Spallanzani's were the principal steps taken in bacteriology, after Leeuwenhoek's discovery of the existence of the germs. Pasteur carried Spallanzani's experiments a step further, determining exactly how high the temperature had to be, and how long the exposure to heat, before the germs were dead. Antoine Béchamp (1816–1895), Doctor of Medicine and of Science, professor of biological chemistry and physics and lecturer at the University of Paris, preceded Pasteur in his development of the germ theory. Contrarily to Pasteur, Béchamp was a humane researcher, and it is interesting to note that as in the controversies between Bell and Magendie, between Tait and Lister (asepsis and antisepsis), between Pasteur and Béchamp and between Koch and Béchamp, time proved the humane researchers right.

For Pasteur and Koch a germ was a disease, and a disease was a germ. Today we know that the germ does not necessarily cause the disease, and the disease can insurge without the presence of that particular germ. Béchamp was among the forerunners who attached more importance to the "soil" (the body) than to the "seed" (the germ). Furthermore, official records show that in regard to many discoveries with which Pasteur was credited, like the origin of silkworm disease, Béchamp had been first.

In fact Pasteur profited like few scientists from the discoveries of others. The Dutchman Leeuwenhoek had first seen a germ, Italy's Spallanzani had shown that germs can only come from other germs and heat kills them, Frenchman Cagniard de la Tour had known ever since 1837 that the fermentation of beer is caused by germs that he had identified, Germany's Schwamm had published a paper demonstrating that meat rots only following an invasion of germs, but in 1864 Pasteur arrogated for himself the merit of all these works by presenting *his* "germ theory," without even mentioning his trailblazers; and he was so convincing that London's great surgeon Lister wrote him a letter of thanks, and today's encyclopedias continue attributing to Pasteur exclusively what by rights belongs to others.

Robert Koch was the first to obtain a pure culture of anthrax germs, responsible for the cattle and sheep disease, and Pasteur made a vaccine from it by reducing the power of germs. Many historians call that the first vaccine in history, as if Jenner and the Orientals had never existed. At any rate, an immediate controversy between Pasteur and Koch ensued, each one accusing the other of plagiarism.

Pasteur then proceeded to develop a vaccine against rabies, or hydrophobia, which may represent the most disconcerting case in the entire disconcerting field of vaccines.

Only an infinitesimal percentage of people bitten by a rabid animal catch the infection. But if it develops, it is supposed to be always mortal. So to be safe, everybody who has been bitten by an animal suspected to be rabid gets the special treatment developed originally by Pasteur. But sometimes the vaccinated person dies anyway. In that case the death is attributed to a defective vaccine. But often it has been demonstrated that the vaccine and not the bite caused the infection —for instance when the animal later on turned out to be healthy. Even if the animal is rabid, the bite very seldom causes the infection—and never causes it if the normal hygienic rules are followed, like the immediate washing out of the wound with water.

In his best-selling *Microbe Hunters,* (Harcourt, Brace, 1926/1953) Paul de Kruif gave a highly fanciful account of 19 Russian peasants who, bitten by an allegedly rabid wolf, traveled to Paris in order to receive the newly announced Pasteur treatment from the old master himself. According to de Kruif, 16 of these Russian patients were "saved" by Pasteur's shots and "only three" died. Pasteur became an international hero after that exploit and contributed substantially to the glamorization of "modern" laboratory Science. Three deaths out of 19 makes over 15 percent casualties. But knowing, as we know today, that not one in a hundred people bitten by a rabid dog is likely to catch the infection, we must infer that at least some and probably all three of those Russian peasants died *because* of Pasteur's vaccine, as did uncounted people later on. Besides, at the time there were no facilities in Russia to find out whether a wolf had rabies. Hungry wolves attacking villagers in winter were a common occurrence; and even today many people, in Italy for instance, believe that any dog that bites them *must* be affected with rabies, otherwise it wouldn't have bitten them.

Some informed doctors believe that rabies, as a separate and distinguishable disease, exists only in animals and not in man, and that what is diagnosed as rabies is often tetanus (lockjaw), which has similar symptoms. Contamination of any kind of wound can cause tetanus, and it is interesting to note that today in Germany those who get bitten by a dog are regularly given just an anti-tetanus shot. According to Germany's most authoritative weekly, exactly 5 Germans are supposed to have died of rabies in 20 years (*Der Spiegel,* 18/1972, p. 175). But how can anyone be sure that they died of rabies? Hundreds die of tetanus.

Among the many doctors I have questioned in the U.S. and Europe, I have not yet found one who can guarantee that he has seen a case of rabies in man. The number of cases reported by the U.S. Public Health Service in its *Morbidity and Mortality Annual Supplement* for all of 1970 was exactly two—among 205,000,000 people. Provided the diagnosis was correct. This compares with 148 cases of tetanus reported, 22,096 of salmonellosis, 56,797 of infectious hepatitis, 433,405 of streptococcal infections and scarlet fever.

Doctors who are faced for the first time with a case of suspected rabies complain that they have no precedents to go by. The main difficulty Pasteur met with in perfecting his alleged vaccine, which often caused paralysis, consisted in finding rabid dogs; finally he had to get healthy dogs, open their cranium and infect them with the brain substance of the only rabid dog he had been able to get hold of.

Pasteur never identified the rabies virus. Today, everything concerning this malady is still more insecure than at Pasteur's time.

Only one thing is sure: ever since Pasteur developed his "vaccine," the cases of death from rabies have increased, not diminished.

Currently, rabies is presumed to be established in autopsies by the presence of "Negri corpuscles," so named after an Italian physician who in 1903 announced to have discovered them in the plasma of the nerve cells and the spinal nerves of rabid dogs. However, Dr. John A. McLaughlin, a prominent American veterinarian who in the sixties was called to investigate a widespread outbreak of alleged rabies in the State of Rhode Island and performed numerous autopsies on dogs during the height of the scare, found animals with "rabies" symptoms that had no Negri corpuscles whatever, whereas dogs that died of unrelated diseases had them in abundance. A veterinarian from Naples, where there is a fixation of fear of rabies, showed me in a textbook the image of a Negri corpuscle—the only one he had ever seen—that looked undistinguishable from the Lentz-Sinigallia corpuscles that occur in dogs who have distemper. Nobody knows how many dogs affected by mere distemper have been killed by order of sanitary authorities whose zeal overshadowed their knowledge.

A few years ago, Dr. Charles W. Dulles, widely-known Philadelphia physician and surgeon and lecturer at the University of Pennsylvania on the History of Medicine, had this to say: "I might cite my own experience in the treatment of persons bitten by dogs supposed to be rabid, which has furnished not a single case of the developed disease in 30 years, and I probably have seen more cases of so-called hydrophobia than any other medical man."

Every real expert is aware that nothing is known for sure except what Hippocrates already knew: that the best protection also against this infection is cleanliness. The No. 523 of the World Health Organization Technical Report Series, entitled *WHO Expert Committee on Rabies, Sixth Report,* 1973 (meaning that there have been no less than five previous WHO reports on the same subject) announces that evidence is accumulating that parenteral injection of antirabies vaccine causes human deaths "under certain conditions" (p. 20), and states (p. 17): "The Committee recommends that production of Fermi-type vaccines, since they contain residual living virus, should be discontinued."

"Residual living virus" is a pretty serious charge to bring from high quarters against a vaccine, but nobody seems to pay much attention to all this, or to understand what it means. It simply means that probably the very rare cases of humans who died of what has been diagnosed as rabies, have not died from something received from a dog but from a doctor.

But the climax of that WHO report is on page 27: "The Committee emphasized that the most valuable procedure in post-exposure treatment is the local treatment of wounds. This should be done by thorough washing with soap and water . . ." And on the next page the point is repeated: "Immediate first-aid procedures recommended are the flushing and washing of the wound with soap and water." So it took no less than 6 reports by WHO "experts" to reach the conclusion that Hippocrates had been advocating.

In fact whoever reads carefully this and other WHO reports, notices that serious students of medicine can rely on very little except Hippocratic hygiene and common sense. But WHO can't admit it, otherwise the public might ask: "What is the use of WHO?" Who is housed in one of the biggest, costliest buildings of modern times, with large, empty halls, libraries lined with every medical publication issued throughout the world, with numerous executives who draw fat salaries to do nothing, and a regiment of smart secretaries to help them. This huge real-estate complex, surrounded by the silence of well-groomed lawns and flower gardens in one of the most beautiful Alpine settings outside Geneva, represents the counterpart of the millions of laboratory animals wasting away under scientific torture the world over.

Lately, still a new vaccine against rabies has been developed, which has been described as a "fantastic breakthrough" by WHO officials. The report in *Time* (Dec. 27, 1976) reads in part: "Writing in the *Journal* of the American Medical Association, a team of US and Iranian doctors last week reported that they recently administered the vaccine in a series of only six shots to 45 Iranians who had been bitten by rabid animals. Not a single victim developed rabies or showed a severe allergic reaction. Reason: the new vaccine, unlike the old, is cultured in human rather than animal cells. Thus, while the patients develop antibodies against rabies, they do not suffer painful reactions to the foreign animal protein."

For the past hundred years antivivisectionists and other sensible people have been saying that there *must* be better ways for medical science than the ones recommended by Claude Bernard, and that Pasteur's alleged antirabies vaccination was humbug. Now official science is at last catching up to this obvious truth, and all the big men want to get into the act.

A headline in Germany's medical news weekly *Selecta* (May 16, 1977), which read "Problem of Rabies Vaccine Solved?" must have surprised many readers who had until then been brainwashed into believing that Pasteur had solved *that* problem long ago, since it has always been presented as his main claim to fame. The article reported a round-table of German virologists, who gave hell to Pasteur's alleged vaccine, and cited one Prof. Richard Haas who had defined it 'an archaic monster."

THE GIANTS WITH FEET OF CLAY

Compared to histrionic, ebullient Pasteur, Koch was a quiet individual. Like Pasteur, Koch also rendered himself useful at the microscope, whereas all his attempts to parallel man and animal were failures that retarded or tragically misled medical research. None the less, Pasteur and Koch are still being presented as the medical giants of our age in the textbooks.

In fact, it was through trusting in animal experimentation that Koch made one of the biggest blunders of his time—one which revealed itself as a blunder only years later, after Koch had received the Nobel Prize for it, and after it had caused the death of innumerable people.

Toward the end of the last century, in the great industrial cities of the north, one person out of seven died of tuberculosis, or TB for short, and usually in youth. Koch's announcement in 1882 that he had discovered and isolated the specific germ was greeted with an explosion of joy the world over. At that early stage of the game nobody had noticed that in those animal species in which human tuberculosis could propagate, the disease took on quite different forms.

The discovery of the tubercle bacillus seemed to sweep away all the other causes for TB that had been advanced: surroundings, air, diet, and the individual physical or psychic disposition, also called the soil. The world had reached the unshakable conviction that medicine had really become an exact science, and that the Six Postulates first enunciated by Koch's teacher Jakob Henle in 1840, later renamed the Six Postulates of Koch, had been proved right.

Those Postulates may be summed up thus:

1. A specific causative organism (*Erreger*) should be found in all cases of an infectious disease.

2. This organism should not be found in other diseases.

3. It should be isolated.

4. It should be obtained in pure culture.

5. When inoculated to experimental animals, it should reproduce the same disease in them.

6. It should be recoverable from the experimental animal.

Says the Encyclopedia Britannica still in our days: "Every modern student of bacteriology learns Koch's postulates as part of his basic training."

Contemporary teachers of medical history report in all seriousness as absolute fact what has long ago been debunked, such as Prof. Dr. Erwin Ackernecht who taught at the University of Zurich (*Kurze Geschichte der Medizin,* 2nd. ed., F. Enke, Stuttgart, 1975, p. 157):

Today we know the utter nonsense of such claims; but the textbooks have given up trying to correct all the mistakes that keep surfacing, and let them ride even in the new editions. We know today that the "specific organism" (or germ) causing a disease in man never reproduces the identical disease in animals: animals can't be infected with our cholera, typhoid, yellow fever, leprosy, smallpox, bubonic plague, our various flus, etc. Not even with our common cold. Koch's contemporaries and the "scientists" who recommended him for the Nobel Prize didn't know that yet.

The universal belief before the end of the last century was this: Since every disease is caused by a specific germ, all we have to do is to identify this germ, cultivate it, infect animals with it, recover it from the diseased animals, obtain a vaccine, and inoculate humanity with it. This had become—for a while—a dogma of the official science, and whoever expressed doubts was a heretic, a regressive fool. No one was allowed to doubt that all the diseases of mankind would be definitely eliminated before the end of the century, which was still 18 years away.

Probably nobody doubted Pasteur when he proclaimed in his emotional voice and flowery style: "If the conquests useful to mankind move your heart, if you are amazed at the effects of electric telegraphy and so many other admirable discoveries, then you should take interest in those sacred sites that are called laboratories . . . They are the temples of the future, of riches and welfare . . . That's where humanity becomes better . . ."

Even while Pasteur was uttering these beautiful words, humanity for the first time in its history was beginning to contract mortal diseases fabricated in laboratories through animal tortures with great effort and at high cost. Eight years after identifying the TB bacillus, Koch had announced to an ecstatic world that he had perfected a vaccine he had named Tuberkulin, which miraculously cured tuberculous guinea pigs. And in the following years, thousands of people rushed to get themselves inoculated with what can aptly be defined the first of the modern "miracle" drugs.

It turned out to work the same kind of miracles that thousands of miracle drugs as yet to come were to achieve: it worked financial miracles for its manufacturers and the medical profession, including Robert Koch, who in 1905 got the Nobel Prize for it; but it spelled disaster for the credulous public. Many years had to pass before the new medicine men had to admit that Tuberkulin cured tuberculous guinea pigs only. Instead of protecting human patients from catching TB, it proved capable of *causing* it in healthy patients, and it invariably activated latent forms of the malady. Tuberkulin has not only long since been discontinued as a vaccine but has even been used as a diagnostic means: The human organism may react so violently to this drug that it can reveal an individual's predisposition to the infection.

Today we know that TB does indeed depend on the environment, on the air, on the nourishment, on individual physical and mental disposition, as proved by the millions of people who come in daily contact with tuberculous persons without catching the disease, and the fact that it is still today four times more frequent among the poor and undernourished than among the well-fed. But meanwhile, in 1901 Koch had already announced to a stunned Congress of Tuberculosis in London that TB is one malady when it occurs in animals and a quite different malady when it occurs in people . . .

*   *   *

Before that, in Alexandria, Egypt, in 1883, an epidemic of cholera had broken out. Immediately Germany and France dispatched their microbe hunters to seek out and destroy the responsible agent. The German team was headed by Koch, the French team by two of Pasteur's assistants, E. Roux and L. Thuillier, each team working on its own and against the other. In a way it was a prolongation of the Franco-German war, as Koch and Pasteur were on a war footing.

In Alexandria, both teams collected intestinal juices from the cadavers of Alexandrians who had just died of cholera and injected them into dogs, cats, monkeys, chickens, and mice. But the animals thrived on those juices. While the microbe hunters were still wondering why, the epidemic, like all epidemics in the past and present, faded away as mysteriously as it had come, and the microbe hunters sailed back home. Not all of them: On the morning of departure, Thuillier developed the symptoms of cholera, and before evening he was dead.

Actually, Koch had already recovered from the intestines of dead Alexandrians the comma bacillus associated with cholera, but as all cultures of it that he injected into animals caused them no harm, he had ruled out the possibility that it was the responsible agent. Today we also know that the comma bacillus dies at once in any animal.

Koch then persuaded the Kaiser to send him to Calcutta, where among the unhygienically crowded populations some cholera epidemics were always smoldering, then as now. Again he found the comma bacillus in the intestines of bodies dead of cholera, but not one in any of the healthy Hindus he examined. So he came to the conclusion that, although harmless to animals, the comma bacillus was the responsible agent in man.

Today we know it is not so; that sometimes the

comma bacillus cannot be found in individuals dead
of alleged cholera, and yet it can be found in people
who are well, in the so-called healthy carriers. At any
rate, the defeat of cholera, which some people ascribe
to the vaccine, others to improved hygiene, was also
retarded by Koch's belief in animal experimentation.

Back from India, Koch received a hero's welcome,
and from the Kaiser's own hands the Order of the
Crown with Star. But at Munich a spoilsport was waiting for him in the person of the old professor of hygiene, Max Pettenkofer, who through the introduction
of elaborate sanitary services had made of Munich the
healthiest city in Europe, and clung to the belief that
not the virulence of the seed but the inadequacy of the
soil was responsible for the infection.

"Your bacillus can do nothing, dear Koch!" the old
lion roared at our puzzled hero. "What counts is the
organism. If your theory were right, within 24 hours I
should be a dead man." He grabbed from Koch's hand
a tube filled with a pure culture of cholera germs,
enough to infect a regiment, and in front of his horrified colleagues he swallowed the entire contents.

But only Koch felt sick.

* * *

Why does a microbe cause a disease in one organism
but not in another? Koch and Pasteur had not yet asked
that question, which today still begs an answer—although the vivisectors have tried to extract it with violent means from millions of animals.

That microbes associated with a malady may abound
in the environment and be present in the human body
without giving rise to symptoms is by now a well-known
fact. In 1909 *Lancet* (Mar 20, p. 848) pointed out:
"Many organisms which are considered to be causal
are frequently to be found in healthy persons. The organisms of enteric fever, of cholera, and of diphtheria,
may be cited as examples of this."

* * *

It is fantastic to note how once science has decided
to give a theory dogmatic validity, it will cling to that

theory, all counterproof notwithstanding. The theory of the Six Postulates, although proven wrong by the experimenters themselves, had been given dogmatic validity. That it has not yet been removed from our textbooks is due perhaps to the recognition that there is no guarantee that any of the other theories which keep cropping up will prove still valid when the next edition is published. Why spend time and money to replace an old bloomer with a new one?

The effectiveness of vaccination is always difficult to determine, because in every case counterproof is lacking. We have no way of knowing whether the decrease of an infection is due to a vaccine or not. For sure we know only what Hippocrates knew: that the most effective and at the same time harmless prevention of contagion is hygiene.

The bubonic plague that caused millions of deaths during the Middle Ages disappeared without any vaccination. Leprosy disappeared from Europe without any specific therapy. The Swiss medical historian Ackerknecht puts it this way: "Leprosy, a rare disease in antiquity, started spreading conspicuously in the 6th Century, reached a terrifying peak in the 13th Century, then vanished mysteriously from Europe." (*Op. cit.* p. 83) Syphilis has lost its erstwhile virulence. Many other infectious diseases underwent mutations in the course of the centuries, to be replaced by new ones. All this tends to prove that the great diseases of mankind have a life cycle of their own—they spring into being, grow, and decline, all without any discernible reason. As usual, man deludes himself that he is the protagonist on earth; but nature is. Medical science today knows nothing with certainty that Hippocrates didn't know already. On the other hand she has forgotten or is neglecting a great many valid notions, by dint of turning out, with unshakable presumption, new biochemical theories almost daily.

In 1931, an article in the Paris daily, *Le Matin,* reported: "Once more the census proves that France's decreasing population is not due to any decline in births but to increased death rate . . . The increasing death rate is greatest among infants, the very class that is being subjected to wholesale 'protective' vaccination."

Dr. G. Buchwald, the German medical director, whose extensive studies of the effects of smallpox vaccination leading to encephalitis eventually were determinant in the German government's recent decision to abolish smallpox vaccination altogether, expressed his suspicion in several scientific works that multiple sclerosis also could be a belated consequence of the smallpox vaccination (*Der Deutsche Arzt,* 1971, Vol. 19, p. 1007, *id.,* 1972, Vol. 3, p. 158, and *Medizinische Welt,* 1972, 23, p. 758).

Prof. René Dubos had already written in *Man, Medicine and Environment* (Praeger, New York, 1968, p. 107): "Smallpox vaccine does produce serious encephalitis in a few persons even when administered with the utmost care. The chance of contracting smallpox is now so slight that the risk of accidents originating from the vaccine is much greater than the chance of contracting the disease itself."

And the French magazine *Vie et Action* (Mar.–Apr. 1966, p. 9) had this comment: "In Great Britain, smallpox vaccination hasn't been compulsory since 1898, and yet five times fewer people have died of smallpox in Great Britain than in France, where this vaccination is compulsory. The same goes for Holland. Now Great Britain and Holland are nations that continuously have contact with hundreds of thousands of seafarers from all over the world, notably from countries where smallpox is frequent. And yet abolition of vaccination and the enforcement of the natural hygienic measures have clearly proven sufficient to eliminate smallpox and the so-called infectious maladies."

The powerful American pharmaceutical lobby was able to oppose much longer than the British drug manufacturers the abolition of compulsory smallpox vaccination. Up to 1971, the millions of people who every year entered the U. S. had to be vaccinated against smallpox, and the vaccination was considered valid only for five years. As ever more cases of smallpox developed among people vaccinated inside that period, the Washington lobbyists actually succeeded in "persuading" the U.S. health authorities that vaccina-

tion was "effective" for only 2 years instead of 5—
insuring new, fabulous profits for the vaccine mongers,
and new cases of encephalitis (severe, frequently
maiming or deadly inflammation of the brain), and
what-have-you among the vaccinated. Unheeded went
a few isolated protests like the one by Dr. Charles
Henry Kempe, famous medical researcher of Chicago
University, who in Philadelphia's *Evening Bulletin*
(May 7, 1965) recommended abolishing smallpox
vaccination, stating that since 1948 there had been
no deaths from smallpox in the U.S., but in the same
period more than 300 had died from smallpox vaccination, including vaccine-induced encephalitis.

A few years later, at last, compulsory vaccination
was quietly dropped by the U.S. It could no longer be
kept from the public that fewer people had died from
smallpox than from the consequences of vaccination.
And immediately many other countries followed suit.

American vivisectionists tried to explain that vaccination was no longer necessary in the U.S. because the
disease had been virtually wiped out by the previous
vaccinations. They neglected to remember that each
year millions of foreigners—including hundreds of
thousands of illegal, unvaccinated immigrants from
Canada, Mexico, Africa, and the Far East—cross the
border into the States.

* * *

All the medical historians of our century, from
Henry Sigerist to Brian Inglis, from René Dubos to
Beddow Bayly to Ivan Illich, agree that the decline of
the epidemics which had wrought havoc in the Middle
Ages was not due to the introduction of vaccination but
of hygiene, for they diminished long before large-scale
inoculations had begun. And hygiene in the broadest
sense of the word—physical, mental, alimentary—is the
only key to health, as the medieval pestilences demonstrated when Galenism replaced the hygienic principles
of antiquity. But most of today's medical journalists
blithely dismiss the major historians and statistical evidence and continue to con the public, stating that the
epidemics have been eliminated thanks to vaccination.

The financially profitable aspect of vaccines for the manufacturerers is undisputable.

The discovery of Salk's polio vaccine was greeted with a wave of enthusiasm comparable with the enthusiasm that greeted Koch's Tuberkulin—when it was first announced. The analogy is not farfetched. But already before Salk developed his vaccine, polio had been constantly regressing: The 39 cases out of every 100,000 inhabitants registered in 1942 had gradually diminished from year to year, until they were reduced to only 15 cases in 1952, the year the vaccination went into effect, according to M. Beddow Bayly, the English surgeon and medical historian.

But soon the Salk vaccine was regarded as dangerous, so much so that it was replaced by Sabin's, which shortly revealed new dangers, to be examined in the chapter on "Cancer Causing Drugs," as they came under suspicion of containing a cancerogenic potential.

Even more confusing becomes the polio question on examination of the basic vital statistics of the New York State Office of Biostatistics (exclusive of New York City) for the period between 1922 and 1962. The death rate per 100,000 population fluctuated only slightly throughout that period. Mass vaccination was administered from 1958 to 1962 in large centers, where polio cases were already on the decline. However, in the large rural areas, especially the Rocky Mountain states where very little vaccination took place, the case rate dropped by the same ratio as in the large centers where vaccination was common. On nationwide debates on radio and TV involving 38 American doctors, not one of them was able to offer an explanation for all this; much less for the fact that polio has almost completely vanished from Europe, where the great majority of the population was never inoculated.

The cholera vaccination also has remained just as dubious as it was in Koch's day. When in 1975 Portugal announced an outbreak of several cholera cases at Porto, the Swiss health authorities recommended preventive cholera vaccination to all travelers to Portugal, but added that vaccination would not guarantee protection. (*National Zeitung,* Basel, Aug. 1, 1975.) The following year a perplexed Swiss population was told that cholera vaccination was effective only in 50 percent of the cases. Thus nonsense is added to nonsense, swindle to swindle. Considering that in every cholera epidemic only a very small percentage of non-vaccinated people get infected, and very few die, and that now vaccination is supposed to be only 50 percent effective, no kind of proof— nor disproof—can ever be brought for this alleged partial effectiveness. In sum, nobody really knows whether vaccines are any good, or how bad they are.

Anybody who thinks that matters are clear should have been in the Naples area during the summer 1973 cholera scare. Together with a modest epidemic, total panic broke out. The local health authorities lost their heads, running in circles and accusing the Rome authorities of neglect, and vice-versa. One terrified doctor, to be safe, inoculated himself three times in a row with cholera vaccine and died—whether from fright or cholera nobody has been able to ascertain. The populace, wanting scapegoats, were meanwhile joyously exterminating stray cats and dogs by the thousands, although Naples strays had always been more efficient in disposing of the city garbage than the municipal sanitary service. But by old tradition the populace attributed the insurgence of the infection to the animals rather than to their own filthiness. In the following years epidemics of salmonellosis and viral hepatitis killed many newborns in the same area, and the circus started all over again.

*   *   *

For centuries, doctors considered it fashionable to take blood out of the patients, and in fact as frequently restored them to health as bled them to death. Today, as fashion demands that blood no longer be taken out of but put into a patient, ever more medical men start wondering whether these transfusions are useful, or even whether they are harmless. Some are convinced that organisms which manage to stay alive after such massive additions of alien blood prove but one thing: the enormous power of resistance that man has received from mother nature.

For various generations, English and American children cried bitter tears into their hated spinach, and were told that if they didn't eat it they would remain physically stunted and mentally retarded. Then one scientist announced that spinach precipitates the calcium in the organism, making for brittle bones and defective brains, that it intoxicates the liver, and its oxalates produce gall and kidney stones. If there was one vegetable to be avoided, it was spinach. Then came the condemnation of the cauliflower. Then came milk, which some scientists considered particularly harmful not only to certain adults, but for entire populations, like South American ones.

At one time it was believed that no food was healthier than meat, giving physical and mental strength. Then new medical schools declared meat unfit for human consumption, since man has the long intestine of the vegetarians, in which meat isn't expelled promptly as by the short intestine of the carnivorous animals, but causes dangerous fermentation, responsible for all ills of mankind, including arthritis, liver and heart trouble, and cancer.

For decades we had been led to believe that smoking is bad for the heart, but only until an American "expert" told in a conference at Zurich University that this was nonsense. As Zurich's daily *Blick* reported on Nov. 10, 1975, Dr. Carl Seltzer, 67, from the U.S., told a startled Swiss audience that sweeping surveys in the U.S., Finland, Holland, Yugoslavia, Italy, Greece and Japan had been unable to turn up any correlation between smoking and heart trouble. In his opinion, the wrong notions have been propagated by the various anti-smoke organizations, which are led by non-smokers. But the fact that Dr. Seltzer was himself an incurable smoke addict—one pack of cigarettes and 10 cigarillos a day—could give rise to the suspicion that here was just another "scientist" indulging in wishful thinking.

From the front of the "official" medicine has come still another news item, indicative of its confused state, which makes it continuously renege today what was yesterday a sacrosanct truth: "Alcohol is not a disinfectant. Its presence in the pharmacies is questionable." Who said that? According to Milan's *Corriere d'Informazione* (Apr. 8, 1974), the President of the Italian Society of Chemotherapy, Carlo Grassi, professor of phtisiology at the University of Pavia, who added:

"We believe in alcohol merely because it burns. That's a crude justification. That it burns means that it irritates, not that it fights germs . . . The alcohol myth is finished."

LIFE EXPECTANCY

Just as the introduction of asepsis, antisepsis, ether, opium, curare, cocaine, morphine, chloroform, and other forms of anesthesia—all of determinant importance for the rebirth of surgery—owe nothing to vivisection, so the thermometer, microscope, bacteriology, stethoscope, ophtalmoscope, X rays, percussion, auscultation, and electronic microscope, all of capital importance for diagnostics, owe nothing to animal experimentation either.

The same applies to the development of vaccination and all the fundamental drugs like digitalis, strophantin, atropine, iodine, quinine, nitroglycerine, radium, penicillin, just to name the best-known ones. In fact, there doesn't exist one single important therapeutic discovery indisputably due to vivisection—whereas books can be filled with the cases where animal experimentation has indisputably spelled disaster for humanity, besides misleading or retarding clinical research.

Thus also the improvement in life expectancy owes nothing to animals. That the discoveries just mentioned have lengthened the average life is obvious. The same goes for the development of surgery. There was a time when an appendicitis could cause peritonitis and death. Today, the appendectomy initiated by Lawson Tait without animal experimentation—for the good reason that animals don't develop appendicitis—

is the surgical operation that saves the largest number of human lives, together with the Caesarean section. Many other lives are saved by the abdominal operations to which the British antivivisectionist surgeons contributed more than any other group—Clay, Fergusson, Tait, *et al.* But still more decisive for the improvement in life expectancy was the massive reduction of child mortality through hygiene.

Toward the middle of the last century, six contagious diseases were responsible for the greatest number of deaths at a young age—puerperal fever, diphtheria, scarlet fever, typhoid fever, cholera and smallpox. All six were practically eliminated, thus lengthening prodigiously the median life, when the main reason for their existence was discovered: The reason was filth, for which Galenism was responsible, as Galen's experiences with animals had taught him that hygiene was unimportant, nothing but superstition.

We saw that not even Pasteur's biographer, René Dubos, thought that the infectious diseases were defeated by modern chemotherapy. He wrote that their decline was "due to a large extent to the campaign in favor of incontaminated nourishment, of pure air and water."

Likewise it is the betterment of economic and hygienic conditions that conspicuously curbed the once very high death rate from TB. New proof that nourishment and hence economic conditions influence this malady was had during World War II: Where food was scarce, all diseases except TB—mainly diabetes and cardiovascular ailments—diminished, while TB experienced a resurgence.

On March 31, 1973, Rome's daily *Messaggero* quoted Prof. Arrigo Colarizi, director of the Pediatric Clinic of the University of Rome and member of the International Society of Pediatry, as declaring: "The physical improvement that we notice is partly spontaneous and partly due to the improved social, economic and hygienic conditions. Drugs have nothing to do with it."

It is hardly a coincidence that today the longest-lived individuals live at a safe distance from the pharmacies.

The frequently heard statement that the median life during the Roman Empire was 20 years, and 30 in the Middle Ages, is a fairy tale, as reliable records have been kept only in recent times, and in few countries. Judging by the historic personalities, there were more people reaching an advanced age in the past, when nobody had heard of miracle drugs. Roman Emperor Tiberius, although sick, lived to be 79, artist-architect-poet Michelangelo 89, philosopher-mathematician Pythagoras 91, tragedian Sophocles 92, rhetor Seneca 94, philosopher Heraclitus 96, writer Isocrates 98, painter Titian 99. In ancient times most of the prominent people who died young were either poisoned, assassinated, or they fell in battle. The exceptionally high age of the past is even more exceptional today.

And yet in the *Temple University News* of September 17, 1976, one more vivisector, Aaron Blumenthal, presented as "a doctoral student and director of project research in Temple's psychological department," had the nerve to declare, disregarding all historical facts, that "the average man lives to be 72 because of the use of animal models in medical research." Fortunately George Bernard Shaw has given the final answer to this sort of statement.

I know that there has never been an epoch in which we could learn something about the physiology of man by torturing animals; we only learned something about animals. And I know that if there is something we can learn from them on the psychological level, it is not by means of steel or electricity, much less so through psychic violences.

The systematic torture of sentient beings, whatever the pretext and in whatever form, can't achieve anything more than it already has: to show us what is the lowest point of debasement man can reach. If that's what we want to know.

Part Five

THE NEW RELIGION

Setting a date for the start of a new period represents a choice that by necessity is always arbitrary, hence disputable. Exactly in what year did the Renaissance in medicine begin? Switzerland's Paracelsus was a typical Renaissance man, but not even an individual of his import could all by himself inaugurate an epoch. Thus Paracelsus may be considered a harbinger, ahead of the times, if only by a few years. As far as medical science is concerned, we may place the beginning of its rebirth in 1543, when Vesalius' book *De humani corporis fabrica* appeared, in concomitance—surely not fortuitous—with Copernicus' *De revolutionibus orbium coelestum*.

In the medieval darkness of Paracelsus' time, the bright light of his intellect would have blinded his contemporaries. When Vesalius and Copernicus came onstage, the dawning of the new day was already visible in many points of Europe, and the contemporaries could view the rising of the new suns without getting frightened.

As far as the New Galenism is concerned—the doctrine founded on vivisection, now imposed by official medical science as the correct method of research, in spite of the crushing evidence to the contrary—we may set its start in the year 1865, when in Paris Claude Bernard's *Introduction à l'étude de la médecine expérimentale* appeared—a book that to this day France regards as one of the two masterpieces of her scientific literature, together with Descartes' *Discours de la Méthode*.

Claude Bernard took vivisection out of the dark basement laboratories of a small coterie of physiologists and raised it to academic status. From then on vivisection started spreading, slowly but irrepressibly.

A doctrine is inseparable from the individual who conceived it. So in order to evaluate fully this New Galenism, which can also be called "Bernardism," it is necessary to know the personality of Claude Bernard, besides his work.

THE APOSTLE

Although all of Claude Bernard's various biographers were fervent admirers of his, yet an X-ray lecture of their accounts, supporting what his critics say, suffices to provide an accurate image of the man's true personality. The two biographies quoted here, both titled simply *Claude Bernard*, were the only ones I found in print in France during the past few years, and represent a distillate of everything interesting the previous biographies contained. One is by Pierre Mauriac (Ed. Bernard Grasset, Paris, 3rd ed., 1954), the other by Robert Clarke (Ed. Seghers, Paris, 1966).

Claude Bernard's bitter disputes with whoever didn't agree with him, his readiness to vivisect any animal, including once his own daughters' pet dog, in order to prove a thesis that someone else dared confute—and usually rightly so—his blindness to his own continuous mistakes, all this bespeaks a vain and narrow-minded personality.

All truly great men have had one trait in common—modesty. Claude Bernard was eminently unburdened by it, which renders his innumerable blunders still less forgivable. Item: Following a great number of vivisections done on dogs, Claude Bernard announced that no sugar is ever found in the portal vein—the one that carries the blood from the intestines, pancreas and spleen to the liver. It was on this wrong observation that he based his assertion that "the liver produces sugar"—since he had found sugar in the veins that convey the blood out of the liver.

With his authoritative voice—as both Clarke and Mauriac report—he once crushed all the other scientists who had dared contradict him, declaring peremptorily to the awed members of the Academy:

"It is a constant and absolute experiment. *Never, never* is there any sugar to be found in the portal vein. I consider it my duty to insurge against all the studies that would like to demonstrate the opposite, and whose superficiality could inspire distrust towards the experimental physiology."

It would be hard to define this as the speech of a modest man. But the worst part about it is that Claude Bernard was wrong. Pierre Mauriac comments thus on the incident: "Among his experiments there is one that Claude Bernard declares *fundamental* and for which he would gladly renounce all others: in fasting animals there is no trace of sugar in the portal vein, the sugar appears only in the vein that issues from the liver. Thus the source of the sugar must be the liver." (p. 138)

Adds Pierre Mauriac: "The experiment that Claude Bernard cites as guarantee is wrong: he considers it fundamental, but instead it has no value. He was misled by the religion of experimentation, which also misled him to affirm the arrest of the heart from systole after puncture of the vagus, and in his analysis of the action of the nerves and muscles of the pupil."

And Clarke has this to say about the error, which is memorable in that it misled whole generations of physiologists: "What a cruel irony! Today we know beyond any doubt that sugar occurs in the portal vein. Claude Bernard had stumbled into one of his own pitfalls, against which he had warned the others."

According to notions that up to a few years ago were considered final—but about which nowadays doubts are arising—the liver condenses a form of sugar, glycogen, and frees it when the organism needs it. We know that the liver does not *produce* sugar. And yet it is mainly on this "discovery"—which has meanwhile proven wrong—that Claude Bernard's great fame has been built. But all his faults, which like Galen's came from his reliance on animal experimentation, were so numerous, and enunciated with such unshakable assurance, that many were unmasked as such only many years after his death.

A century later, on July 5, 1951, another comment about his errors was heard in the fifth Addison Memorial Lecture, delivered at Guy's Hospital Medical School by F. G. Young, professor of biochemistry at Cambridge University: "Since Bernard found that piqûre was still effective after section of the vagi, and since the idea of reflex secretion was dominant, he was led to build up a wholly incorrect theory, according to which a nervous stimulus to the secretion of sugar by the liver originated in the lungs . . ." (*British Medical Journal,* Dec. 29, 1951, p. 1537)

*   *   *

A frustrated playwright, Claude Bernard stumbled into his true vocation by chance. Born to a family of farmers near Lyon, grown up in a Jesuit boarding school at Villefranche, where he was a mediocre student, he started working in Lyon as the assistant to a pharmacist, who taught him to mix a profitable elixir against all ills. That inspired the young apprentice with an incurable contempt for all medical art and its practitioners.

At the age of 21 he went to Paris, determined to win literary fame with two plays he had written. The first influential person who read them persuaded him to forget the theater and rather to enroll at medical school, since he had already worked in a pharmacy.

He was as mediocre in medical school as he had been in his earlier studies. Writes Pierre Mauriac: "Disappointed in his literary ambition, he decided to study medicine . . . It seems that he was a second-rate student, punctual but lazy, ill prepared for the tests and examinations." (p. 20)

But suddenly, the miracle: at *Collège de France,* the laboratory of the university's medical school, Claude Bernard sees for the first time an animal being cut open alive—and the enthusiasm he displays from then on for vivisections is such that the college's director, François Magendie, soon makes him his assistant.

Robert Clarke puts it this way: "Medicine has never interested him: research immediately excites him with passion." (p. 12) And Pierre Mauriac: "He was less interested in the hospital than in the laboratory, except when he took a fancy to a patient." (p. 207)

* * *

In 1843, aged 30, Claude Bernard graduated at last, with scarce distinction, ranking 26th in a group of 29, and the next year he failed the exam for the habilitation of practicing the medical profession. His thesis was defined "less than mediocre" by Prof. J. L. Faure, another of his biographers. Thereafter, setting the trend for many medical students who flunk their final examinations today, he dedicated himself exclusively to the vivisection laboratory, eventually becoming Magendie's successor.

Magendie, who contributed to forming Claude Bernard's philosophy of life besides his professional outlook, was then and is today greatly admired by vivisectionists, including the physiologists in charge of compiling the encyclopedias. "A superb experimenter and a bold vivisectionist . . ." Thus the Britannica describes him.

But there are other testimonies that reach beyond Magendie's official titles. Dr. John Elliotson, professor of physiology in London, who had visited Magendie's courses, wrote: "Dr. Magendie cut living animals here and there with no definite object, but just to see what would happen." This must be what prompted the Britannica writer to define Magendie a "bold vivisectionist."

There was a bitter controversy between Magendie and Sir Charles Bell, the Scottish doctor and scientist who had come to one of the most important physiological conclusions ("Bell's law") by sheer observation of the normal functions, and by exercising his intellectual powers.

Bell was a humane person. But he was taunted by the vivisectionists for making affirmations that had not been confirmed by animal experiments. When he finally decided to demonstrate through an experiment what he already knew, it was in the hope that this would put an end to any controversy and prevent further vivisectionist experiments. He wrote (*Op. cit.* p. 29):

"My conception of this matter arose by inference from the anatomical structure; so that the few experiments which have been made were directed only to the verification of the fundamental principles on which the system is founded. In France, experiments without number and without mercy have been made on living animals; not under the direction of anatomical knowledge, or the guidance of just induction, but conducted with cruelty and indifference, in hope to catch at some of the accidental facts of a system, which, it is evident, the experimenters did not fully comprehend. After delaying long on account of the unpleasant nature of the operation, I opened the spinal canal of a rabbit, and cut the posterior roots of the nerves of the lower extremity; the creature crawled, but I was deterred from repeating the experiment by the protracted cruelty of the dissection."

At the end of this classic work of his, on pages 377-378, Bell wrote: "In a foreign review of my former papers, the results have been considered a farther proof in favour of experiments. They are, on the contrary, deductions from anatomy; and I have had recourse to experiments, not to form my own opinions, but to impress them upon others. It must be my apology that my utmost efforts of persuasion were lost, while I urged my statement on the grounds of anatomy. I have made few experiments; they have been simple, and easily performed; and, I hope, are decisive."

They were indeed decisive, but Bell did not reckon with the vivisectional mind, the malady that was pervading the physiologists' world—the endless ritualistic repetition of well-known experiments, reported in all physiological textbooks.

Contrarily to Bell, Magendie made no apologies, had no qualms, knew no scruples: "He sacrificed 4,000 dogs to prove that Sir Charles Bell was correct

in the distinction he drew between sensory and motor
nerves; but later he sacrificed 4,000 more to prove
that Bell was wrong." It was vivisector Flourens, who
was to become Claude Bernard's successor, who said
this, as reported by still another vivisector of those
days, H. Blatin, in *Nos cruautés* (1867, p. 201).
Blatin also confirmed that Bell was right from the outset, adding: "I also have made experiments on this,
vivisecting a large number of dogs, and I have demonstrated that the first opinion is the only true one."

Other testimonies help reveal the true personality of
Magendie, but science writers charged with compiling
the encyclopedias did not care to include them in their
biographical columns. One was by French doctor
Latour, in *L'Abeille Médicale:*

"Magendie performed experiments in public. I remember once, amongst other instances, the case of a
poor dog, all bloody and mutilated, who escaped from
his implacable knife; and twice did I see him put his
forepaws around Magendie's neck and lick his face. I
confess—laugh, *Messieurs les Vivisecteurs,* if you
please—that I could not bear this sight." (*British
Medical Journal,* Aug. 22, 1863, p. 215)

On another occasion, Magendie immobilized a small
cocker spaniel to the dissecting table by driving nails
through the paws and the long ears, in order to demonstrate to his pupils the cutting of the optic nerves,
the sawing of the cranium, the dissection of the backbone and the exposure of the nerve stems: and, as
after all that the puppy was not yet dead, Magendie
left him in that condition in order to use him again the
next day.

In one of the following chapters we see how vivisections even aroused Magendie's laughter. And
Claude Bernard, the apostle of today's vivisectional
method, was a pupil who surpassed his master on every count.

*   *   *

Claude Bernard considered physiological research
an end in itself. He stated so repeatedly. So in *Principes
de Médecine Expérimentale,* his big, posthumous work

published for the first time only in 1947 (Ed. Presses Universitaires de France, Paris) which contains his ultimate thoughts, his definite outlook on life, he wrote: "We wish to establish that professional medicine must be distinct and separate from the scientific medicine, theoretical and practical, and as such it must not enter into the framework of our teaching, which is purely scientific." (p. 35) He also revealed his contempt of the medical profession: "Medicine is considered an industry by the majority of the practicing physicians. They consider it a necessity to act as they do. I think it is in consideration of this that sometimes they can look at each other without laughing." (p. 18)

Of Claude Bernard's activity, his former assistant, Dr. George Hoggan, wrote in his now famous letter that appeared in *The Morning Post* on Feb. 1, 1875: "After four months' experience, I am of the opinion that not one of those experiments on animals was justified or necessary." And the *Report* of the Royal Commission of Enquiry, appointed in 1875 by Prime Minister Disraeli to investigate vivisection, included a testimony by Dr. Arthur de Noë Walker, another British doctor who had worked in Bernard's laboratory. After describing one of Bernard's experiments to the Royal Commission, Walker said:

"I decline myself to criticize this horrible experiment. I feel too much contempt for the experimenter and disgust with the experiment. I would have deprived that man of his position as a lecturer and teacher of physiology." (Par. 4888)

Claude Bernard's vivisections kept giving everchanging results, prompting him to multiply the experiments and the ensuing confusion. And prompting his followers to repeat them, in an effort to capture some glory of their own.

Claude Bernard constantly criticized or ridiculed his colleagues' experiments. And when they unmasked one of his numerous errors, he had no qualms about reneging his own words. Says Pierre Mauriac: "His errors originated from his cult of experimentation. He paid little attention to the objections of his colleagues, and in the discussions he was capable of denying the evidence and contradicting himself without shame. In 1854, he affirms that the sugar produced by the liver is destroyed by the lung, and draws a scheme showing blood arriving to the capillaries of the lung where it is almost entirely destroyed. But in 1859 he writes: 'They lend me an opinion that isn't mine, that I have never written . . .' " (p. 143)

But although many doctors or even his fellow vivisectors—Figuier, Pavy, Schiff—were exposing his mistakes, nobody listened, for Claude Bernard's fame overshadowed all others.

*   *   *

From South America news had come of a lethal arrow poison, curare, and Claude Bernard had some of it sent to him. Trying it out on animals, he discovered that curare acted in a different way from any other known poison. It caused paralysis, acting upon the motor nerves only, without influencing the sensory nerves. So the victim, however paralyzed, retained all its capacity to suffer. In modern "scientific" terminology, "curare blocks inhibitory synapse, thus allowing the excitatory synapses to make the nerve cell more excitable." (From *Effects of Curare on Cortical Activity,* Morlock and Ward, University of Washington, Seattle, *E. E. G. Journal,* Feb. 1961, p. 60)

In other words, curare is a muscle relaxant, which not only lacks any analgesic effect, but enhances sensitivity, so that pain is even more keenly felt by an animal under curare than one with no medication at all—a discovery that inspired our hero to flights of lyricism, in an article for the *Revue des Deux Mondes* (Sept. 1, 1864). Excerpt:

"In every type of death that we know there are always, towards the end, some convulsions, cries or gasps indicating sufferance, a struggle between life and death. In the death by curare, nothing of the sort: there is no death struggle, life appears just to fade away. A mere slumber seems to be the transition from life to death. But it isn't so: the appearance is misleading. If we enter, by means of experimentation,

into the organic analysis of the extinction of life, we
see that this death is, on the contrary, accompanied
by the most atrocious sufferings that human imagination can conceive . . . When somebody is poisoned
by curare, the intelligence, the sensibility, the will, are
not affected by the poison, but they lose by and by
the motive instruments, which refuse to obey. The
most expressive movements of our faculties are the
first to go: first the voice, then the motions of the
limbs, finally those of the eyes, which, as in dying
people, function longest . . . Can anyone conceive of
a more horrible sufferance than that of an intelligence
which has to witness the successive failing of all the
organs designed to serve it, but finds itself, so to say,
locked up, completely alive, inside a corpse? When
Tasso describes Clorinda incorporated alive in a ma-
jestic cypress, he left her at least the power of complaining with tears and sobs, and move to pity
those who made her suffer by injuring her sensitive
bark . . ."

Clearly, the idea of sufferance turns Claude Bernard into a poet; however, as the conscientious scientist that he was, he would never have allowed himself
to be swayed by tears and sobs if his victims had still
been capable of that much, rather than being, fully
conscious, paralyzed into total immobility. From the
day he had discovered the properties of curare—its
use on laboratory animals is officially forbidden today
in Europe, because "too cruel", but it is nonetheless
almost as widely employed as in the U.S.—this drug
became Claude Bernard's favorite means for rendering
his victims helpless.

Since the laboratory of the *Collège* wasn't roomy
enough for stabling large sized animals, Claude Bernard and Magendie sometimes made excursions to the
veterinary school at Alfort, outside Paris, where they
could "work" on horses and mules, or visited the
municipal abattoir, where the two cronies were allowed to do anything they pleased with the cattle.
And so as not to get bored in the evenings and on
Sundays, Claude Bernard kept up in addition a private
laboratory in the basement of his home.

From Ernest Renan, one of his close friends, occupant of a chair in Hebrew at the *Paris University* and author of a noted *Life of Christ,* we can gather what squalid rites, what grisly shows took place in Bernard's private torture chamber. Every Monday night Claude Bernard used to give a "reception" in that basement playroom of his, which for the occasion became what his biographer Clarke defined "a scientific salon." There four or five physiologists convened, including sometimes Ernest Renan, the only man of letters who frequented that laboratory. Clarke doesn't say anything else about those "receptions." But we know that in that "scientific salon" there were in every corner dogs in their death throes, dogs that had been poisoned, dogs from which various organs had been extirpated. And what claret was decanted in that salon so different from other Parisian salons of the time, what music could be heard there, we can gather from Ernest Renan's inaugural speech on April 3, 1879, when he was admitted into the French Academy, and commemorated his recently deceased friend:

"It was an impressive spectacle seeing him at work in his laboratory, thoughtful, sad, absorbed, allowing himself no distraction, no smile. He felt that he fulfilled the task of a priest, that he celebrated a sort of sacrifice. His long fingers, plunged in the bleeding wounds, seemed those of an augur of yore, pursuing in the intestines of the victims some mysterious secrets . . ."

* * *

Claude Bernard's favorite method for "discovering life's mysterious secrets" was one he had learned from Master Magendie: It consisted in "destroying" an organ, as he himself said—meaning to extirpate it— and then simply to observe the animal thus mutilated by keeping it alive as long as possible, up to giving artificial respiration or letting it inhale ammonia to revive an agonizing heap of flesh that was only asking the mercy of being allowed to die. In vain did he sacrifice thousands of dogs, in an attempt to discover through them "the secret of diabetes," and he

even published a treatise on this disease. His contemporaries were impressed, but today we know how
far from the mark all his ideas about diabetes were.

By a variety of violent interventions, such as knif-
ing a dog into the fourth ventricle (Clarke, p. 85)
or sticking a big pin into the cranium of a rabbit, he
succeeded at times in producing an "artificial diabetes," *i.e.* causing sugar to appear in the urine of his
victim; but the next time he tried he did not succeed,
and he never knew why. Neither did he ever guess,
not even vaguely, the cause of the disease. "Diabetes
is a nervous ailment," he announced once with unshakable assurance after producing the symptoms of
diabetes by puncturing the spine of a dog. But when
he tried repeating the experiment, he failed once
more.

Claude Bernard had one of the more important
secrets about diabetes right there at hand, for many
years, just begging to be lifted: in the thousands of
unanesthetized dogs from which he extirpated the
pancreas along with the entire bundle of nerves surrounding that gland—one of the severest surgical operations extant—and on which he then made until death
all sorts of experiments—except one.

It never occurred to Claude Bernard to analyze
the urine of one of these depancreatized victims. He
would at least have discovered that there was a correlation between diabetes and a defective pancreas.

*   *   *

Claude Bernard's private life gave him fewer satis-
factions than his "scientific" activity. As in his day
vivisection brought in more fame than money, Claude
Bernard had married the well-to-do daughter of a
physician, to be able to dedicate all his time to the
laboratory without worrying about how to make a
living.

They had two daughters and two sons, but both
sons died a few months after birth. Claude Bernard
never understood why, medicine having always been
a closed book to him, and this realization rankled
in one who tortured thousands of animals under the

pretext of discovering the secrets of nature. It rankled indeed so deeply that when their second son died, he sought a scapegoat and flung at his wife—disregarding her own grief at that hour—a terrible but very characteristic accusation: "If you had taken care of our son as you take care of your dogs, he wouldn't have died!"

It was surprising that such a marriage did last all of 17 years. Biographer Clarke reports indignantly that Claude Bernard's wife tried to sabotage her husband's experiments and incited the animal-protection leagues to sue him, and Pierre Mauriac reports just as indignantly that his wife's and daughter's love of animals prompted them to found at Asnieres a shelter for dogs saved from the tortures of vivisection.

Claude Bernard sometimes took one of his suffering victims up into the bedroom for the night, to observe it without having to get out of bed. His wife was not amused; which caused Mauriac to write (p. 26):

"His wife protested when dirty, malodorous animals under experimentation were imposed upon her as tenants." It didn't occur to this biographer, who had the title of professor, that Marie-Françoise may not have objected so much to the filth of those animals as to the torments they had to endure.

Her husband's indifference to animals' sufferings is further evidenced by the fact that all his experiments were done without the slightest anesthesia, and usually lasted a very long time. From his writings we know that the dogs which had to serve for demonstrations were cut open an hour or more beforehand, and that they were not destroyed afterwards, but left to the students "for other operations."

Another insight into Bernard's personality is inadvertently provided by Robert Clarke, who relates that during the lectures at the *Collège*, Bernard's thoughts sometimes strayed, and he lost the thread of his discourse. Then he would ask his preparator, d'Arsonval, whether he didn't have a rabbit on hand with the sympathetic spinal cord severed.

"There was always some such rabbit prepared," writes Clarke in his memorable biography. "Claude

Bernard would get hold of it and make an experiment, during which he could leisurely get his train of thought back and resume his discourse."

Thus, inflicting additional torments upon a hapless creature that had been languishing with its spinal cord severed exerted on Claude Bernard the same effect as does a cigarette or a cup of tea on an ordinary person.

*   *   *

The question of sadism shall be examined in a coming chapter, where we'll see that probably not all vivisectors are sadists; that many are simply handicapped by very limited intellects, making them too callous and obtuse to realize what they are doing—unless they suffer from some other mental disorder.

Let us examine Claude Bernard from that viewpoint as well.

A mediocre lower-grade pupil, a cynical and contemptuous pharmacist's helper, a frustrated playwright, a dense and lazy student of medicine—a subject that never interested him—among the last of his group at graduation, then flunking his conclusive medical test, Claude Bernard suddenly wakes up from his chronic apathy at the first vivisection he is made to witness. From that moment on he is seized by an unquenchable thirst for experimentation, involving always and exclusively the torment of animals. No other activity or branch of learning arouses his interest, ever, throughout his entire life. In the light of these facts, the diagnosis of Claude Bernard's mental state is all too obvious.

But in the course of time, like all sadists who are allowed to indulge their weakness, he became insensitive to everything except his personal glory and the praise of the rich and the mighty. He was elected to the Academy of Sciences, won its prize in experimental physiology four times, was made a senator of the Empire, and was admitted among the immortals of the French Academy—every Frenchman's ultimate ambition. And his literary training enabled him to clad in splendid clothing a squalid doctrine, the falsity of which only the passage of time was to reveal.

* * *

"Descartes' *Discourse on Method* and Claude Bernard's *Introduction to the Study of Experimental Medicine* constitute two magnificent moments of French thought. And this could seem a banal statement, without adding that the French spirit which has been able to derive from the ancient languages the most beautiful form of expression of human thought that exists in the world, namely the French language of the 17th Century, created at the same time the most beautiful scientific language—the prose of *Discourse* and of *Introduction*."

Thus declaimed Ferdinand Brunetière in 1894, the foremost literary critic of France, inaugurating the statue that the city of Lyon had erected to Claude Bernard. More than half a century later, Dr. Léon Delhoume, laureate of the same medical academy as Claude Bernard, used equally grandiloquent terms in his preface to Bernard's posthumous book, *Principes de Médecine Expérimentale* (ed. Presses Universitaires de France), first published only in 1947:

"Descartes! Claude Bernard! In the misfortunes of the fatherland, what consolation it is to listen to the voices of these two great geniuses! . . . It is in their thoughts that through the centuries the real soul of France appears to us; it is in their thoughts that are preserved, for our safe formation as men, the eternal truths of art, of beauty, of reason, of sense, of judgment, of moral and physical sanity, of human progress . . ."

When the literary critic Brunetière pronounced his eulogy, he couldn't yet guess on what shaky stilts his hero had edified his doctrine; nor that in his final writings, as yet unpublished, Claude Bernard had advocated the vivisection of human beings, probably because he had discovered the uselessness of animal experiments. And Dr. Delhoume, who knew about it, didn't mention it in his lengthy preface.

Now let us examine what hides under the splendid

clothes so admired by the various Brunetières and Delhoumes. Let us listen to Claude Bernard's own words.

THE DOCTRINE

First, we scan *Introduction à la médecine expérimentale,* from now on called *Introduction* for short; the page numbers refer to the Garnier-Flammarion reprint, Paris, 1966.

"Everything that is obtained with animals is perfectly conclusive for man." (p. 153)

"Experiments made on animals, with noxious substances or in detrimental conditions, are perfectly conclusive for the toxicology and the hygiene of man. The research on medical or toxic substances are also entirely applicable to man from the therapeutic point of view." (p. 180)

None of the innumerable errors that Galenism had imposed upon the western world for 15 centuries is comparable, in seriousness and consequences, to this fundamental error on which Claude Bernard erected his entire doctrine; an error he affirmed and emphasized and reiterated innumerable times and in every possible form, transmitting it to the following generations of doctors and physiologists and biologists; an error which, the enormous and constantly growing evidence to the contrary notwithstanding, has firmly established itself as a dogma in modern medical science.

The notion of "animal experimentation" consists of two words and innumerable errors, so far as medical science is concerned. "Experimentation" presupposes the deliberate infliction of a morbid state, of a pathological condition. But this, having been obtained artificially, has nothing in common with a spontaneous disease. The second mistake, compounding the first, lies in the fact that the reaction of animals differs from man's.

Today every medical man knows that individual vitality and the psyche and other imponderable factors influence, in always different ways, the reactions of every living creature; in spite of this, Claude Bernard's dogma has not been repudiated, and Bernardism has become a new Galenism, equally full of mistakes and misconceptions, but far more disastrous. A world that Descartes had recently awakened from the long night of medievalism, making it ready for every mechanist cause, had enthusiastically embraced Claude Bernard's conviction that medicine was an exact science like mathematics, and that any medical conquest was not only possible but imminent, provided that one repudiated the idea that "life" or individual "vitalism" had any influence on the organism, since they were abstract terms, designating something impalpable, which could not be mathematically formulated, measured, weighed; something that was alien to mechanism—the new deity.

"Vitalism, which can have as many nuances as there are individuals, is the negation of science and the abdication of every kind of research, in order to surrender to the fancies of imagination," wrote Claude Bernard on page 202 of *Introduction,* and on page 258 he thus criticized a "vitalist" colleague: "According to Gerdy, the vitality of one individual is not the same as the vitality of another, and consequently there must be differences between individuals that are impossible to determine. He refused to change his mind, he retrenched himself behind the word 'vitality,' and it was impossible to make him understand that it was a word devoid of meaning, a word that answered nothing."

According to Claude Bernard, everything belonging to the living organism could be reduced to a precise formula, like any *corps brut*—brute body, inert matter. And already before the publication of *Introduction* it was fashionable for the intellectual Parisians to attend the lectures at the university of a man who presented such revolutionary ideas. Among the visiting celebrities, there were in turn the Prince of Wales, the Count of Paris, the Emperor of Brazil. They didn't witness the actual experiments, of course, which were regular failures. They just listened to the conferences, to the abstract Bernardian theories. And those conferences,

some reprinted by the *Revue des Deux Mondes,* formed
the basis and body of the *Introduction,* the book that
was to give Claude Bernard the fame which the theater
had denied him.

*   *   *

The ethical aspect of vivisection was dismissed by
Claude Bernard in a few lofty lines, in which he
stated that, since man uses animals for all the tasks of
life, it would be "very strange" to prohibit him from
using them in order to "instruct" himself. The thought
of the sufferings, deliberately inflicted, never seems to
have entered his mind.

Is it necessary to point out that, personally, Claude
Bernard bore pain and discomfort very poorly? It is,
for the trait is common to all vivisectors. "You should
see some of those wretches (*ces misérables*)," a French
dentist told me, "pale and shaky with apprehension
when they enter my office, imploring me for heaven's
sake not to cause them any pain!"

Of course, no one likes to suffer. But one can bear
pain and discomfort with more or less fortitude, or
dignity. And it would be surprising indeed if vivisectors did not belong to the kind of individuals who constantly wail over the little annoyances of everyday life.
About Claude Bernard, Mauriac writes: "From 1877
on, his correspondence is nothing but one long complaint. 'I continue to live, thus to suffer.' Sciatic pains,
a chronic enteritis, an abnormal irritability, a great
scepticism towards all therapeutics, made of him a defeated patient."

Claude Bernard's real or imaginary sufferings were
aggravated, as at the time of his sons' deaths, by the
realization of his own nullity as a physician, of his
total ignorance in diagnostics and therapeutics; an ignorance that the thousands of animal experiments had
not helped to dissipate, but only to aggravate.

At one point, he attributes his own mysterious ailment to psychic reasons—to his grief over France's
recent defeat in the war against Germany; without realizing that just by making this diagnosis, which may

have been quite right, he was shattering the very pillar of his mechanist doctrine.

* * *

Looking into Claude Bernard's posthumously published *Principes de Médecine Expérimentale*—consisting of the notes he took from 1862 up to his death in 1878, and which from here on will be called *Médecine* for short—reveals even more about the man than the book that established his fame.

At the beginning we find in it the apostle's previous convictions, as yet unshaken: "I demonstrate that one can act upon living bodies like upon inanimate objects; this is the basis." (p. 19) But then, progressing in the years of Claude Bernard's experiences, we discover that growing doubts begin deranging a mind that can no longer shrug off the evidence of individual "vitalism."

Claude Bernard has actually made the startling discovery that "inert matter" and "living bodies" are not one and the same thing. He writes (p. 145):

"Inert matter has no spontaneity of its own, no individual difference, so one can be sure of the result one has obtained. But when we deal with a living being, individuality brings on an element of frightening complexity: beyond the external conditions, it is necessary to consider also the intrinsic organic conditions, those I call the interior setting (*le milieu intérieur*)."

Claude Bernard had begun to understand. And his discovery was obviously due to an endless string of failed experiments, in which he never succeeded in obtaining twice in a row the same result—a discovery that couldn't help frightening him, threatening to reveal the uselessness of his whole life as a "scientist."

Perhaps the pitiless disproofs emerging continually from his vivisections have already unbalanced his mind. At any rate they impair his literary vein, clouding his style and hamstringing his reasoning. For if *Introduction* expressed clearly ideas that only the passage of time would prove wrong, in *Médecine* even the thinking is often nebulous and the author doesn't make sense, as at the end of this passage (p. 249):

"It has been said: how can one come to any conclusions since there are substances that are poison for
certain animals but not for others, and substances that
poison man but not animals. It has been mentioned
the porcupine that doesn't get poisoned by prussic
acid, the goat that eats belladonna, the sheep that
swallow enormous quantities of arsenic, the toads
which don't get poisoned by their own venom, the
electric fish which don't resent their own electricity,
the sea animals which don't suffer the influence of the
salt. All these things are wrong as explanations. Because if one admitted this, science would be impossible."

Rereading this conclusion, Claude Bernard must
have realized that it badly needed clarification, and
he added a footnote—making it worse:

"One must be slave to a fact; one says it's a brutal
fact, as if one were saying something very scientific.
Certainly, one must believe in facts, but one mustn't
believe in them blindly. We have reasoning to shed
light on facts, and facts to moderate imagination and
stop reasoning. So an experimenter who poisons a toad
with his venom without result, or a goat with belladonna without result, will say: I am consistent; yes,
but there are facts that one can't believe because the
mind has the certainty that things are different. For
this reason I couldn't believe in the toad. If I had not
succeeded, I should have given my resignation as
physiologist."

Dr. Delhoume, who otherwise abundantly annotated
the volume, chose to ignore this Bernardian gaffe, perhaps hoping that it would go unnoticed, for no matter
how twisted and muddled, it reveals that the author
realizes that the facts ridicule his theory. Hence he
decides simply to ignore "the facts" of the toad and
goat; otherwise he would have to give his "resignation
as physiologist." Like so many famous vivisectors after
him, Claude Bernard lacked the greatness to admit
that his whole pseudoscience was erected on a gigantic
blunder.

So he, of all people, makes the extraordinary statement that "there are facts that one can't believe be-

cause the mind has the certainty that things are different." Then what kind of "facts" are they? Or what kind of "mind" is it? It can't possibly be the same mind that once stated: "If a fact is in opposition with a reigning theory, one must accept the fact and abandon the theory, even if the latter, endorsed by great names, has been widely adopted."

* * *

"I don't admit that it is moral to try on sick people dangerous remedies without having them first tested on dogs, for I shall demonstrate further on that everything one obtains on animals can be perfectly conclusive for man if one knows how to experiment well." So had written Claude Bernard in *Introduction* (p. 153).

His contemporaries who had sung the praise of that book couldn't know, as we know today, that this dogmatic affirmation of the apostle was wrong on two counts. Scientifically it was wrong because Claude Bernard went on to demonstrate exactly the opposite of what he had promised: He proved with his experiments that nothing obtained on a dog is "perfectly conclusive for man." And it was hypocritical because Claude Bernard had no qualms about advocating human vivisection, so the humane reasons he had professed were nothing but a pretext to justify his exercises on animals—the same hypocritical pretext today's researchers resort to.

In fact, in *Médecine*—which he had not prepared for publication and which contained his personal notes, his genuine thoughts—Claude Bernard revealed a different morality. On page 147, after oddly remarking that "the pathological anatomy has not the importance that certain people would like to attach to it"— up to that point, we always thought that nobody attached so much importance to it as Claude Bernard— he goes on advocating human vivisection as the ultimate objective of experimental medicine, as we shall see in one of the following chapters.

In those days Bernard couldn't guess that some 60 years later, the dehumanization to which he had so

effectively contributed by deeds and words would lead
to vivisectionist experiments upon tens of thousands of
human beings that were as helpless as the animals in
his squalid laboratory—the political prisoners in the
Nazi camps of extermination. And not at the hands of
SS guards, but of Claude Bernard's scientific heirs, all
titled physicians, trained in the vivisectional schooling
of which he had been the loudest apostle.

* * *

In the light of his continuous failures, the memory of
his heated controversies with the "vitalist" doctors and
scientists clearly rankled in Claude Bernard. They included many a famous name, like the great naturalist
Cuvier, and Pasteur himself. Claude Bernard had derided every adversary of organic mechanism in his *Introduction*. And now those words stood in print,
indelible, published, undeniable.

But the High Priest of vivisection could not disown
the false deity that he had foisted upon a credulous
world. At stake was the honor of France, the prestige
of Science, but most of all the vanity of a man who
at the expense of other creatures' sufferances had been
acclaimed as the founder of a new epoch, and had
been heaped with honors.

Only in a letter to Madame Raffalovich, his friend
and confidante who later on will donate to the Academy of Sciences their private correspondence, did
Claude Bernard confess toward the end of his days:

"In the autumn of life the illusions fall from the
soul one after the other, like leaves falling from the
trees in the autumn of the year."

Words that could sound very touching indeed if we
didn't know how bloody the hand was that wrote
them, what ravages had been necessary to cause those
illusions to fall from a vain and cruel mind. And the
illusions continue falling, like so many autumn leaves,
until the tree is entirely bare; and on his deathbed,
without any member of his family being present, but
only surrounded by other vivisectors—including
d'Arsonval, his preparator—Claude Bernard confesses

at last: "Our hands are empty, and only our mouths are full of promises."

Perhaps for all vivisectors the hour of truth comes only in the face of death? Too late, ladies and gentlemen.

Claude Bernard was the first French scientist to be given a state funeral, and his biographers tell us that the day he died "all of France wept." But this is an exaggeration. There were at least three people in France who didn't weep that day: his wife and his daughters.

POSTSCRIPT TO CLAUDE BERNARD, DIABETES AND THE LIVER

Up to date the major encyclopedias and textbooks in the western world continue calling Claude Bernard a "genius" and indicate as his major claim to fame his alleged "discovery" of the role of the pancreas and of the "glycogenic power" of the liver.

But the thousands of dogs he had mutilated didn't reveal anything that had not been described previously, and with much more adherence to the truth, by the U.S. Army doctor, William Beaumont, in a book that in 1833 became part of the history of medicine. (Sigerist mentions it in *Grosse Aerzte*, p. 364.) In fact William Beaumont had discovered more about digestion than all the world's vivisectors put together, by clinically observing a single human patient who was accidentally afflicted by a gastric fistula—an opening in the stomach that enabled the doctor to observe the digestive process over a period of years; without propagating the vivisectors' innumerable fatal errors.

Claude Bernard had not understood—any more than today's vivisectors—that by extirpating a dog's pancreas, which means inflicting one of the most brutal injuries possible, the experimenter does not duplicate the condition of a diseased pancreas, but puts the thus mutilated organism in a completely different condition; that through the severity of the injury and the pain he inflicts, he causes organic reactions that are entirely different in nature from those caused by a

pancreas that has gradually become defective through
alimentary errors or excesses.

In fact today, as in Hippocrates' day, diabetes is
preventable through appropriate diet. Although a
ruined pancreas cannot always be restored to full
efficiency, the only effective treatment, if the damage
is not too far gone, consists in a simple diet—which
is of no advantage to anyone, except to the patient.

Diabetes is a very serious disease. It can lead to
acidosis and hence definitive, irreversible lesions of the
arteries. It can lead to gangrene, uremia, angina
pectoris, blindness, and the most serious infections,
including pulmonary TB. The cause of diabetes is
clear, well known to all those that haven't clouded the
issues with animal experiments. The highest incidence
of diabetes is in the United States, where the mortality from it is rising and has recently reached 27.8 per
100,000 inhabitants; the lowest in Japan, where mortality is only 2.4 per 100,000. And the Japanese diet
contains on average 5 percent animal fats and meat,
the American 35 percent. When Japanese take on
American eating habits, they develop the same diabetic trouble. So the cause is not racial but nutritional.
In one and the same country, like India, mortality
from diabetes is very high among the rich, who
consume large quantities of meat and animal fats,
very low among the poor, whose staple diet is rice
and vegetables. So statistics confirm the conclusions
reached by the Hippocratic doctors through sheer intellectual activity, whereas animal experimentation
keeps obscuring or misleading our sure knowledge, in
all fields.

Facts and statistics have clearly shown that a pancreas can be ruined and chronic, incurable diabetes can
be established by improper nourishment—heavy and
rich. Hence we know how it can be prevented and
treated. Already nearly half a century ago doubts
were expressed about the usefulness of insulin, as in
this statement by Dr. J. E. R. McDonagh, a distinguished surgeon, in *The Nature of Disease Journal*
(Vol. I, 1932, p. 1): "Diabetes is a symptom, not a
disease, and insulin does no more than palliate this

symptom. The drug throws no light upon the cause, it does not act in the manner described, and, had the cause been found and eradicated as it can be, there would have been no need to use it." The treatment with insulin and other drugs since developed has the effect to efface the symptoms and thus contributes to masking the cause of the malady. Insulin treatment has done more damage than it has brought benefits, has killed more people, especially among the old, through insulinic shock, than it has saved, has shortened more lives than it has lengthened.

In fact deaths by diabetes have not diminished but have increased since the discovery of insulin. In 1900, 22 years before its discovery, deaths from diabetes in the United States were 11 for each 100,000; in 1954 they were 15.6; in 1963, 17.2; ten years later, 27.8. And the rate keeps rising. Some success . . .

This caused French Academician Jean Rostand, one of Europe's best-known biologists and himself a vivisector, to write that "medicine cultivates disease. The health situation is worsening . . . Therapeutics is a purveyor of ills, it creates individuals that will have to take recourse to it . . . An impressive example is hereditary diabetes. Since the discovery of insulin, this disease has markedly increased." (From *Le Droit d'être Naturaliste,* éd. Stock, Paris, 1963).

Wrote Brian Inglis in *Drugs, Doctors and Diseases* (1965): "Further study has shown that diabetes is more complex than it appeared to be and that intrinsic diseases of the pancreas may not, in most cases, be the primary cause after all . . . The cause, or more probably causes, still elude researchers." (p. 70)

And to quote a vivisectionist journalist, Ulrico de Aichelburg, writing in the authoritative Italian magazine *Epoca* (Sept. 21, 1974): "The more we study diabetes, the more we discover the contradictory aspects of this malady. Fifty years ago, when insulin was discovered, we thought that the mystery of diabetes had been resolved. But now the mystery keeps getting more mysterious." Aichelburg failed to add: "But only to us vivisectionists."

And so now the whole subject is up again for review. Not since Banting and Best were presumed to have solved the problem has there been so much milling around.

Of course, there is no money in it for research if everybody followed the proper, well-known diet. But money can be asked for working on dogs to "solve" the diabetic mystery once more—and never mind that the dogs' alimentary habits and organic reactions differ radically from ours, and that the very diet which being the wrong diet, *causes* diabetes in man (lots of meat and fat) is the *proper* diet for dogs—the favorite animals of the experimenters on diabetes.

I know personally diabetics who have been living very well for years without taking insulin or any other "anti-diabetic" drug—just following the proper, Hippocratic diet. One of them is Ursula von Wiese, aged 72, who just finished translating this book into German.

But never underestimate the enterprising spirit of died-in-the-wool experimenters. So, the Jan., 1971, issue of *Surgery, Gynecology and Obstetrics* had a report by Drs. L. Beaty Pemberton and William C. Manax, who in their attempt to solve what to them seemed the "mystery" of diabetes, subjected still another 74 dogs to complicated transection of the body of the pancreas, transplantations, and grafts, whereafter irritant drugs were administered. Four dogs were lucky enough to die comparatively soon from pancreatitis and peritonitis. Sixteen died from abnormally high concentration of sugar in the blood. Eight died from thrombosis, one of kidney failure and another of lung congestion. It isn't clear what the end of the other dogs was. Much less what was the practical result of the experiment. Perhaps it was to bolster the feeling of self-importance, produce the usual entertainment value or pecuniary advantages for the pseudoscientists involved.

And a 14-page report in the April, 1975, issue of that same *Surgery, Gynecology and Obstetrics,* indicated that three doctors from London and three from Denver, Colorado, were at it again, with 123 dogs all told, and the usual result: *nil.*

But meanwhile, to confuse still further the scientists' ideas concerning diabetes, an editorial in the *Journal of the American Medical Association* questioned even the notions that had been considered definitely acquired, like the long-accepted theory about insulin and blood sugar. *According to the editorial, more insulin does not always mean less sugar, nor less insulin more sugar.*

A splendid reason for starting to research diabetes all over again, as if Claude Bernard had never extirpated a dog's pancreas.

* * *

The other major achievement attributed to Claude Bernard is the alleged "discovery" of the "glycogenic" function of the liver—based on his mistaken experiment reported earlier, which made Claude Bernard believe that the liver fabricates sugar out of nothing, since he ruled out the existence of sugar in the vein leading to the liver. According to more recent theories, the liver is a filter for impurities and has antitoxic functions, which Claude Bernard had never suspected. Many physiologists assume that the liver—through some processes that they define "very complex," because they haven't clarified them—has the power to "store" sugar and "liberate" it again when needed. Or at least this was the "official" belief a few decades ago. For presently all these notions have become doubtful again, as the Italian medical encyclopedia (*Edizioni Scientifiche Sansoni,* 1952) indicates on page 928:

"Numerous and recent investigations have cast serious doubts on everything that had been 'discovered' up to now about the function of the liver."

And the Encyclopedia Britannica puts it this way: "The construction of the liver is extremely simple, yet almost nothing was known about its microscopic structure prior to 1949 and almost nothing was known of its gross anatomy before 1952. The numerous functions of the liver are all carried out by the Kupffer cells (so called after their discoverer), but it appears that the more details are learned, the less is understood about their astonishing variety of function."

And we thought that the great Claude Bernard had solved it all with the help of thousands of dogs ages ago!

THE RED CANKER OF BERNARDISM

Great Britain was the first nation that promised to restrict vivisection by law, with the Cruelty to Animals Act of 1876. It established that for each experiment authorization had to be obtained beforehand from a special board, which would grant it only if the absolute necessity of the experiment was proved. It further established that the animals had to be spared unnecessary suffering, and that the number of experiments had to be made public. The promise has not been kept—neither in Great Britain nor elsewhere.

The year before this act went into effect, about 800 experiments had been performed in Great Britain. Since then, the number of experiments the British vivisectors have managed to have acknowledged as indispensable to the welfare of mankind has kept rising relentlessly, with slight fluctuations. It reached in 1973, at the hands of 16,759 licensed researchers, in 607 licensed laboratories, a total of 5,363,641 during that one year alone. Over 4.5 million experiments or 85 percent were performed without any anesthesia, and fewer than 4 percent of the anesthetized animals were destroyed before waking up again to suffer to the bitter end.

And yet these figures are modest compared with American and Japanese figures. Since the number of vivisections is directly related to the possibility of gains and to the subsidies for so-called scientific research, it is inevitable that the U.S. should be in first position. In Russia, where there is no money in subsidies and drugs, vivisection is today almost nonexistent, in spite of some widely advertised experiments of the recent past, as when a Prof. Demichov implanted a small dog's head into the neck of a large German shepherd; both heads were shown drinking water the next day, but finally the man-made freak had to be destroyed, because the pain-crazed smaller head kept biting furiously the host animal.

Said Owen B. Hunt, director of the American Anti-Vivisection Society, whom I interviewed in Geneva in 1976: "In our country the prime reason for the growth of vivisection is money. Take the money out of vivisection and 90 percent of its projects would collapse overnight. Awhile back, somebody sold the government on the idea that you could buy anything with money, including health. All you had to do was spend enough money. This was great news for the researchers, especially for the biological scientists. President Johnson was our most recent high official to fall for it, though every president since the last war must share the blame. Johnson made extravagant promises that in a few years we would conquer cancer, heart disease and what have you. He has seen his promises along with billions of dollars of groaning taxpayers' money go down the drain. He has also experienced hardening of the arteries and angina pectoris at the comparatively early age of 61. All those dead experimental animals have done him no good. Nor have the squandered tax dollars done anybody any good—except the venal vivisectors and their sycophants in the National Institute of Health, the Department of Health, Education and Welfare, and other governmental bodies dedicated to the proposition that the American citizen is a sucker to be taken."

According to Rutgers University, New Jersey, in 1971 the various U.S. laboratories sacrificed 85,-283 primates, 46,624 pigs, 22,961 goats, and approximately 190,000 turtles, 200,000 cats, 500,000 dogs, 700,000 rabbits, 15-20 million frogs, 45 million mice and rats. However staggering, these figures probably stand below reality, since just one American breeder boasted the next year to have sold 220 million mice to laboratories in a twelve-month period. And in spite of the new alternative methods that are constantly being developed because they prove superior to animal tests, the number of animals annually sacrificed to the profits of industry and to the experimental folly of a comparatively small number of individual experi-

menters keeps growing on a worldwide scale of about
5 percent annually.

These are the figures. Now let us see what could
lead mankind to such aberration.

* * *

During the last century, the western hemisphere
had gone into raptures of enthusiasm over the great
discoveries and inventions that were changing the face
of the earth—for the better, it was still being hoped.
At that time the faith that the majority was placing
in the Bernardian dogmas was understandable, even
though many scientists were ridiculing them. Today,
the absurdity of Claude Bernard's doctrine is being
demonstrated daily. But meanwhile the vivisectionists
have modified their argumentations, like Claude Bernard kept modifying his, in order to mask his continual failures.

Today's "researchers" admit that one can't experiment on organic life equally as on inert matter, and
that animals don't react like man; but blithely ignoring logic, they argue that this calls for an intensification of vivisection rather than for abolition. So the
aberration of Bernardism is as firmly entrenched in
our current social structure as the aberrations of
Galenism were during the long medieval night.

There are two major explanations—the one material, the other psychological—why official medicine
won't admit that it has taken the wrong road. The
first is the financial profit of the drug industry and its
willing agents—the practicing physicians. The psychological explanation was furnished by Claude Bernard
himself when he wrote that "man is always inclined
to accept as absolute truth what he has been taught."
(*Médecine,* p. 214)

In the U.S., in the name of liberty and democ-
racy, no less, the vivisectionists have imposed the
principle of "complete freedom of vivisection," as if
it were the equivalent of freedom of thought or the
rights of man. Vivisection is glorified in the States;
its rare outspoken adversaries risk the ostracism of

the community, are accused of being antisocial and inhuman, much like those who would have opposed the witch hunts of the past, but did not dare to, lest they join the victims at the stake.

Continual efforts are made today to indoctrinate the children with the new religion. Its phony priests dedicate much study to the matter. The New Jersey Science Teachers Association, for example, conducts an annual essay contest in which money prizes are awarded to children from the 6th to 12th grades. Among the topics in 1974: "How Medical Research Using Animals Saves Millions of Lives" and "The Need for Continued Progress in Medical and Scientific Research Using Animals."

As a result of this early brainwashing of American children, although there are severe laws against the maltreatment of animals in the U.S., the so-called "Science" is free from any inhibitory laws.

In the U.S. a man who whips a horse faces a stiff penalty. But if he wants to find out, under the pretext of scientific research, how many blows are needed to kill a horse, he can club to death a hundred horses and reap admiration from his equals for doing it, for this is "Science."

Part Six

BIOCHEMICAL BERNARDISM

The eminent doctors and scientists who reveal, intentionally or not, the folly of vivisection as a method of medical research are countless. They can be found simply by reading the old as well as the recent issues of the world's leading medical journals, such as Britain's *Lancet* and the *Journal of the American Medical Association*, or the general press of various countries. Some of their statements have already been cited in this treatise, notably in the part on Surgery. Others will appear later on in part Nine, relating to the Stilboestrol tragedy. Here are a few more, by way of example and in chronological order, to show that the warnings don't date from yesterday, and that they were as deliberately ignored in the past by the health authorities as they are being ignored by today's "official" medicine, which clearly has a huge vested interest in the current swindle.

* * *

"Chloroform is so toxic to dogs, especially the young, that had that anesthetic been first tried on them it would have been withheld for many years from the service of man. Flourens, in consequence of the fatal effects that he observed in animals, discarded chloroform altogether as an anaesthetic, and Sir Lauder Brunton's experiments on dogs led to results which were ridiculed by all the leading English anaesthetists." (Dr. Benjamin Ward Richardson, *Biological Experimentation*, 1896, p. 54)

* * *

On March 20, 1904, the Paris edition of the *New York Herald Tribune* published a long article that began, "The assertion made by Dr. Ph. Maréchal and published in these columns last week, that the anti-vivisectionist cause, to succeed, should originate in the medical body itself, is thoroughly endorsed by a large number of eminent French physicians, as the following opinions obtained during the last few days by the *Herald* prove."

Excerpts from some of the opinions reported by the paper:

Dr. Paquet, formerly doctor-inspector of the *Enfants Assisté de la Seine:* "Vivisection is useless for the study of medical science. It is also useless for the study of physiology, for, if we are today cognizant of the functions of the organs, it is through having treated them when injured. It is in the *clinique,* and not in the vivisection room, that we have learned the physiological role which each organ in the human body plays. In order to study the action of medicinal matters, would it for a moment enter into the head of a serious practitioner to imagine that what passes in the body of a healthy animal would be the same as in that of a sick person?"

Prof. Dr. Léon Marchand: "It is an error to suppose that vivisection has given any true scientific notions to either surgery or medicine. It is quite the contrary. I have always found what are called 'scientific experiments' not only strange and inhuman, but illusory and dangerous."

Dr. Edgard Hirtz, of Necker Hospital: "I am decidedly hostile to it. It is a useless torture, and a sterile cruelty."

Dr. Nicol: "From the scientific point of view I consider that vivisection cannot do otherwise than divert right judgment into error. As to the moral point, no beneficial result for humanity can be obtained by practices so cruel and barbarous. The only good result which could be obtained would be to vivisect human beings, and my advice to vivisectors is that they should commence by operating upon each other."

Dr. Salivas: "I consider that vivisection is as useless

as it is immoral. The immortal Hippocrates never vivisected, yet he raised his art to a height that we are far from attaining today, in spite of our alleged great modern discoveries, which are the result of introducing extravagant theories which it will be most difficult to eradicate."

Dr. C. Mathieu: "During my medical studies I was charged with preparing the physiological experiments in the hospitals. They are useless cruelties, which have taught me nothing."

The *Herald Tribune* article contained several other similar opinions, and concluded by listing 17 more well-known French doctors who had all declared themselves opposed to vivisection on all counts. Interestingly, not one vivisector came forth in praise of vivisection.

* * *

A revealing insight was furnished by Prof. Dr. Felix von Niemeyer, Germany's most famous doctor at the turn of the century and author of several medical treatises, who in his manual *Handbuch der praktischen Medizin* (7th edition), differentiated between "scientific" results, designed to satisfy personal vanity or curiosity, and practical results, which may benefit the patient: "In spite of their scientific value, animal tests of medicaments have remained totally fruitless in the treatment of diseases, and the practicing physician hasn't learned anything useful for his patients that he didn't know fifty years ago."

* * *

"An experiment on an animal gives no certain indication of the result of the same experiment on a human being." (Dr. Robert Koch, *Report of the Second Royal Commission on Vivisection*, 1906–1912, p. 31, par. 48)

* * *

The well-known German physician, Dr. Wolfgang Bohn, in the medical journal *Aerztliche Mitteilungen* (No. 7/8, 1912): "The proclaimed purpose of vivisection has not been achieved in any field, and it can be predicted that it won't be achieved in the future either. On the contrary, vivisection has caused enormous damages, has killed thousands of people . . . We have a great number of medicines and therapeutical techniques which have been perfected without torturing animals, but they have not been used and propagated as they deserve because our generation of researchers don't know any other method than the vivisectionist one."

* * *

"The tuberculosis of the guinea-pig is not the tuberculosis of man, anymore than the cancer of the mouse is the cancer of man. It is just because in the laboratories so many animals are killed without reason that research is bearing no fruit. Sacrificing hundreds of guinea-pigs, I also, like so many other scientists, have demonstrated one thing only: that results obtained on animals are not remotely applicable to man." (Prof. Dr. Doyen, Paris, *Abolitionist,* No. 5, May 1, 1912, p. 117)

* * *

"The discovery of anaesthetics owes nothing to experiments on animals." (*Report of Royal Commission on Vivisection,* 1912, p. 26)

* * *

Writing in the *New York Daily News* (Mar. 13, 1961), the long-time staffer William H. Hendrix recalled an interview, printed many times before, of the famous Dr. Charles Mayo (not to be confused with today's Dr. Charles Mayo): "I abhor vivisection. It should be abolished. I know of no achievement through vivisection, no scientific discovery, that could not have been obtained without such barbarism and cruelty. The whole thing is evil."

* * *

Dr. Abel Desjardins, president of the Society of Surgeons of Paris, the foremost surgeon of his time in

France, and professor of surgery at the *École Normale Supérieure:* "I have never known a single good surgeon who had learned anything from vivisection." (*Intransigeant,* Paris, Aug. 25, 1925)

* * *

"The young doctor is made to believe that human beings in health and disease react in the identical way in which animals used for experimental purposes are reacting. That mistaken idea has been very harmful to the art of healing and to the patients themselves. This has been proved also by Prof. Hans Much, who has criticized this error in detail." (Dr. Erwin Liek, one of the most eminent German doctors, Surgeon of Danzig, in *The Doctor's Mission,* John Murray, London, 1930, p. 5. Prof. Hans Much of Hamburg University, author of a score of medical tomes and the discoverer of the granules of the tubercle bacillus, is one of this century's most distinguished medical scientists.)

* * *

". . . It is only by the study of the effects on patients that we can hope to understand the effect of radium." (Dr. J. A. Braxton Hicks, *British Empire Cancer Campaign,* Seventh Annual Report, 1930, p. 58)

* * *

"It has long been recognized, by those who have had most experience in the propagation of tumours by cell-grafting, that the whole process is absolutely artificial and has no counterpart in the natural genesis of a tumour." (Dr. W. E. Gye, *The Cause of Cancer,* London, 1931, p. 22)

* * *

"We do not venture to say that guinea-pigs are better or worse than people; but they are different, so different indeed, that had not the experiments been conducted under the auspices of the National Institute for Medical Research, we should have been inclined to describe them as futile, if not silly." ("The Effects of Alcohol," *The Morning Post*, July 9, 1932)

*   *   *

"In recent years research workers have been distracted and misled by animal experiments claiming to show that vitamin deficiency was the cause of this, that, or the other thing, when indeed the actual cause may have been intercurrent disease resulting from the animals being kept in quite unnatural captivity (laboratory), and apart from vitamin deficiencies, fed on unsatisfactory diets, and deprived of exercise, fresh air, sunlight and perhaps warmth." (Dr. J. Sim Wallace, King's College, London, *Report in Medical Press and Circular,* Sep. 21, 1932, p. 229)

*   *   *

"It so happens that the whole of our knowledge of the structure, symptoms, diagnosis and treatment of the neoplasias (cancers) of man comes from those who approach the subject by direct clinical methods. To this extensive knowledge the contribution of laboratory experimentalists is practically nil." (Dr. Hastings Gilford, Surgeon, *Lancet,* Jul. 15, 1933, p. 157)

*   *   *

"My own conviction is that the study of human physiology by way of experiments on animals is the most grotesque and fantastic error ever committed in the whole range of human intellectual activity." (Dr. G. F. Walker, *Medical World,* Dec. 8, 1933, p. 365)

*   *   *

"For many years, at great expense, cancer research has been carried out by large numbers of devoted workers in the laboratories of this and other countries. The continued failure of distinguished scientists to obtain any useful results, so far as the disease in man is concerned, shows that they must be working on unfruitful lines." (Dr. W. Mitchell Stevens, *British Medical Journal,* Feb. 24, 1934, p. 352)

*   *   *

"To show by further example the completeness with which observations on man himself must govern the establishment of medical remedies, digitalis is named, than which there is no more valuable remedy in the pharmacopoeia today . . . The most essential information, the profound effect which digitalis is capable of exerting in auricular fibrillation, could not have been won through observation on the frog or normal mammal, but only as it was won, by observation on patients." (Dr. Thomas Lewis, Surgeon, *Clinical Science*, Shaw and Sons, Ltd., London, 1934, pp. 188-9)

*   *   *

"Then there is the physiologist. Here we are up against the most flagrant example of the uselessness of animal experiment . . . Such experiments lead us nowhere. In fact they hamper the progress of medical science." (Leading article, *Medical Times*, Mar. 1934, p. 37)

*   *   *

"They [gastric and duodenal ulcers] never occur naturally in animals, and they are hard to reproduce experimentally. They have been so produced, but usually by methods of gross damage that have no relation to any possible causative factor in man; moreover, these experimental ulcers are superficial and heal rapidly, and bear little resemblance to the indurated chronic ulcers we see in our patients." (Dr. W. H. Ogilvie, Consulting Surgeon to Guy's Hospital, *Lancet*, Feb. 23, 1935, p. 419)

*   *   *

"Digitalis is invaluable in cases of cardiac insufficiency associated with arterial sclerosis. Too long we were taught otherwise, thanks to erroneous application of the results of animal experiments to man." (Review, *Medical World*, Feb. 8, 1935, p. 724)

*   *   *

"The wasted time and energy over the modern lines of cancer research are greatly to be deplored. We are sorry to think that so many able research workers are being tricked into believing that the cause and cure of cancer will be discovered by animal experiment." (*Medical Times*, Jan. 1936, p. 3)

* * *

"The problem of dental caries is essentially one affecting the human race . . . for it has not been possible to produce with any certainty, in animals which can be kept in a laboratory, dental caries in a form comparable with that occurring naturally in man." (The Imperial Bureau of Animal Nutrition, *Nutrition Abstracts and Reviews*, Vol. 5, No. 3, Jan. 1936)

* * *

Commenting upon experiments on dogs, cats and pigs, the *Medical Times*, Dec. 1936, said: "The experimenters state that it must be frankly admitted that human peptic ulcers are not caused by such drastic alterations of the gastro-intestinal canal as were occasioned in the animals experimented on. Then why were those experiments performed at all? . . . The entire business sounds somewhat ridiculous to anyone with a really critical mind." (p. 187)

* * *

"Clinical research is the only key to progress, in the sphere of medicine at least." (Review, *Medical World*, Feb. 12, 1937, p. 847)

* * *

"The stomachs which he had examined postmortem in human beings who had died of pernicious anaemia showed severe atrophy of the fundic region . . . but practically no change in the pylorus or duodenum—a finding completely the reverse of that which he had anticipated from his animal experiments." (Report, *Lancet*, June 12, 1937, p. 1404)

* * *

"We wish to know when the medical profession will unite in expressing their dissatisfaction at the way in

which they are being misled by the published results
of experiments on animals in physiological and pharmacological laboratories." (Editorial, *Medical Times,*
Apr. 1937)

* * *

"The sooner we relegate the pure laboratory worker
to his proper place in medicine the more likely we are
to advance in our diagnosis and treatment of disease.
At present we are being grossly misled by the experimentalists." (Review of the *Medical Annual,* 1937,
Medical World, May 28, 1937, p. 462)

* * *

". . . Let us by all means get back to the bedside,
and leave the laboratory worker to his experiments
and his often hopeless contradictions." (Editorial,
Medical Times, Nov. 1937, p. 170)

* * *

"It is well known that it is almost impossible, in an
experimental animal, to reproduce a lesion or a disease at all comparable to such as is found in the human subject." (Dr. Lional Whitby, *Practitioner,* Dec.
1937, p. 651)

* * *

Dr. A. J. Clark, writing upon "Individual Response
to Drugs" in the *British Medical Journal,* Aug. 14,
1937, stated that (to discover the lethal dose of a
drug): "Until about twenty years ago the method employed was to give varying doses to a dozen or a few
dozen animals . . . As soon as systematic investigations
were made it was found that animals showed a considerable individual variation in their response to
drugs, and that consequently the methods that had
been in use for a century were inherently inaccurate."
(p. 307)

* * *

"The entire teaching of pharmacology is wrong at
the present time. The reason is that it is being taught

by experimentalists accustomed to the laboratory and animal experiments instead of, as it should undoubtedly be, by clinicians with experience of human disease." (Editorial, *Medical Times,* Jul. 1938)

* * *

"Take the comparatively recent drug, acetylcholine. As a result of animal experiments this is stated to be of great value in paralytic ileus. We now know that it is by no means safe in this condition in humans, and has actually caused death when administered after operations." (Editorial, *Medical World,* Apr. 15, 1938, p. 246)

* * *

Medical World, Apr. 15, 1938, in its editorial (p. 246) declared in regard to the teaching of the medical student: "We calmly assert that he is taught little or nothing that will be of any ultimate value to him. He is lectured to about decerebrated cats, nerve-muscle preparations of the frog, the theories of fatigue in muscle and similar matters, all of which are hopelessly useless for his practical requirements as a medical man."

* * *

"Cats are no good for scientific research, because each gives different results from the other. We gave powdered glass to see how it affected their lungs. They lapped it up and thrived on it." (Dr. A. E. Barclay, Nuffield Professor of Medical Research at Oxford, at a conference on TB, as reported by the *Sunday Express,* Apr. 10, 1938)

* * *

"Even when a drug has been subjected to a complete and adequate pharmacologic investigation on several species of animals and found to be relatively non-toxic it is frequently found that such a drug may show unexpected toxic reactions in diseased human beings. This has been known almost since the birth of scientific pharmacology." (Dr. E. K. Marshall, Balti-

more, *Journal of the American Medical Association,*
Jan. 28, 1939, p. 353)

* * *

"All sulphonamide compounds, though singularly
free from toxic reactions demonstrable in animals,
have proved as clinical experience widened to be capable of causing peculiar and undesirable effects in the
human patient." (Leading article, *British Medical
Journal,* Aug. 19, 1939, p. 405)

* * *

Dr. Erwin E. Nelson, in his presidential address to
the section on pharmacology and therapeutics at the
1939 Annual Session of the American Medical Association, asserted that the minimum lethal dose of a
drug, determined by injection, as in the case of digitalis, only applies to 50 percent of animals tested,
for "actually any individual animal may be killed by
an amount which is much smaller than this, or it may
require a considerably greater amount . . . Some cats
require more than two and one-half times the dose
required for others." (*Journal of the American Medical Association,* Oct. 7, 1939, p. 1373)

* * *

"Vivisection is mostly undertaken in the expectation
that the goal which has been mentally erected is attain-
able. The results never justify the means, as erecting
goals is an idle pursuit, as evidenced by research conducted on these lines retarding instead of advancing
progress." (Dr. J. E. R. McDonagh, Surgeon, in *The
Universe Through Medicine,* Heinemann, London,
1940, p. 371)

* * *

"For years I have carefully studied the annual reports of the Ministry of Health, the Medical Research
Council and the two Cancer Research bodies, but I
have been unable to discover what benefits they have
conferred on the community, although I must confess
I have often admired their easy flowing rhetoric and

their naive assumption of the value of their own efforts
as essays in subtle propaganda for the extraction of
yet more money out of the generous and credulous
British public." (Dr. W. Mitchell Stevens, *Medical
World*, Jul. 5, 1940, p. 465)

* * *

"At present, the many contradictory reports of animal experimentation becloud the issue for the clinician, and only too often create an almost hopeless
confusion." (Dr. Harry Benjamin, *Medical World*,
Jan. 17, 1941, p. 505)

* * *

In *Lancet*, Oct. 10, 1942, (p. 431) reference is
made to the work of Duncan and Blalock in producing 'experimental shock' in dogs by various crushing
injuries. The comment is made in the Annotation that
all these experiments were inconclusive since the renal
failure, usually the cause of death in man, did not occur at all in dogs.

* * *

"In the old days we were taught, as the result purely
of animal experiments, that digitalis raised the blood
pressure. We now know that this is utter nonsense.
Indeed, it is a remedy of very great value in certain cases when the blood pressure is found to be abnormally high." (Dr. James Burnet, *Medical World*,
Jul. 3, 1942, p. 388)

* * *

"No experimental shock in animals can be completely identified with clinical shock as we do not know
in what the latter consists." (Dr. G. Ungar, Paris,
Lancet, Apr. 3, 1943, p. 421)

* * *

"The great onrush of laboratory and animal experiment is in so many respects threatening the very
foundations of practical medicine. Diseased conditions
cannot be correctly imitated in experimental animals,

so why persist in making such experiments?" (Extract
from *Medical World,* May 18, 1945, by Dr. James
Burnet, one of the best known British physicians,
late Examiner to the University of Aberdeen.)

* * *

"Tuberculosis in human beings and tuberculosis in
animals are distinctly different, although they are produced by the same micro-organism. The disease in animals is relatively simple in character, and fairly
predictable in its course, whereas in the human being it
is far more complex; so one must not assume that a
drug that is effective in the laboratory animal will be
equally effective in man." (*Lancet,* July 20, 1946)

* * *

"The characteristic effects in leukaemia were de-
tected solely as a result of clinical observation. The
various leukaemias in the mouse and rat were relatively refractory to the influence of urethane, and the
remarkable effect in the human might have eluded
discovery if attention had been directed to the animal alone. That illustrates the hazards of such work."
(Prof. Alexander Haddow, *British Medical Journal,*
Dec. 2, 1950, p. 1272)

* * *

"Localization is an artificial observer-made attribute of the brain . . . The brain and its ordinary owner
have no knowledge whatever of localization, and, except for those interested in it as a subject for study, it
is of supreme indifference to the individual and his behaviour. Localization in a rigid sense is an abstrac-
tion of the sort which may take us further and further
from reality." (Dr. William Goody, Assistant Physician to National Hospital, and Consultant Neurologist,
University College Hospital. *Lancet,* Mar. 17, 1951,
p. 627)

* * *

"There has never been any justification for the assumption that a given experimental operation reveals

the natural function of the cortex. What the experimentalist has produced is a disorder of natural function—what the clinicians would call a symptom—and we may not assume that a symptom is the same as a normal function or process. Yet that is the assumption that generations of cortical stimulators have made, and this is predominantly why we have not yet got a satisfactory generalization as to the control of purposive movements by the cerebral cortex." (Dr. F. M. R. Walshe, *Lancet*, Nov. 17, 1951, p. 898)

* * *

"As the years pass, cancer seems to be on the increase. The search for the cause has up till now met with a very poor result, largely owing to the fact that cancer research has been and is being conducted on laboratory animals . . . We believe that until research switches over to the clinician and leaves the laboratory investigator of cancer to grieve over his failures, no real progress will be made." ("Cancer, an Abstract Review," *Medical Review*, Feb. 1951)

* * *

". . . results obtained experimentally in such animals [guinea pigs] certainly cannot be taken to hold also for rheumatic fever in man, since argument by analogy of this sort has only too often proved fallacious in the past." (Leading article, *British Medical Journal*, Jul. 7, 1951, p. 37)

* * *

"The gastro-intestinal tract in man is unfortunately very different from that of animals, and the results of a new operation for gastric disease cannot be predicted from operations on dogs." (Editorial, *Lancet*, May 5, 1951, p. 1003)

* * *

". . . Much of the work consists of long feeding tests on the experimental animals, but the results can be strictly applied only to these animals—usually rats."

(Leading article, *British Medical Journal,* Oct 13, 1951, p. 897)

*   *   *

"It was difficult to foresee from experiments on animals how far a muscle relaxant was likely to affect respiration in man . . . It was equally difficult to foresee, from laboratory experiments, the duration of the effect of the drugs in man." (Dr. H. O. Collier, chief pharmacologist at Allen and Hanburys, Ltd., *British Medical Journal,* Feb, 17, 1951, p. 353)

*   *   *

"Vaccines prepared from animal brain tissue, containing either killed or mixture of killed and live virus, are capable of protecting animals, but are potentially dangerous for man when inoculated parenterally. Feeding live virus to animals is quite another matter from doing so to man." (Leading article, *British Medical Journal,* Sept. 6, 1952, p. 551)

*   *   *

"In the pursuit of discovering the cause of cancer it cannot be gainsaid that organized research has failed. In every civilized country in the world innumerable scientists of all grades, working indefatigably in all manner of institutions and laboratories, are using up uncountable man-hours, irreplaceable materials and millions of pounds—all to agonizingly small human profit . . . Many of our greatest discoveries resulted not from endless experimentation but from the processes of native thought." (Article "Ab Ovo Cancer," *Medical World,* Jan. 25, 1952, p. 576)

*   *   *

"I will not discuss the research work that has been done to find the cause of peptic ulceration, because it leads to nowhere. Most of the work has been done on animals, and animals do not get peptic ulcers." (Sir Heneage Ogilvie, M.D., Surgeon, *Nursing Mirror,* Oct. 21, 1952)

*   *   *

"When Forssmann, in 1929, by repeated cardiac catheterisation upon himself, showed that the procedure was not only possible but apparently without undue danger, a new era in cardio-vascular investigation began." (*Practitioner,* July, 1952, p. 40)

* * *

"Any work which seeks to elucidate the cause of disease, the mechanism of disease, the cure of disease, or the prevention of disease, must begin and end with observations on man, whatever the intermediate steps may be . . . Man is a species that in many respects is quite unlike any species kept in cages and subject to the kinds of experiments that can be made by any discipline other than clinical science." (Sir George Pickering, M.D., University of London, *Lancet,* Nov. 8, 1952, p. 895)

* * *

"Vagotomy is unsound, in the way that any procedure based chiefly on animal experiments is apt to be unsound . . ." (Sir Heneage Ogilvie, M.D., Surgeon, *British Medical Journal,* Aug. 9, 1952, p. 302)

* * *

"Warning is given not to carry over, without reservation, to man, the conclusions based on animal experiments. In the monkey none of the powerful carcinogens has been shown to produce cancers." (Review, *Lancet,* Aug. 9, 1952, p. 274)

* * *

"Experimental evidence may be dangerously misleading; for in the words of one gastric surgeon, 'not all of our patients behave exactly like dogs'." (Annotation, *Lancet,* Sep. 20, 1952, p. 572)

* * *

"So long as the research worker plays about with mice and other animals and becomes completely divorced from the clinician and the pathologist no progress will ever be made with cancer research. So far it is a total failure, and is likely to remain so for so long as it is conducted on what we consider to be entirely wrong and fallacious lines." (Notes on Books, *Medical Review*, Nov. 1952)

* * *

"Most of our knowledge of transplantation is based upon experiments in animals; but these, it seems, differ as much from man in their response to homografting as in the diseases from which they suffer . . ." (Leading article, *Lancet*, Nov. 29, 1952, p. 1068)

* * *

"Well-established facts about human disease have been ignored by experimentalists and have had to be re-discovered before fallacies were recognised and corrected." (Dr. Clifford Wilson, *Lancet*, Sep. 19, 1953, p. 579)

* * *

"It is readily granted that a fracture and a burn on a dog are not the same as on a human." (Drs. Harvey S. Allen, John L. Bell and Sherman W. Day, Chicago, Illinois, *Surgery, Gynecology and Obstetrics*, Vol. 97, Nov. 1953, p. 541)

* * *

"The folly of founding the actions of drugs on animal experiments cannot be over-emphasized. This is the case with chloramphenicol (chloromycetin). This drug was tried out for long periods on dogs and was found to produce only a transient anaemia, but fatal results have followed its use in human disease . . ." (Editorial, *Medical Review*, Sept. 1953)

* * *

"The hypothesis that acid acting on nerve-endings in the floor of the ulcer is the primary cause of ulcer pain is based upon unnatural experiments, false anatomy, and faulty pathology . . . Many patients with 'ulcer pain' have no nerves in the ulcer floor, some have no acid, and some even have no ulcer . . ." (Dr. V. J. Kinsella, Sydney, *Lancet,* Aug. 22, 1953, p. 361)

*   *   *

"Although lung tumours have been described in many species, there is no laboratory animal which spontaneously develops tumours comparable to the ordinary squamous or anaplastic carcinoma of the bronchus of man . . ." (Dr. Richard Doll, *British Medical Journal,* Sept. 5, 1953)

*   *   *

"One of the newer antibiotic drugs, chloramphenicol, has been recorded as a cause of fatal aplastic anaemia in human beings. But extensive experiments on dogs have failed to show any evidence of injury or disease to the canine species." (*Bulletin,* Easton, Massachusetts, Apr. 2, 1953)

*   *   *

"Mice were used in the initial toxicity tests because of their small size, but what a lucky chance it was, for in this respect man is like the mouse and not the guinea-pig. If we had used guinea-pigs exclusively we should have said that penicillin was toxic, and we probably should not have proceeded to try to overcome the difficulties of producing the substance for trial in man . . ." (Dr. Howard Florey, Nobel laureate, co-discoverer of penicillin, "The Advance of Chemotherapy by Animal Experiments," *Conquest,* Jan. 1953, p. 12)

*   *   *

"I am particularly concerned not with the wickedness but with the folly of experiments on animals . . . To apply the results of experiments on dogs to the aetiology and treatment of peptic ulceration in man is as scientific as to base a course on post-natal lectures to mothers on a study of the maternal habits of the female kangaroo." (Address by Sir Heneage Ogilvie,

M.D., Surgeon, to Leeds Medical Society, Dec. 12, 1952, *Lancet,* Mar. 21, 1953, p. 555)

* * *

"It must never be forgotten that the results of animal tests may be of little value in forecasting the effects of a substance on man . . ." (Dr. J. M. Barnes, World Health Organization Monograph No. 16, 1954, p. 45)

* * *

"The argument from man is so much more convincing than the argument from mice—which, indeed, may be completely misleading as in the case of urethane, which has some inhibitory action on human tumours, but a marked, though temporary one on chronic human leukaemias." (Dr. C. G. Learoyd, Surgeon, *Medical World,* Aug. 1954, p. 172)

* * *

"No experimental worker can provide a single fact about human disease." (Dr. D. A. Long, London, from the National Institute for Medical Research, *Lancet,* Mar. 13, 1954, p. 532)

* * *

"Few neurological and probably no psychiatric disorders can be adequately reproduced in animals." (Review, *British Medical Journal,* June 12, 1954, p. 1364)

* * *

"Let us not deceive ourselves. The guinea-pig's reputation is spurious." (Editorial, *The Medical Press,* Jan. 19, 1955, p. 45)

* * *

"Recently, Dr. Harald Okens, Professor of Anatomy in the University of Copenhagen, stated that there is no compelling argument which can justify scientific experiments on dogs. For his part he categorically prohibited such experiments at the Institute of which he was head. In his opinion much good would be won if such experiments were forbidden by law." (*Dog's Bulletin,* Feb. 1955)

* * *

". . . Largely as a result of animal experiment, during which parts of the hypothalamus have been stimulated or destroyed, a concept of its function in its different parts has been built up. Results of these experiments may be confusing since a destructive lesion may produce an entirely different clinical state from that caused by an irritative lesion . . ." (*The Medical Press,* Sept. 21, 1955, p. 272)

* * *

"It must be pointed out that a phenomenon observed in a given organism under normal condition . . . is one thing, and a phenomenon observed under pathological conditions, especially when they are produced in the laboratory, as, for example, the stimulation of the brain, is another thing. They are, of course, absolutely different phenomena." (Ivan Petrovich Pavlov, *Selected Work,* Foreign Languages Publishing House, Moscow, 1955, p. 383)

* * *

"The evanescence of our knowledge is something we rarely mention. We go from one cocksureness to another. Read your lecture notes of 1928 or 1929 if you have any. It is embarrassing to see how little those giants knew. But we are just as ignorant now. We have acquired a great many more wrong data since, if we have tried to keep up to date. Only we won't admit it, even to ourselves." (*Lancet,* Nov. 24, 1956, p. 1100)

* * *

"The intensive research on carcinogenic substances which has been undertaken during the past quarter of a century has complicated rather than simplified the problem." (*Lancet,* Feb. 16, 1957, p. 334)

* * *

"Pacatal was tested in animals by Nieschultz et. al. (1954) and found to be well tolerated. Unfortunately, the high incidence of toxic side-effects in this group of patients suggests that the widespread use of pacatal is unjustifiable . . ." (Dr. P. H. Mitchell, Dr. P. Sykes, Surgeon, and Dr. A. King, Surgeon, *British Medical Journal,* Jan. 26, 1957, p. 207)

* * *

"Contrary to a widespread belief based on studies in the lower animals, the xanthine drugs consistently produce significant cerebral vasoconstriction in man." (Dr. Seymour S. Ketty, Chief, Laboratory of Clinical Science, National Institute of Mental Health, Bethesda, Maryland, *Triangle,* Vol. III, No. 2, June 1957, pp. 47 and 51)

* * *

"It is a melancholy thought that hundreds of research workers spending hundreds of millions of money have been at work for well over thirty years on this problem, tobacco-smoking and lung cancer, and at the end of this period we have advanced so little, if at all. The very volume of money and effort has built up an organized research which is no longer original. Its very bulk forces it through well-worn channels." (Dr. W. A. Ball, Surgeon, *Lancet,* July 6, 1957, p. 45)

* * *

"How are we to know that when a drug has been tried on 15 different species of animals, including primates, and shown to be harmless, it will be found harmless to man? The reverse consideration also applies. How are we to be sure that a drug shown to be toxic to 15 different species of animals will also be toxic to man?" (Dr. A. L. Bacharach, Wellcome Chemical Research Laboratory, in *Quantitative Method in Human Pharmacology and Therapeutics,* Pergamon Press, London, 1959, p. 196. Report of symposium held in London, Mar. 1958)

* * *

"There really exists no logical basis for translating the results in animals to man." (Dr. L. Goldberg, Department of Alcohol, Karolinska Institute, Stockholm, Sweden, *Quantitative Method in Human Pharmacology and Therapeutics,* Pergamon Press, London, 1959, p. 197. Report of symposium held in London, Mar. 1958)

* * *

"It is not possible to apply to the human species experimental information derived from inducing cancer in animals." (Dr. Kenneth Starr, Honorary Director of the special unit for investigation and treatment of cancer for the New South Wales Cancer Council, *Sydney Morning Herald,* Apr. 7, 1960)

* * *

"The idea, as I understand it, is that fundamental truths are revealed in laboratory experimentation on lower animals and are then applied to the problems of the sick patient. Having been myself trained as a physiologist, I feel in a way competent to assess such a claim. It is plain nonsense." (Sir George Pickering, Regius Professor of Medicine at the University of Oxford. *British Medical Journal,* Dec. 26, 1964, pp. 1615–1619)

* * *

"Another basic problem which we share as a result of the regulations and the things that prompted them is an unscientific preoccupation with animal studies. *Animal studies are done for legal reasons and not for scientific reasons.* The predictive value of such studies for man is often meaningless—which means our research may be meaningless." (Dr. James D. Gallagher, Director of Medical Research, Lederle Laboratories. *Journal of American Medical Association,* Mar. 14, 1964)

* * *

"We are sorcerer's apprentices, especially in the scientific field. We boast of discoveries which poison us. I think the future generations will need much time and courage to get rid of the disastrous consequences of our research." (Prof. Pierre Lépine, head of the Pasteur Institute's bacteriology department, member of the Academy of Sciences and the National Academy of Medicine, in an interview in the French daily *Alsace,* Mar. 17, 1967)

* * *

"Much of the experimental animal work on atheroma has held back our progress rather than advancing it." (*Medical News Tribune,* London, Sept. 18, 1970)

* * *

"No animal tumor is closely related to a cancer in human beings." (*Lancet,* Apr. 15, 1972)

* * *

Lancet made one more monotonous admission barely one week later (Apr. 22, 1972): "We know from drug toxicity studies that animal tests are very imperfect indicators of human toxicity; only clinical experience and careful control of the introduction of new drugs can tell us about their real dangers."

* * *

"It is almost a cliché among research workers that findings in animal studies cannot be extrapolated to man. Nevertheless, the temptation is ever present . . . Dutch investigator H. G. S. van Raalte blended recent laboratory findings with data from human epidemiology and experience from clinical medicine, to conclude that any inference from animal experiments that dieldrin causes hepatomas in man is unwarranted." (From an article in *Medical World News,* Aug. 24, 1973—the medical magazine published by McGraw-Hill, New York, financed by the pharmaceutical industry, and sent free of charge to 237,000 American physicians.)

* * *

The 1970 Nobel laureate for Medicine, Ulf S. Euler of the Karolinska Institute in Stockholm, declared at the International Medical Conference in Manchester in 1973 that "if drugs were tested on people and less on animals they might be better and safer. Proper caution would have to be taken with human testing, but in the long run it could give increased security on the side-effects of drugs and increase the prospect of new and better drugs." (*Yorkshire Evening Press,* York, Sept. 20, 1973)

* * *

The April 1973 issue of *Anesthesiology* pointed out that fluroxene, a form of ether, when used as an anesthetic in man produced no untoward results, yet when used in dogs, cats and rabbits, they all died of ataxia, hypotension, seizures, etc.

* * *

An editorial in *The Economist,* London, Jan. 6, 1973, opened thus: "Thalidomide is not the first nor the last drug to have brought heartbreak where it was meant to bring help. There have been quite a number of other tragedies since Thalidomide went wrong thirteen years ago."

* * *

"Can we justify cruel experiments on animals on the grounds that psychologists can learn more about behavior? I do not believe any of the suffering I have caused to laboratory animals—and, alas, there has been some—has helped humanity in the slightest." (Dr. Richard Ryder, senior clinical psychologist at Warneford Hospital, Oxford. *Sunday Mirror,* London, Feb. 24, 1974)

* * *

If drugs tested on animals vary from one human to another, then certainly what happens to animals tells nothing about human reactions. That the entire mode of research could be called ridiculous, if it didn't serve profit purposes, is demonstrated once more by the following news item:

"A study panel reported Friday that the same drug

made by different manufacturers may produce varied results in different patients. In critically ill patients, this can mean the difference between life and death." (Arthur J. Snider, Science Editor, in *Chicago Daily News,* July 12, 1974)

* * *

"At a time when millions are starving in the world, and our economy is in great trouble, Congress is allocating billions of dollars annually in grants for 'basic' no-goal research on living animals. Careers in torture are as financially rewarding as they are morally bankrupt. Reports in the medical journals recorded by the experimenters themselves are indisputable indictments of their gross inhumanity." (Barbara Schultz, a member of the Attorney General Louis Lefkowitz's advisory committee on the treatment of animals in New York State, writing in *Newsday,* July 12, 1974)

* * *

"Unfortunately we shall learn the effect on our health of the thousands of chemical compounds at some unforeseeable future date only, for they act very slowly, in the course of time, and by accumulation." (Dr. John Higginson, head of the International Agency for Cancer Research, as reported by Milan's *Corriere della Sera,* Oct. 22, 1974)

* * *

"A plant should not be considered safe simply because a pet animal nibbles on it without ill effects; it could still be harmful to humans." (From an article in *Time* Magazine of Mar. 1, 1976, quoting Dr. Guy Hartman, veteran pediatrician and caretaker of a garden of popular but poisonous plants at the pediatrics clinic of the Kaiser-Permanente Medical Center in Fontana, Calif.)

* * *

"Modern medicine is a negation of health. It isn't organized to serve humans' health, but only itself, as an institution. It makes more people sick than it heals." (Famed Yugoslav-born Ivan Illich, sociologist, philosopher and theologian, author of *Medical Nemesis,* in an interview at the Italian-Swiss TV station of Lugano, in 1975.)

*   *   *

"With only a few notable exceptions, such as some senior official of the American Medical Association, almost everyone agrees that modern medicine is as sick as the patient it treats." (Opening sentence of the book review of *Medical Nemesis* in *Time* Magazine, June 28, 1976.)

*   *   *

"In praxis all animal experiments are scientifically indefensible, as they lack any scientific validity and reliability in regard to humans. They only serve as an alibi for the drug manufacturers, who hope to protect themselves thereby. . . . But who dares to express doubts of our much-vaunted technological medicine, or even just to ask questions, without meeting the solid opposition from the vested interests of science, business, and also of politics and news media?" (Dr. Herbert Stiller and Dr. Margot Stiller, doctors of neurology and psychiatry, in *Tierversuch und Tierexperimentator,* Hannover, Germany, 1976.)

*   *   *

In sum, I can hardly claim to be making a discovery when I affirm that today's so-called "medical research," driven by profits or personal vanity, is disastrous not only for human morals but also for human health, and thus represents a criminal activity. The warnings that have been ignored, and of which the above are only a few examples, are so numerous that they can no longer be called isolated cries in the desert; they form a veritable chorus. And yet this stolid but lucrative research goes on and on, and keeps spreading, while continuing to prove directly responsible for the majority of modern diseases, foremost cancer. And the culprits should be brought to court.

In the following parts we shall see not only some

specific cases of laboratory fabricated ills, sold to the public for profit motives, but we shall also see on whom the major responsibilities rest.

SOMEBODY UP THERE IS LYING TO YOU

It would be difficult to find more naive commentators on today's science and scientists than news reporters. Unless they are being paid. In fact the mass media are always readily at the disposal of the official medicine, reporting any kind of news coming from that quarter—the more extravagant the better. Most news media people, who normally are skeptical of everything and everybody, who would pillory a saint before accepting a word of his as truth, genuflect to anyone who has been defined a scientist. Especially in the U.S., the most obviously sadistic and worthless of vivisectors has no difficulty, by the simple means of donning a "scientist's" white frock, in being accorded the reverence of a saint, of a savior of mankind.

In most cases even the most seriously documented adverse criticism faces a veritable censorship. That's a result of the religion-like veneration for official science that has been inculcated into the majority since tender age, when a veritable brain-washing takes place. The head of the mass media seem to take it for granted that every criticism of the vivisectionist method is based on wrong information or is maliciously attempting to mislead them. Worse, they often deliberately withhold from the public crucial facts with the pretext of not shaking a confidence which these very facts show to be misplaced.

But ignorance is only one explanation. The other is money. In many countries, most mass media couldn't exist without the advertisement revenues from the drug industry, which doesn't sell only little liver pills, but also cosmetic products. And the huge sums these firms have at their disposal for promotion and public relations enable them to hire news writers and influence the press and politicians.

Vivisection would have been abolished long ago if

it were championed only by the vivisectors, whose motives are all too transparent. The real obstacle to abolition is the smokescreen produced by the mass media, which influence public opinion, governments and legislators, by constantly advertising "medical research" as an intelligent and humanitarian enterprise, useful and necessary.

Example: A TV program shows a child whose blood is "regenerated" by letting it stream through the liver of a live pig or baboon. Then the "scientist," who acts as master of ceremonies for this sleight-of-hand trick worthy of a three-ring circus, explains to the unprepared audience that this child's life has thus been saved: another "miracle" of modern science. Nobody informs the public that the child was dead within three days, probably as a consequence of this performance. If the child survives, it survives in spite of this science-fiction show, not because of it. It will represent one more proof that nature endows most human beings with fantastic stamina at birth, and that the real "miracle" consists in surviving the interferences of the experimental doctors.

Christiaan Barnard's first heart transplant caused an earthquake of enthusiasm throughout the world. It was presented as if Modern Science had offered palpable proof that she can triumph over nature and insure eternal life, health and happiness for all. As we know today, that first heart transplant marked just the beginning of a new series of sufferings for mankind, unknown in the past—to say nothing of the increased suffering it meant for millions of animals.

The real experts knew that Barnard's operation presented no serious technological obstacles; that it had been feasible long before; and that it had not been attempted before owing to the danger of rejection. The matter has been sufficiently examined in the first part. Once Barnard had broken the spell, other surgeons, sensitive to such publicity, decided to get in on the act, with the results that are by now all too well known.

The perusal of old newspapers shows that at regular intervals the final solution to one of the various nightmares weighing on mankind was "just around the corner," with news items beginning usually with: "Animal tests have demonstrated that . . ." Announcement of miraculous cures *just about to be made* are the manna of vivisectionists, even if they don't materialize, like the various cancer cures, or turn out to wreak havoc.

More than half a century ago Pavlov's announcement that he had found a serum against epilepsy was advertised as a colossal medical conquest. He had achieved this by allegedly causing "epileptic attacks" in dogs after freezing parts of their brains and trying on them a special poison which, injected into sane dogs, enabled him to extract from them a "serum" which rendered epileptic patients refractory to future attacks. So his widely advertised story went. Unfortunately, the men at the head of the mass media didn't know then as they don't know now that serums are prepared differently from the way Pavlov described, today's epileptics show the identical seizures they showed before Pavlov's time, and their number has increased steadily since Pavlov pocketed his Nobel prize in 1904.

A few decades later the world was thrilled to learn in a report by the British Empire Cancer Campaign that "following the very recent discovery of the *complete control* of cancer by this campaign in *one* site of the body, intense investigations are now proceeding to *completely control* cancer in *all* sites of the body." (*The Times,* Nov. 24, 1944)

And then again on October 31, 1950, in the debate of the House of Commons, rebutting a speech that had pointed out the uselessness of animal experimentation in cancer research, a Dr. Charles Hill did not hesitate to make the startling statement that "at least one form of cancer *is now curable* as a result of animal experimentation."

Both the 1944 and 1950 statements had reference to the treatment of prostatic cancer by the potent estrogen (sexual hormone) Stilboestrol, which had been synthesized in 1938. The two statements have meanwhile ridiculed those who made them. The cancer of the prostate has increased; and Stilboestrol has not only proved ineffective in curing it, but has been *proved* to be the *cause* of a new type of cancer, which didn't exist a few decades ago.

Who cares? Far more than in failures, the public is interested in the various medical miracles *that are just around the corner*.

The cover design of *Newsweek* of March 31, 1958, showed a human heart, and the legend: 'Special Medical Report: HEART DISEASE BREAKTHROUGH AT HAND.' Of course it wasn't at hand then, and it isn't now— many years later.

*   *   *

In 1973 a Reuters dispatch about flu made headlines once again. The *International Herald Tribune* (Feb. 7), under the title "Pasteur Institute Reports Discovery: Vaccine for All Strains of Influenza," stated without laughing that "A French medical research team said today it has discovered a vaccine against influenza that will be effective against all strains of the disease. Production of the revolutionary vaccine has already started, and it will be available in France shortly, researchers at the Pasteur Institute here said. Prof. Claude Hannoun, who heads the Pasteur research team, told reporters that the new vaccine differs from all others in that it anticipates future strains of influenza. Prof. Jacques Monod, famed head of the Pasteur Institute and a winner of the Nobel medicine prize, called it 'a revolutionary discovery.'"

Whoever has been reading newspapers for the past few decades, and whose memory has not been too weakened by the miracle drugs, must have experienced an eerie, very strong déjà-vu feeling.

However, in the fall of 1975, the whole Italian press announced that a vaccine for flu had this time really been found, and called for massive inoculation. Nobody knows exactly how many Italians followed suit, but the records show that more working hours were lost during the following winter due to flu than in preceding years. Then in the following spring the Rome daily *Tempo* (Apr. 25, 1976) reported that

Dr. Albert Sabin had said at a press conference in Salsomaggiore, Italy, that no reliable flu vaccine existed, all press reports notwithstanding.

Too bad President Gerald Ford hadn't heard Sabin's opinion when, at about the same time, his advisers convinced him that he might get himself reelected if he launched a mass-inoculation program against a possible outbreak of swine-flu. "We cannot afford to take a chance with the health of this country!" cried he patriotically, announcing the $135 million program to the American people. However, it backfired badly, when the swine-flu didn't develop, but there were casualties among the Americans who had followed their President's call to get inoculated. A goodly number died, and many more merely developed paralysis. "They were mainly old people," parried the medical "experts" who had got the President into this mess, which may have cost him the decisive votes, for all we know; and they hoped the public would forget that inoculation had been recommended particularly for the elderly. "Federal officials indefinitely suspended the nationwide effort," wrote *Time* Magazine on December 27, 1976, in its obituary titled "Roll Down Your Sleeves, America!"

Coming back to Sabin, ever since he had perfected his own "vaccine" for an infection that was already on the wane (polio), the good doctor had been making headlines at regular intervals with sensational announcements. One concerned "research" he had done together with one Dr. Giulio Tarro of Naples University between 1967 and 1973, on the usual mice, and which had led the two "scientists" to the usual belief that they were about to lick cancer for good.

But 18 months later, Dr. Sabin published in the *Proceedings* of the National Academy of Sciences a paper retracting his claims. "Sabin's retraction comes as something of a shock to Tarro," commented *Time* Magazine. (Sept. 30, 1974)

Meanwhile, on April 8, 1974, the same magazine had reported the following item on cancer: "Dr. Sol Spiegelman, director of the Institute of Cancer Research at Columbia University, was encouraged enough about progress in virology research to make a bold prediction: that 1974 will bring the isolation and identification of two viruses that cause specific human cancers."

Why didn't *Time* notify its readers on December 31, 1974 that Sol Spiegelman's had been one more empty promise? Because failures don't make news. And so the merry saraband goes on, and on, and on . . .

THE GRAND ILLUSION

Already Claude Bernard used as an alibi for his constant failures the "unpredictability" of living organisms. Since he died—of a malady that neither he nor his colleagues or successors have ever been able to diagnose—a whole century has gone by and the difficulties created by Bernardism have multiplied. And they started spreading at an unprecedented rate ever since the medicine men of the western world decided to solve their self-created problems by compounding them with a new error of even greater magnitude: resorting to biochemical theories to treat human ills. This means trying to apply an exact science, like chemistry, to biology—to organic life, living bodies which are heavily subject to psychic influence—and furthermore by extrapolating to man the inevitably misleading answers obtained from animals.

A medical science edified on theoretical biochemistry was from the outset doomed to fail for the same reason that Bernardism was doomed to fail: Because *there is no standardization in biology*. In organic life, individual reactions always vary—be it human, animal, or plant.

So constant strains of bacteria do not exist, since they are subject to continual mutations. When science has developed a supposedly effective chemical weapon against a particular bacterial strain, some of these bacteria always manage to survive—and precisely the strongest of the lot, according to Darwin's law of the survival of the fittest. These surviving bacteria undergo a mutation by effect of the means that have been employed on their forebears, and form new strains, different from the preceding ones and more resistant than they. Furthermore, at a velocity with which no kind of research can ever keep up.

Bacteria multiply in geometric progression, doubling their number every half hour. So in a few days there could be theoretically enough of a new strain to infect the world population with an entirely new malady. But just to identify it, man requires years, then more years to perfect an alleged remedy to the disease that he himself has created. In sum, the only protagonist on earth is always nature. Man deludes himself into believing that he is the protagonist. This is a fact that the philosopher has always understood. The scientist hasn't. In his blind arrogance, he presumes to dominate the earth and harness nature, and has managed to make others believe it, too.

Since 1871—when R. Maly began issuing in Germany the *Jahres-Bericht über die Fortschritte der Tier-Chemie*, which appeared in yearly volumes up to 1919, abstracting from various scientific journals all the papers with a primarily biochemical content—the field of biochemistry has spread to such an extent that no individual can ever hope to know it in its entirety, much less to keep up with its continual changes.

Today a researcher can investigate only a small area of the big field. But even this small area may turn out to be so intricate at closer examination as to require several specializations, over which the whole is forgotten, or at least neglected: the cliché of not seeing the forest for the trees. It may happen that the specialist doesn't even see the trees, being too close to the branch. That he doesn't see the branch, being too close to the leaf. He doesn't see the leaf, being distracted by the stalk. And looking closer at the stalk he discovers a whole new world that contains many new worlds, of which each requires new specializations.

This situation is bound to worsen in the future, as the notions multiply, as new theories spring into being, facts and figures multiply, techniques proliferate. All of which have mainly theoretical value, and remove the scientist further and further from understanding biology, life, and health. As the number of items that should be learned increases, the shortsightedness of the scholar worsens. It is like using glasses with thicker and thicker lenses in order to see smaller and smaller insects—insects within insects within insects. But with such glasses one can no longer see the world at large.

The medical student, having to choose a branch of learning, is taught by a specialist, whose notions are vast only numerically; but in actual fact they are restricted to his own, severely limited field, which in his eyes appears magnified and distorted by the lenses of specialization that blur the surroundings. A specialist in biology will know everything about a certain type of cell, but little about other types, and much less about the whole organism.

"Today," proudly wrote Prof. Ulrico di Aichelburg, medical columnist of *Epoca* (Nov. 11, 1973), the influential Italian weekly editorially connected with the *Time/Life* group, "the physician has at his disposal an enormous quantity of diagnostic tests. So far it has been possible to identify and frame no less than 8,000 syndromes, meaning sets of manifestations or symptoms, which represent as many specific morbid states (*quadri*), and each of those syndromes requires a corresponding curative treatment . . . The necessity is being envisaged to resort to electronic computers in order to disentangle the boundless congeries of new notions that arrive like drumfire from the thousands of publications and hundreds of medical conventions."

The real maladies—those that nature has planned with definite purposes, and not the daily new ones fabricated in the laboratories by incompetence—can be counted on the fingers of one hand. The remedies to those maladies are to be found in nature herself, or else they can't be found. And yet, modern science was supposed to have "identified and framed" no less than 8,000 syndromes—8,000 assemblages of symptoms—and obviously any doctor who wanted to find his way out of this labyrinth needed an electronic computer. Who could remember, much less recognize, 8,000 syndromes?

Aichelburg's article was dated 1973. By now the 8,000 must have doubled, and are bound to keep mushrooming, thanks to the current biochemical fad that runs wild like cancer cells, and prompts the industry to produce always more drugs, ever more poisons, which affect human health in unknown ways, causing new maladies—and offering the pretext for perfecting still more new drugs.

In 1975 the number of specialties recognized by the American Medical Association included 67 fields, each with its specialized nurses, technicians, theoreticians, journals, congresses, etc. But nothing evidences better the rapidly worsening case of elephantiasis (an incurable disease) which afflicts present-day medicine than the major international conventions. Often as many as 5,000 "scientists" register to intervene, 8,000 arrive, the program is as thick as a city telephone directory, and some 2,000 reports are delivered *in 6 to 32 parallel conferences,* in which each lecturer reads from a paper printed months in advance, keeping his voice low so as not to disturb his sleeping colleagues.

And yet, if today a sick man gets well, it happens in spite of the drugs his physician or advertisements have prescribed, not because of them.

An architect is not afraid of building a house for his children, knowing that his is an exact science, not guesswork or superstition. But a medical doctor, if his own child gets seriously ill, will call in other doctors, because he mistrusts his own science. And right he is. He hears increasingly of maladies that were believed to have been rooted out but come back with a vengeance, clearly as a result of the interferences of modern research.

One case in point is malaria. A few years ago, this disease was believed to have been practically eliminated in South Asia. But in 1975 the World Health Organization admitted that its victory bulletins were premature. India, which had cut its cases to only 125,-000 by 1965, expected to record 4 million cases in 1975. Pakistan, which then included Bangladesh, had reduced its annual toll from tens of millions to only 9,500 in 1961, but estimated 10 million cases in 1975. In the same year the former Ceylon, which counted only 6 victims in 1963, recorded at least 500,000 cases.

(*Time* Magazine devoted its "Medicine" column of Dec. 1, 1975 to this problem.)

Hippocratic good sense and wisdom are irreconcilable with the technological arsenal on which today's official medical science feeds. When some courageous and intelligent voice is heard, it is studiously ignored by the health authorities and the public at large, as when Prof. Roger Mucchielli of Paris University wrote, "Official medicine keeps disregarding the signs heralding its own ruin, but it is already imbued by a current that finds again the profound Hippocratic inspiration." (*Caractériologie à l'Age Scientifique*, ed. Griffon, Neuchâtel, 1960)

Another French physician, Prof. Maurice Delort, did some plain talking at the inaugural session of the Academy de Bourges (Dec. 16, 1962): "Today's medicine is at the end of its road. It can no longer be transformed, modified, readjusted. That's been tried too often. Today's medicine must die in order to be reborn. We must prepare its complete renovation."

THE CAGE

Being by nature a conformist, besides an imitative and gregarious animal, man tends to pattern his inner habits no less than his outer appearance on the rest of the crowd. That's understandable: It makes him feel safe. Less easy to explain, in view of his unshakable conviction that he possesses a rational mind, is his persistence in refusing to recognize an error even when it has been proved to him. And when he has at last acknowledged an error, likely as not he will replace it with a new error, often more serious than the preceding one. That's what caused Roscommon to say, "The majority is always in the wrong." So the majority has blandly replaced Galenism with Bernardism. And man's errors are almost all, and maybe all, due to his reasoning, rather than to his intuition or instinct.

According to Aristotle, whose thoughts were long considered the topmost achievement of human intelligence, a heavy stone must fall faster than a lighter one.

More than the error in itself, what surprises us today is that it never occurred to Aristotle nor to anyone else for many centuries after him to find out whether it was true. Why? Because the range of human thought has always been limited by a cage, conforming to the period. In the course of time, slowly, the cage moves— not necessarily ahead, but move it does—with the pushes and shocks it receives from some rebellious individualist inside, and so covers some partly new ground; but the way of thinking remains confined within the bars of the cage, from which it cannot evade.

During Aristotle's time and for nearly 2,000 years thereafter the cage prevented the human mind from advancing to the concept of the experimental method. Mankind had to wait for Descartes to enunciate it, and the spirit of enterprise of a few of his contemporaries to illustrate it. One of them was Galileo, who decided to verify Aristotle's theory of the two stones, and startled the world by his discovery that the light stone falls just as fast as the heavy one. Humanity had waited millions of years for this simple observation.

Descartes, a geometer, had pushed the cage over new ground, teaching mankind another way of thinking, which is called for him Cartesian. Thanks to Descartes, today's cage dwells on a territory that was unknown to Aristotle; but it has also moved beyond the range of certain notions and values which are at least as important for the understanding of the world and of life as any chemical or mathematical formula.

While rapidly extending the borders of human knowledge, the Cartesian technique of thinking, spurning all intuition and philosophical thought, substituted a new, macroscopic error for all the preceding ones; an error which contained from the inception the seed of future defeat, because it led the scientist unawaredly away from the truth of life, and thus away from the scientific ideals.

By denying the importance, and even the very existence, of anything that cannot be weighed or measured, they divorced themselves from reality.

So the idea of roasting in an oven live animals in order "to discover the secret of fever" could be conceived only by a caged mind, one rigidly limited by a mechanist conception of life and health, like Claude Bernard's. The founder of today's vivisectionist method thus demonstrated that he was unable to distinguish between cause and effect—had failed to understand that the raised temperature of a diseased individual was the consequence, not the origin, of a malady. And in the same way modern medicine presumes to cure diseases by masking their symptoms—which very often, as in the case of fever, are nature's way to reestablish health.

* * *

In a public debate organized in the fall of 1973 by the Italian weekly *Epoca,* a "scientist" asserted that "in a laboratory it is possible to reproduce exactly a natural estrogen." The claim came from Prof. Silvio Garattini, head of the Institute of Pharmacological Research "Mario Negri" of Milan, which had been defined by *Epoca* as "one of the most important centers of Europe for research on cancer, on the nervous system, on arteriosclerosis: more than 400 published and internationally distributed papers testify to the results of its 10 years' activity."

Apart from our wondering what the "results" of that alleged research could possibly be—since conditions in the three fields mentioned by *Epoca* hadn't ceased to deteriorate during the decade of that institute's activity —Prof. Garattini clearly personified the type of today's scientist whose mind moves within the narrow confines of the cage that we may call Bernardism, being limited by Claude Bernard's dogmas.

In fact the assertion that "in a laboratory it is possible to reproduce exactly a natural estrogen," is to be put on the same level with Claude Bernard's claim that "results obtained on animals are perfectly conclusive for man."

So a laboratory mechanic analyzes a natural estrogen, meaning a sexual hormone produced by a living organism, and establishes its chemical formula. Basing itself on this analysis, the laboratory then manufactures a product that *theoretically* contains the same

chemical ingredients as the original, with which it thus
has a *theoretical, conventional* similarity. But in fact
the two products won't be identical, because the analysis has identified only the inert, lifeless ingredients of
the original—those *corps bruts* which were always
foremost in Claude Bernard's reasoning; but it has not
identified the most important elements, those that
elude any chemical analysis for the very reason that
they constitute the *vital* part and not any *inert* part
of the organism: those ingredients that derive from life
itself and are conditioned by that very "vitalism"
which, by refusing to be pinned down, identified and
pigeonholed, eventually drove Claude Bernard out of
his mind.

But there is more: The synthetic imitations of natural products, besides lacking the vital ingredients of
the original, usually contain deleterious substances,
which don't occur in the natural substances that they
pretend to duplicate.

Already two decades ago, the head of the Chemotherapy Division of the British National Institute for
Medical Research wrote an article on "Modern Chemotherapy" in *Medical World* (Mar. 1956, p. 437) in
which he said that "the toxic effects are now becoming
evident and the medical papers are full of instances
where the patient has suffered more harm from this
treatment than he would have experienced from his
original infection."

Thus many years ago top experts in the field have
pointed out that the continuous output of new drugs
is not beneficial, but harmful to mankind. And the
situation has only grown worse since then. And yet
the public health authorities have not intervened.

Clearly, the prevailing system is too profitable to
too many persons.

THE DEVIL'S MIRACLES

In 1961, Dr. Walter Modell, of Cornell University
Medical College, whom *Time* had defined "one of
America's foremost drug experts," wrote in *Clinical
Pharmacology and Therapeutics:* "When will they re-

alize that there are too many drugs? . . . No fewer than 150,000 preparations are now in use, of which 75% did not exist 10 years ago. About 15,000 new mixtures and dosages hit the market each year, while about 12,000 die off . . . We simply don't have enough diseases to go around. At the moment the most helpful contribution is the new drug to counteract the untoward effects of other new drugs; we now have several of these." (*Time,* May 26, 1961)

Considering his high professional standing—he is still today the top authority—Dr. Modell couldn't have made a more candid and revealing confession. But why don't so many already existing drugs suffice? Obviously they don't suffice because they don't cure. They are nothing but palliatives, at best harmless, but usually more harmful than the disease they are supposed to cure; they simulate recovery by suppressing the symptoms, but poisoning the organism and upsetting still further its natural balance.

The analgesics (pain killers) put the nerves to sleep, weakening them, but the trouble that causes the pain continues to develop, without the patient being aware of it, until the damages are irreversible. If a person has a headache as a consequence of intestinal trouble, the drug may sometimes—not always—drive the headache away, but the intestinal trouble will manifest itself later, in a more serious manner. If a person suffering from constipation takes laxatives, these will render the person ever more prone to constipation.

ACTH and Cortisone, hailed as cures for rheumatism and many other ailments, have been found not only to be, at best, short-lived palliatives, but to have effects on the heart, kidneys, liver and nervous system that are much worse in many cases than the original ailment.

The feeling of a "full stomach" is a warning from nature that one has eaten too much, so the valve that insures the passage from the stomach to the intestine refuses to open. Among the so-called "digestives" that are flooding the market, some take over the stomach's digestive task, thus causing it to lose the habit of producing digestive juices of its own, and rendering it less and less efficient; moreover, they intoxicate the liver, aggravating the condition still further. Others artificially cause the opening of the valve, so the food passes into the bowels although not ready for it. Both remedies may afford momentary relief, so the immoderate eater learns to disregard the warnings offered by nature and to listen to the advice of publicity, eating more instead of less, relying on those "miracle drugs": until the intestines develop an ulcer—often a prelude to cancer.

If a person suffers from arteriosclerosis that manifests itself through heart cramps, no heart medicine will be able to prevent further trouble, such as a renal cirrhosis or a stroke. If an agitated person resorts to tranquilizers, they will in the long run ruin the liver, so the person becomes more nervous, or may suffer from mental trouble; to say nothing of the irreversible damages the tranquilizers cause to the eyesight, damaging the retina as well as the cornea.

Arthritic patients who prefer to forget their pains by swallowing pills rather than taking up regular exercise can be sure of only one thing: that their condition will deteriorate; and they can consider themselves lucky if they don't wind up in a wheelchair within ten years. Even more deleterious is the administration of drugs against simple head colds or flus—drugs like antihistamines, which mask the symptoms, or antibiotics, which deprive the organism of its natural defenses and are bound to transform an occasional malady into a chronic one. To say nothing of the suspected cancerogenic effect of most antibiotics: a suspicion that is gaining ever more ground. Just as overdoses of vitamins can cause a variety of diseases including cancer.

A medical commission nominated by Chile's President Salvador Allende, himself a medical man, shortly before his assassination in 1973, had come to the conclusion that in the whole world there are only about two-score medicaments that have a demonstrable therapeutic effectiveness, and that the world's pharmacopeia could be reduced accordingly. (*Nouvel Observateur,* Oct. 20, 1974)

Of course that commission's report remained without any practical effect. Geneva's WHO, the multinational pharmaceutical giants, the health authorities in the various countries, the official medical science, meaning the world's most lucrative professional-industrial complex, have all pretended not to hear.

And it is logical that those who have no scruples about ruining people's health to gain money or fame, can view with indifference, and even with satisfied smiles, the torture of millions of animals. And in fact the pharmaceutical industry bears the heavy responsibility for the constant expansion of vivisection, along with the steady deterioration of public health during the last decade.

In *Drugs, Doctors and Disease,* Brian Inglis wrote that "the figures for animal experiments have continued to rise every year, not because ever better and safer drugs have been coming on the market, but simply because *more* drugs have been coming on the market. Paradoxically, the increase in tests on animals have reflected the growing recognition of how inadequate the tests have been in the past. 'It is a commonplace of biological research,' the 1963 Report of the British Pharmaceutical Industry's Expert Committee on Drug Toxicity has admitted, 'that information from one animal species cannot be taken as valid for any other.' . . . It is no longer, then, a matter of balancing the cruelty of suffering animals against the gain to humanity spared from suffering; because that is not the choice. Animals die to enable hundreds of new drugs to be marketed annually; but the gain is to industry rather than mankind."

* * *

In August 1973, Hoffmann-La Roche, one of the three Swiss pharmaceutical giants—the same one that originated the chemical disaster of Seveso, Italy, in the summer of 1976—announced that it was about to build still another plant near Basel, at the cost of 200 million Swiss francs (more than 60 million dollars), for the exclusive production of Vitamin C.

Vitamin C is most easily available in all the world's drugstores as well as in our daily diet. However, having 200 million loose francs, Roche couldn't imagine a more profitable investment for them than an additional drug manufactory. Meanwhile in nearby Sisseln another commercial enterprise had sprung into being: a breeding center for laboratory animals, mainly beagles and cats, to supply all three Swiss chemical giants— Roche, Ciba-Geigy and Sandoz. By causing some of those animals to fall sick and eventually to die by feeding them artifact diets, which never occur in real life, Roche will "prove" to a gullible public that its synthetic Vitamin C product is indispensable to human health.

Some three decades ago the American public was promised that the daily ingestion of large doses of Vitamin C would surely do away with the majority of ills; that it would at any rate increase resistance to infections, to the common cold and the various flus.

Result: during the decades since then, the number of working hours lost as a result of the common cold and flu have steadily increased—along with the consumption of Vitamin C, which has been present in practically all medicines purporting to cure colds.

A senator from Wisconsin, Gaylord Nelson, charging that widespread promotion of cold medicines "is nothing short of scandalous," conducted hearings in December 1972. On that occasion three prominent doctors warned the Senate Monopoly Subcommittee that there is no known cure for the common cold, that highly advertised cold relief medicines can be dangerous, and that a bowl of hot soup is of more use in fighting runny noses, coughs and sneezes than so-called remedies on the market. (Reuters, *International Herald Tribune,* Dec. 6, 1972)

A leading American doctor, who made numerous studies on the subject between 1942 and 1974, came to the conclusion that "Vitamin C is useless against colds." It was Dr. Thomas Chalmers, president of New York City's Mount Sinai Medical Center, who reported this at the 58th annual meeting of the Federation of American Societies for Experimental Biology, contradicting 1954 Nobel laureate Dr. Linus Pauling. Dr. Chalmers warned against taking Vitamin C pills for a long time, "as there are as yet no data on long-term toxicity." (AP, *International Herald Tribune*, Apr. 11, 1974)

If adding unnecessary doses of Vitamin C to the average diet were merely useless, the advertising of it would represent just another fraud, customary to the industry. But it's worse than that. On August 29, 1974, a medical article in Milan's authoritative *Corriere della Sera* included this item:

"Excessive doses of Vitamin C can cause scurvy in newborn infants, who after birth find themselves suddenly deprived of a high concentration of ascorbic acid."

This is a stunning case. The history of medicine has shown us that intelligent clinical observation has taught that the lack of fresh foods can bring about serious illnesses. The living organism automatically extracts from any natural, unsophisticated and fresh or fairly varied diet whatever vital substances it needs, and eliminates the superfluous. We don't have to find out what a "balanced" diet is. The organism, given half a chance, does its own balancing. But our medicine men fell for the propaganda of the industry, and several years ago started prescribing overdoses of synthetic vitamins to pregnant mothers—especially Vitamin C, which had not yet caused visible ill effects as had other synthetic vitamins.

Meanwhile, however, it has been revealed that overdoses of synthetic Vitamin C also can cause serious damage. It works this way: both the pregnant mother's organism and the fetus learn to eliminate the artificial Vitamin C surplus. When the child is born, it suddenly no longer receives the overdoses of Vitamin C, but its organism is trained to eliminate Vitamin C, and eliminates even the necessary doses of C in its normal nourishment. Thus fatal cases of scurvy have been produced in newborn children, through the same vitamin that, never absent in an average diet, is an insurance against the insurgence of scurvy. Another of the devil's miracles.

But there is more and worse: "There have been reports of excess Vitamin A intake retarding bone growth and causing tumors; excess Vitamin D can lead to damage of the kidneys and the nervous system, sometimes with fatal consequences." So wrote Brian Inglis in his previously mentioned *Drugs, Doctors and Diseases.*

And in fact even the much-vaunted vitamins belong to the miracle drugs that have worked miracles for the maufacturers only.

While Brian Inglis was merely a medical historian, Prof. Guido Fanconi of the University of Zurich was a practicing pediatrician and a medical authority of great renown when he published his own history of medicine, *Der Wandel der Medizin* (Verlag Huber, Berne, 1970). In it he blamed synthetic Vitamin K as having caused, just like sulfa drugs, "acute haemolitic anemia" (often a prelude to leukemia), and denounced overdosages of Vitamin D as responsible for a great number of ills, including severe kidney damages, high blood pressure, and other health hazards.

On pages 141-142 of his book, Prof. Fanconi vents the suspicion that "idiopathic Hypercalcaemia of Infants with failure to thrive" might be attributable to overdoses of Vitamin D—Hypercalcaemia having furthermore proved to be often associated with heart defects and severe damages to the pulmonary arteries.

THE PUSHERS

The just mentioned Prof. G. Fanconi states on p. 59 of his book: "Really frightening is the addiction to drugs among young laboratory workers, secretaries, *et al.* The doctors and the pharmaceutical industry are mainly to blame for this, because the easily influenced youngsters are helplessly in their power."

Of course, the manufacturers of drugs that are not merely inefficient but deleterious to health and often addictive, the doctors who prescribe them, and the druggists who sell them, ought to be arrested and led to jail handcuffed, under heavy escort, as happens to the manufacturers, pushers and peddlers of dope. Most of the patent drugs openly sold by the ton are far more ruinous for human health in the long run than, say, marijuana, which is outlawed in many countries. But what about the governments and legislators who have permitted, regulated, imposed, and usually also subsidized the instauration of such a medical system —which turns millions of consumers into addicts to drugs that are usually very harmful and frequently deadly?

Of course, the system could not have been established without the complicity of the patients themselves. Man has always believed more in the power of magic than of science. Hippocrates' teachings were strictly scientific, based on logic and experience. But they were *too* logical and especially too uncomfortable to follow for a humanity that was growing rich and lazy, liked to overeat and overdrink, and as a consequence was beginning to contract a variety of self-inflicted diseases, like gout, liver and kidney trouble. So the magicians moved in—to stay. They are still here today, having taken over the reins of medical government.

It was in the 13th Century that Frederick II of Hohenstaufen, King of Sicily and Germany, promulgated the first edicts designed to protect the patients from the charlatans and to legalize only the activities of recognized, state-approved "doctors"—a term that was coined in that period. In the course of time, the charlatans took over, making sure that the honest, Hippocratic doctors, who threatened to ruin the lucrative medical trade with simple, natural treatments that benefited only the patients, were outlawed. And, like squids, the state-approved "doctors" started protecting themselves with clouds of impenetrable ink.

Today, "miracle drugs" described with complicated and "scientific" looking chemical formulas have replaced the mysterious abracadabras of the Dark Ages and the magic concoctions that had to be drunk out of church bells to be most effective; and the more in-

comprehensible the new formulas look, and the more
expensive the products are, the more evident is their
psychosomatic effect bound to be, just as in the Middle Ages.

But the fact that the patients themselves are mainly
responsible for this state of affairs is no alibi for
governments and legislators. It is a principle of the
modern, supposedly illumined state that the citizens
should be protected from their own gullibility and
foibles. The state does not allow its citizens to ruin
their health with dope, it does not contend that it is
their own business what they do with their health in
every respect, or even with their money. The modern
state makes it its duty to protect the less intelligent or
more gullible citizens from swindlers. The most notable exception is the medical field, for the governments
themselves have become victims of the prevailing system, partly without realizing it. As a result, the most
powerful professional-industrial complex in the world,
the medical-pharmaceutical, can get away with anything, for whenever something goes wrong, it is called
in to repair the damage it has caused, for a price—
thus doubling the profits. And the medical authorities
deny anyone else the right to sit in judgment over
them, claiming that they themselves are the only "experts" in the field. And this is how they can get away
with producing cancer-causing drugs, selling them at
huge profit, and then to be asked to "treat" the cancers they themselves have produced. The Stilboestrol
tragedy, which is probably only just in its initial stage,
is a case in point.

The responsible government agencies, meaning the
so-called health authorities (the various nations' Ministries of Health, the U.S. Food and Drug Administration, its Geneva-based European extension known
as WHO—World Health Organisation) intervene only
when the deleterious effects of a drug approved after
long animal tests can no longer be concealed, but
then immediately allow it to be replaced by another
drug, which will inevitably prove equally damaging or
more so after a certain time, because obtained with
the identical, fallacious method. This system is today

more firmly established than any other medical system ever was in the history of mankind, although no system has ever been proved to be more harmful. And its basis is the profit motive.

* * *

It all started shortly after World War II, when the affluent society had the possibility of spending large sums of money to allay its constant dread of pain and disease, of aging and death, and made of the drug industry the most profitable enterprise in the world. The manufacturers decided to take over the role of medical education, instructing the doctors directly on how to treat their patients—and in the process on how to make more money. Thus "a drug on the market" became the most familiar cliché for any commodity that is overabundant or in excess of demand.

A steadily growing number of laboratory workers who, like Claude Bernard, had flunked their final examination to practice medicine and had never spent five minutes at a sick man's bedside, but only dealt with mice, rabbits, guinea pigs, dogs, cats and monkeys, were commissioned to concoct "miracle drugs" with which to replace those that were no longer profitable after the public had realized their uselessness or the health authorities could no longer ignore their noxiousness. A massive propaganda financed by growing profits persuaded the doctors to prescribe those new drugs, each of which was advertised as more efficient and less harmful than the predecessors—an evident contradiction, for the more effective a product is in one respect, the more harmful it is bound to be in another.

In May 1961, Dr. Pierre Bosquet had written in France's *Nouvelle Critique:* "Research is strictly subordinated to an immediate commercial profit. Currently, disease is one of the major sources of profit for the pharmaceutical industry, and the doctors are willing agents of those profits."

Of course, not all doctors act in bad faith; on the contrary, they are themselves victims of deceit, of

misinformation received through their formal medical
formation. And since they see that this system is legal,
is agreeable to the patients, and furthermore highly
profitable to themselves, they see no reason to insurge
against it.

However, in September 1974, during an international Congress of Pharmaceutical Sciences in Rome,
Dr. A. Bédat, president of the Swiss Pharmacists
Federation, charged in a press conference that the doctors overprescribe medicaments to such an extent that
the druggists in Switzerland had begun protesting. Dr.
Bédat pointed out that the patients themselves were
not blameless: they refuse the traditional cures, they
want to get well immediately and demand medicines,
the more the better. And the doctors, lest they lose
their clients, humor them.

Like other unionized organizations, whose principal
purpose is to foster their own interests, the medical
class also has fallen into the trap set by the industry.
The trap was baited with the sweet smell of money.

*   *   *

When at the end of the forties the price of penicillin suddenly dropped owing to overproduction, the
doctors began using it indiscriminately, even for minor
flus or common colds, thus depriving the organism of
the faculty to develop its own natural defenses. The
doctors used the available antibiotics—many of which,
like Chloromycetin, were in some cases going to prove
lethal—even prophylactically, before, during and after
operations, without realizing that they were not only
weakening the human organisms, but at the same
time strengthening the various strains of bacteria, to
such an extent that some of them would eventually
defy every type of antibiotics. So modern science had
begun in the forties already producing stronger and
stronger bacteria, and weaker and weaker humans.

The lesson started coming in the fifties, when various hospitals registered outbreaks of epidemics that
no kind of antibiotic was able to control. Brian Inglis
reported that in the U.S. there were over a hundred
such epidemics in a single year, of which one killed

22 patients in a Texas hospital. Official medical science tried to argue that the use of all those antibiotics was justified in spite of the recognized damages, having saved so many lives. But once more the facts speak differently.

John Lear, former science editor of the *Saturday Review,* wrote in a "miracle drugs" article about a study made by Dr. Charles Henry Kempe, University of Chicago medical researcher: ". . . The record shows that prophylactic antibiotics do more harm than good. Dr. Kempe's study cited in this connection the results of 250 'clean' operations. Of these 250 cases, 154 did not receive antibiotic therapy. Among those 154, only 7.8% developed bacterial aftermath. The remaining 96 patients in the test group of 250 cases all got prophylactic antibiotics. Bacterial complications arose in 37.5% of the 96 cases *while they were receiving antibiotics.* 'In our own experience,' Dr. Kempe reported, 'bacterial complications in clean operations are five times as high in prophylactically treated patients.' "

* * *

Gonorrhea, a comparatively minor venereal infection, can become chronic and crippling if untreated. In antiquity, the Romans cured it successfully with a Hippocratic prescription that was slow, but safe and inexpensive: *lectus et lac*—bed and milk, *i.e.* enabling nature, *suprema guaritrix,* to righten the wrong. In my school days it was cured with long-winded and violent antiseptic treatments. Then came the miracle drugs—a pill or a puncture, and within a day the patient was ready for new adventures. But in this case, too, the surviving bacteria developed more vicious and resistant strains, refractory to antibiotics, and perhaps even refractory to bed and milk. In other words, the ancients knew how to cure gonorrhea; today, thanks to modern science, the disease has been reinforced and is spreading. To a point where in 1976 Geneva's WHO felt compelled to sound the alarm, calling for precocious treatment. A recent article in *Le Figaro* (Paris,

Sept. 18, 1976) was titled "A Warning from WHO: Penicillin No Longer Cures Gonorrhea," and read in part: "WHO's warning is particularly important inasmuch as gonorrhea, after a massive withdrawal following World War II, has been staging since 1960 a full comeback. It has become the world's most frequent contagious disease, excepting the influenza epidemics." Another devil's miracle.

And *Time* Magazine had the following to report on November 22, 1976: "Though gonorrhea has already reached epidemic proportions—an estimated 3 million cases in the U.S. alone and perhaps 100 million worldwide—doctors have usually been able to treat it effectively and inexpensively with a large dose of penicillin. In recent years some gonococci strains with a measure of resistance had emerged, but even those stubborn bacteria eventually succumbed to still bigger dosages of the antibiotic. Not the new strains; for the first time, gonococci are figuratively gobbling up penicillin . . . Nobody knows for sure how the gonococci acquired their disturbing new capability."

*   *   *

The damages caused by antibiotics, and by the failure of modern science to understand health, nature and biology, are countless and can no longer be denied. An abstract of a series of articles published between 1962 to 1963 by Dr. Raiga in France's *Bulletin de l'Association Générale des Médecins de France* ("Bulletin of the General Association of the Doctors of France") reads:

"For the past ten years, the number of staphylococcal strains resistant to penicillin has been steadily growing, especially in the hospitals, where we witness a constant increase of the number of serious staphylococcal infections that arise while maladies of a quite different nature are being treated. This is particularly evident in the maternity wards, where epidemics of such infections have reached catastrophic proportions. These current therapies carry definitely the heavy and tragic responsibility of having generalized and aggravated the staphylococcal pathology, whereas they were destined, at least at the outset, to eliminate them . . . These accidents appear even more dramatic when they are caused by antibiotics prescribed for harmless afflictions which eventually would have resolved themselves without any treatment. In such cases the medicament is undisputably *a cause of therapeutic death.*"

It took the so-called medical science in the U.S. ten years longer to catch on than its European counterpart. It was only in December 1972, testifying before the Senate Monopoly Subcommittee, that some Food and Drug Administration officials urged drastic reforms "to deter physicians from prescribing antibiotics for diseases against which they are ineffective and for diseases for which safer therapy is available."

Dr. Harry F. Dowling, presented as an "infection specialist," professor emeritus at the University of Illinois, and former chairman of the Council on Drugs of the American Medical Association, cited data indicating that doctors prescribe 10 to 20 times as much antibiotics as is medically justified. Dr. Dowling went on to say: "A few years ago we were resting secure in the knowledge that we had two effective drugs for use in typhoid fever: chloramphenicol and ampicillin. Then a strain of typhoid bacilli was found that was resistant to chloramphenicol, and now one is resistant to ampicillin. Before too long we may be back to the 1930s, when we had no effective therapy for this disease." Echoing the earlier warnings from France, Dr. Dowling then informed the committee that "resistant bacteria are increasing blood poisoning in hospital patients treated with antibiotics." (*International Herald Tribune,* Dec. 9-10, 1972)

* * *

The number of medical men who are awakening to antibiotics reality is evidently growing, but they just don't know what to do about it, having been led much too far along the wrong road to find the strength or the courage to turn back. According to Rome's conservative *Il Tempo* (July 31, 1976), Nobel laureate James Banielli has declared that "the antibiotics have caused damages that are far superior to their benefits," having been found responsible for chronic conditions, for specific infections, for allergic reactions, cellular toxicity, and vitamin deficiencies.

It isn't possible, not even approximately, to ascertain how many people die as a consequence of medical prescriptions. No doctor is willing to expose himself to a malpractice suit by admitting that a patient died from a drug he had prescribed. Nor will his colleagues like to testify against him, for they are constantly exposed to similar risks. And the cause of death cannot always be ascribed with certainty to a single factor. Drugs don't necessarily cause sudden death. Usually they upset the organism's balance and gradually harm vital organs, eventually leading to precocious death, often in conjunction with other causes.

A disquieting article in the German weekly *Welt am Sonntag* (July 29, 1973) by Dr. Werner Lehmpfuhl, practicing physician in Hanover, stated that "every month a million people are being damaged by treatments that are supposed to help them."

And this applies to Germany only, where 1.5 million people afflicted by rheumatisms keep being treated with medicaments containing Cortisone, although for over ten years now warnings against the danger of this drug have been issued.

A mass of similar charges were brought recently in Germany by a science writer, Kurt Blüchel, who had been press representative for a German medical association and for a drug company, and editor-in-chief of a respected medical journal. His book *Weisse Magier,* "White Magicians," (Bertelsmann, Munich, 1974) raised a storm of angry outcries from the drug industry, which threatened an avalanche of lawsuits and the seizure of all copies. Nothing came of it. On the contrary, the book was reissued in 1976 in paperback (Fischer), its authority strengthened by the industry's failure to make good on its threats. As to the German doctors, they didn't disclaim the author's assertions, but angrily accused him of having "disturbed the rapport of trust that the patients must have with their doctors."

*   *   *

According to Ivan Illich's carefully researched *Medical Nemesis* (Pantheon, New York, 1976) at least 60,000 people died in 1974 in the U.S. because of medicaments, and in some years many more may have died. That new drugs are particularly hazardous for no other reason than that they are preventively tested on animals, was inadvertently confirmed by Dr. William Bean of Iowa State University in his testimony to the Kefauver Committee as far back as 1957:

"The richest earnings occur when a new variety of a drug is marketed before competing drugs can be discovered. Under this system it is impracticable to do tests extending over a long period to establish the range of usefulness and potential dangers from toxicity . . . *Thus after extensive laboratory tests on toxicity and pharmacological properties, but sometimes with a minimum of clinical trial, a drug may be marketed."*

The sense of the discourse couldn't be clearer: Apart from the consideration that we do not need new drugs, as we have far too many as it is (as the topmost pharmacological authority, Walter Modell, has stated), the only valid tests are the clinical experiences, with human patients, which have to be carried out with utmost caution. The "extensive laboratory tests" Dr. Bean mentioned are the trials made on animals, and they are unreliable, hence dangerous for man. But they enable the manufacturers to keep flooding the market with new products—of which the ultimate effect on man only time will tell.

All this could not have been made possible without connivance from above—the various governments' health agencies.

*   *   *

It is of course very difficult to prove complicity between industry and high-placed government officials, but two news writers succeeded in bringing a case in the open that goes a long way toward showing the deviousness of money-greedy individuals. One news writer was Richard Harris who wrote a series of articles in *The New Yorker;* the other was John Lear in the *Saturday Review,* and the high government official involved was no less than Dr. Henry Welch, head of the powerful Food and Drug Administration's antibiotics division, which imposes animal tests for all drugs, and thus influences the health ministries in most other countries.

The articles revealed that Welch was part owner of *Medical Encyclopedia,* an annual antibiotics symposium, and editor-in-chief of two medical journals, *Antibiotics and Chemotherapy,* and *Antibiotic Medicine and Clinical Therapy*—both journals relying heavily for their profits on advertising from the pharmaceutical industry.

Questioned, Dr. Welch said it was "unimportant," since he only received a "honorarium" from those journals. But he declined to disclose in what amount. Dr. Welch was furthermore linked with the promotion campaigns of Pfizer's: His *Medical Encyclopedia* did colossal propaganda for some of Pfizer's new drugs, such as Sigmamycin.

Asked to explain himself before the Kefauver Commission, Welch pleaded illness, but said he would show up nonetheless should his integrity be in any way questioned. His integrity was heavily questioned, but he did not show up.

A witness from the General Accounting Office, who had checked subpoenaed records of his financial affairs, testified that Dr. Welch's honorariums between 1953 and March 1960 amounted to $287,142.40. Shortly before this was revealed in the hearings, Dr. Welch filed an application for retirement, which was quietly granted.

* * *

When Congress provided federal campaign funds for the 1976 presidential election, but not for Senate and House campaigns, special-interest groups simply poured their money through the still open gates of Capitol Hill. And who were the top givers in Senate and House races? According to *Time* Magazine (Feb. 28, 1977), *the medical associations topped all the other special-interest groups,* with $1,790,879, against $1,362,159 given by the dairy committees and $996,-910 by the AFL-CIO committees. And that probably helps explain why some senators and congressmen passionately defend vivisection.

Collusion between health authorities and industry is very widespread, as wherever a great deal of money is at stake, and can take on many facets. In its January 26, 1976 essay, "What Causes Cancer?", *Newsweek* Magazine announced that the Department of Health, Education and Welfare had decided to look into conflict-of-interest charges involving scientists who act as paid advisers to regulatory agencies while getting consultant fees from private companies. And the same year, Rome's daily, *Paese Sera,* reported that a doctor in Palermo was questioned by the local health authorities as to why he was in the habit of prescribing some 30 percent fewer drugs to his patients than his colleagues. When he explained that he considered most drugs useless or harmful, he was put under investigation.

Thus the mental troubles that prompted the first vivisectors of the last century to form generations of disciples to whom "research" became synonymous with animal tortures, were not alone responsible for the spread of the new barbarism which is being palmed off as science. As time went by, to the experiments clearly inspired by sadism or capable of furthering a career were added all those that could increase profits. And from the moment it was discovered that the systematic torture of animals could bring in more money than any other legal activity, there was no hope left for those unfortunate creatures.

Part Seven

DEHUMANIZATION

The Summer 1971 issue of *American Scholar* published an article-debate between monkey-head transplanter Dr. Robert White from Cleveland University and microbiologist Dr. Catherine Roberts. At one point, Dr. White ironized in the following terms about his opponent: "Dr. Roberts repeats with relish the often-used phrase of antivivisection literature 'dehumanization'—of the scientist participating in animal research. This should obviously be classified as a psychiatric syndrome. Fortunately, psychiatrist literature and I are ignorant of this spectacular clinical diagnosis—since it does not exist." (p. 512)

However, Dr. White himself had just used this very term on the preceding page, thus: "I can only assure the readers of the *Scholar* that I have participated for over two decades in animal research in all the areas Dr. Roberts so selectively portrays (behavioral, neurophysiological, parabiosis, and organ transplantation,) that I have visited institutes for experimentation all over the world, and have not witnessed the cruelty or dehumanization that she insists characterizes biomedical animal research."

As I added this article to my file relating to the famous vivisector, my eyes fell on the image of a convalescent little monkey he had operated on—part of an illustrated article in the German weekly *Stern* (Mar. 1, 1973). Dr. White's monkey displayed an impressive scar, which began at the tip of the chin and ran all the way down to the top of the chest. Through that opening the fearless surgeon had cut the monkey's carotid arteries, had drained its brain of all blood, had kept the brain refrigerated for an hour, then had pumped the blood back into the brain and sewn up the mess, to see whether the monkey would survive.

Alas! The poor monkey survived. This experiment was just the beginning of a whole series of new horrors to come, on uncounted other monkeys, eventually leading to the actual transplantation of monkeys' heads upon other monkeys' bodies. I join all those people who regard these performances as nothing but laboratory spectaculars, with no other purpose than, at best, satisfying White's "scientific" curiosity, and probably just providing him with world-wide publicity—which he amply got, at the expense of untold suffering caused to countless monkeys.

And all this clearly is a prelude to new horrors to come for man—when head transplants will be tried on people. Dr. White played it safer than most rainmakers, setting the practical application of his exercises at some 30 to 50 years from now—when he won't be there to answer.

Of course, no thinking person's happiness, much less the salvation of mankind, depends on the feasibility of head transplants. Many thinking individuals believe that the salvation of mankind depends much rather on the speedy elimination of the mentality that spawns individuals like Robert White.

But that is not the point of my discourse. The little monkey of the image was clearly in agonizing pain. Its facial expression could have symbolized the sum of human sufferings through the ages. Half crouched, devoured by pain, it clung desperately with its little hand to the wiremesh of its cage. The lips looked thin and drawn very wide, in an agonized grin. The huge eyes, staring at an incomprehensible world, seemed lost, and looked enormous in the emaciated, fleshless face, its skin clinging to the bones. One foot, which had served for god only knows which "scientific" investigation, was bandaged, and clumsily so.

My point is the following: An individual such as Dr. White who has admittedly toured vivisection laboratories all over the world and performed practically every senseless animal experiment extant, including parabioses, and is nonetheless able to declare that he has never witnessed cruelty, demonstrates that he has reached a degree of dehumanization as total as can ever be reached.

THE BIG LAUGH

This chapter could be long, but it shall be limited to just a few items. The first I found in Robert Clarke's enthusiastic biography of Claude Bernard:

"Magendie, the director of the *Collège de France,* never prepared his lessons, but gave his pupils the spectacle of his doubts, and then he interrogated nature. When he ventured to foretell a result, the experiment proved exactly the opposite. Magendie, then, joined in his audience's hilarity."

What an idyllic description! It could evoke some jolly picnic among the beauties of nature—provided we didn't know that the *Collège de France* was the Medical School's physiological laboratory, and the experiments through which its director "interrogated nature" —and whose always unexpected outcome made professor and pupils burst out laughing—were vivisections.

Dr. Du Prel relates a "comical" incident that he witnessed at the University of Munich. For an experiment on nephritis, a dog already solidly fastened to the operating table was carried in and set up in front of the students. Blood was trickling from an empty orbit. The professor in charge explained to his students that the wound they saw was not related to the experiment on the program, but that a while ago another professor had needed an eye. This explanation, according to Du Prel, caused a burst of hilarity among the students.

Other medical students laughed, as German Dr. Herbert Frische wrote, recalling the first period of his university studies, when on witnessing the classical experiment of Pavlov's dog, they saw the look of pained surprise on the hungry animal on discovering that the food it was swallowing dropped at its feet through the severed gullet.

Also Prof. Otto Cohn found the endlessly repeated

Pavlov's dog experiment "very amusing." (*Münchner Medizinische Wochenzeitschrift,* Mar. 30, 1902)

On January 31, 1903, a debate took place at the Institute of Physiology of Bern University, Switzerland, between its director, Prof. H. Kronecker, and Magnus Schwantje, German writer and philosopher. Only medical students were present: The disgust that the argument always inspires had once again kept away the general public. When Prof. Kronecker said, "It is impossible that vivisectors perpetrate the cruelties you accuse them of, because, being physiologists, they respect life more than anyone," Schwantije countered simply by reading out loud from the vivisectors' own published works. That was before the time the experimenters had learned to clad their reports in anodyne language and benign euphemisms. At every mention of animals being boiled or skinned alive, of organ extirpations, of exposure of the spinal cord and other sick deeds, the students burst into howls of laughter, making it impossible for Schwantje to continue.

I have collected plenty of evidence showing that experiments that cause sudden death to animals represent a source of merriment for the "scientists" involved. A picture in *The New York Times* of November 26, 1973, showed two such researchers identified as Dr. Bernard Lown and Dr. Richard L. Verrier at Harvard laboratory, laughing delightedly as they tease a dog suspended from a body sling. The dog receives electric shocks until he dies. The experiment "proved" that it takes less electricity to electrocute a dog helplessly suspended than when he is resting on the floor of his cage.

This chapter could be illustrated with photographs published in various papers, such as the German weekly *Quick* (Dec. 26, 1965), taken at the Medical Academy of the University of Tulane, New Orleans, when 200 rhesus monkeys were sacrificed to "study" crash accidents. As if there were not enough medical histories of real car accidents the scientists could have used if they were seriously interested in what happens to man, and not to monkeys—who are many times more resistant and elastic than man, and thus can only give misleading answers.

Each monkey was strapped to an impact sled and sent crashing against a wall. Some died from a broken neck or smashed chest, or were merely severely injured, so the pseudoscientists could make further studies on them at the taxpayers' expense.

The little monkeys of Tulane knew what was in store for them, having witnessed their companions' smash-ups, and were terrified. And in several images that showed them struggling with the white-robed scientists who were tying them to the vehicle, these men—identified as "pathologists of the University of Tulane" in the captions—were laughing heartily at the useless efforts of their little victims. And one of those laughing "pathologists" was furthermore tickling the screaming rhesus under its armpit.

* * *

P. S. The Tulane experiments inspired another "scientist," Dr. Warren M. Crosby of the University of Oklahoma, to repeat them with pregnant baboons, for which he was awarded a federal grant of $103,800 and an article in *Medical Tribune* (Sept. 5, 1968).

No images of Dr. Crosby's experiments were released, so we don't know whether the Oklahoma pathologists also laughed while tying their pregnant baboon ladies to the impact sleds. We only know that other American scientists thereafter felt that they, too, rated a slice of the federal pie. So in its June 1969 issue, *Clinical Medicine* reported still another smash-up test, in which numerous monkeys were subjected to whiplash and other impact injuries "to ascertain the amount of energy needed to produce brain concussions." The "scientists" involved in this project concluded that "velocity determines the degree of damage" —something any three-year-old who ever pedaled a tricycle could have told them.

Of course these experiments were an inspiration to the rest of the confraternity, who went about demolishing vehicles and monkeys all over the United States and Japan. Smash-ups with pregnant baboons especially fascinated the mad scientists and editors of the pseudo-scientific journals. The November 1972 issue of *Surgery, Gynecology and Obstetrics* reported one more such "experiment."

This time the pretext for sponging more federal or private funds was the alleged testing of safety belts that wouldn't cause injury to the fetuses of women involved in car crashes. Of course, these experiments revealed nothing that the airlines hadn't known for many decades, when they decided to adopt safety belts, which had not been tested on animals but had been developed by the simple exercise of uncorrupted mental faculties.

CORRUPTION GROWTH

That vivisection, being inhuman, has a dehumanizing effect on those who practice or even just stand by it, is self-evident, inescapable. In its March 1932 issue, *Medical Times* stated: "The moral damage caused by vivisection isn't only general but individual. What is the inevitable effect on the medical students' morals? It isn't difficult to provide examples showing that vivisection causes the vivisectors' moral sense to degenerate."

It isn't indeed difficult to provide examples, on a world-wide scale. Among the mass of complaints that reached the Italian Anti-Vivisection League, one letter concerned the case of a rabbit which after an experiment at Milan's University had been left bleeding all afternoon and through the night, bound to the contention board, for culinary reasons: one of the attendants wanted to cook it the next day.

After a demonstration to the students, the professor usually deems the postoperative observation necessary, allowing the victim to recover from its more or less effective anesthesia, or else goes to lunch, abandoning the dying animal to the attendants. These are no tenderhearted animal lovers, otherwise they would seek a different employment. And seeing how their superiors —who are bigshots, famous surgeons, university professors, presumably personalities of culture and substance —treat the animals, the attendants all too often feel encouraged to let out on the helpless victims those famed sadistic instincts that lurk in so many human beings and keep coming to mind whenever the topic is vivisection.

In Rome, by order of the sanitary authorities, the animals that die in the laboratories must be buried in special inhumation pits, located off the city limits, alongside the road to Ostia. Oftentimes, vivisected dogs are found buried alive in those pits. Following one such finding, charges were brought against Rome's health department, Rome's municipality and one of the city's major hospitals, *Istituto Tisiologico Forlanini*. Reporting the news, the *Messaggero* (Dec. 22, 1971) included this description:

"From one pit, the head and half the chest of a German shepherd protruded, its eyes wide open, its tongue hanging out. All around, the ground bore the signs of the animal's desperate attempts to dig itself out before dying."

In general, the small animals that have served their purpose are killed by getting their heads banged a few times against the sharp edge of a table. An Oxford professor assured Richard Ryder, the clinical psychologist at Warneford Hospital, that in his laboratory the rats were "humanely" destroyed through quick disemboweling.

Another example of how alien the concept of compassion is to the laboratory subculture, and how incomprehensible the motives of their critics: When the U.S. Army caused a public outcry in 1974 for wanting to test new poison gases on hundreds of beagles, the Army "scientists" in charge of the lucrative project proposed to use pigs instead of beagles.

Surgeon Stephen Smith contributed this testimony to the second *Royal Commission Report*:

"The first time I saw a brutal experiment on an unanesthetized animal I wished to leave the room, I was sickened by it. The next time I was less affected, and with every experiment I was less affected, and eventually I was able to look on at the most terrible things without my emotions being moved in any way . . . I submit that what occurred in my own case probably occurs to everybody . . ."

* * *

The progressive blunting of human feelings, which occurs inescapably in all those who engage in systematic torture, is an extremely serious matter. As vivisection is being practiced on an increasing scale and in ever more countries—in the Third World's new republic, medical teachers trained in the West nowadays show off their "scientific" prowess by repeating before their gaping pupils the experiments of Claude Bernard and Company—there is a constant, world-wide increase of the number of individuals who get conditioned to disregard the sufferings of other sentient beings, and to perpetrate inconceivable cruelties as if they were commendable acts.

Since this attitude has been allowed to spread from the physiology classes to all the other fields of medicine, the scientific torture has now come to loom large even in psychology teaching. A growing percentage of psychologists and psychiatrists are made to witness or participate in experiments in which all sort of animals are being driven to insanity through every physical or psychological torture that diseased human minds are able to devise.

Thus the miasma of dehumanization is contaminating also those medical people to whom mental patients look for help—and the law makers studiously ignore the danger of such a state of affairs. The international health authorities—starting from the thoroughly infected World Health Organization and the United States Health Department, who provide the guidelines for all other countries—are not merely blind to this danger, but are part of it.

The callousness of present-day medical scientists manifests itself also in the way they express themselves, as when in the scientific publications the patients are referred to as "the material." Or when in his *New Horizons in Psychiatry* (1971), Prof. Peter Hays writes (p. 103): "The screening of new substances by means of animal tests is at present rather primitive in spite of the elegance of the experiments themselves." Clearly, for today's medical scientists the term "elegance" must have a different meaning than for common mortals.

Of course, Dr. Robert White of Cleveland also merits to be cited in this connection. In relating some of his monkey-brain transplants in the July 1971 issue of *Surgery,* he used with deep earnestness such grotesque technicalese newspeak as: "These experiments demonstrated that it is possible to vascularly transplant the isolated cephalon to the isolated body at the primate level." And further: "All four of the cephalic exchange transplantation preparations survived; their periods of viability ranged from 6 to 36 hours. In 3 to 4 hours each cephalon gave evidence of awareness of the external environment by attempting to chew or swallow food placed in its mouth. The eyes tracked the movement of individuals, and the cephalons remained basically pugnacious in their attitudes, as demonstrated by their biting if orally stimulated." (Though noting the monkeys' hostility when further plagued by "oral stimulation," Dr. White at least didn't seem offended, as his colleague H. F. Harlow would doubtlessly have been, that the cephalons felt no desire to kiss the hand that had severed them from their original bodies.)

But then, during the already mentioned debate published in *American Scholar,* Dr. White fearlessly ventured into the dangerous realm of abstract thought:

"I believe," philosophized the famous vivisector, "that the inclusion of lower animals in our ethical system is philosophically meaningless and operationally impossible, and that consequently antivivisectionist theory and practice have no moral or ethical basis." And further: "The preoccupation with the alleged pain and suffering of the animals used in medical research may well represent true psychiatric aberrations."

As the term "alleged" means "asserting without proof," and Dr. White applied it to the sufferings of laboratory animals, he showed a total ignorance of animal physiology—a very serious scientific aberration in a neurophysiologist; but not surprising, since in time vivisectors lose all sense of reality, and hence move further and further away from the scientific truths. And then our hero went on record with the following statement:

"Perhaps both Dr. Roberts and I owe the readers of this journal an apology for having consumed so many pages on discussing a topic of such little relevance today"—the topic in discussion, which Dr. White considered irrelevant, being whether man has the right to torture.

Dr. White belongs furthermore to the growing number of medical "researchers" who think that censorship should be exerted over "scientific" news. So when Italy's Oriana Fallaci reported for an American magazine the carnage she had witnessed during one of his experiments with monkey heads, Dr. White not only lamented in a paper that the reporter had "tried to humanize the baby gorilla by comparing it to a child" (clearly a heinous crime in Dr. White's eyes), but also referred to her report as an "unauthorized article."

Long before that, Clarence E. Richard, who very effectively directs Chicago's National Anti-Vivisection Society, had cited another memorable phrase by a famous American vivisector of his town, Prof. George Wakerlin of the University of Illinois Medical School (Chicago): "I want nothing to do with anything having the word 'humane' connected with it." (*The National Magazine*, June 1954)

If there are individuals who share Dr. White's view that a sense of humaneness and compassion "may well represent true psychiatric aberrations," there surely is a larger number of people who think that the total absence of these human qualities, as admitted by Robert White and George Wakerlin and others of their ilk, represents a far more worrisome form of psychiatric aberration.

CONSEQUENCE AND CAUSE OF MENTAL TROUBLES

"The physiologist is not a man of the world, he is a scientist, a man caught and absorbed by a scientific idea that he pursues; he no longer hears the cries of

the animals, no longer sees the flowing blood, he sees
only his idea; organisms which hide from him problems that he wants to discover. He doesn't feel that he
is in a horrible carnage; under the influence of a scientific idea, he pursues with delight a nervous filament
inside stinking and livid flesh that for any other person
would be an object of disgust and horror . . ."

So wrote Claude Bernard in his classic *Introduction*
(*op. cit.*, p. 154), and English writer John Vyvyan
surmised that if the high priest of modern vivisection
had lived in our Freudian days he would not have
published those lines, for they afford a textbook example of one of the gravest mental diseases known to
psychiatry, of which Claude Bernard represented a
typical case, and of which probably no vivisector is
entirely free: paranoid schizophrenia.

As a mental patient Claude Bernard had plenty of
company among vivisectors. So his famous Russian
disciple, Elia de Cyon, wrote in *Methodik der Vivisectionen* that "the vivisector must approach vivisection with a sense of joyous excitement."

Now it shouldn't be very hard for anyone to find the
exact definition of the "sense of joyous excitement"
with which that Russian physiologist used to approach, knife in hand, his trembling victims, securely
strapped down to the Czermak table.

E. E. Slosson, professor of chemistry at the University of Wyoming, wrote in *The Independent* (New
York, Dec. 12, 1895), under the title "The Relative
Value of Life and Knowledge": "A human life is
nothing compared with a new fact. The aim of science
is the advancement of human knowledge at any sacrifice of human life. If cats and guinea-pigs can be put
to any higher use than to advance science, we do not
know what it is. *We don't know of any higher use we
can put man to.*" So here is one more vivisector to
whom the value of a human life—excepting, of course,
his own—is unimportant compared to a new fact and
figure. And once more the endless repetitious tortures
are not even thought of.

Dr. Ludimar Hermann, late professor of physiology
at Zurich University, had the honor of being quoted

by Lord Dowding in the House of Lords on October 14, 1952, for having gone on record with this statement: "The advancement of knowledge, and not the utility to medicine, is the true object of vivisection. No true investigator thinks of the practical utilization of his research. Science can afford to dispense with this justification with which it is still obliged to defend itself in England." (Contradicting his own words, this same Prof. Hermann proclaimed on another occasion: "Each dog that you subtract from vivisection costs you a human life.")

In 1953 another university figure declared: "The infliction of the most acute agony on an infinite number of animals is justified if in the opinion of the least member of any medical faculty there is the slightest chance of adding to the sum total of human knowledge, and this without reference to the question whether this additional knowledge promises to be of any practical value or not."

Words of an insane individual? Clearly. However, this individual was Dr. Walther Meek, at the time research professor of physiology at the University of Wisconsin, and it was in this official capacity that he testified before a Senate committee of the Wisconsin legislature at a hearing in Madison on a bill as to whether or not to turn impounded dogs over to medical laboratories.

Even when they were not familiar with Freud, most of the people I saw reading a list of experiments couldn't help exclaiming sooner or later: "But these people are crazy!" One said: "The main impression one gets is one of stupidity."

In the language of psychiatrists, the term "craziness" does not exist, nor does "stupidity"; but in the vocabulary of common mortals they do. And whatever term one wants to use, it is clear that the major number of vivisectors are mentally deeply deranged people. According to Austrian philosopher Johannes Ude, "The vivisector is a morally underdeveloped individual with pathological tendencies." Which means, in poor man's language: "The vivisector is mentally very sick."

On August 27, 1928, long before Prof. Ude made

that statement, the *New York Daily Mirror*'s medical columnist, who signed himself "Medicus," had written: "Does it not seem that those who are cruel to animals are diseased? Ought they not to be secluded in mental homes?"

In many asylums for the criminally insane, for example the *Manicomio Criminale* at Aversa, near Naples, the registration form includes the question whether there are any precedents of animal abuse in the patient's medical history—animal abuse being a familiar symptom of insanity in psychiatry.

As a rule, when a vivisector, who otherwise seems normal, discovers that he is confronted with some investigating antivivisectionist, his face undergoes a sudden alteration, he may be seized by uncontrollable anger, may start trembling, stuttering, and inevitably manifests deep mental agitation, exactly like a schizophrenic whose "id" is suddenly exposed, or certain insane persons accused of madness. I have seen this happen time and time again.

It happened to me not long ago with a neurologist from Zurich, university professor Konrad Akert. My polite request for an interview about the results of his experiments on the brains of apes elicited from him a furious tirade against antivivisectionists, and he slammed down the phone; nor did he acknowledge my letters in which I repeated my request. Equally unanswered went my inquiries addressed to that university's rector, a biologist. Although Zurich University operates with public funds, in matters of vivisection it considers itself justified in imposing censorship upon a Swiss citizen like myself who wishes to find out what goes on in its animal laboratories. In Switzerland, as in other countries, medical science is the hegemony of an arrogant, presumptuous clique which sets itself above public opinion, above government, above laws, restrictions or regulations, to achieve a totalitarian dictatorship of their guild, in which no outsider may interfere.

A short time later, on Oct. 23, 1973, Zurich's daily *Neue Zürcher Zeitung,* officious mouthpiece of Switzerland's Establishment, reported a symposium denominated "Foundation for Fundamental Research of Human Sciences," no less, to which convened "scientists of nature and of thought, of different directions."

The neurobiologists were represented by the above-mentioned Prof. Konrad Akert, and the newspaper carried excerpts from his address, including:

"It is important that man should know better the extension and limits of the stage on which the human drama takes place, before we start developing new ideologies, philosophies and ethics."

So this Prof. Akert, who at Zurich University contributes to forming tomorrow's physicians and scientists, thinks that we shouldn't allow ourselves to be hampered by any ideology, philosophy or ethics. He considers it more important that man should prod into the animal brain, by means of vivisectionist experiments; although they evidently haven't taught him anything about man, for he went on saying:

"Modern brain research tries to investigate the structure and function of the brain. Since it must work on the live brain—we already know the dead one, and it hasn't advanced us—modern research must take recourse to animal experimentation. Hence we experience a continuous embarrassment, as it wasn't possible to extrapolate directly on man the information obtained from animals."

It gets wearisome to read vivisectors' conclusions over a period of 150 years, all stating the same thing: That results obtained on animals cannot be extrapolated to man. But it certainly isn't half as wearisome on the readers as on the animals involved.

INSANITY IMPARTED

Didactic or pedagogical vivisection, with which teachers repeat ad nauseam for their students experiments already described in the course of the last century in countless physiological treatises, represents the elementary training of obtuseness and insanity.

To illustrate his assertion that a fire requires oxygen, a teacher may cover a burning candle with a glass bell, so the students may see the flame gradually fading out; this is an intelligent demonstration, which makes an academic lesson stick. But when a teacher drops dogs or rats into a tankful of water to prove that over-exertion eventually leads to a heart attack, he merely demonstrates his own stupidity, for he does not realize, or does not care, that he is conditioning his pupils to cruelty, and that the students hate to see this kind of spectacle, unless they are already mentally deranged. Any sane student is willing to take the teacher's word rather than being forced to witness the drowning of helpless animals.

In the *Yorkshire Post* of Aug. 13, 1975, the paper's education correspondent Mark Parry wrote that the cutting up of animals by children in school laboratories could be such a gruesome business that some children had nightmares, others had fainting fits in the classroom. Some children have been known to run away from school. One instance was cited where a boy who had been looking after a guinea pig heard that it was to be cut up in the next biology class. He ran away, and later was found in a barn sheltering the guinea pig.

On June 26, 1975, Elizabeth McGill of Maryland's *Westminster Times* devoted her column to the subject of vivisection in American public schools and colleges. Among many students who were appalled by what they had to witness, she cited Ellen Berkenblit, 17, of Yorktown Heights, N.Y., who told her: "Dipping a live frog in ether during sophomore biology was really disturbing, especially since the frog came to life during surgery. If I had a choice I would have gotten out. Other kids also felt it wasn't appropriate. The teacher told us it would teach us to appreciate life, which I found ironic."

The columnist stated further: "Educators such as George K. Russell, an Adelphia University biology professor, contend that biology has largely forgotten that organisms are alive. He has been asking his college freshmen to write their reaction to experiments. Over half support his view—that vivisection leaves the young with 'feelings of disgust, disrespect and alienation.' Russell and others argue that such experiments teach little that could not be found in an elementary textbook, but much more about the insensitivity toward life."

The professor who stimulates the nervous system of an animal to demonstrate to his students its functions —an excruciatingly cruel exercise, which of course rules out any anesthesia—has blunted his own feelings about the matter, having performed the same experiment many times before; and by and by this indifference infects his pupils.

Furthermore, a double inversion of values takes place: 1) Personally insensible (so far as the sufferings of his victims are concerned, of course—not his own), the teacher has convinced himself that the animals are insensible, and reassures his students to that effect; and most students are glad to believe him, also because "man is always prone to accept as an absolute truth what has been taught him" (Claude Bernard). 2) Obviously affected by some serious mental disorder, the teacher has convinced himself, and tries to convince his pupils of it, that the psychopaths are not the vivisectors, but those who oppose them.

The students who refuse to conform have usually no choice but to renounce the study of medicine, as many talented individuals like Johannes Ude and C. G. Jung were obliged to do, although they would have been eager to serve medical art.

Ude, the Austrian, withdrew after four years of studying, because he was increasingly appalled by the vivisections he was made to witness, but then obtained four other doctorates, was ordained a Catholic priest, and became professor of philosophy at the University of Graz. Jung—the Swiss psychoanalyst who made such terms as archetype, extravert and introvert universally familiar—withdrew from the study of medicine and chose psychology instead (before psychology also embraced vivisection) because he couldn't suffer the vivisectionist exhibitions, which in his book of memories, *Erinnerungen, Träume, Gedanken,* he defined "barbarous, horrible, and most of all superfluous."

A recent American news item read: "A teacher in a Minneapolis public school classroom, performing biology-class experiments, hits two puppies on the head with a hammer to 'anesthetize' them, and slits the animals' bellies to show his tenth-grade students the intestinal tracts. Periodically, the puppies revive and are promptly hammered into unconsciousness again." This item, which appeared in the *St. Paul Dispatch* of February 22, 1973, also stated that after a horrified student had told his parents about it, they informed the Minnesota Humane Society, who couldn't do more than see to it that the teacher was blandly admonished.

A vivisectionist teacher doesn't pass on to his students merely his own callousness, but something much more serious. The first vivisection the pupil is made to witness means a shock to an as yet uncorrupted juvenile mind. The young persons feel with sure instinct that they are witnessing a dastardly crime; but their teacher says it isn't so, that the act is right and necessary, and thus he or she upsets the entire ethical world in which the young people have been raised. The cruel deed not only hurts their natural feelings; it also makes light of all the ethical precepts received up to date. Point-blank, the young persons are told that might makes right, and that the worst cruelties are justified if a hypothetical advantage can be derived from them. Who says so? The teacher, who speaks on behalf of the country, the authorities, the parents. Thus the students, however horrified, keep silent.

As more such shocks follow, the young persons become calloused—a new, different personality is created in the young mind, starts emerging from the original personality, and doubles for it. Outside the laboratory, the students know that they should respect the laws, which claim to be based exclusively on justice and humanity. But inside the laboratory they witness and participate in acts of abominable cruelty as if they were the most natural things in the world, and even commendable; until the young psyche is irreparably split, dissociated in two separate entities. The student—tomorrow's physician, surgeon, biologist—has contracted one of the most serious mental diseases known to psychiatry: schizophrenia, usually of the paranoid type.

Jung was among those who managed to escape, changing over to a different subject; but he didn't have the courage to protest until many years later. And like Jung, the other students didn't dare dissent, any more than most of today's students dare dissent: thus allowing the red canker of Bernardism to spread and perpetuate itself in the seats of learning that form our society.

* * *

Schizophrenia is the most frequent, but hardly the only mental illness that afflicts vivisectors. Claude Bernard, in his terminal years, suffered in addition from manic depression (a psychiatric term not yet coined in his day), as his letters and the unexpurgated edition of *Médecine* clearly indicate.

A colleague of his, Prof. Blanchard, having become blind, kept seeing the eyes of the cats he had tortured staring at him from out of the dark, until he went out of his mind, and on his deathbed kept raving and imploring his family to remove all those eyes that surrounded him. And Flourens, Claude Bernard's successor, roamed during the final years of his life at nighttime the *Jardin des Plantes* in Paris, howling and barking like the dogs in his laboratory.

But there have also been vivisectors who woke up to the realization of their own past follies when faced with the final reckoning. One was John Read, the Scottish physiologist mentioned at the beginning of Part Three. As he lay dying in early middle life of cancer of the tongue, and the spreading cancer affected the very nerves he had so frequently experimented on, he wrote: "This is a judgment on me for the pain I have inflicted on animals."

Small consolation for the victims of his past exploits. And surely many interesting cases could be revealed about our contemporary "scientists."

* * *

While many medical students are appalled by their teachers' show of inhumanity, others inevitably get hardened and, by and by, feel encouraged to try out the instruments of their future profession on stray animals. In many medical schools the professors advise or demand some vivisectionist exercise as the basis of the final dissertation.

Example, among the mildest: Dip the rear half of a live rabbit into boiling water. When the scalded part has become one big hairless sore, you can graft pieces of skin on it and apply several types of ointments, then report how the sore reacted during the few days the rabbit can be kept alive.

Of course, this sort of exercise isn't of the slightest use to the student's future profession; on the contrary. The animal's skin reacts quite unlike human skin; for instance, it becomes edematous, instead of developing the boil that is the usual feature of burns in man; but the experiment serves to obtain the degree. And it will provide a degree to an individual who through this experiment will have acquired dangerously wrong notions in respect to the treatment of human patients.

Now one of those rabbit experiments was done in Naples, Italy, by a medical student I know personally. And in a speech on vivisection at the House of Lords on July 18, 1957, Air Chief Marshal Lord Dowding told his peers the case of a doctor friend who was appalled by the inhumanity he had found prevailing among laboratory workers:

"What particularly struck him was the callous attitude of people who were otherwise normal, decent members of society . . . When a young man who was joining together rats was asked, "What on earth can be the use of this experiment to humanity?", he answered: 'I don't know what good it is going to do to humanity, but I know what good it is going to do to me: it is going to get me my degree.' "

In 1974 Germany's largest paperback publisher, DTV, flooded the newsstands with a book titled *Zoologische Experimente,* explicitly aimed at "school children between 14 and 18 years old," and containing instructions on how to vivisect various small animals, like mice and guinea pigs. Example: "You place the mouse on the table and hold it fast by the tail. If you suddenly pull up the tail while you exert pressure on the neck of the mouse by means of a closed pair of scissors, you will hear a crack, which indicates the fracture of the spine." (p. 367)

So the systematic blunting of the human qualities doesn't begin at university level, but much sooner. And the trend comes from the U.S.

"Each year about a million high school students compete for prizes in science fairs where they are encouraged to conduct horrifying, gruesome and inhumane experiments on animals," wrote Dr. Barbara Orlans in America's muckraking *National Enquirer* (Sept. 3, 1972). "These students are taught a kind of sanctified torture, and they are rewarded for these efforts. More than 50,000 animals a year are mutilated tortured and subjected to terrible pain by these young hands. And it's all being done under the protective guise of 'science.' The judges of these fairs are usually science teachers, scientists or school officials."

At an International Science Fair in Cobo Hall, Detroit, an 18-year-old high-school boy demonstrated a dying monkey with pus-exuding holes in its head as an example of his skill at implanting brain electrodes; he won first prize and a mention in *The New Scientist* (Jan. 9, 1969).

Are we quite sure this is the society we wish to build? Is this the world we want to leave to our children?

SADISM

Sadism is one of mankind's most appalling mental diseases. Like all serious illnesses it should be treated, and in many cases, if caught early enough, it can be cured. The practice of vivisection not only fosters this disease, but is likely to cause it.

There are mentally sick individuals whose quirk makes them take delight in murder—often just because it amuses them to "observe" how the victim reacts when stuck with a knife. In the past such individuals were hung or quartered, or at least held in irons to the end of their days, to protect society. Nowadays, they are put into specialized institutions for the criminally insane and subjected to psychiatric and also chemotherapeutic treatment.

But when this same killer instinct is directed not against man but against animals, including primates whose intelligence and sensitivity, according to psychologists, can equal and sometimes surpass that of some human beings, then it is encouraged and rewarded by the present-day Establishment—as evidenced by the fact that nowadays it seems difficult to obtain a Nobel prize in biology or medicine without torturing animals.

Dr. François Dejardin, former chief surgeon of the hospitals of Liège, Belgium, wrote these revealing words: "Every sane person trembles at the sight and smell of blood, and resents the sacrilegious shudder that in these individuals is a sign of delight. I have seen horrible looks in their eyes, exultant and proud of the spilled blood, and in which one could read the satisfaction for the advantages obtained: pecuniary advantages, or of renown."

François Dejardin has been dead many years. But there is a more recent document, a 392-page volume published in 1962 by the U.S. government, oddly titled *Humane Treatment of Animals Used in Research: Hearings before a Subcommittee on Interstate and Foreign Commerce, House of Representatives.* (U.S. Govt. Printing Office, Washington, D.C.)

The word "sadism" kept cropping up during testimonies of the many different people belonging to government, universities, or industry. Most of them had been eyewitnesses and all are named.

Sample extracts:

Page 218. "In any class of medical students you can always spot a certain number with sadistic tendencies."

Page 264. "There is no check whatever upon the wasteful repetition of experiments for which the taxpayer pays; no check on careless planning; no check on the outright sadist, who surrounds his real subconscious motive with a fog of scientific terms."

Page 250. "Trying to produce convulsions in dogs is terrible. I know they wouldn't let you see that, though. Shock experiments, removal of organs, blocking intestines, or the urine outlets so the bladder ruptures are only run of the mill . . . You'd be surprised to hear what professors and some students can think up. At night I keep thinking about the dogs. Imagine, after you have major surgery and you are between life and death . . . your little square of cold, draughty, cement flooring is cleaned by having a hose of cold water squirted over you. The dogs are soaked by this cold water—dogs right after recovering from surgery. No wonder most of the dogs die. If they live, within a couple of days or a week, they are used for a different experiment. One dog survived seven experiments."

Page 251. "I am a student studying veterinary medicine. I was never and am not now in the employ of any humane society . . . This is a cry and a plea from a young person still holding on to a few ideals I have grown to believe in—and I am beginning to wonder if there is any real humane goodness among humans. I am not a sentimentalist, a crusader, or a fanatic; but I cannot, under any code or way of human life, condone what I, in a few short years, have seen."

Page 311. "I recently asked a young physician how the newer medical students can judge the need for sedatives if the dog has been 'devocalized,' as the scientists phrase it. His answer was startling. He said: 'It is the prevalent attitude in medical schools now that dogs can't feel pain—dogs do not suffer.' The prevalent attitude: meaning, in the simplest terms, that medical students are encouraged to believe that drugs to relieve the animals' pain are not required . . . they cannot feel it. That theory is an astounding example of scientific hypocrisy. If a research worker can seriously reject the idea that animals suffer, how dependable are his conclusions from the results of his experiments? . . . Without a basic understanding of pain, its causes and its significance, what kind of doctors are being turned out by the medical schools today?"

Page 346. "I attended Chicago Medical School last September. I withdrew of my own accord . . . One of the conditions which led to my contempt towards this school was the cruel treatment which was given to the experimental animals."

*   *   *

At times it is hard to decide whether experiments invented in American medical colleges, then promptly imitated elsewhere, ought to be ranged under the heading, "Dehumanization" or under "Insanity"; like some of the cases reported in those House of Representatives Hearings of 1962; of experiments which had no other purpose but the infliction of unprecedented mental agony and physical pain—university teachers and students banding together in devising brand-new, drawn-out tortures for the favorite scapegoat of their own mental troubles: the hated cat. And then they rushed to publish the "results" in the pseudoscientific journals whose only reason for existence is the publication of suchlike reports.

Following, a transcription from page 226 of the U.S. government publication of those hearings: "We come now to some of the methods by which animals are tormented by an amazing variety of 'noxious stimuli' or, to put it plainly, stimuli that hurt. At the University of Oregon [a footnote reads: *Journal of Neurophysiology*, 21: 353-367, 1958] noxious stimulation was applied to cats by means of 'a noxious level of heat in wires on the floor . . . and pin prick.' The responsiveness of some of the animals to the pricking of their paws would cause them 'to leap into the air and frequently hit the top of the test apparatus. If they landed on the pins, they would jerk their paws aside vigorously on every contact, sometimes even trying to balance on the forepaws with the hindpaws in the air.'

"Since 1928 researchers at Johns Hopkins University [footnote: *Proceedings of the Association for Research in Nervous and Mental Diseases*, 27: 362-399, 1948] have been inducing fear, rage, and other manifestation of distress in cats. In a typical study, the researchers report: 'Postoperatively, quite intense and nociceptive stimuli were applied . . . During the 139 days of survival she was subjected, every 2 or 3 days, to a variety of noxious stimuli . . . On one occasion her tail, shavened and moistened, was stimulated tetanically through electrodes connected with the secondary of a Harvard inductorium. When the secondary coil was at 13, she mewed; at 11 there was loud crying . . . At the end of the 5-second stimulation she screamed loudly and spat twice. The last of these stimulations produced a third-degree burn of the tail."

We are still on the same page 226 of the official U.S. document: "At Cornell University [footnote: *Archive of Neurology*, 1: 203-215, 1959] researchers destroyed the sight, hearing, and sense of smell in cats and then *for a period of 10 years* applied such stimuli as (*a*) electric shocks delivered via a metal grid covering the floor, (*b*) blows to the face with a plastic fly swatter, and (*c*) pinching of the tip of the tail."

So in one of America's highest seats of learning a group of cats have been mutilated—made deaf, dumb, and unable to smell, through massive surgical operations—and then further systematically tortured for a duration of 10 years, at the hands of so-called scientists presumably engaged in the noble task of "alleviating mankind's sufferings." Is it really surprising when we learn that in the pediatric ward of that same university, various prematurely born babies (human) have been submitted, at an age varying between 5 and 8 days, to "noxious stimuli" by a team of "scientists"? Probably to "alleviate the sufferings of mankind."

* * *

Vivisectionists are never at a loss for an alibi, and experience tells that when they can't palm off as "scientific experiments" examples of sadism run wild such as the aforementioned, they will say that they represent aberrations of the past.

Not so. On the contrary. These aberrations are spreading, multiplying, fostered and spread by the medical colleges and university faculties, mainly in the

U.S., from there corrupting the rest of the world. A recent example was revealed by Roger Simon in the *Chicago Sun-Times* of July 25, 1976, with an article titled "Is There a 'Demonstrable Practical Value' in Killing Cats?", and beginning thus:

"I have never written a story about animals. I just have never met one with something interesting to say. Now, I have changed my mind. There was a story the other day in a New York newspaper about animals. It was not your typical story.

"It was about experiments being conducted on cats by a very famous New York museum.

"The experiments, which were financed with half a million dollars in U.S. tax money were to find if the following things, when done to cats, affected their sex lives:

Blinding by the destruction of the optic nerve;

Deafening by the destruction of a portion of the inner ear;

Eliminating the sense of smell by the destruction of the olfactory center of the brain;

Removing nerves in the male sex organs of kittens;

Surgically injuring sections of the brain:

"Electrophysiological" testing in which the cats die after electrical stimulation to their genitals.

"Now you and I, not being scientists, would look at these experiments and say something stupid like, 'Well, of course, these things would affect the sex life of a cat!' Or, we would say something silly like, 'Do we really need to spend half a million dollars to find out?'

"But then you and I are not scientists.

"The American Museum of Natural History has conducted these experiments for 14 years. In 1974 it did these things to 74 cats. It continues to do them today. And it would like an additional $200,000 in tax money so it can continue to do them for the next five years.

"The sex lives of cats are apparently more complicated than any of us thought. I suppose there is some value to studying the sex lives of cats—if you are another cat, for instance, or running a feline dating service. I'm just not sure how badly we need to know these things.

"So before the museum moves on to higher mammals, I would like to give them a hand. Speaking from my own area of expertise—I have been a human for a number of years—I can tell the museum right now not to bother experimenting on human beings.

"I can assure the museum that blinding me, that deafening me, that destroying parts of my brain, and that electric-shocking me would have a very definite effect on my sex life—it would, at the very least, make it tougher to get dates.

"It is just a shame that the cats couldn't speak up and let somebody know.

"The museum has been picketed by some bleeding hearts who claim that these experiments serve no useful purpose, that they do not solve any pressing medical problem, and that they are not designed to cure any disease or save any lives. But the museum was ready for that kind of nonsense.

"The director, Dr. Thomas D. Nicholson, said, 'If anything has distinguished this museum it has been its freedom to study whatever it chooses without regard to its demonstrable practical value. We intend to maintain that tradition.' "

RELIGION

Every religion can and should contribute to refining the human spirit by including in its teachings the idea that the love of animals is one of the many facets of universal love, and by condemning the opposite as a sin against creation. Perhaps because it evolved in a land or in a population—the Mediterranean—that by tradition wastes little love on animals, the Catholic Church has chosen to take the opposite stand. And yet there are enough grounds in the Scriptures for advocating compassion toward animals, apart from the touching scene of the infant Jesus warmed by the comforting breath of the ass and the cow, the frequent reference to Jesus as the Lamb of God, and the extraordinary story of the ass of Balaam, which saw and understood what its master was incapable of seeing and understanding.

Saint Thomas Aquinas, whose anthropocentric teachings flattered human vanity and justified the worst abuses of animals, provided a doctrinal basis for the Church's contempt of animals, and for deriding St. Francis of Assisi's invocations that animals are worthy of man's respect and love. St. Francis—whose altruism, not limited to animals, prompted him to despoil himself of all earthly goods to help his destitute fellowmen—had centered an important scientific target by listening only to his intelligent heart. He had already discovered in the period of darkest obscurantism that the animals are even closer to man on the psychological than on the biological level. Obtuse vivisectors keep resorting to cruel experiments without end in order to "discover" this obvious fact.

*   *   *

To Schopenhauer, "Christian morality contains the great and essential imperfection of taking into consideration only man, and leaving the entire animal world without rights."

In ancient Egypt the cat had been declared sacred by the clergy, in order to protect this most persecuted of all animals from the blind hatred of the mob. Five centuries before Christ, Gautama the Buddha was preaching compassion for all creatures, man and animals alike: "I shall teach pity to the human beings and shall be the interpreter of all dumb creatures and soothe the boundless suffering, which is not only of man." And the Koran: "There is no beast on earth nor bird which flieth with its wings but the same is a people like unto you . . . All Allah's creatures are his family."

Man's cruelty to animals is exclusively a result of

ignorance and moral turpitude; but there are some religious laws that try to thwart the manifestations of those sick instincts, and in this the eastern religions are superior to the western ones.

In Italy, the rare prelates who have tried to intervene in favor of the animals have always been promptly discouraged from on high. Not so outside Italy. Some hundred years ago in England, Cardinals Manning and Newman were among the major promoters of the first antivivisection society, and in many countries today there are a good number of Catholic clergymen, low and high, who participate prominently in the antivivisection movements.

The English cardinals minced no words in their condemnation of vivisection. Cardinal Newman: "Now what is it moves our heart, and sickens us so much at cruelty shown to poor brutes? I suppose this: First, that they have done us no harm. Next, that they have no power whatsoever of resistance. It is the cowardice and tyranny of which they are victims, which makes their sufferings so especially touching. There is something so very dreadful, so satanic in tormenting those who have never harmed us, and who cannot defend themselves, and are utterly in our power."

No less forcefully did the Austrian priest and philosophy professor Johannes Ude express himself when he wrote: "A God who would approve vivisection would only frighten me immeasurably. If vivisection were permitted by Christian ethics, I would turn my back on Christianity." Johannes Ude died in 1965, just in time not to hear the Vatican's spokesman endorsing vivisection.

In France, Jean Gautier, a writing and teaching priest with a doctorate in Canonic law and philosophy, wrote a bestselling book about his dog: *Un prêtre et son chien* (1957), "A Priest and his Dog." Together with other French priests he addressed in vain requests to the Vatican to denounce vivisection.

And in *Revue Défense de l'Homme* (Cannes, France, Sept. 1971) one René Ansay wrote:
"The Catholic Church doesn't like animals and

doesn't hide it: she has never wanted to spend one word against vivisection, nor against any of the other cruelties that man commits against animals. But the Church blesses the fox hunts, usually reserved for the affluent devout, and blesses their hounds. This is one of the rare occasions when the Church invokes the divine protection upon animals—when man lets them participate in his own cruel games. And the Church continues to maintain in the *plazas de toros* the chapels where the torturers confess themselves and invoke the Virgin's protection before initiating their infamous exercises."

Alas! René Ansay has committed the sin of optimism. The Church of Rome has not merely ignored vivisection, but has bestowed upon it her seal of approval if it is true, and it is, that the Archbishop of Perugia, Monsignor Ferdinando Lambruschini, the Vatican's spokesman, has written in the Vatican's Sunday paper:

"There are some propaganda campaigns that the Church cannot approve, for instance against the experiments of a scientific nature on living animals. The Church isn't even opposed to the vivisection of the beasts, from which so much help comes to the progress of medical science." (*Osservatore della Domenica*, Mar. 13, 1966)

It wouldn't be charitable to point out to the Church of Rome that she has allowed herself to be hoodwinked in regard to the alleged help that has come to medical science through the torture of those creatures that by inveterate habit she calls "the beasts": She is not alone in having been so deceived. But she must be blamed for having thus missed still another opportunity of proving herself the Church of the oppressed and the helpless, rather than of the rich and the mighty.

In his article, Monsignor Lambruschini did not forget the pious recommendation that the beasts' sufferings should be "kept down to a minimum, which nowadays can be easily achieved through general and local anesthesia." But to make sure that he wouldn't thus be suspected of being an animal lover, the Archbishop promptly added: "On the other hand, it is certain that the sufferings of beasts, devoid of intelligence and liberty, cannot be put on the same level as the sufferings of men, who are endowed with reflection . . ."

So it was to nobody's surprise that in a round-table debate on vivisection arranged by one of Italy's state radio stations in May 1971, the Italian vivisectors obtained moral approval from a Jesuit Father Giuseppe De Rosa, S.J., who was introduced to the listeners as a "moralist" of *Civiltà Cattolica*—the official paper of the Jesuit order. This "moralist" did not limit himself to support in his official capacity the vivisectors present; he deplored the attitude of antivivisectionists. Then he added the usual sanctimonious admonition that "the beasts should, of course, be spared unnecessary suffering."

No such gingerly tip-toeing was evident in the opinion the head vivisector from Cleveland, Dr. Robert White, obtained from his spiritual comforter for the debate in the Summer 1971 issue of *American Scholar*. Dr. White, who in numerous interviews had proclaimed himself "a good Catholic," knew whom to consult in order to get an ecclesiastical endorsement of his views. "I took the liberty," he wrote, "of forwarding a copy to the Jesuit theologian, Father Nicholas A. Pedrovich, of John Carroll University in Cleveland." This "theologian" gave the vivisector his full approval, furthermore ridiculing the humanitarian arguments of his adversaries.

And in his yearly pilgrimages to Rome, this same Dr. White has so far never failed to be received in private audience by the Pope. And one might well wonder what the two rich and mighty talk about, while millions of innocent animals with cannulas in their skulls and drains in their abdomens languish in their wire-mesh prisons, their only unconscious hope being that death will release them before the white-robed devil comes around again to submit them to one more experimental session.

Another gentleman who had no difficulty in being received by the Pope was Monsieur Ricard, famous in France as the manufacturer of the namesake *apéritif*, for promoting bullfights, and for his contributions to the Vatican's coffers.

But when in 1967 an interdenominational delegation of Catholic and Protestant high prelates, including eminent representatives of the Catholic Bishopry of Westminster and the Anglican Bishopry of Worcester, went on pilgrimage to Rome to plead for more humaneness toward animals, they were not even received by the Pope, who delegated his secretary, Cardinal Cicognani, to ward off the bothersome petitioners with mealy-mouthed banalities.

*   *   *

To have produced a handful of universal geniuses like Leonardo da Vinci, who shone as a writer, artist, scientist, engineer, inventor, augur, philosopher is considered by many thinking individuals the only justification for the existence of the human species on earth. He prophesied—and in the meantime most of his forecasts have come true—that some day men will look upon the killing of an animal as today we look upon the killing of a human being. If recognition of the animals' moral value is any token of progress in man's own moral evolution, the Church of Rome has moved backward, especially in our century.

In his Papal Bull *De salute gregis* of November 1, 1567, Pope St. Pius V formally forbade bullfights, threatened excommunication against the princes who organized them, and ruled out ecclesiastical burials for the men who had been killed in them, stating: "We consider these spectacles contrary to piety and Christian charity, and we wish to abolish these bloody and shameful spectacles which are worthy of demons and not of men." In the following centuries, the Vatican tacitly continued to show its disapproval of bullfighting by every Pope's refusal to receive officially people connected with the corridas. But in 1972 Pope Paul VI broke this humanitarian tradition by receiving, addressing and blessing a delegation of Spanish bullfighters.

The Church's longest step backward was, of course, her official endorsement of vivisection in 1966 under the reign of that same Pope. Actually, it was the ultimate effect of a "new" policy that began when the Church, in an ill-advised effort to "modernize" her battered image after the blunder committed with Galileo—who had been forced by the Holy Inquisitors to recant his assertion that the earth moves—decided that it would be smart to let the pendulum swing all the way in the opposite direction, and embraced blindly the new "scientific" spirit that was sweeping Europe, evidently not realizing that from religion mankind expects guidance of a different sort.

The Church's present attitude puts her on a spot. For just as she was eventually obliged to recant her own view on the motion of the earth, she will sooner or later have to recant her view on animals in general and vivisection in particular, and the sooner she does so the better for her. Such pious recommendations as "anesthesia should be used wherever possible" only aggravate her position, adding hypocrisy to inhumanity. Nothing short of total, official repudiation of vivisection can help her at this point.

Ironically, while the Catholic Church openly despises animals, denying not only that they have a soul but even a "free will," the behavior of most animals comes much closer than man's to the ideals so fervently and so unsuccessfully preached from the pulpits. So, excepting the domestic species that for millennia have lived in close contact with man, most animals lead strictly monogamous lives. The wolf is monogamous, but its domestic derivative, the dog, is quite the opposite, probably due to its long association with man. When a robin's mate dies, it will live on usually in a widowed state to the end of its remaining life. Animals know gratefulness, one of the qualities most notably lacking in man, and compassion, which in praxis is none too frequent in human beings.

And who is closer to the Christian concept of God—the cats which following their Creator's design spend several days in vocally anguished courtship, or the outraged monsignori who periodically order all the cats and their litters clubbed to extinction by the Vatican's gardeners? The stray bitch that goes hungry in order to feed her offspring, or the priest who smashes this bitch's head against the sacristy wall because "the

beast had desecrated the House of the Lord" by leaving
her calling card under the pews? The swordfish which
for days follows the trawler that has captured its mate
and finally, unable to free it, dashes upon the beach to
die at her side, or the fishermen who blind their catches
to keep them fresh and alive but unable to escape?

The argument that animals allegedly don't have an
immortal soul doesn't justify our abuse of them, but
aggravates it. The knowledge that they won't be indem-
nified in another world for their sufferings in this one
should prompt us to treat them more kindly, not less. It
is hard to understand how the alleged ownership of
spiritual immortality could excuse the torture of creatures whose terrestrial existence is the only gift they
have received from their creator.

"To a man whose mind is free," wrote Romain
Rolland, the French Nobel laureate author, in *Jean-
Christophe,* "there is something even more intolerable
in the suffering of animals than in the sufferings of
men. For with the latter it is at least admitted that
suffering is evil and that the man who causes it is a
criminal. But thousands of animals are uselessly butch-
ered every day without a shadow of remorse. If any
man were to refer to it, he would be thought ridiculous.
And that is the unpardonable crime. That alone is the
justification of all that men may suffer. It cries vengeance upon all the human race. If God exists and
tolerates it, it cries vengeance upon God."

Convinced that in the whole universe nothing is as
important as *his* life, *his* well-being, *his* pleasure, man,
self-styled Crown of Creation, takes it for granted that
he may inflict any suffering he chooses upon the dumb
animals; and a Church that barely a century ago considered it normal to celebrate All Saints Day in Italy
by burning barrels full of live cats in the town squares
(young vandals still do it in Rome and other Italian
cities today, and not only on special holidays), has
contributed notably to such an attitude. Strange
charity, which excludes the most defenseless creatures,
and sanctions the atrocities committed against them on

the contention that the torturer is made in the image of God. Some Image!

An Italian nun used to write me touching letters from her remote convent, adding newspaper clippings about animal abuses, and recommendations never to write to her, so as not to compromise her, "because love for animals is not viewed favorably here." One day all her literature on animals was confiscated and she was transferred.

So the love for animals is not only discouraged by the Church of Rome, it seems to be feared. Is the Church perhaps afraid that the Devil—whose existence or non-existence was passionately debated by nine top-notch theologians in the *Osservatore Romano* of December 17, 1972—hides among "the beasts"? Although I am no theologian, I can assure the Church that if the Devil exists, it is not among the animals that he will be found.

But there is little doubt that if the animals believed in the Devil, to them he would look remarkably like a human being.

P.S. Vivisection is practiced in a steadily growing number of American parochial schools.

Part Eight

THE REBELLION

Each action causes a reaction: And so it is no coincidence that the same man who first succeeded in palming systematic torture off as science, Claude Bernard, also provoked the first organized antivivisectionist movement in the world—the British one. And then his widow and daughters, first-hand witnesses of so many horrors that had taken place in their own home, started the French antivivisection league, of which Victor Hugo, who embodied not only the intellect but also the spirit of France, was proud to accept the presidency in 1883, declaring in his inaugural address: "Vivisection is a crime!"

The British movement was sparked one century ago by Dr. George Hoggan, the English physiologist who had studied in France and whom Claude Bernard had engaged as his laboratory assistant. But four months later a nauseated Dr. Hoggan gave up his job, returned to England, and in a long letter that appeared in the *Morning Post* on February 1, 1875, denounced the horror and uselessness of the experiments he had witnessed, and the inhumanity and cynicism of those who performed them. Excerpts:

" . . . I am of the opinion that not one of those experiments on animals was justified or necessary. The idea of the good of humanity was simply out of the question, and would have been laughed at, the great aim being to keep up with, or get ahead of, one's contemporaries in science . . . I witnessed many harsh sights, but I think the saddest was when the dogs were

322

brought up from the cellar to the laboratory. Instead of appearing pleased with the change from darkness to light, they seemed seized with horror as soon as they smelt the air of the place, apparently divining their approaching fate. They would make friendly advances to each of the three or four persons present, and, as far as eyes, ears and tail could make a mute appeal for mercy eloquent, they tried in vain . . . Were the feelings of experimental physiologists not blunted, they could not long continue the practice of vivisection . . . Hundreds of times I have seen when an animal writhed with pain, it would receive a slap, and an angry order to be quiet and behave itself . . . To this recital I need hardly add that, having drunk the cup to the dregs, I cry off, and am prepared to see not only science, but even mankind, perish rather than have recourse to such means of saving it . . ."

When Dr. Hoggan wrote this, nobody could guess that vivisection not only lacked the power to "save" mankind from anything, but that it was going to harm it more and more, through the wrong information it was going to provide, and by corrupting the vivisectors' character; but there were already many other people who considered that if humanity was willing to take recourse to such sordid means in order to save itself, it wasn't worth saving.

Hoggan's letter set on fire the public reaction of the nation that was in the vanguard not only of all humanitarian causes but also of medical science. Immediately an antivivisection league was founded, with the support of some of the most illustrious names of the day, including Tennyson, Ruskin, Carlyle, Browning, Lord Shaftesbury, Wagner, Victor Hugo, and Queen Victoria, who charged her Prime Minister Disraeli with naming a *Royal Commission of Inquiry into Experiments on Animals*.

The Commission interrogated a long line of the most eminent doctors and scientists, including Charles Darwin and Robert Koch, and its *Report* effected the approval within the coming year of a bill aimed at restricting severely all vivisection experiments by subjecting each one to previous approval. Known as the

"Cruelty to Animals Act, 1876," that legislation provided the basis for similar laws in all countries that have since decided to regulate vivisection.

The most notable exception is the United States, where well-paid lobbyists, with huge sums from the pharmaceutical industry at their disposal for influencing votes of both Houses, have managed to defeat any bill that was being introduced. And yet the United States had been second in time only to England in organizing an antivivisectionist movement.

However, even where regulations existed, experiments kept spreading. The laws designed to protect the animals are nowhere fully enforced; not even in Great Britain, where at the time of this writing there are only 14 inspectors, who lack both the time and the will to act in the spirit of the law and pay surprise visits to the laboratories. They are busy sitting at their desks, examining the requests from 18,000 licensed British vivisectors, and writing out permits for the approximately 5.5 million yearly experiments palmed off as "necessary" to the welfare of mankind.

In Great Britain, not even a member of Parliament, on which legislation of vivisection depends, has access to the laboratories. Vivisection in Great Britain is no different from other countries, nor could it be. Just as elsewhere, the secrecy demanded by the vivisectors is endorsed by the government: It is forbidden to take pictures or films of experiments done in Great Britain —proof that the government hasn't a clean conscience about it.

* * *

All animal causes have one big handicap compared to other humanitarian causes. The first advocates of social justice could unionize the working classes, who had a selfish interest in the cause. Those who first advocated women's equality in England could rely on the women as allies, just as those who first fought for Negro rights in the U.S. knew that the Negroes themselves would eventually take on the brunt of the fight and insure success. But those engaged in animal causes get no help from the animals, and have only themselves to rely on.

As far as the abolition of vivisection is concerned, the cause faces an additional handicap, as it can't even rely on all the animal lovers, because most of them find the subject too horrible to approach. And then, like many average citizens, there are also a good number of so-called animal lovers who hope that *some* good might come to them from the vivisection of animals after all.

Having never taken the trouble to investigate that kind of experimentation, and thus never discovered the unmitigated barbarism and quackery it represents, many uninformed people resent the antivivisectionists, and bandy about words like "progress," which must not be thwarted by "sentimentalism"; just as in the Dark Ages their likes viciously attacked as antihumanitarians and heretics those who disapproved of witch hunts and religious torture, since the tortures allegedly served to save the sinners' souls; and up to the last century those who had vested interests in slavery accused their adversaries of hating humanity, of wanting to wreck the economy, and the children to starve as a consequence.

Konrad Lorentz, supposedly an animal lover and Nobel Prize-winner (1973) for his studies on animal psychology, never held forth against vivisection. Although his reports of his own observations and experiments don't seem to imply any cruelty, in the original (German) edition of his most famous book, *Das sogenannte Böse,* ("On Aggression" is the English title), he cited without disapproving it a particularly cruel and senseless experiment done by his two "assistants," W. and M. Schleidt, who surgically "destroyed" the sense of hearing in turkey hens, to "study" how that would affect their behavior toward their newly hatched chicks. "The deafened turkey mothers immediately hacked their newborn to death," Konrad related (p. 174), adding that this unmotherly behavior must not be necessarily ascribed to their inability to hear the chirps of their young, for the surgical injury might have affected the mother instinct in other, unknown ways. Not for a moment did it occur to the Nobel Prize psychologist that the turkey hens may have preferred to see their chicks dead rather than helplessly exposed to the whims of man, just as the baboon mothers prefer to decapitate their children rather than surrender them to the laboratory workers. Even without criticizing it, Lorentz thus gave one more example of vivisectionist folly and futility.

In 1975 Prof. Bernard Grzimek, another world-famous German "animal defender," endorsed vivisection in an editorial in *Das Tier,* the zoological magazine of which he was editor-in-chief together with Konrad Lorentz, using the very same words and arguments of vivisectors. Thus he showed, in my estimation, that he had never bothered to investigate the question from the scientific and historic point of view, let alone the humane point of view. Vivisectionist propaganda presented by supposed animal-defenders like Lorentz and Grzimek are the most formidable bulwark against abolition.

Whenever abolitionists want to advocate their cause, they find all the most important doors closed to them, including the Vatican's. When famous vivisectors, disguised as philanthropists, set forth to sing the praise of animal experimentation they find the most important doors open to them, including the Vatican's.

*   *   *

Antivivisectionism is a one-way street. Those who opt for abolition after studying the question never change their minds again, whereas many vivisectionists, and even vivisectors, have been prompted to recant by experience and maturity.

The antivivisectionist movements don't depend necessarily on people who are particularly fond of animals, but they rest on normal, intelligent humanitarian concepts, like the movements that in the past fostered the individual liberties, and the abolition of religious, racial, and sexual discrimination. Someone who intervenes against a sadist who abuses a child need not be inordinately fond of children. Said John Vyvyan, the

Shakespearean scholar who wrote two great books denouncing vivisection*: "You may wonder why I wrote those books. I am not an animal-lover to any unusual extent. I loved my dog, now dead, but every normal human being loves his dog if he has one. But when I discovered this particular form of cruelty, it did more to shake my faith in human nature than anything else. To me this was a blot on our civilisation. I felt I had to try to do something to get that blot removed."

Albert Schweitzer is better known as a philanthropist than animal lover. But the last of his famous "messages to the world" from his bush hospital in Lambaréné, delivered a few weeks before his death in 1965, concerned vivisection. Addressed both in French and German language to the World Congress for Abolition, which was being held in Zurich, it was also read on the Swiss TV station and said:

"We must fight against the spirit of unconscious cruelty with which we treat the animals. Animals suffer as much as we do. True humanity does not allow us to impose sufferings on them. We have come too late to this realization. It is our duty to make the whole world recognize it."

It is because even a man as great as Albert Schweitzer had needed the experience of a long lifetime to come to such a conclusion that I said before that antivivisectionism is a sign of maturity, and by the same token its counterpart is a sign of infantilism, of mental retardation, when not of something much worse.

THE MORAL SENSE

Man is a moral creature. The moral sense is so deeply rooted in human beings that no thief, no murderer has ever asked the abrogation of the penalties against theft and murder.

All the laws that have ruled human organization in

---

* *In Pity and in Anger*, 1969, and *The Dark Face of Science*, 1971, both published by Michael Joseph, London.

the past and rule them at present are based on the
moral sense: on what is right and wrong. And no religion, no legislature has ever deemed it necessary to
define right and wrong, because no one has any doubt
as to the meaning of these terms.

Only the worshippers of the pseudoscience of modern times regard morality and immorality, justice and
injustice, good and evil, as anti-scientific concepts,
*since it is not possible to reproduce them in a labora-
tory*.

Anybody who like Italy's Prof. Silvio Garattini can
declare that an artificial hormone, fabricated in a
laboratory, is identical—in every respect—with a
hormone produced by a living organism, will never
comprehend the moral law, as the moral law can't be
exposed by a surgeon's lancet nor reproduced in a
test tube. And that explains also how monkey-head
transplanter Dr. Robert White from Cleveland can
affirm that "dehumanization does not exist," only because, having himself lost or never possessed the notion of humaneness, he is incapable of noticing its
absence; and can say that the animals don't suffer,
simply because he is not sensitive to their pains—
only to his own. Asked Thomas Wolfe: "Is there no
light because the blind can't see?"

The reasonings of the vivisectionists are unscientific
because they don't take into account the intangible re-
alities of life. The moral law is one such intangible
reality: And it is the incomprehension of this reality
that marks the inescapable failure of experimental science when applied to living beings, with its inevitable
sequence of tragic errors.

* * *

The moral sense is at the root of pity. Pity means
compassion—the capacity to resent someone else's
suffering as if it were one's own. The absence of pity is
a mark of obtuseness: incapacity of identifying oneself with those who are in pain or downtrodden.
Worthy of pity are mainly mistreated or bereaved
children, the old, the sick, all those that are helpless
and abused. This includes the majority of animals.

And we mustn't ask ourselves whether or not they are able to go to heaven, whether or not they are able to reason, or to speak, or to count, or to vote, but we must ask ourselves only one question: "Are they able to suffer?" And it is their misfortune that they are only too able to suffer.

"Pity dwells not within a fool, but in wise men," wrote Euripides 25 centuries ago, and in modern times Thomas Wolfe dressed up this ancient thought in rich and splendid robes when he wrote in *Look Homeward Angel:* "Pity, more than any other feeling, is a 'learned' emotion; a child will have it least of all. Pity comes from the infinite accumulations of man's memory, from the anguish, pain, and suffering of life, from the full deposit of experience, from the forgotten faces, the lost men, and from the million strange and haunting visages of time."

People who have suffered and yet have no pity, evidence a worrisome callousness of the intellectual and human faculties. Among the survivors of the Nazi concentration camps there were some former vivisectors, who—including a woman—went straight back to the laboratories as soon as they were liberated . . .

Centuries of anthropocentric religious education—indicating man as the central fact, the final aim and end of the universe—have taught us to regard pity as an exclusively human quality. But it isn't so, for we have seen that the animals are also capable of compassion—and this proves that pity, whatever Thomas Wolfe said, is also a natural feeling, or an instinct, so the individuals who lack it are unnatural beings. And unfortunately, such unnatural beings occur mainly in the human species.

Animals can kill their offspring or let them die by refusing to nurse them, but only when they are captive of man (in the zoos, on transports, in the laboratories) or if circumstances make it impossible to raise them. Those are true cases of euthanasia. But man is the only being in the world able to kill his own child because it disturbs him in his sleep. In England 700 children die every year from parental beatings. And nobody can tell how many other times this cause of death is not discovered, not to mention how many children survive the maltreatments.

Dr. Theo Solomon, director of the Institute of Law and Social Process of Teaneck, N. J., told a seminar at Texas Woman's University: "Violence is built into our society, and child abuse, unrecognized as a major problem until the early 1960s, is a part of it. There are 7 million abused children in the United States today." He added that New York City had 86 child-beating deaths the preceding year; 240 more deaths might have been caused by abuse or neglect, he said. (*International Herald Tribune,* Apr. 13, 1974)

On February 14, 1975, the same paper reported in an AP article by John T. Wheeler: ". . . And Dennis became one of an estimated 30,000 to 50,000 children who died in 1974 as a result of child abuse. Approximately 45% were under the age of four. Many thousands of others are crippled, maimed, twisted psychologically or rendered mentally defective by child abuse. Dr. Ray Helfer, a nationally recognized authority, says the number of children under five who die each year because of this growing problem in the United States exceeds the number of children in that age range who die of disease."

If we are to judge by the way the offspring is treated, animals, overwhelmingly as a whole, are much better than people. It will be difficult to prove that they are worse than people. And that we have a moral right to submit them to tortures.

*   *   *

History teaches that when a new religion takes hold, the gods of the old one become the devils of the new. Love, or sentiment, or whatever, used to be the gods of the former religion, the supreme ideal of all thinking and feeling individuals. Now for some people Science has become the new established religion, and scientists are its priests. The most prestigious profession among the youths of those countries that are considered "progressive," such as the United States, is the scientist's; and science is the new religion to which sacrifices—both human and animal—are callously brought by stolid, white-robed priests, and which is unquestionably accepted by an unthinking herd-population, for whom "sentiment" has become a dirty word.

Sentiment, of course, survives. In fact, it is as in-eradicable as sex, which for centuries had to hide, could not be openly discussed or shown. But as sex has recently come out into the open, and one can at last speak about it and show it, sentiment had to go underground. It is no longer socially acceptable. Even the various "help-for-the-starving-third-world-children" appeals must be advertised as being ultimately profit-able for the givers. If they were based on sentiment and neighbor's love alone, they would cause suspicion or derision. In today's world, sentiment has taken the place of sinfulness that used to belong to sex. Not only is "sentimentalism" the principal charge brought against the antivivisectionists, but it is also the charge that is most heatedly denied by the antivivisectionists themselves, as if it would brandmark them as social lepers.

The majority of vivisectors blandly invoke the argu-ment of Herod and Hitler that the aim justifies the means. But apart from the fact that the alleged advan-tages of vivisection do not exist, the argument that cruel acts are no longer despicable if we can derive a material advantage from them is simply unacceptable.

In fact the only justification for the vivisection of animals that I can think of is religious—if one ac-cepted the blind point of view of Descartes and the Church of Rome in regard to animals, based on St. Thomas Aquinas' contempt of them. The religious question is irrelevant anyway, because it cannot be proved empirically that we humans have an immortal soul any more than it can be proved that animals have not got it. What has been proved time and time again is that St. Thomas, who was so influential in forming the opinion of today's Catholic Church, couldn't have been more wrong in regarding the animals as creatures devoid of reason, will, and sentiment, and Voltaire—one of the brightest intellects mankind has produced—didn't hesitate to accuse him of smallness and narrow-mindedness. Incidentally, and characteristically, to St. Thomas' mind women, too, were devoid of soul.

But actually few vivisectors would endorse the theological opinion of total difference between man and animals. On the contrary, their similarity is the very pretext for the entire vivisectionist practice. However, people who affirm that there is no difference between man and animal on the biological level, and not even on the psychological one—as the continuous behaviorist experiments prove—how can they claim a total difference on the moral plane?

Vivisectionists have a very simple answer: Since man is the most intelligent species—and *they* have no doubt about this—he has *ipso facto* the right to do what he pleases with all other living beings.

But if intellectual superiority really constituted a moral right, then it would also be permissible to vivisect the idiots, the retarded, the illiterates, the gypsies, the blacks, the communists, the capitalists, the Protestants, the Swiss, and indeed all those people that someone, according to one's personal opinion, considers inferior on the intellectual, moral, religious, political, racial, national, cultural and any other level. And doubtless it would be permissible to vivisect vivisectors, whose intellect, according to many psychologists, is below that of many apes.

Moreover, if it were right to torture laboratory animals for the benefit of mankind, then it would also be right to torture one man for the benefit of a hundred men. In fact any argument that justifies the vivisection of animals is equally valid for the vivisection of human beings.

People willing to allow unlimited animal tortures for a hypothetical advantage for themselves would probably be equally willing to let other human beings suffer for such a hypothetical advantage. "After all, some good might come out of it for *me* someday," seems to be the reflection of this silent majority, whose moral sense can be put at just about the same low level as their scientific knowledge.

And yet I am convinced that if everything that goes on in the laboratories were known to all the people, the overwhelming majority—except the outright sadists and animal haters—would for once forget the natural human selfishness and call for a halt.

* * *

In all countries the antivivisectionists are divided into two factions—"controlists" and "abolitionists," who both accuse each other of hampering the progress of the cause. The controlists include some doctors and veterinaries who claim that they want the "abuses" of vivisection outlawed, but not the "indispensable" experiments, usually without going on record as to which ones they consider "indispensable."

Abolitionists point out that the whole history of medicine hasn't brought forth one single case of an animal experiment that has been irrefutably useful for man, whereas the misleading answers, causes of immeasurable harm and endless tragedies, can't even be counted. And since vivisection is also morally wrong, it can only be outlawed, not "regulated."

If something is morally wrong, no amount of legislation can make it right. The abolitionists further contend that abolition would immediately cause medical science to progress, obliging it to abandon the wrong road, and to concentrate on the more dependable alternative methods of research, and especially on the far more effective preventive medicine, which harms nobody, not even the citizens' pocketbook—but is therefore financially unrewarding.

* * *

Vivisection is responsible for other sufferings than the ones directly inflicted upon the uncounted animals and human victims of an erroneous medical science. It is also responsible for the very real, drawn-out sufferings of all those who can't shut out of their minds the thought of the continuous tortures deliberately inflicted. Only vivisectors and animal haters will shrug or laugh off those sufferances.

"This daily crime, which keeps us awake at night," wrote Dino Buzzati, the Italian author. And the thought of it was so unbearable to Richard Wagner that he felt it influenced his entire creative work. In one of his three essays on vivisection he wrote: "The thought of their sufferings penetrates with horror and dismay into my soul, and in the sympathy evoked I recognize the strongest impulse of my moral being, and also the probable source of all my art. The total abolition of the horror we fight against must be our real aim. The vivisectors must be frightened, thoroughly frightened, into seeing the people rise up against them with stocks and cudgels. Difficulties and costs must not discourage us."

I was reminded of Wagner the day a very beautiful young woman from France, a schoolteacher, came to see me in Rome just to ask me for a word of hope; my assurance that I believed the horrors would really be stopped someday. At the moment of leave-taking, this young woman, who could have had the world at her feet, suddenly burst into tears and said in despair: "This thing just takes all the joy out of living!"

How Wagner's joy of living was also clouded by the vivisectors' continuous and unpunished crimes transpires from his open letter to Ernst von Weber, a leader of antivivisectionism in Germany: "If vivisection should spread, then there will be one thing at least for which to thank its advocates: although the *Deutsches Requiem* will not be played for us when we pass away, we shall be glad and willing to leave a world in which not a dog would want to live."

*   *   *

Nobody realizes better than the vivisectors themselves that the systematic torture they practice, for whatever motive and with whatever results, would not be acceptable to the overwhelming majority, no matter how selfish mankind is, if everybody were fully informed: And that is why they insist, even in the U.S., on working behind barred doors, hiding the evidence. And this alone should suffice to disqualify them.

There may well be controlists in good faith. But I know that if I were a vivisector, I would advise my colleagues to declare themselves antivivisectionists, but of the controlist party—as the surest way to perpetuate vivisection.

ALTERNATIVE METHODS

This is an enormously wide, highly specialized and technical field: much wider, in fact, than vivisection itself. I shall touch upon it only briefly to give the reader a general idea of it. Actually, the whole question of alternative methods is irrelevant to the basic idea of this treatise, which is quite content to demonstrate that animal tests are misleading for science and corruptive for morals and must therefore be abolished by law. Furthermore, advocating a proliferation of "alternative" research methods implies advocating the continued proliferation of new drugs in addition to the hundreds of thousands already developed; and this for just a handful of diseases, which can be cured by natural means if they are curable, and can't be cured if they are incurable. However, it is important to show the reader what can be done, and what could have been done from the beginning in the realm of medical research, without resorting to animals.

When in the last century vivisection began its dismal spread, a great many opponents said, "There *must* be better ways than vivisection for the progress of science." And as has been demonstrated in the course of this century, they have been proven right.

Human tissue, cell and organ cultures—obtained from biopsies, aborted fetuses, umbilical cords, placentas, etc.—find many uses in medical research and are of particular value in immunology and toxicology, where for the most part animals are still being used. Other areas of application are cancerology, embryology, endocrinology, genetics, pathology, pharmacology, virology, radiobiology, and teratology (study of fetus malformation). Tissue samples taken at autopsy from the thousands of people who die every day are available for study of practically any disease that can be named, and in greater quantity than needed.

Until recently, the study of arthritis—a very wide-spread disease of the joints which can cause pain, swelling, loss of movement and sometimes deformity —is still today largely carried out on animals, by injecting material into their muscles and joints or injuring them traumatically. This is obviously a senseless method, as in humans the disease is not the consequence of injections or arbitrary injury. A better way to study arthritis with a view to curing it is the examination of arthritic cartilage normally removed from human patients following injury cases that require the joint to be surgically opened so that corrections can be made, or from people who have died in accidents. This abnormal cartilage can be kept alive in the laboratory for several days or weeks, during which its reactions to the various drugs can be observed.

In medical research, computers are not limited to diagnosis and data processing, but can be used for the testing of drugs, conditioned reflexes, kidney function, heart disease, and in crash and growth studies.

Combined techniques of chromatography and mass spectrometry detect minute traces of drugs and their breakdowns in humans, thus allowing unerring study of metabolism of a drug directly in man without any danger to him, rather than in other species, which give unreliable answers.

Pregnancy tests can now be made chemically in minutes; it is no longer necessary to wait ten days, using rabbits. Culture tests have made it possible to dispense with routine guinea pig inoculations in tests of patients suspected of having TB.

Mice used for the assay of tetanus antitoxin and of yellow fever vaccine can now also be advantageously replaced. Lower organisms can be used in the screening of drugs for side effects, in nutritional studies and in connection with investigation of anesthetics.

Dummies simulating human anatomical features including flesh, muscle and bone structure can and have been used by Volkswagen in car-crash studies, one of them giving far more reliable results than all the rhesus monkeys and pregnant baboons sacrificed so far put together.

A new cell culture technique tests the effectiveness of treatments for the inactivation or killing of tumor cells.

Particularly dramatic was the demonstration of the superiority of one of these replacement methods in the Thalidomide case. It was provided by Turkish Prof. S. T. Aygün, virologist of the University of Ankara. Using chicken embryos, he discovered within weeks the danger that Thalidomide represented for fetuses, and while the drug was being marketed in a score of countries, he prevented its being licensed for use in Turkey. And Dr. Ross Nigrelli, who directed the Laboratory of Marine Biochemistry and Ecology in New York, has been widely quoted as saying: "In testing drugs we use sea-urchin eggs. We could have told them about Thalidomide quickly had we tested it on sea-urchin eggs." (Margaret B. Kreig, in her book *Green Medicine*, 1964 Rand McNally, Chicago.)

The March 20, 1972 issue of *Newsweek* Magazine reported that a new vaccine developed without resorting to animals by Dr. Leonard L. Hayflick, Professor of medical microbiology at Stanford University, had satisfied the Division of Biologics Standards, a United States agency: "Dr. Hayflick set out to develop a strain of human cells using cells taken from the lungs of a fetus aborted in Sweden. This strain, known as WI-38, produced a virtually limitless number of completely uniform cultures that could be stored in a frozen state for periods of years and thawed out when needed to provide the growth medium for vaccines anywhere in the world. By contrast, culturing vaccines with monkey kidney cells requires a fresh set of cells for each new batch of vaccines."

World-wide tests on humans have failed to reveal any cancerous content in WI-38. Extensive tests were made in Yugoslavia and Britain. In 1960 Bernice Eddy of DBS discovered that a viral impurity in kidney cells of African green monkeys, which were used to culture live polio vaccines, produced cancer in hamsters. "Fortunately, the impurity caused no harm to humans, but to Dr. Leonard Hayflick of Philadelphia's Wistar Institute, [before he moved to Stanford University] the episode suggested the need for a safer approach to vaccine production. Dr. Hayflick's work on vaccines finally received approval from the DBS responsible for regulating vaccines. Approval was granted to each vaccine and it licensed Pfizer Laboratories to produce a live oral polio vaccine named Diplovax, grown in human cells." *Time* Magazine published a similar report (Apr. 17, 1972).

Formerly, anti-rabies vaccine was produced on the spinal fluid of rabbits or the brains of sheep. Then it was discovered that ducks' eggs gave a safer product. But a substratum of human tissue or cell culture has proved still safer. In Russia, 90 percent of all vaccines are nowadays produced with replacement methods, which prove far superior to animals, confirming the antivivisectionist thesis of long standing.

The above are just a few examples of the various replacement techniques that have been perfected in the past years and that now number thousands.

England leads in this field, too, expanding it faster than elsewhere, with the support of various foundations. One of these sets out to meet the need for information and communication on the subject and maintains direct contact with researchers everywhere; others make available to scientists awards and grants-in-aid in support of research projects not involving the use of live animals.

The field of replacement techniques is spreading rapidly, not only because of monetary grants by these foundations, but because they prove to be better. Many such techniques have been developed and are put to use in major pharmaceutical laboratories; but often animals are sacrificed even when alternative methods exist, sometimes because backward laws demand animal tests.

The replacement techniques are not spreading as fast as they could and should, also because the university brains who prepare the coming scientists, and the pathologists who use animals, have not been taught the sciences, like advanced mathematics, needed for some of these new methods, nor to study cultures of live cells in human tissues; they are only trained to examine dead human tissues or else animal tissues.

If vivisection had been prohibited from the start, all these progressive techniques would have been developed and adopted much sooner, benefiting medical science incalculably, and humanity would have been spared the countless tragedies derived from the wrong answers given by animal experimentation.

As expected, the traditionally backward, vivisectionist *Journal of the American Medical Association* (JAMA)—which a few years ago caused a scandal in the U.S. when it was reported that it had invested all its $6,000,000 loose cash in drug shares—ridiculed the new, more humanitarian and scientific techniques. A 1972 editorial discussing Britain's FRAME—Fund for the Replacement of Animals in Medical Experiments—said that "FRAME might be better called FRAUDS; FRAME's intentions seem pure, but there is good reason to believe that its basic motives are antivivisectionistic." Having aired his terrible suspicion, the editoralist made this very pertinent remark: "Just how these methods might substitute for animal experimentation in neurophysiology, for example, is difficult to comprehend."

Neurophysiological experiments are those exemplified in various chapters of this treatise, and they are of the particularly cruel, stupid and useless kind—if cruelty, stupidity and uselessness are worth grading; and they have done nothing but aggravate the already worrisome mental condition of the experimenters performing them. So the humanitarian foundations that alarm *JAMA* indeed won't be able—or willing—to find alternatives for those experiments. But they might provide for having those sick neurophysiological experimenters institutionalized, and perhaps even restored to sanity.

So it is clear that vivisection can be abolished only by the force of law, and not by the alternative methods alone, no matter how superior they are; too many researchers deliberately reject any type of alternative.

Owen B. Hunt of the American Anti-Vivisection Society in Philadelphia gave an interesting slant on this in his speech at the Hotel Méditerranée in Geneva on July 26, 1975:

"Lederle Laboratories found a non-violent vaccine in a duck embryo six years ago—a vast improvement on the Pasteur treatment where painful and dangerous shots are administered to the patient for weeks. But the Pasteur violent method is still being used in the United States. Why? Easy government money. Salk and Sabin vaccine taken from monkeys—over a million monkeys used so far. Dr. Hayflick's human cell culture can produce enough vaccine to last the world forever, the vaccine cells reproduce themselves and can be permanently frozen until used, and every laboratory in the world has access to these cells. Yet monkeys are still used by the tens of thousands. Why? Easy government money. The U.S. Army and Air Force got $3.5 million in July 1973 to test gases on 600 beagle puppies, who would eventually all die. But a quick method of identifying pollutant gases in the air has been devised by Bell Laboratories scientist Lloyd B. Kreuzer. Using a laser and a computer, his system is capable of identifying concentrations of gases as low as one part in 10 million, a ten times greater sensitivity than most present regulatory standards require. The Army and Air Force were fully aware of this and many similar, previous information when they requested the $3.5 million appropriation, insisting on using beagles for experiments that would last as long as two years."

But not only money is involved. Some experimenter's driving motive is not money but what they euphemistically call "scientific curiosity." They would lose interest in research if they could not use live animals.

For such people vivisection has become a fixation devoid of any logical basis. This was demonstrated by Dr. Robert White, the monkey-head transplanter, when he wrote in the *American Scholar* (Summer 1971) that "our advanced technological society and increasing population have produced additional serious health hazards through industrial and human pollution of our air, water and land, and the use of laboratory animals to establish acceptable levels of biological contamination and to design methods of control and decontamination for humans represents a new dimension of biomedical research that may prove to be utterly crucial to human survival."

When he wrote this, Dr. White had already fathered ten children. Having thus done his manly best to contribute to the world's over-population and consequent pollution, what remedy did Dr. White recommend? To no one's surprise, using innocent animals as scapegoats for his own inconsiderate excesses.

Now a question. For decades, chemical methods have existed for measuring biological contamination and consequently for designing methods of control and decontamination far more accurately than any animal tests could ever do. Is it possible that a "scientist" like Dr. White was not aware of it? Or could it be that he belongs to that category of individuals for whom animal experimentation has become an incurable paranoid obsession?

Example: Chinese acupuncture, which was perfected several thousand years ago without animal experiments and is highly effective in expert hands—to the point of providing total anesthesia in case of surgical operations—has not changed, because there was no need to change it. But ever since it has been "discovered" by the vivisection maniacs, it is being "tried out" on animals, which can't report to us what they feel, and react differently from man anyway. So for the first time in history even that branch of medicine, which for thousands of years had been exemplary for clearness and utility, is beginning to grow nebulous through the vivisectors' doings.

Unfortunately, awed by western airplanes and nuclear weapons, the Chinese assume that our technological superiority must also apply to medical art. So they start abandoning the millenarian wisdom of their barefoot doctors, replacing the tried and proved herbal medicines with our cancerogenic miracle drugs, while the universities start forming a Bernardian laboratory subculture in imitation of ours for the first time in the history of China.

A LOST CAUSE?

Some time ago an Italian schoolteacher in Tunis wrote to tell me, "Your articles against vivisection are very disturbing to me and other people like me. When we think we have at last succeeded in blotting out all thought of vivisection, there you go reminding us, and we suffer again. Why don't you forget about it, and let us live in peace? How can you ever hope to defeat the three strongest forces in the world—human stupidity, cruelty, and greed? Abolitionism is a lost cause."

Considering the spread of vivisection since Claude Bernard took it out of the squalid cellars of a few physiologists and raised it to academic status, abolitionism may well seem a lost cause. Being still just a leaderless, disorganized protest movement from a bunch of well-meaning but harmless amateurs, it seems destined to fail. But many times in the past, apparently powerless causes have succeeded in upsetting political and social organizations that seemed immovable. So the early Christians ("a bunch of exalted, unrealistic visionaries"), devoid of any power, contributed more to fashioning Europe's civilization than the Roman Empire, the Hebrew orthodoxy and the warlike hordes of Nordic, Asian, and Moslem invaders. It was only when their organization became rich and numerous, and accordingly weak in spiritual values, that Christendom lost decisive influence.

A recent survey has made the surprising discovery that of late many more young people admire Albert Schweitzer than the astronauts. This is quite a shift from a few years ago. Even as French philosopher Joseph Joubert (1754–1824) wrote that the poets, in their quest for beauty, have discovered more truths than the scientists in their quest for truth, so today ever more people begin to feel that the philosophers, writers and artists have done more for the world than the scientists ever will.

"So this is the little lady who made the big war,"

said Abraham Lincoln on meeting Harriet Beecher Stowe, whose *Uncle Tom's Cabin* had rocked America and taught the world what racism is. If the little lady did not start the war, her book went a long way in preparing the mood for it.

But Charles Dickens once wrote a novel which shattered the British Empire's complacency, prompted London-based Karl Marx to write a sociological treatise that turned the world's social outlook upside down, and eventually effected the Bolshevist Revolution. Marx's ideas were then incorporated in a social system by Adolf Hitler, providing the pattern for Roosevelt's Social Security, which in turn served as guideline for most other nations, regardless of political labels. All this sprang from a single work of art, philosophy, esthetic thought: not science; just as the most momentous step by far in modern medicine—Semmelweis' rediscovery of the importance of ancient hygiene—was not the result of science, but of feeling and thought; in other words, a philosophical conquest. And it met, like all momentous innovations, with the opposition and derision of the very category that should have been the first to hail it.

The policy of most present-day antivivisectionist organizations is to bend over backward to avoid appealing to the public's emotions, to make no "sentimental" plea for the suffering animals. And herein they err, they greatly err, as the failure of those movements proves—for not even the greatest optimist could claim that they have been a success so far. The great majority of people have always been more accessible to emotion than logic—but there is always a logical basis for strong emotions. All the popular leaders who have changed the course of history have realized that.

Those who choose to ignore the power and importance of human emotions and sentiments, as if they didn't exist, are as unrealistic, as unscientific, as the disciples of Claude Bernard who assert that one can experiment on living organisms as on inanimate matter.

But it is also unrealistic to expect that the justness

of a cause facilitates the fight. On the contrary. A just cause presupposes strong opposition from vested interests firmly entrenched in the existing social, political and educational structure. All good causes have had rich, mighty and ruthless opponents: It is by its enemies that the goodness of a cause is demonstrated. But it also means that the cause can't win by wish alone.

It was the unflinching determination of a few undauntable humanitarians or "hysterical visionaries" that eventually obtained the abolition of slavery, child labor, bear-baiting, cock-fighting, and the like. Very few people today disapprove of the laws barring those abominations; yet at the time the great majority, including Church and governments, were opposed to their abolition. So the antivivisectionist movement should not be measured by the number of its members. These are but the leaven in the dense public conscience, which it will transform to intellectual sanity. A little spark can cause a great deflagration.

For centuries, the Catholic Church perpetrated the torture of human beings, and the few who dared criticize her were put in irons as crazy or dangerous, because it was all allegedly done to save the sinners' souls; but as Illuminism spread, public opposition grew so strong that a Papal Bull had to abrogate all religious torture. Thus, as information about the cruelty and damage of vivisection spreads—and it is our duty to spread it—the day will come when the public will revolt against this practice, and official medicine will no longer be able to absolve itself of its own crimes, but will have to bow to the majority and choose new ways if it wishes to continue reaping its fat profits.

*   *   *

George Bernard Shaw, Richard Wagner, Mark Twain, who were among the many great men uncompromisingly opposed to vivisection, had steadfastly refused to use the weapon of its uselessness.

Wrote Wagner: "If we abolish vivisection only because we have proved its uselessness, humanity will have gained nothing." And Shaw: "If you abandon the dogmatic humanitarian attitude, if you say that this is a question which has to be decided by the benefit the practice confers or may confer, then you put yourself hopelessly in the wrong . . . If you attempt to controvert a vivisectionist by showing that the experiment he has performed has not led to any useful result, you imply that if it had led to a useful result you would consider his experiment justified. Now, I am not prepared to concede that position." (From *Shaw on Vivisection,* Allen & Unwin, London, 1949)

Naturally most of today's "scientists" contend that moral considerations are not pertinent; that pity is not the yardstick by which human progress should be measured. But then what should be the yardstick of human progress? Violence? If so, let the antivivisectionists by all means use violence against the vivisectors.

Twain, Wagner, Shaw, and the others of their mind, like the recently deceased John Vyvyan, were right in demanding that vivisection should be abolished on ethical grounds only and that humanity would lose if it were abolished because of its uselessness. However, today not even an incurable optimist would affirm that since Twain and Wagner's day, or even since the much more recent time of Shaw, humanity has become more humane. At the end of the last century, John Ruskin resigned his seat at Oxford University in protest at the opening of a Physiology (vivisection) Department. And when on July 15, 1879 Lord Truro unsuccessfully introduced in Parliament a bill for total abolition, one of the most noted political men of the time, the Seventh Earl of Shaftesbury, read in support of the bill a quotation from the records of Prof. Friedrich Goltz, the vivisector from Strasbourg, who had boasted of a particularly clumsy, revolting and long-lasting experiment on the nervous system of a young bitch. Lord Shaftesbury concluded his address with the comment, "I would rather have been the dog than the professor." It is hard to imagine an important politician today going on record with a similar statement.

So it might seem that if vivisection wasn't abolished during the last century, when it was practiced by few and criticized by many, now that it is being studiously ignored by the majority, tacitly accepted by the politicians, and fueled by the most lucrative industry in the history of mankind, the outlook must be hopeless.

But meanwhile something new has come up.

Vivisection has proved far worse than merely futile; it has proved directly responsible for damages to public health that are increasing and proliferating in geometrical progression and can no longer be buried, as other medical mistakes have been buried in the past. These damages have been ascertained by the same "scientists" who cause them through the erroneous methodology hammered into their heads like a religious dogma from the first day of their schooling.

It is significant that the staunchest denouncers of vivisection as dangerous because totally unreliable have not been Shavian humanitarians, but outstanding surgeons and physicians—from Britain's Lawson Tait to America's Henry Bigelow to Germany's Erwin Liek to Austria's Joseph Hyrtl to Italy's Antonio Murri to France's Abel Desjardins.

If I have decided to abandon Shaw's exclusive humanitarian stand and to invoke abolition on scientific grounds also, I have two reasons. First, having revealed at least some of the harm done to animals, I must by the same token advertise the damage that is done to mankind—to its physical no less than to its mental health.

The other reason is that digging into medical history, in order to understand how an aberration like vivisection could be spawned and be allowed to proliferate, I came upon that phrase of Charles Bell's which makes it clear that even if abolition comes merely out of practical, scientific considerations, because it has been proved harmful to health, humanity will nonetheless be able to claim a victory. When Sir Charles declared: "I don't think that men capable of such cruelties have the faculties to penetrate the mysteries of nature," he established a second "Bell's law" which has meanwhile proved as correct, and far more important, than the first. The humanitarian genius that was Bell had realized that calloused individuals, devoid of humanity, are intellectually deficient; and that the type of people who feel attracted by a research based on systematic torture would be the least apt for conducting intelligent medical research, namely useful research.

That vivisection is an inhuman practice is self-evident; that an inhuman practice dehumanizes those who practice it is axiomatic. And the havoc that has been wrought—not merely on animals but on humanity —by the arrogant hegemony that constitutes the western hemisphere's "health" authorities, starting from America's FDA and its main European base, Geneva's WHO, is evidenced in the following, final part, from which it emerges that if ever there was a lost cause, it is vivisection.

Part Nine

THE COMEUPPANCE

"Vivisection is a school of sadism, and a generation of medical men educated in this practice justifies the most serious concern on the part of the public."

Thus wrote French doctor G.R. Laurent a few decades ago, and his words have turned out to be equally as prophetic as Germany's Dr. Wolfgang Bohn's, who had written in the medical periodical *Aerztliche Mitteilungen* as far back as 1912 (No. 7):

"The asserted purpose of vivisection hasn't been achieved in any field and it is predictable that it won't be achieved in the future either. On the contrary, vivisection has caused grievous damages, has been fatal to thousands of people . . . The constant spread of the vivisectionist method has achieved but one thing: to increase the scientific torture and murder of human beings. We can expect this increase to continue, for it would just be the logical consequence of animal vivisection."

And exactly this has come to pass.

"Human experimentation has become a major industry in America." Millions of baffled Americans heard this statement on the hour-long *NBC Reports* TV program that Robert Rogers wrote, produced and narrated on prime time of the evening of May 29, 1973. And columnist Bob Cromie wrote in the *Chicago Tribune* of January 19, 1974, as a result of his extensive studies done on American experimentation habits: "My personal opinion is that many of the experiments being conducted are supervised by sadists, idiots, or those greedy for the federal grants involved . . . It seems obvious that some scientists no longer are content with the use of lower animals, in view of recent experiments conducted on inmates of prisons and other institutions, and the quicker this Nazi mentality is curbed the better."

Of course, the only experiments on human beings that are ethically justifiable are experiments on volunteers—but on such volunteers as are fully capable of giving intelligent consent, without any sort of psychological pressure. This rules out all children, all mentally retarded or unbalanced persons, all inmates of penal institutions, all military personnel, and all the members of any organization on whom any kind of psychological pressure can be exerted.

Apart from the fact that health is no secret, so that continual experimentation is either a sign of infantilism (still at the game-playing stage) or of greed for easy money, surely no one can object to medical doctors or researchers experimenting on themselves and on each other, should they consider it necessary. And these should be the only lawful experiments, because only the medical people are fully capable of appraising the risks involved and benefits to expect; at least let us presume that.

When doctors damage patients or imperil their health through an unauthorized experiment, they commit an obviously criminal act, and the law should intervene without waiting for the patient or the survivors to bring malpractice suits. Instead, such criminal acts are at present tacitly accepted by the judicial system, which apparently has come to be as complacent about wild, stolid experimentation on patients as the editorial staffs of the medical journals who report them.

The German doctors tried in Nüremberg by the Allied court for experimenting on prisoners explained that since they had practiced animal vivisection, it was "logical" that they wanted to experiment on human beings as well. They were not SS troopers, but respected physicians, and the entire planning of the experimentation on prisoners was in the hands of such leading medical authorities as Dr. Sievers, deputy

chairman of the Reich Research Council; Prof.
Rostock, head of the Surgery Department at Berlin
University; Prof. Rose, head of the department of
Tropical Medicine at the Robert Koch Institute; and,
of all people, Dr. Gebhardt, president of the German
Red Cross (!), among many others.

In Nazi Germany experiments had been performed
on prisoners even before the war, but the first war-
time experiments are supposed to be those suggested
by a surgeon in the Luftwaffe, Dr. Rascher, who on
May 15, 1941, wrote to Himmler asking whether it
would be possible to have "two or three professional
criminals" test life-saving equipment for parachutists
who would have to jump from altitudes of 12 kilo-
meters. In his letter Rascher called these experiments
"absolutely essential for the research on high-altitude
flying and cannot, as has been tried until now, be
carried out on monkeys, as monkeys offer entirely different test conditions."

Himmler agreed at once, but when the final report
was handed in, not two or three but over 200 persons
had been used, and more than 70 had died. These
experiments were carried out at Dachau.

Then when the Russian campaign raised different
problems, like survival in freezing water and ways
of resuscitation, another 300 prisoners were allocated
for these new trials. It was found that anesthetics introduced unnatural conditions, so they were dispensed
with. Many of the prisoners screamed as parts of their
bodies froze. But the performing doctors were used to
screams—from the animal laboratories.

The legal records of the Nüremberg trial include
letters that the chemical giant IG Farben addressed
to the concentration camp of Auschwitz. They read,
according to *Frankfurter Rundschau* (Feb. 10, 1956):

"We received your reply, but we consider the price
of 200 Mark per woman exaggerated. We propose a
maximal price of 170 Mark per woman. We need approximately 150."

"We have received your letter of agreement. Prepare
150 women, in as good health as possible. As soon as

you let us know that they are ready, we will take them over."

"We acknowledge receipt of 150 women. They are not in very good health but we have decided to consider them acceptable. You will be informed as to the progress of our trials."

"The trials have been carried out. All test objects have died. We will be in touch with you shortly in regard to another delivery."

*   *   *

The American prosecutor at Nüremberg, who denounced with pious indignation the German experimenters, chose to ignore the continual appearance of reports in his own country of hospital patients being used as test material, for experiments not connected with their ailments, but just to prove or disprove a theoretical point. And since then, such experiments have kept increasing in number and scope, like an ineluctable malediction upon a species that has tacitly accepted organized torture as a matter of social principle and public policy.

HUMAN GUINEA PIGS

Inevitably, the tortures society permits to be inflicted upon animals fall back upon society itself, as if by the workings of some mysterious moral law. So Pavlov's "conditioned reflexes" experiments, which caused pain or acute distress to thousands of animals, are now being constantly repeated, with variations, on human subjects. And, as usual, on such humans as are unable to protest, strike back, or sue—the orphaned or abandoned children, the mentally handicapped, the destitute dependent on public welfare; in sum, all those who are as helpless as laboratory animals.

Between the two World Wars, while Nobel laureate Pavlov's experiments on animals were eagerly being followed and imitated in laboratories the world over, a book titled *Behaviorism* (Norton, 1925, and The People's Institute Publishing Company, New York, 1930) appeared in the U.S., by a Dr. John B. Watson, at one time director of the psychological laboratory of Johns Hopkins University. He described dropping new-born children just when they were falling asleep, to test "loss of support"; robbing of toys; letting them be bullied; placing acid in their mouths; and it states the amazing (!) fact that burning or pricking or cutting produced crying and screaming and an attempt to escape the pain by withdrawing the body, etcetera, etcetera, etcetera.

"We were rather loath at first to conduct experiments in this field," sanctimoniously wrote this "researcher," who then overcame his qualms arguing "but the need of study was so great that we finally decided to build up fears in the infant and then later to study practical methods for removing them. We chose as our first subject Albert B., an infant weighing 21 pounds at 11 months of age . . . He had lived his whole life in the hospital. He was a wonderfully 'good baby.' In all the months we worked with him we never saw him cry until our experiments were made!"

To make Albert cry, a white rat, which had been his playmate for weeks, was presented to him, and just as he reached for the rat a steel bar was struck with a carpenter's hammer right behind his head. Albert jumped violently, burying his face in the mattress. The experiment was repeated until the infant was a nervous wreck: He began to cry as soon as the rat was shown, fell over, raised himself on all fours, and began to crawl away so rapidly that he was caught with difficulty before he reached the edge of the mattress. Finally the infant was frightened by everything he had played with. The experiments came to an end because he was adopted.

So here are more instances where a vivisector, under the pretext of "Studying practical methods for removing fears," just *inflicts* fears, submitting the hapless infants to such traumas that their psyches will probably be scarred forever, and that they might have grown up into adults as twisted as their torturers. (In 1923, a sum of Rockefeller money was granted to enable those new Pavlovians, the Behaviorists, to experiment on 70 children ranging in age from three months to seven years.)

* * *

Another among the many callous abuses of small children was solemnly reported in the American *Journal of Pediatrics* in 1939 (Vol. 15, No. 4, p. 485) by the experimenters themselves. With no other purpose but to satisfy their curiosity, they had subjected 42 infants ranging from 11 days to $2\frac{1}{2}$ years of age to repetitious, terrifying experiments of submersion in water. The average number of "observations" on the same child was more than 10, and went up to 51. "When submerged," read the report, "the movement of the extremities are of the struggling order. The infants clutch at the experimenter's hand, try to wipe the water from the face . . . Often the ingestion of fluid is considerable, and the infant would cough or otherwise show respiratory disturbances when taken out of the water. At no time did any baby show himself capable of raising his head above the water for the purpose of breathing."

I myself saw similar experiments in American newsreels in the mid-forties—babies were dropped into a large glass tank, which was suspended in mid-air, so that the camera could record their struggles from below. I well remember the terror-stricken, contorted little faces.

Everywhere, the cases of doctors deliberately putting human beings in danger, inflicting maladies on hospital patients, or withholding drugs from them in order to "study" a malady, have become so frequent that they can no longer be shrugged off as exceptional. The dehumanizing process that begins with the first vivisectionist experiment the student is made to witness is affecting widening segments of the medical world.

A warning about this was sounded more than two decades ago by Dr. O. E. Guttentag of the University of California Medical School, who wrote in *Science* (1953, *117*, p. 207):

"Experiments on the sick, which are of no immediate value to them but which are made to confirm or dispute some doubtful or suggestive biological generalization, have recently become more and more extensive."

Particularly frequent are experiments performed on mental defectives, preferably orphans, or on seniles. With the pretext that the state or the community is paying for their upkeep, the health authorities and the researchers in general consider those helpless creatures fair game. For example, the Buffalo *Courier Express* reported on March 7, 1958, that 40 inmates from 5 to 10 years of age, of the Willowbrook State School for Mental Defectives, on Staten Island, New York, were used as experimental material to be infected with hepatitis viruses, which may cause death, or permanent damages, and inevitably a long period of sufferance.

Another typical example out of thousands: London's *Sunday Express* of November 22, 1959 gave details of experiments in a mental home in Gloucester on old women who were so senile that they were described as "cabbage-like." They were given convulsions to see if the brain could be jarred enough to make it start working again—but the results were so bad that the experiment was stopped.

Experiments done on patients without their knowledge have been impressively denounced, but without any practical effect, by Dr. M. H. Pappworth, the London physician and internationally known teacher of clinical medicine. In *Human Guinea Pigs* (Pelican Books, London, 1969) he revealed hundreds of cases involving thousands of patients, which he had uncovered simply by perusing British and American medical journals. For instance (p. 125): Three doctors of the University of Arkansas Medical Center in Little Rock injected radioactive iodine intravenously into 46 healthy newborn infants in order to "study" thyroid function, regardless of the well-known and "undoubted risk" that this medicament can produce cancer in the thyroid gland; then they calmly reported their exploit in the *American Journal of Diseases of*

Children, (1962, *103,* p. 739) without giving any indication as to what happened to the children.

Dr. Pappworth pointed out that the worst experiments, and all those that have caused damage or death, are obviously never reported by the "researchers."

The experimental fixation is not confined to the English-speaking world, of course. Writing in *Animali e Natura* (June, 1972) Italy's Dr. Alda Antonaz cited several cases in her own country:

"In a Naples hospital, concentrated solutions of cortisone have been instilled in the eyes of 20 women, hospitalized for other diseases, in order to 'study' the formation of an experimental cataract. That means an attempt was made to cause almost total loss of eyesight. Fortunately the experiment was a flop—probably because previous experiments made on dogs, a species in which cataracts occur much more frequently, the desired effect had been easily obtained. In Rome, an attempt was made to cause experimental paralysis to a group of women hospitalized for various diseases. Charges have been brought against Prof. Sirtori, President of Milan's Carlo Erba Foundation, for administering, to several children hospitalized for viral hepatitis, drugs which block the natural defenses of the organism and thus facilitate the spreading of the hepatitis virus."

Prof. Sirtori is, of course, an enthusiastic animal vivisectionist. Incidentally, he was absolved of any wrongdoing by the Italian judges.

* * *

While abuses against human patients are nowadays common in all those countries "civilized" enough to glorify animal experimentation, they are most frequent where animal experimentation is most widespread. So, inevitably, the U.S. takes the cake in this field also.

For the *NBC Reports* series mentioned at the outset of this part, Robert Rogers had made a thorough investigation of American research methods. So he knew what he was talking about, as he continued:

"*Normal* research volunteers are seldom available,

particularly normal children. As a result, researchers have often used retarded childen as subjects, not because the experiments would benefit the children, but *because they were available*. Until recently, the children of Florida's state-run homes for the retarded were *very much* available. We found most doctors reluctant to talk about testing among the retarded . . . Obviously, a retarded child cannot be a volunteer in any meaningful sense of the word. However, they continue to be a major source of human subjects for pediatric research."

Lately, the U.S. Public Health Service was obliged to admit that it had withheld a proven remedy from 425 syphilitic patients in order "to study the effects of syphilis on the human body." And who were the victims that were allowed to go untreated? *All* were poor, uneducated, and black—recruited through local clinics in Alabama. (*Time*, Feb. 7, 1975)

As this "study" lasted 40 years, a great many doctors must have known that it was going on; but the fact came to light only when some smart lawyer smelled the financial possibilities and persuaded the victims, or the families of those who had meanwhile died of the disease, to slap a $18 billion suit against the federal government—which acknowledged its moral obligation to those it had failed to treat, and paid.

* * *

Dr. Bernard Barber, chairman of Columbia's Department of Sociology, recently made a thorough survey of the ethical stand of American research doctors. His results were reported by *Scientific American* and the *Sunday News* of Feb. 1, 1976. Since the survey was done simply by direct interviewing or sending out questionnaires, the researchers' answers must be suspected of being slanted in their own favor, to say the least. Still, they are revealing. For example, 28 percent of the researchers answered that they would remove a patient's thymus gland (currently believed to be an important part of the immunological protection system) to determine the effects on the survival of an experimental skin graft, and 14 percent said they would inject radioactive calcium into children, increasing the risk of leukemia, even if the odds were only one in 10 that an important medical discovery would result. (Important medical discoveries have not resulted since Hippocrates' time—Author's Note.)

"What little ethics training there is is apparently not very effective," Barber said. "Research is their business. Research is their mission and predominant interest, not applied ethics or active advocacy of patients' rights."

All this sounds sophomorically obvious. And the indifference to ethical behavior of the so-called scientists seems well matched by the public's indifference.

In the light of the above, and of the fact that the U.S. Army sponsored tests with the hallucinogenic drug LSD on monkeys and cats at Tulane University in the 1950s, it was not surprising when an Associated Press report of July 22, 1975 announced that the Army also admitted to having sponsored LSD tests on about 800 civilians during that period.

That was only the tip of the iceberg. The Department of Health, Education and Welfare gave millions of dollars in grants to more than 30 university researchers for LSD experiments with human subjects, while themselves conducting LSD tests on some 2,500 prisoners, mental patients and "paid volunteers."

* * *

The growing dehumanization in the field of research through the legalized torture of animals has led to current exploits that most people expected to find only in horror movies. Some researchers buy from hospitals live, just-aborted fetuses. It is conceivable—in fact sooner or later it is inevitable—that such fetuses can be raised in the nutritional jars that play the role of the maternal placenta, up to the period of natural birth: After which the experimenter has a complete, laboratory child at his disposal.

Whether this has already happened behind the locked doors or not we have no way of knowing. But we know that some hearts of embryonic children, withdrawn alive from their mothers' bodies and sold to researchers, have been implanted into the bodies of dogs.

London's *Daily Telegraph* of August 25, 1970 had this report: "Progress in the storage of hearts intended for transplantation is being made in the department of surgical sciences at the Royal College of Surgeons, says Mr. J. Keith Ross, consultant surgeon at the National Heart Hospital today. A member of the hospital's heart transplant team, Mr. Ross writes in *Hospital Management* that recently two hearts stored 72 hours were transplanted into dogs. They comfortably supported the circulation of the recipient dogs in a stable manner."

Whether this particular report also concerned the heart of fetuses I was unable to establish. But the *Chicago Tribune* of March 14, 1975, reported that "Dr. Eugene Diamond of the Loyola University Medical Center testified in favor of the Kelly bill, telling committed members that a new law is necessary to prevent 'horrors perpetrated on living fetuses by a minute percentage of researchers.'"

All this is but the logical consequence of far more numerous and horrifying experiments done on animals, authorized and financed by the governments of the so-called civilized countries—where the medical students are taught that the principal apostle of vivisection, Claude Bernard, was a "genius" (Encylopedia Britannica), but whose teachings, which have been determinant in shaping the behavior of the current medical researchers, included the following:

"Experimental medicine must have as its object: 1) to perform on living, healthy individuals vivisectionist and physico-chemical experiments which will reveal the property of all organs, of all histological [pertaining to tissue structure] elements in their normal state; 2) to perform on the living and sick individual, in different ways, parallel vivisectionist and physico-chemical experiments which show the modifications of the properties that have undergone the organs, or the histological elements in the pathological state." (Claude Bernard, *Principes de Médecine Expérimentale*, Presses Universitaires de France, Paris, 1947, p. 147)

TEN THOUSAND LITTLE MONSTERS

So we have seen what the new barbarism is doing increasingly to the general public, after it has been made acceptable through the indoctrination by the medical faculties and fueled by the drug industry. It is evident that the researchers have realized that animal experimentation is useless for man, otherwise they would not be experimenting increasingly on man. If animals gave definite answers, no further experimentation on man would be necessary. But all the died-in-the-wool experimenters—as said before, still at the game-playing stage—want to experiment on animals *and* people, because the game fascinates them.

After seeing the moral havoc wrought by the spreading of this new barbarism, let us see a few instances of the physical havoc. No science-fiction writer had foreseen what the laboratory gnomes have managed to effect through a "simple" tranquilizer—one that had been advertised as *the most harmless in the whole history of modern therapeutics.*

It is necessary to analyze the Thalidomide disaster because it illustrates better than anything else the stubborn reluctance, both of the laboratory subculture and the authorities, to learn anything from previous lessons. In fact the tragedy of malformed births is still going on today, and keeps growing, owing to the same mistakes, undeterred by logic and experience.

The Thalidomide case is to date by far the best known, the most widely advertised tragedy of modern therapeutics. But public opinion has been led to believe that it represents an exceptional case. This is not so. Rather than being exceptional, the Thalidomide case is typical, and as such it merits a closer examination.

Thalidomide had been tested on many thousands of animals before being thrown on the market. In its February 23, 1962 issue, when the first warning signs of the tragedy were appearing on the world horizon, *Time* Magazine reported that Thalidomide had been marketed "after three years of animal tests."

Invented by the West German pharmaceutical company Chemie Grünenthal, it was not just another of the many already existing sedatives re-edited with a slight variation under a new label, but a truly new product. So the preliminary animal tests had been particularly thorough and extensive before Thalidomide was introduced on the German market under the name of Contergan in October 1957, and then sold by licensees in 7 African, 17 Asiatic and 11 western hemisphere countries.

On August 1, 1958, Grünenthal sent a letter to 40,-000 German doctors describing Contergan (Thalidomide) as the best medicament for pregnant women and breastfeeding mothers, as it damaged neither mother nor child.

In the previously mentioned final version of Kurt Blüchel's *Weisse Magier,* which must be regarded as an accurate, because undisputed document, by 1961 the firm had already received as many as 1,600 warnings of various damages attributed to the new drug. In fact in the Alsdorfer trial, the German prosecutor charged that the firm had enough information to withdraw the drug from the market as early as 1960.

Why didn't it do so? Contergan had already conquered 40 percent of the German tranquilizer market, animal experiments kept giving negative results, and so the firm clung to its belief that the drug was harmless to man also.

But there is more: In several European countries, such as England and Sweden, the licensees of Thalidomide had undertaken animal tests of their own, independently from the German firm, and came to the same results as Chemie Grünenthal. So in October 1961 the British licensee, Distillers Company, brought Thalidomide on the market under the name Distaval, accompanied by the following assurance:

"Distaval can be given with complete safety to pregnant women and nursing mothers without adverse effect on mother or child."

Result: an estimated 10,000 children—but probably many more—born throughout the world as phocomelics, deformed, some with fin-like hands grown directly on the shoulders; with stunted or missing limbs; deformed eyes and ears; ingrown genitals; absence of a lung; a great many of them still-born or dying shortly after birth; parents under shock, mothers gone insane, some driven to infanticide.

The discovery of the drug's effect on man had required years. While the first birth defects in human beings were becoming increasingly evident, the resumption of animal tests just didn't confirm the suspicions, no matter how high the concentration given —thus confirming for another long, fatal period the assumption of the drug's harmlessness, and so the manufacturers saw no reason to withdraw it. Until the evidence became overwhelming: Although harmless to animals, Thalidomide caused malformations in man, and Chemie Grünenthal was incriminated for having marketed a harmful drug.

Now comes the interesting part: Even while the trial was grinding along, the German and other manufacturers continued the animal tests, constantly increasing the doses of Thalidomide that were force-fed to various strains of dogs, cats, mice, rats, and as many as 150 different strains and substrains of rabbits, with negative results. Only when the white New Zealand rabbit was tested, a few malformed rabbit babies were obtained, and subsequently also some malformed monkeys—after years of tests, hundreds of different strains and millions of animals used. But researchers immediately pointed out that malformations, like cancer, could be obtained by administration of practically any substance in high concentration, including sugar and salt, which will eventually upset the organism, causing trouble.

In December 1970, the longest criminal trial in Germany's judicial history—2½ years, 283 days in court—ended with the acquittal of Chemie Grünenthal, *after a long line of medical authorities had testified that the generally accepted animal tests could never be conclusive for human beings.* This was unprecedented, for the testimonies came from an impressive array of individuals whose careers and reputations were practically built on animal experimentation, in-

cluding the 1945 Nobel laureate biochemist Ernst Boris
Chain, co-discoverer of penicillin with Fleming and
Florey.

Even Prof. Widukind Lenz, the German scientist
who through posthumous tests with primates had been
able to obtain some malformed offspring, testified at the
trial that "there is no animal test capable of indicating beforehand that human beings, subjected to
similar experimental conditions, will react in identical
or similar fashion."

In substance, a long array of research authorities
confirmed in court, explicitly or by implication, what
Dr. Raymond Green had written in *Lancet* (Sept. 1,
1962):

"We must face the fact that the most careful tests
of a new drug's effect on animals may tell us little
of its effects on humans. There can be no doubt that
Thalidomide was subjected to the most careful scrutiny. I myself took part in a trial to investigate its
possible goitrogenic effect on man, even such improb-
able hazards having been considered by its British
distributor . . . There are no drugs which do good
which do not sometimes do harm. Animal experiments
cannot obviate the risk and may even prevent the use
of excellent substances. We must accept some risk
or—perhaps the wiser course—do without new drugs."

Apart from the consideration that the only need for
still another tranquilizer, of which there existed already 1,200 on the German market at the time, was to
boost a manufacturer's profits, if the health authorities
had not regarded animal experimentation as reliable,
Thalidomide would have been tested clinically, with
the necessary caution, on a few individuals, as new
drugs used to be tested in the past, and so the victims
would have been few. Thus not only the Thalidomide
tragedy in itself, but the extent of the disaster was due
solely to the stubborn presumption of manufacturers
and health authorities that animal tests give valid answers for human beings.

Incredible vivisectionist reaction: They came up
screaming that the Thalidomide case "proved the necessity of expanding animal experimentation," instead

of repudiating it, and they advised to add to the usual tests some specific "teratogenic" tests (capability of damaging the fetus) on animals. Of course they know full well that such specific tests can never be reliable.

Meanwhile the trial had revealed that Thalidomide had also caused irreversible peripheric polyneuritis in adult humans: another drawback the many animal tests had failed to reveal. And it was lucky that the Thalidomide damages were apparent at once. What if Thalidomide had the power to cause, say, retarded children? Or genetic cancers? The animal tests would not have revealed that, either. And we would still be using it.

So in spite of the monotonous confirmation that animal experimentation multiplies the medical problems instead of clarifying them, the industry now adds alleged "teratogenic tests" to their usual preventive experimentation, just so that they may reassure the consumers in the descriptive leaflets with phrases such as "studies in mice, rats and rabbits have not shown teratogenic effect"—an assertion that promptly appeared in the advertisement of Valium Roche (*Pharmacopeia* 1967, British Encyclopedia of Medical Practice, 2nd. ed.), which meanwhile has been shown to stunt the psyche no less than Thalidomide has stunted the fetuses.

This means deliberately misleading the public and the doctors into using dangerous drugs. Any tests on animals can only demonstrate that a drug is harmless for the particular species on which the drug is tried; it doesn't mean it is harmless also to man. And vice versa. *This rule has no exceptions.*

According to the Washington *Science News-Letter* of Aug. 22, 1970, three French scientists had made pregnancy tests forcing a great number of animals to take the hallucinogenic drug LSD. The fetuses and the newborns showed no evidence that the drug produced deformities, but the scientists cautioned that "it is impossible to conclude from these experimental data that LSD may not be teratogenic (producing malformation) in man."

The London *Times* reported on Oct. 15, 1970 that pregnant rats, forced to inhale marijuana smoke at a New Yory laboratory, produced malformed offspring, but Dr. William Geber, who conducted the experiments, made the point that "as a rat is not a human being, no positive conclusions could be drawn."

And Dr. Robert L. Brent of Jefferson Medical College made a by now monotonous point when he wrote in *Prevention* (July 1972): "Some drugs that are teratogenic in the human in therapeutic doses are innocuous to many pregnant animals," while "some drugs that are innocuous to a pregnant woman are teratogenic to some animal species." (It's the case of aspirin and insulin, harmless to human fetuses, causing birth defects in mice.)

And in a supplement to West Germany's judiciary weekly, *Zeitschrift für Rechtspolitik* (vol. 12, 1975), Prof. Dr. Herbert Hensel, director of the Physiological Institute of Marburg University, wrote on the subject of animal tests: "Currently there is absolutely no possibility for a scientifically based prediction. The situation is even less favorable than in a game of chance, in which the odds are known . . . According to our current notions, it is not possible to establish through animal tests the effectiveness or harmlessness of medicaments for man . . . The Thalidomide disaster is often cited as an argument for stricter tests. But today a similar disaster cannot be avoided with sufficient certainty through animal tests anymore than in the past."

And finally the *Journal of the American Medical Association* of October 20, 1975 revealed that man had been found to be 60 times more sensitive to Thalidomide than mice, 100 times more sensitive than rats, 200 times more than dogs, and 700 times more than hamsters—all favorite test animals.

So why make such tests at all? The eternal question elicits the eternal answer: Because there is money in it. Money by the ton.

*   *   *

"Persisting on the wrong road, the pharmaceutical industry—in collusion with health departments and the silence of official medical science—continues to prepare new pharmacological calamities."

The preceding prediction is from an article of mine on the Thalidomide case, in the October 1973 issue of the Italian monthly, *Animali e Natura*. Alas! I was an easy prophet.

In May 1975 London's *Sunday Times* reported under the title "These Drugs Can Deform Babies but Mothers Are Not Warned" that "thousands of pregnant women each year are unknowingly risking malformed births by taking hormone drugs prescribed by their doctors. About 100,000 prescriptions a year are being written for pills such as Primodos and Amenorone Forte, which a woman can take as a way of testing for pregnancy." The article went on to say that if the woman is pregnant, the fetus is exposed to a large dose of these powerful hormonal drugs at the most sensitive stage in its development, that a warning had recently appeared in a terse letter in the *British Medical Journal* (Apr. 26), but that "only 4 out of 10 general practitioners read every issue of the journal and about 3 out of 10 read it only occasionally or not at all." Then came the long story of how those drugs had been under suspicion ever since 1967, when more and more women who had used them had borne malformed babies.

Whoever knew the Thalidomide story had a sickly déjà-vu feeling in reading the rest of that article by the *Sunday Times'* medical correspondent, Oliver Gillie. And of course what was happening in Great Britain was happening wherever synthetic drugs were being produced and palmed off on a credulous public.

In West Germany's authoritative medical journal, *Münchner Medizinische Wochenschrift* (No. 34, 1969) Dr. W. Chr. Müller of the nation's First Gynecological University Clinic reported that a sweeping survey by German doctors had revealed that "for 61% of all malformed children born alive and 88% of all stillborn children the intake of various drugs had to be held responsible."

In *Weisse Magier*, Kurt Blüchel reports the following figures relating to West Germany: "Twenty-five years ago the malformations were three in each 100,000 births, now they number 5 in only 1,000—*meaning a more than hundred-fold increase.*" (p. 259)

Further on in the same book, we find the monotonous information that "the organism of animals reacts often entirely differently from man's . . . Many products that damage the animals' fetuses don't harm human fetuses, but with others the opposite holds true —and therein lies the great danger. Many of these medicaments may well turn out to be time-bombs someday." (p. 357)

Now the question is: How much longer will the pharmaceutical industry be permitted to continue those criminal activities? How much longer will the people let themselves be exploited by a medical-industrial organization that speculates on their sufferings and on their constant anxiety, cowardice and ignorance? The obvious answer is: as long as they are not fully informed on all the aspects of vivisection—moral and medical.

The necessity for full information is demonstrated by an incident in 1973 that sheds a very unfavorable light upon the competence of the then British Minister of Education and Science. It happened when 151 Members of the House of Commons were ready to support the introduction of bills proposed by Kenneth Lomas and Douglas Houghton, aimed at reducing animal tortures. The bills they proposed would have obliged the government to develop alternative methods for medical research, or obliged the manufacturers to use only the alternative methods where such methods already existed. On July 18, 1973, Mrs. Margaret ("Iron Doll") Thatcher, Minister of Education and Science under the Heath government, was presented with a petition bearing 120,000 signatures of people who thought they could count on her help and were "urging the Government to make specific investigations into the entire field of alternative methods of research not involving living animals."

Clearly self-conscious of her role as an ambitious politician (who was soon to become the first woman at the head of her party), Thatcher rejected with icy disdain what she thought was merely a plea for humaneness, and sailed into an impassioned there-must-never-be-another-Thalidomide speech. Not one of the hundreds of supposedly well-informed and educated men and women in the House of Commons was able to retort on the spot that the Thalidomide tragedy was, like uncounted other tragedies, directly attributable to animal experimentation, that further such tragedies could only be avoided by abolishing the vivisectionist method of research, and that Turkey had in fact been spared the Thalidomide tragedy because virologist S. T. Aygün of the University of Ankara always and only used alternative methods and had therefore discovered the danger of it in time.

And yet, perpetuating the public deception, the American-owned Encyclopedia Britannica calmly continues to affirm under "Animal Experimentation": "The use of animals to test drugs and biologicals for safety and potency is widespread and necessary."

THE SO-CALLED TRANQUILIZERS

The term tranquilizer has come into general usage for all drugs that act on man's nervous system, although the laboratory workers, in their constant effort toward obscurantism, prefer more "scientific"-sounding words like hypnotics, ataractics or psychotropics. Whatever their name, those drugs were at first all widely advertised as harmless, well-tolerated and non-addictive—on the basis of extensive animal tests. In time, all those that were effective proved very harmful, ill-tolerated and addictive, so by and by the manufacturers had to change their descriptive leaflets and issue warnings.

Here is how the supposedly "tranquilizing" effect of a new drug preparation is ascertained: Some 200 "control" cats, confined to a small space, receive electric shocks through the metal floor grid. By dint of shocks, the cats eventually, after a carefully controlled lapse of time, become crazy with pain and terror, and not knowing whom to blame, they attack each other. Then those crazed cats are replaced with fresh, unused cats, to whom the presumed tranquilizer has been administered; if it takes this new bunch a longer time to go crazy, the tranquilizer is considered "effective." The longer time it takes the cats to fall upon each other can be due, of course, to a variety of drug-induced mutations having nothing to do with tranquility, but this consideration doesn't disturb today's pseudoscientists in the least.

A way of testing analgesics is by squeezing the tails of cats by means of a surgical clamp and "scientifically" recording their pained screech, *i.e.* registering the decibels, which is a measure of sound. Then each cat receives the supposed analgesic, whereafter its tail is squeezed again and the decibels are registered and compared to the previous results. It would be laughable if it were not so sad: sad for the victims, of course, but sad for humanity also, which has developed individuals capable of devising such means of "research," and of executing them.

Another way is by the usual electrode implanted through the skull to register the "brain waves" of the cats subjected to pinching, squeezing, puncturing—in vivisectors' jargon all called "noxious stimuli"— before and after administration of the "new" analgesic to be tested.

Then come of course the LD-50 tests to establish the new drug's "toxicity," not less barbarous, obtuse and misleading, which has been illustrated earlier.

A case in point is Metaqualone, a hypnotic that in 1973 was found to have caused serious mental derangements, hundreds of them with fatal outcomes, not only in the U.S., where it originated, but in other countries where it had been marketed. Of course, Metaqualone is neither the first nor the last sedative that brought to its users no other lasting peace than the peace of the grave. In that same year, 1973, a "commission of experts" of the Yugoslav authorities published a list of 200 drugs that had just been forbidden to all motorists. The list included tranquilizers, painkillers, and other "psychotropics." The Yugoslav authorities had belatedly discovered that those drugs were particularly dangerous if taken together with an alcoholic beverage. But evidently these drugs had not proved troublesome for the cats on which they had been preventively tested.

Could the reason be that the cats are not in the habit of driving motor vehicles? Let alone after tippling?

Nobody knows how many fatal accidents, how many tragedies had to happen before those "experts" had issued the official warning, after imposing the dangerously fallacious animal tests in the first place. And probably they continue imposing them, in Yugoslavia as elsewhere, to wash their hands of any responsibility.

How many more tragedies must occur before the leading health authorities the world over recognize the truth? Provided they are interested in the truth. Nobody will ever be able to ascertain how many millions of the fatal or maiming car crashes that have occurred in the past decades everywhere were caused by those drugs, which the laboratories continue to turn out on the basis of animal tests.

A fairly recent discovery is that even the blandest tranquilizers and painkillers, besides harming liver and kidneys and exerting untoward influences on the nervous system in connection with alcohol, cause irreversible damage to the eyesight—another danger that the animal tests had failed to reveal. Inevitably, still other drawbacks will be discovered in time—giving the industry a reason to turn out once more "new" drugs, which will be advertised as "free of any side-effects, as extensive animal tests have demonstrated." At least for a while.

*　　*　　*

"Animal tests," writes Kurt Blüchel in *Weisse Magier,* "reveal very little about psychic effects: we don't know if a rat feels happy or depressed. On the other hand a long time may pass before we discover the side-effects of a new drug. It took us 80 years to discover that Aspirin can cause internal hemorrhages . . . . Nobody has attained lasting happiness through psychodrugs. Countless people have suffered serious physical and mental damages through the usage of those drugs, and many have died from them. Among the side-effects of tranquilizers, Dr. H. Häfner of the Psychiatric and Neurological Clinic of the University of Heidelberg has cited for instance: vertigoes, delirium, epileptic fits, allergies, liver complications, thrombosis."

Blüchel goes on to say that at the end of 1972 London psychiatrist Dr. Simon Behrman had warned in *Journal of Psychiatry* against the use of Phenothiazin, another tranquilizer much used in the psychiatric institutions, as he had found it capable, in normal dosage, of causing loss of speech. But the most dangerous side-effects of the Phenothiazin combinations is the so-called agranulocytosis, an extremely serious, frequently deadly disease of the blood, which manifests itself mainly in women above the age of 35, within 5 to 10 weeks after the first administration of that drug. (*Op. cit.* pp. 358-359)

Now all these are pretty serious charges against a group of drugs that once upon a time had all been advertised as "harmless," but it is by far not all. Recently another psychodrug has been accused of causing malformations: Lithium, according to a report in France's *Revue de Médecine* (Mar. 29, 1976). It read: "The hypothesis, formulated a few years back, that lithium salts are responsible of fetal malformations has now been confirmed by Prof. Schow. This chemical substance, which has been used increasingly since 1970 for its curative action in cases of mania and for the prevention of manic-depressive psychoses, crosses the placental barrier and causes cardiac and vascular deformations in the children whose mothers have been administered lithium during the first months of pregnancy. These malformations have been discovered in 16 children out of 150 that have been examined."

This news item had been previously published by the two Paris dailies, *Le Figaro* of January 22 and *Le Monde* of January 23, 1976.

Let me add that with the thousands of new drugs coming on the world market every year, only our descendants will know what genetic side effects they can cause, and the full truth will presumably never be known, as every combination can have different effects. What we know for sure already is that the effects are not good—and that humanity has grown noticeably more nervous, not less, since the so-called tranquilizers have been flooding the market.

But all this is nothing when compared to the news from the cancer front.

CANCER

"To the question as to whether experimental research on cancer has led to new means or indicated new ways for an effective fight against this disease, not even the greatest optimist could answer yes."

This can be said today. And it was said half a century ago by Prof. Bruno Bloch of Zurich, to an assembly of other doctors, as reported by *Schweizerische Medizinische Wochenschrift* (1927, No. 51, p. 1218).

It was Frank Burnet, Australian virologist and immunologist, who first formulated a general theory explaining how the living organism fights off diseases: with an inborn capacity to recognize and fight germs, viruses, cells and bacteria that are alien to that organism and likely to harm it. A few years later, together with Lewis Thomas of the Sloan-Kettering Cancer Institute, Frank Burnet advanced the hypothesis that there could be a relationship between this immunological system and cancer. The human body, according to Burnet and Thomas, continually generates many abnormal cells, genetically different from the normal ones and potentially cancerogenic. The immunological system usually destroys them before they can multiply. But when, for some reason or another, the natural defenses are weakened or hampered and are unable to recognize and destroy the abnormal cells, these cells multiply rapidly, invading the healthy tissues and destroying the organism.

Since everything that could conceivably be tried to defeat cancer has been tried in vain—mainly by inflicting the disease upon billions of animals, then submitting them to various tests while they painfully waste away—the major cancerologists have now finally come to at least one conclusion: that while the cancer scare will remain for a long time the best pretext for extorting money from the public, science will probably never single out the agent that provokes the malady, and thus will never be able to perfect a "miracle drug" that eliminates it overnight; but that the best remedy lies in the natural defense system with which every living organism is provided by nature.

In the fall of 1973, exactly two centuries after Peyrilhe had inaugurated the experimental fight on cancer, using a dog, the Swiss Anti-Cancer League awarded first prize to Jean-Charles Cerottini of Lausanne and Robert Keller of Zurich, whose published works the League had considered the most important of the year for the fight on cancer. And what were they all about? Essentially, in recognizing that a strengthening of the natural defensive power of the organism is the best way to ward off cancer.

This is also an admission that everything that had been tried up to then has been useless; that the fantastic expenditures, the gigantic efforts, the incredible tortures deliberately inflicted not upon millions but billions of animals, represented a total waste of money, time and sufferings.

Clinical experiments which seem to confirm that the immunological system also eliminates cancer have long been made. Such tests were, of course, highly reprehensible. At any rate they confirmed the theory that nature takes care of diseases, so long as it is not ruined by unreasonable interference.

At the Sloan-Kettering Institute cancerous cells have been injected into human patients, some of them cancer patients in the terminal stage, others healthy individuals. Only in a few cases did the cancerous cells injected in healthy individuals continue to grow, but within 2 to 3 weeks they had all been eliminated by the organism. The result with the cancer patients was quite different: They evidently had an immunological defect, because they required several weeks, up to eight, before their organism had rejected the implanted cancerous tissues. Details of these experiments have appeared in the *Bulletin* of the New York Academy of Medicine (1958, *34*, p. 416) and in *Annals of the Academy of Science* (1958, *73*, p. 635).

But meanwhile international cancer research continues stolidly working on animals. And what keeps surprising the outside observer is the automatism of the current method of research, its perverse persistence in the ancient errors— for the warning signs are not of recent date. But modern Bernardism is just as reluctant to recognize its errors as was the ancient Galenism. Today, as in the Middle Ages, the ignorance of the scholars is particularly long-lived.

Before showing how modern "medical science," far from defeating cancer or even just checking its rise, has directly contributed to the propagation of this disease, let us briefly look at the cancer situation at the time these lines are written. Since comparative figures on a world scale are lacking, we shall examine the U.S. figures, which cover a reasonably large number of individuals.

* * *

A vast analysis concluded in 1972 has established that in the United States more women between the ages of 30 and 34 years die from cancer than from any other cause. In spite of the alleged progress in early diagnosis, surgery, irradiation and chemotherapy, mortality from breast cancer has remained unchanged over the past 35 years.

More children between 3 and 14 years of age die from cancer than from any other disease. Among men, cancer has increased 40 percent between 1936 and 1971.

Since 1933, the year the U.S. government first began gathering cancer-mortality figures nationwide, the overall death rate from cancer had increased 66 percent. In 1972 the cancer death rate rose at the fastest pace in 22 years. The rate of increase was 3.35 percent, or about triple the annual average since 1950.

The side effects (including bone-marrow depression, kidney damages, liver necrosis, cerebral hemorrhages, etc.) of the anti-cancer treatments are so severe that a sizable percentage of patients haven't the time to die from cancer because the side effects of the treatment kill them before cancer can.

Apart from the known damages the anti-cancer treatments cause, there must of course be a great many as yet unknown damages, which will be discovered someday; for instance, genetic damages—to children conceived after or while one of their parents was under treatment for cancer.

So for years now, cancer has been on the increase, and the rate of increase is quickening. Medical science, to hide its impotence, puts up smoke screens like this statement from Dr. Frank J. Rauscher, Jr., director of the U.S. cancer program: "Much of the increase is due to the increasing percentage of our population that is 55 years of age or older, an age group that is at high risk to cancer." (*International Herald Tribune,* Apr. 10, 1973)

Irresponsible deception, of course, as people don't get older in the U.S. than they used to 20 years ago. The worst sign of all: The major increase is in infant and juvenile cancer.

So there is no alibi for this increase, no matter how you twist and turn it. Most modern maladies are fabricated by today's misled medicine men, and cancer most of all.

At the end of 1975, the world press reported that "The number of cancer deaths in the U.S. is rising faster than it has in decades. The National Center of Health Statistics has reported a 5.2 percent jump in the mortality rate in the first 7 months of 1975. In past years the rate had increased at a steady 1 percent. This increase has been attributed by Frank Rauscher, head of the National Cancer Institute, to the rising consumption of chemical products." (*Tages-Anzeiger,* Nov. 8, and *Time,* Dec. 8.) Could it be that even the head of the National Cancer Institute is finally catching on?

A dispatch from Washington, DC, datelined July 29, 1976, read: "60 percent of cancer cases in U.S.

women and 41 percent in U.S. men are related to dietary habits, a National Cancer Institute researcher told a Senate committee yesterday . . . Cancer of the colon and breast have been linked to a high-fat diet and other dietary factors correlated with cancers of the stomach, liver, kidneys and prostate, the researcher, Dr. Gio Gori, told the Senate Select Committee on Nutrition and Human Needs . . . Asked by committee members what Americans should do to decrease risk factors for cancer in their diet, both Dr. Gori and Dr. Mark Hegsted, a nutritionist from Harvard's School of Public Health, said they should eat less, cutting down on fat, meat, sugar, and salt." (*International Herald Tribune,* July 30, 1976)

So this was news in America's capital in 1976, although some 25 years previously two leading British physicians, Sir Arbuthnot Lane and Lord Moynihan, had written innumerable articles asserting "there is no doubt that cancer arises from something we eat"—and this includes food and medicaments. Since animals have different alimentary habits and alimentary tracts than we have, it is difficult to understand the rationale prompting the researchers to discover "the secret of cancer" by animal tests. Once more, this whole research sounds useless, done by retarded individuals. Except for the money angle, of course.

It takes some strength of character to cut down on the intake of meat and "miracle" drugs, and renounce the lucrative grants for "research." It is much easier to continue indulging in one's favorite foods, meanwhile using animals as scapegoats for one's own foibles, and hope for the best.

CANCER-CAUSING DRUGS?

A synopsis of a detailed article in *Science* (May 19, 1972, pp. 813-814) by Dr. Leonard Hayflick, formerly with the Wistar Institute in Philadelphia, Pa, then professor of Microbiology at Stanford University, Calif., reads:

"Vaccines against human viruses are mostly produced on monkey kidneys and on cultures of chicken embryos; both may be contaminated. Several people have died as a result of handling monkeys or their cultured cells. A substantial number (25 to 80 percent) of monkey kidneys processed for vaccine manufacture must be discarded because of extensive contamination with one or more of 20 known viruses. The annual slaughter of monkeys for primary cultures has reached such proportions that several species are endangered. At least several hundred thousand people in the U. S. have been inoculated with live SV-40 virus found in polio vaccines produced in monkey kidney cells. This SV-40 virus produces tumors in hamsters and converts normal human cells to cancer cells in vitro."

This information gathered from Prof. Hayflick's article simply means that the overwhelming majority of people vaccinated all over the world have been inoculated with potentially cancerogenic substances, *i.e.* theoretically capable of producing cancer.

Not only has the SV-40 virus, which occurs in monkey kidneys, proved capable of altering normal human cells "in vitro," modifying them into cells that have all the attributes of cancer cells, but this SV-40 virus is not killed by formaline, meaning that it survives the normal processes of formalinization required for the production of vaccines of killed polio virus. (For more technical details, see *American Review of Respiratory Disease,* vol. 88, no. 3, Sept. 1963, and *Postgraduate Medicine,* vol. 35, no. 5, May 1964.)

It was to prevent this fatal risk that more than 10 years ago Dr. Leonard Hayflick, who at that time was with the Wistar Institute of Anatomy and Biology, Philadelphia, developed that vaccine substrate named WI-38 obtained from a human fetal tissue mentioned in the chapter "Alternative Methods." The results of Prof. Hayflick's research were announced by him at the 10th International Congress of Microbiology (Prague, 1967), and have been discussed extensively in the medical press. Here is a summary from an article in *Laboratory Practice* (Jan. 1970, pp. 58-62):

"Canine kidney now used for production of measles vaccine in the U. S. is also not without a potential adventitious viral flora. Puppies, whose kidneys are the source of these cells, have been found infected with infectious canine hepatitis virus. Infectious canine hepatitis occurs as a common infection which most dogs have during the first year of life where the virus is known to persist in the kidney. One strain of infectious canine hepatitis virus has been reported to produce tumors in hamsters. Canine Herpes virus also can occur in canine kidneys. Several canine cancerogenic viruses are also known, including those causing canine papillomas, canine venereal tumor, and canine mast cell leukemia . . ."

The following statements in the same article are of particular relevance: "It is common knowledge that the most important cancerogenic animal viruses (those that can be isolated from primates; SV-40 and the cancerogenic adenoviruses) are *only* cancerogenic when they *do* cross the species barrier. No primate cancerogenic virus is known to produce tumors in the animal species to which the virus is indigenous, but such viruses can produce tumors in heterologous [other, different] animal species. Thus the SV-40 and the cancerogenic adenoviruses are cancerogenic, not for their natural hosts, but for other animal species. In respect to the safety of human virus vaccines, the only conclusion that can be drawn is that *the risk for cancerogenity of human virus vaccines is greater for those vaccines produced in animal cells than for those vaccines produced in human cells:* the potential cancerogenity for any vaccine is diminished if the vaccine is produced in the cells of the animal species to which the vaccine is to be administered."

* * *

Thus we are gradually discovering that the biological antagonism between species is so powerful that viruses indigenous to one species, and therefore harmless to it—for example, the SV-40 is harmless for monkeys, in which it occurs naturally—may "go crazy" when transferred to a different species, such as man, to the point of becoming cancerogenic, capable of producing cancer. Which also helps to explain why the sorcerer's apprentices of our Bernardian epoch have been so eminently successful in "inoculating human cancers into animals"—or so they believed. Whereas it is likely that in many cases not the cancerogenity of the diseased cells inoculated into the animals but the biological difference of the species have caused these animals to develop cancer.

Conversely, the vaccinations with which we had hoped to immunize ourselves and our children from polio and other infections we fear, have transmitted to us and our children a cancerogenic potential which is gradually manifesting itself on a world-wide scale, as the death rate from cancer seems to indicate. It would be ironic indeed if we got proof some day that the alleged elimination of polio—which was already disappearing on its own before the vaccine was introduced, and which caused comparatively few victims at that time—was obtained at the expense of thousands of cancer deaths.

As Prof. J. Clausen of the Institute of Preventive Medicine of the University of Odense, Denmark, declared in March 1973: "Millions of people have been inoculated with the anti-polio vaccine contaminated with the tumoral SV-40 virus, which in origin was present in the monkeys. It is possible that it will take 20 or more years before the eventual harmful effect of this virus will manifest itself."

Once more, our sorcerer's apprentices can't say that they haven't received sufficient warning. Instances of warnings against the cancerogenic danger from smallpox vaccination:

"The vaccination causes furthermore an explosion of leukemia," wrote Dr. B. Duperrat, physician at the Hospital of Saint-Louis, France, in *Presse Médicale* as far back as March 12, 1955.

The January 1958 issue of another French medical magazine, *Revue de Pathologie Générale et de Physiologie Clinique,* stated: "The vaccine modifies the terrain of the vaccinated, driving it towards alkaline and oxydized terrain—the terrain of cancer. The fact can no longer be denied."

And Professors Julian Aleksandrowicz and Boguslav

Halileokowski of the Medical Academy of Cracow, Poland, have written (as reported by *Lancet,* May 6, 1967): "Already published reports as well as our own observations indicate that smallpox vaccination sometimes produces manifestation of leukemia. In children and adults observed in the clinics of Cracow, small-. pox vaccination has been followed by violent local and general reactions and by leukemia."

Smallpox vaccination can also cause cancer in the form of malignant tumors, as has been found in 38 persons whose tumors originated from the vaccination scar. This was front-page news in 1969 in *Medical News*. Dr. Willard L. Marmelzat, University of Southern California, had told the 2nd International Congress of Tropical Dermatology that at no time had any of these people been exposed to chemical carcinogens, nor were any related, nor had any sustained injury or mechanical trauma to the vaccination site.

Vaccines are not, of course, the only suspects or culprits among the drugs. An excerpt from an article by Dr. Freda Lucas in *Medical World,* July 1957, page 47, reads: "In England and Wales, total death rates from all forms of leukemia have increased more than six times between 1920 and 1952 . . . According to Wilkinson, sulphonamides stand convicted as one of the contributing factors even when fairly low dosages were exhibited. In cases quoted in detail, the tragic path from agranulocytosis to haemolitic anemia and *acute monolytic leukemia* is revealed in black and white."

So even if we were to abandon the current Bernardian method this very day, the growing death rate from cancer is most unlikely to be halted before a new generation comes to life. And it also explains why the pseudoscience which has brought the human species to such a pretty pass makes great efforts to conceal most of its recent findings.

But the figures stand. And mathematics—contrarily to what passes for medical science today—is no moot point. And the figures demonstrate that cancer continues to increase.

It would indeed be ironic if some day we had

mathematical proof that the decrease of infections,
or other trouble that the human organism can overcome on its own, had been paid for with the increase
of cancer. And new indications that exactly this is
happening come up all the time, abreast of the industry's increasing output of new drugs. Of course,
only a few detailed examples can be cited in a treatise
like this, which must cover various fields. Let us examine just one of the latest cases—of a drug that the
"official" medical science has discovered to be directly responsible for a new type of juvenile cancer,
non-existent a few decades ago.

THE STILBOESTROL CASE
OR THE CANCER MONGERS

"It's worse than a crime: it's a mistake."

Talleyrand

Modern medical science, to which most of the civilized world's population looks up for its "salvation"—
though salvation from what isn't quite clear—has developed in the laboratory and then marketed on a
world-wide scale alleged estrogens (which is medi-
calese for sexual hormones, the secretions produced
by the sex glands). Among the various reasons why
these synthetic estrogens are administered by the modern medicine men is to insure the successful outcome
of pregnancies. Over the past several decades millions
of women all over the world have been prescribed
them by their doctors, with the assurance that it might
help prevent miscarriages.

A natural, spontaneous miscarriage is clearly a
safety valve built in by Mother Nature, eliminating at
the fetal stage individuals who are inapt for survival,
not quite viable; thus spontaneous miscarriages contribute to strengthening the species and keeping it in
good health. But such obvious considerations have
never disturbed scientists who must either justify their
high fees or satisfy their experimental curiosity, and
who have been led to believe through their vivisection-

ist training that they can circumvent nature as easily as they can deceive public opinion.

Of course, no doctor in the world can guarantee that the administration of a drug will prevent a miscarriage, nor that the successful outcome of a pregnancy has ever been due to a particular drug. But since 1973 there is one thing medical science now knows for sure.

In that year, Italy's internationally known vivisector Prof. Silvio Garattini asserted in a public debate (*Epoca*, Oct. 14, 1973) that "we are able to reproduce in a laboratory exactly a natural estrogen." But at about the same time, WHO in Geneva was printing in all haste a warning in English to medical circles: It had been indisputably proved that the prototype of those synthetic estrogens, Stilboestrol, had caused cancer in humans.

The WHO paper was authored by Robert W. Miller, director of the epidemiology branch of the National Cancer Institute of Bethesda, Maryland: it was titled *Transplacental Carcinogenesis*, and bore the No. 4 of IARC's (International Agency for Research on Cancer) Scientific Publications, Lyon, 1973.

On page 175, in the chapter titled "Prenatal Origins of Cancer in Man: Epidemiological Evidence," Dr. Robert W. Miller wrote:

"Transplacental Chemical Carcinogenesis. Less than 6 months ago the dramatic announcement was made that cancer could be induced in the child by a drug that the mother had taken during pregnancy. (Herbst *et al*, 1971a) Never before had such an occurrence been observed. A particular form of vaginal cancer (clear-cell adenocarcinoma), a disease of the elderly, was reported in 8 young women in the Boston area. They were 14 to 22 years of age. The mothers of 7 had been given Stilboestrol during pregnancy. In a matched control group of 32 mothers, none had been given the drug. Five additional vaginal cancers of the same type in young women were found immediately thereafter through the New York State Tumor Registry. (Greenwald *et al.*, 1971) All 5 of the mothers had received synthetic oestrogens during pregnancy. In commenting on still another case reported by Newman (1971), Herbst *et al.* (1971b) stated that they knew of more than 20 cases since publication of their 7 cases. Various studies are being planned to evaluate the health status of children whose mothers received Stilboestrol during pregnancy. *In any event, there is now no doubt that transplacental carcinogenesis has occurred in man after a latent period of 14 to 22 years.*

"Prezygotic Determinants. Genetic influences can operate in a similar fashion. Years or even decades may pass free of symptoms before genetically determined cancers show themselves."

* * *

So it isn't anymore a question as to if and when and how and at what cost so-called medical science is going to present us with the miracle pill that eliminates cancer once and for all: Modern science *causes* cancer. The WHO document is the first "scientific proof" of it, by the scientists' own standards, and furthermore proof that it has created a kind of cancer that did not exist before. Since this has been proved true in one case, it must be true also in many other cases, not yet "scientifically" ascertained. And this of course helps explain the relentless rise of cancer in the past decades: a rise that proceeds abreast of the rising consumption of the endless variety of new medical drugs.

Excessive doses of synthetic vitamins have caused bone tumors, medicines designed to relieve mild cases of high blood pressure make women far more prone to breast cancer, vaccines cultivated on animals have shown cancerogenic potential, antibiotics long considered safe have produced leukemia, and recently it has been proved "scientifically"—by the vivisectionists' own standards—that a synthetic estrogen, administered for decades to humans because it had proved harmless for animals, hasn't merely retarded bone growth or caused liver and kidney damages, cataracts, heart and mental troubles in man, but has been the incontrovertible cause of malignant tumors in the offspring.

As in many other instances, the responsibility for the Stilboestrol tragedy also rests squarely on the vivisectionist method of research. And it appears to me that medical science has pleaded guilty in Dr. Miller's report, and its responsibilities are so much the heavier in that in the course of the preceding four decades endless warnings have been sounded that it is dangerous to judge the effects of hormones in general and sexual ones (estrogens) in particular by animal tests. All these warnings were once more scorned by the various national institutes of health, who perhaps are not pledged to respecting ethics, but are responsible for public welfare.

The following public warnings are just a few examples among the many that have been sounded when there was still time to heed them.

* * *

"As pointed out by Halban, the placenta stimulates the growth of the genitals and the breast glands. While this is true for animals, it does not hold good for human beings." (J. P. Greenhill, *American Journal of Obstetrics and Gynecology,* Feb. 1929, p. 254)

* * *

A. M. Mendenhall, M. D., Head of the Department of Obstetrics, Indiana University School of Medicine, in an article entitled "Solution of Pituitary and Ruptured Uterus":

"It is a powerful drug even when greatly diluted, and no method has yet been developed that will positively insure a given strength. Too much cannot be said in warning those who persist in using this powerful drug that there is no dependable way of knowing the degree of effect they may expect from it until they try it out on the patient herself." (*Journal of the American Medical Association,* Apr. 20, 1929, p. 1341)

* * *

"The injection of adrenalin into the heart is particularly reprehensible, and when patients afterwards recover, it is in spite of, and not because of, the injection. Grave harm may be done by the production of haemopericardium or pericarditis. Intravenous injection of adrenalin is known to provoke dangerous cardiac irregularities." (Dr. L. J. Witts, *Medical World*, Jan. 23, 1931, p. 565)

* * *

"Pituitrin [a hormone] is a diuretic in cats, having the opposite effect in human beings." (*Journal of Physiology*, Vol. LXXVI, Nov. 1932, p. 384)

* * *

"It is almost a hundred years since Raynard, a veterinary surgeon at Lyons, discovered that removal of the thyroid gland in dogs was rapidly fatal. Fifty years later Schiff showed that while this was true of cats as well as dogs, it was not true of rabbits and rats." (Leading article, *Lancet*, Dec. 2, 1933, p. 1267)

* * *

"Regarding the endocrine preparations, although there have been lately some very important discoveries, great care must be taken in using them. There has been much dangerous misuse in this respect because of the hurried application of animal experiments to man, and because also of the streams of propaganda flowing from the various pharmaceutical firms." (Dr. A. P. Cawadias, *Medical World*, Apr. 5, 1935, p. 191)

* * *

As to the induction of labour by the injection of ovarian extracts: "Such experiments have been almost uniformly successful when applied to animals such as the rodents, but they have been a complete failure in the human subject." (Drs. A. Leyland Robinson, M. M. Datnow, and T. N. A. Jeffcoate, Hon. Surgeons, Liverpool Hospital for Women, *British Medical Journal*, Apr. 13, 1935, p. 749)

* * *

"Of very considerable importance is the attempted treatment of prostatic enlargement by means of male hormones. Experiments with mice and monkeys un-fortunately proved misleading when their results were applied to man." (Review, *Medical World,* May 3, 1940, p. 226)

* * *

"Another form of substitution therapy for men is injection of male hormone solutions, of which syn-thetic products have recently been put on the market . . . At present, many contradictory reports of animal experimentations becloud the issue for the clinician, and only too often create an almost hopeless confu-sion." (Review, *Medical World,* Jan. 17, 1941, pp. 504-5)

* * *

Medical World, January 16, 1942, in a review of *Essentials of Endocrinology* by Dr. Arthur Grollman: "So much of the work done in connection with these various substances has necessarily had to be carried out on laboratory animals, and when these results have been applied to humans they have been found to be hopelessly misleading and even dangerous in not a few instances." (p. 482)

* * *

"The practical results of treatment with sex hor-mones fall far short of what might be wished. One rea-son is that the results of animal experiments cannot be applied to women." (Dr. Alfred Gough, Hon. Consult-ing Surgeon to the Leeds Hospital for Women, in *Medical Press and Circular,* Mar. 14, 1945, p. 169)

* * *

". . . Facts incontrovertible in the laboratory are applied to clinical medicine in a manner quite unwar-ranted. The best examples are the indiscriminate use of hormones and the ready acceptance of the biased blurbs of research propagated by commercial travel-lers." (Dr. Ffrangcon Roberts, *British Medical Jour-nal,* June 16, 1945, p. 848)

* * *

"We well remember how there was a boom in hormonal therapy. Much of the vaunted good results obtained was wrongly deduced from animal experiments . . . These results, when applied to humans clinically, were found to be not only erroneous but in some cases highly dangerous." (Review, *Medical World*, June 6, 1947, p. 471)

* * *

"The sensitivity of animals varies from laboratory to laboratory, and therefore it is impossible to compare potencies arrived at in one laboratory with those of another. It has been usual to assume that the sensitivity of all mammals is roughly the same for oestrogen, but there is now considerable evidence that such is not the case, and that it is most unwise to assume that the human female will react in the same way as laboratory animals. This work is of very great interest in that it shows the folly of applying results obtained on animals to the human being." (Prof. Dr. E. C. Dodds, *Journal of Pharmacy and Pharmacology*, Vol. I, No. 3, 1949, pp. 143-45).

* * *

"When oestrogen first became available for clinical use, there was an understandable over-enthusiasm for its application . . . If one depends on the beautifully embossed brochures which exhort the practitioner with every mail, one falls, unhappily, into the security of the illusion that there are neither contra-indications nor side-effects in the use of oestrogen." (Drs. Robert A. Kimbrough and S. Lion Israel, *Journal of the American Medical Association*, Vol. 138, Dec. 25, 1949, p. 1216)

* * *

"It seems clear therefore that one is not justified in depending on the result of animal assays to determine the relative potency of oestrogens in the human subject." (Drs. P. M. F. Bishop, N. A. Richards, M. B.

Adelaide, and Neal Smith, *Lancet*, May 6, 1950, p. 850)

* * *

"Thomas Addison's monograph of 1855 opens with the words: 'It will hardly be disputed that at the present moment the functions of the suprarenal capsules, and the functions they exercise in the general economy, are almost or altogether unknown.' Like so much of his writings, these words are still true. We have accumulated a mass of facts, but we still can say little about the organism." (Dr. F. G. Young, professor of biochemistry, University of Cambridge, *British Medical Journal*, Dec. 29, 1951, p. 1541)

* * *

"At the CIBA Foundation, London, on July 3rd, Prof. Houssay reviewed his group's work on the influence of sex hormones on the incidence and severity of experimental diabetes in the rat; but he first warned his audience not to accept these results for other animals or for humans." (Annotation in the *Lancet*, July 14, 1951, p. 70)

* * *

"I cannot overemphasize the fallacies inherent in the efforts to apply directly to man the results of animal experiments in the field of hormones." (From the testimony of Don Carlos Hines, M. D., before the Delaney Committee of the House of Representatives, Jan. 31, 1952)

* * *

"There were important differences between the reactions of the uteri of different species to pituitary hormones and between in vivo and in vitro experiments. Great caution was therefore necessary in making any inferences about the action of drugs on the human uterus from such data." (Prof. G. H. Bell, at the 13th British Congress of Obstetrics and Gynaecology: *British Medical Journal*, Aug. 2, 1952, p. 281)

* * *

"The discovery of the ovarian hormones, oestrogen and progesterone from 1917 onwards, and later the gonadotrophins of the anterior pituitary, opened a wide new field in physiology. The astonishing effects of all four hormones when given to small laboratory animals led to great expectations of their therapeutic value in obstetrics and especially gynaecology. These early hopes have been disappointed." (Dr. Alec Bourne, Surgeon, *Medical World*, June 13, 1952, p. 400)

* * *

"Knowledge of the endocrine control of these processes is derived mainly from experimental studies on a number of different animal species. So great is the variation in response of these species to the hormone concerned that it would be imprudent to assume that the human breast behaves in a manner similar to the mammary gland in any particular species studied." (Dr. P. M. F. Bishop, *The Practitioner*, June 1956, p. 630)

* * *

Dealing with the assay of oxytocic drugs (*i.e.* drugs supposed to hasten parturition): "With the exception of drugs acting on the soul, the most striking differences between animal and human experiments are probably to be found in drugs acting on the uterus. Much time and effort have been spent in trying to find new oxytocic drugs by experiments on animals, which later proved to be completely inactive when tested on the human uterus. There is thus a need for assay methods by which oxytocic drugs can be tested on the human uterus." (Dr. H. O. Schild, reader in pharmacology, University College, London; joint author of Clark's *Applied Pharmacology: Quantitative Method in Human Pharmacology and Therapeutics*, Pergamon Press, London, 1959. Report of a Symposium held in London, Mar. 1958, p. 154)

* * *

"Dr. P. Richter, of the famed Phipps Psychiatric Clinic at the Johns Hopkins Hospital, conducted controlled experiments with drugs and hormones commonly in use and his results were published in the August issue of *Proceedings of the National Academy of Sciences*. His conclusions are a warning that, while certain drugs and hormones may have an immediate beneficial effect, the patient may suffer permanent damage which will not appear until months after discontinuance of the medication. These medicaments had already been 'proved' by the usual tests on animals, chiefly rats, to be perfectly harmless." (Cited from *News-Post*, Baltimore, Aug. 5, 1959)

* * *

The preceding citations prove that also in the field of synthetic hormones the bankruptcy of the current research method had been clearly predicted. Eminent specialists had explicitly warned of the danger. But not even the greatest pessimist among them had expected that someday this antiscientific method might prove guilty of causing cancer.

How many women have been administered these cancer-causing estrogens? How many people who will die of cancer in the coming decades are today already carrying in their systems an early death sentence received through their mother's placenta? We shall never know. Of course thousands of other synthetic medicaments all over the world must be capable of causing the same effect as Stilboestrol.

For West Germany alone, Kurt Blüchel lists in *Weisse Magier* 173 basic medicaments that represent hazards for the fetus if administered to the mother, and some of these medicaments occur in many products under different labels. What we know for sure is that the rate of acceleration of cancer and malformations has been increasing during the past 30 years, abreast of the increase of drug consumption.

The colossal fraud that today's official "research," speculating on human suffering and especially on people's fear of suffering, is perpetrating against public health—no matter whether from greed or incompetence—has assumed almost inconceivable dimensions. And it is the more intolerable in light of the fact that the herborist who sells some natural decoction (always less harmful and usually more useful than any chemical drug) can be indicted in many countries for unlawfully practicing the medical profession, as happened lately in Italy; while the confessed culprits of cancers and of the innumerable "diseases of civilization" are not only left free to move, but receive applause and fat subsidies with which to continue their criminal activities.

Let us return to the elucubrations of Dr. Robert Miller in the historic WHO paper. With that acumen that inevitably derives from long years of vivisectionist activity, Dr. Miller informs us that "when the tumor is present at birth, there can be no doubt that it arose *in utero*." (p. 177)

The illustrious scientist continues: "Considering all deaths under 5 years of age over the 8-year interval, 13,782 were due to neoplasia [tumors] that arose *in utero* or soon thereafter."

But now the author ruins his thriller with a cliché: He reveals that the butler did it. In fact, on page 181 near the end of his paper, Dr. Miller writes: *"Experimental animal studies. There was no correlation between the types of tumors obtained in experimental models and types of childhood cancer."*

In vivisectionist jargon, of course, *experimental models* means "laboratory animals subjected to experiments." So, in poor man's language, Dr. Miller might as well have said: "From the great variety of cancers that we have succeeded in causing through the years in uncounted millions of animals we haven't received the slightest hint about the danger of Stilboestrol for the fetus, so that for decades now we thought that we could administer this estrogen with impunity to pregnant women. Well, anybody can make a mistake."

*   *   *

And now, as had been the case with Thalidomide and the variety of other drugs first experimented with on animals and then proving ruinous for humans, how did the vivisectionist brotherhood react to this new

tragedy they had caused? Not by admitting that this
new tragedy demonstrated the folly of their method,
but by advocating an intensification of animal experiments. It is difficult to believe, but Dr. Miller actually
adds that "other animal species than the rodents might
profitably be employed. In particular, the use of non-
human primates was suggested." And he concludes his
remarkable paper with these words:

"*Recommendations to IARC.* IARC, through its
world-wide sources of information, can collect and
publicize reports warning of human transplacental
hazards from particular substances. IARC could carry
out investigations where the incidence of tumors and
malformations, or other circumstances, hint at transplacental carcinogenesis or teratogenesis. Finally, IARC
should compile a list of drugs and environmental con-
taminants which may represent a human prenatal
carcinogenic hazard in various areas of the world."

At this point, considering that every year thousands
of new drugs are thrown on the world market, and
Dr. Miller's own previous warning that "years or even
decades may pass free of symptoms before genetically
determined cancers show themselves," his recommendations to continue exactly along the old, proven road
to disaster and expand the experiments might at first
glance seem a sign of delirium. Not so. The illustrious
cancer artist is also a hard-nosed businessman. And
here's why.

The U.S. government's yearly expenditures earmarked for "research" amount to billions of dollars
every year. First, no "scientist" of Dr. Miller's standing can admit that everything he has believed, taught
and propagated during his entire lifetime is humbug.
Then, the Bethesda Institute of which he is one of
the most prominent directors is one of the leading
vivisection laboratories in the world, and as such gets
a fat slice of the Federal Pie every year, in addition
to sizable private subsidies. To renege the vivisectionist method in medical research would mean putting
tens of thousands of honest torturers out of work.

That would be inhuman. So it is preferable to go
on torturing millions of scapegoats—also to preserve

one's image of the "great scientist," who can step upon the podium reserved for the Saviors of Mankind in the medical congresses to the applause of thousands of colleagues convened from all over the world, and produce new "miracle drugs" like Thalidomide, Stilboestrol, *et al.* After all, the animals can't vote, can't protest—especially when they have been "devocalized,"—can't strike, can't call meetings, can't organize marches on the Capitol, can't throw bombs. If, then, the consumers are born malformed or retarded or epileptic or cancerous, that's just too bad.

Since Dr. Miller's warning published by WHO, the ascertained cancer casualties caused by Stilboestrol are no longer just a handful, but are now counted by the hundreds, and the number is inevitably bound to rise much further.

SORCERER'S APPRENTICES

Beyond figures and statistics, let's look for once at some of the victims of the sorcerer's apprentices that are taken for scientists. One case was reported by *Newsweek* (Jan. 26, 1976):

When Mrs. Grace Malloy from California read in a newspaper report that Stilboestrol was linked to a rare but deadly form of vaginal cancer in young women whose mothers had taken the hormone during pregnancy, she remembered that she had been prescribed this drug while she was expecting her daughters, Patti and Marilyn. By the time she read this they were 19 and 14. She had them examined and the result was bad news: Marilyn had vaginal cancer.

In an operation lasting more than 12 hours, Marilyn's vagina and nearby lymph glands were removed. An artificial vagina was constructed using skin grafts from her legs. A year later the doctors discovered that the cancer had spread to one lung, the esophagus and the lining of the heart. Following another operation, Marilyn seemed to recover, but soon her condition worsened again. Tests revealed that the cancer had reached her pituitary gland, and Marilyn underwent a grueling six-week regimen of "whole head" radiation. When all her hair fell out as a result, she kept up a brave front and started wearing a bright scarf over her head. But at night her mother could hear her moaning in pain as the cancer continued its lethal spread through her arms, legs, spine and brain. Soon she was blind and confined to a wheelchair. Marilyn died on May 26, 1974, two weeks before her high-school class' graduation.

Mrs. Malloy said: "I had no way of knowing what those pills would do. Thousands of women took them, because our doctors prescribed them." The article went on to say: "Grace Malloy is not without bitterness about what happened to her family—and what still may lie ahead. Her older daughter, Patti, now 25, has been diagnosed as having vaginal adenosis, a lesion that appears benign but could be the precursor of cancer . . . For the time being, Patti can only wait —like thousands of other young women with the same history—and pray that the killer that claimed her sister may pass her by."

So mass media like *Newsweek* do often reveal the bankruptcy of modern medical science. But they regularly fail to reveal that the therapeutic disasters, which are bound to increase over the next decades owing to the long "latent" period (sometimes 35 and more years) of the drugs' cancerogenic effect, are due to the wrong information attributable exclusively to the vivisectionist method of current medical research.

* * *

Indications that modern drugs, believed to be safe following animal trials, sweepingly contribute to diseases in general, and especially to the rise of cancer, are innumerable. In 1974 it became known that a Boston University team had analyzed the records of 25,000 patients admitted to 24 hospitals in the Boston area in 1972, and found that women aged over 50 who take certain types of medication to relieve mild cases of high blood pressure run a threefold increased risk of developing breast cancer. Determined not to be alarmist, the Boston group asked eminent specialists in England and Finland to run a similar check. Their

results were essentially the same. *Lancet* suggested
that doctors now would have to weigh the apparently
greater risk of breast cancer against the advantages of
lowering blood pressure for mature women.

Although this matter had been discussed in an editorial in the world's leading medical publication and
reported also by the general press, such as *Time* Magazine, more than a year later I hadn't yet found a
single doctor in Italy, France or Germany who had
heard about the matter. Most of them told me they
hadn't even had the time to *open* the medical literature that the drug manufacturers kept sending to
them.

As reported by *Newsweek* (Jan. 26, 1976), the use
of estrogens by middle-aged women to alleviate symptoms of the menopause increases their risk of uterine
cancer nearly five times. If the doctors are too busy
prescribing medicines to read the warnings, there is at
least some hope for patients who take the time to
read the general press.

There are indications that at long last the American
public is not willing to be taken much longer—and
American reactions usually foreshadow what happens
in other countries. *Time* reported in 1975 (June 9)
that patients' malpractice suits, once rare, were becoming so common that the average annual premiums
for high-risk specialists in California, for example,
soared in one year from $5,377 to $22,704.

And that was even before the Yugoslav-born,
Mexico-based sociologist, Ivan Illich, announced the
findings of his long, meticulous study of current
medical practice. From his book, *Medical Nemesis*
(Pantheon Books, New York, 1976), and his interview on the Italian-Swiss TV station of Lugano on
May 25, 1975, the public learned:

"In the American hospitals, between 18% and 30%
of all patients have pathological reactions induced by
the medications they receive . . .

"During the one-month strike of the Israeli hospitals,
the death-rate of the population was the lowest
ever . . .

"Dr. Salvador Allende, the late President of Chile

who was also a physician, proposed a reduction of the pharmacopeia to the few dozen items that had been proved to be of any value, and which are about the same ones carried by each Chinese barefoot doctor. Many of the minority of Chilean doctors who tried to translate the ideas of their president into practical programs were murdered within one week after the take-over by the junta on September 11, 1973 . . .

"The deliberately produced belief that people can't overcome a malady without a modern medicine causes more damages to their health than the doctors who impose their services upon the patients . . .

"The evaluation of medical efficacy formulated in down-to-earth terms shows that the diagnoses and treatment can be perfectly understood by every layman, but the constant usage of specialized language practically prevents the deprofessionalization of medicine . . .

"The precocious treatment of incurable diseases has no other effect than to aggravate the patient's condition . . .

"Doctors who discover in their organism the symptoms of cancer, delay longer than any other professional people of the same educational standing the recourse to diagnosis and professional treatment, being well aware that they have mainly a ritual meaning . . .

"The much advertised acrobatics of the surgeons, which are referred to with reverence as medical 'miracles,' have added up to one solid fact during the last 20 years: higher expenses and more new sufferings, without any effect on the life expectancy . . .

"The rising cost of medical care in the U.S. has run parallel with another event: the life expectancy for adult American males declined, and is expected to decline still further. The same thing is happening in Great Britain, in Japan and in most countries of the Common Market."

* * *

The researchers know that failures must be publicized as amply as successes, in order to educate the public about the priorities and politics of allocations. And so when they denounce the danger of medicaments, they do so only to call for an intensification of animal tests, meaning a multiplication of the errors and horrors.

Then was vivisector Markowitz right in considering the anti-vivisectionists' position "at the outset hopeless, for they could *not possibly succeed against an industry with billions of dollars at stake*"? Whether he was right or not depends on the rest of humanity.

SUPERB SALON AND MORAL LAW

"True science can be compared to a superb salon resplendent with lights, which one can reach only through a long, horrible kitchen." (Claude Bernard, *Introduction,* 1865, p. 44)

Ever since the apostle of modern vivisection palmed off this sophism upon a credulous world that was still groggy from the long sleep of medievalism, the horrible kitchen has widened immeasurably, its horrors have multiplied, taking on forms that not even Claude Bernard's deranged brain had conceived of, its miasmas have engulfed half the globe, spreading incurable diseases among mankind; but the "superb salon" has receded further and further, making room for ever larger hospitals, where increasingly perplexed priests in white robes perform mechanistic rituals that have replaced yesterday's and will be replaced by tomorrow's, and are as incomprehensible to the performers as to the patients on whom they are inflicted.

The moral law, whose existence the vivisectionists deny because they can't reproduce it in a laboratory, much less grasp it intuitively, operates in many different ways, most of them extremely subtle, but all equally devastating in the long run.

To believe that the crimes which humanity is committing against the animals in the pseudoscientific laboratories can go unpunished is not just a sign of obtuseness but of folly. The child who is born retarded or malformed or dies of cancer or leukemia because its mother was prescribed a harmful hormone or tranquilizer that had been proved harmless in drawn-out, cruel animal tests—this child pays for crimes committed by others. But so have billions of animals had to pay in the cruelest way for the callousness not only of vivisectors but of humanity at large, which bears at the very least the guilt of indifference: indifference to the infinite tortures other sentient creatures have been subjected to; and many people bear the responsibility of having actively supported the inhuman methods that now fall back on them and their offspring. A great many innocent human beings must equally pay for the continual violations of the moral law, simply because they are members of the human race, and that can't be helped. The moral law, once it starts operating, lets the chips fall where they may, and all we can say is that those chips are very effective.

The prolonged sufferings people are subjected to before being allowed to die are among the more obvious, short-term demonstrations of the moral law at work. Richard Kunnes, the young doctor who once declared that the American Medical Association (AMA) should be renamed the American Murder Association. and set fire to his membership card at an AMA convention, wrote in *Your Money or Your Life* (Dodd, Mead, New York, 1974):

"The 1960–1970 decade was the period of greatest U.S. health *research* expenditures in history and yet produced the least results." ("Research" has been put in italics by me here to remind the reader of something Dr. Kunnes didn't consider necessary to point out: that the research activity which looms so importantly in his reflections involves mainly, and often exclusively, animal experiments.) And further: "What can be predicted with utmost certainty is that the continued diversion of resources towards *research* will render health care more and more unavailable, resulting in the needless deaths of thousands, and cause undue sufferings to hundreds of thousands every year. Many medical schools have had to drain money allocated for patient services in order to put it into *research,* so as to attract more money and more *research.*"

Dr. Kunnes' book was destined to be just one more cry in the desert, especially as he offered no solution, had no explanation, gave no indication of having realized that the deplorable state of present-day medicine was the direct result of a method that corrupts the researchers' character, impairs their intelligence, and thus spells ruin for the science of health. Neither have most of the other authoritative medical scholars or historians I have cited—Sigerist, Rostand, Hayflick, Dubos, Inglis, Ryder, Blüchel, Illich—apparently understood where the basic error lies: in today's "basic research."

As hinted in the beginning of this treatise, if the current approach to the cure of disease were valid, we should long ago have entered an age of universal health. But just the contrary has come to pass.

There is a constant increase of cardiovascular diseases, of the arthritic and rheumatic maladies, of diabetes, psychoses and cancer, especially infantile cancer—meaning exactly those ills on which the vivisectionist research has concentrated most of its efforts. And as a consequence, life expectancy—which had increased prodigiously thanks to the control of infections and infant mortality when ancient hygiene found its way back into medical art—has ground to a halt, or is regressing.

Actually, a high life expectancy is not an indication of sound health. People can live long in very poor health. As Ivan Illich put it, "The true miracle of modern medicine consists of making whole populations survive on unhumanly low levels of personal health."

Many other investigators into the present state of medicine have had to admit that humanity has never been so unwell as today. Of conditions in West Germany, which are fairly typical for all "civilized" nations today, Kurt Blüchel has reported on page 174 of *Weisse Magier:* "In the Federal Republic, damages deriving from therapeutic methods employed or recommended by doctors represent today the most frequent cause of disease." And on page 257: "Today the average German citizen consumes about five times more medicaments than just before World War II. Is he five times healthier? Of course not. On the contrary: on the average the West German population is nowadays ill far more frequently than at that period . . . Inadvertently, an industry that was meant to cure disease has become the cause of disease."

And Prof. Guido Fanconi of the University of Zurich: "The doctors manage to make many patients sicker, and to make even healthy people sick." (*Op. cit.* p. 79)

Small wonder that life expectancy for a man of 45 has barely changed since the beginning of this century, and in many countries of the western hemisphere it is actually regressing, in spite of WHO's optimistic or misleading predictions. Life expectancy today is rising only in those nations where infant mortality can still be drastically reduced through introduction of early hygiene.

According to France's authoritative *Nouvel Observateur* (Oct. 28, 1974), the French population's life expectancy has not increased since 1965, but the mortality rate among the 15- and 20-year-olds is increasing at a rate of 2 percent a year. For the men aged 40 to 50, the rate of mortality has increased in the past 10 years in all industrialized nations. The paper went on to report that among British workers the mortality rate is higher today than it was in 1930. So one can't attribute the increase of chronic diseases, as many medical authorities try to do, to the fact that the average citizen reaches a higher age, for this does not apply.

And as far as the U.S. is concerned, for all the formidable therapeutic arsenal at the disposal of its citizens and the feverish activity of their doctors, Americans don't live longer today than their parents—but they suffer much more. In fact they go into retirement earlier because of ill health, and a far larger percentage of them are ailing than in the past, and for a longer time. Most of them spend the terminal years of their existence in the antechamber of death, in that purgatory that is the hospital, kept artificially alive—

if one may call that life—by intravenous feeding, injections, transfusions, oxygen tents, transplants, and violent medicines that produce such side-effects as painful gastritis, nausea, vomiting, renal and hepatic colics (the sudden, violent abdominal spasms that vivisectors artificially inflict upon thousands of laboratory animals) and often severe bone marrow depression or cerebral hemorrhages that paralyze the patient partially or totally.

Official figures show that 80 percent of all Americans now die in institutions, and that ever more public funds are being spent on extending with various technological means the dying process, meaning to make the sufferances last longer. Ivan Illich informs us that " 'Consultants' sanctimoniously select one in every five Englishmen who are afflicted with kidney failure and condition him to desire the scarce privilege of dying in protracted torture on dialysis. Much time and effort during the treatment is used in the prevention of suicide during the first and sometimes the second year that the artificial kidney may add to the lives of patients." (*Medical Nemesis,* 1975, London, p. 51)

Already in August 1972, Senate hearings had been conducted in Washington on "Dignity and Death." A long line of instances of incompetence and inhumanity of a medical class raised on vivisection and experimental fixation came to light in those hearings, as reported by Nancy L. Ross to the *International Herald Tribune* (Aug. 9, 1972):

"There was the committee chairman, Sen. Frank Church, D., Idaho, who recalled how 25 years back, in 1947, doctors had given him six months to live when he had cancer . . . There was 94-year-old Dr. Arthur E. Morgan, former president of Antioch College, who wept when he told of how nurses forced his dying wife's jaws open to make her eat . . . Dr. Kubler-Ross said that the worst place to die is a large teaching hospital. If physicians can't learn from the dying, the patients cease to be medically interesting and are shunted off to the custodial care of students."

*   *   *

All over the civilized world, when they get close to death, the rich and the mighty are made to pay more dearly than others, in sufferings and money, for the right to pass on. When Greek oilman Aristotle Onassis died in 1975 after a long illness, his doctors boasted that their famous client had been "clinically dead" three times in his final hours, but they resuscitated him each time.

Much less was Spain's Francisco Franco, afflicted by 20 different diseases, allowed to die in peace. After several heart attacks, already in his death throes, the almost 83-year-old dictator was submitted to a series of torments and indignities against which he had no strength left to protest. The press kept the world informed about the "miracles" that were being performed to pull the moribund old man out of his coma and stretch his agony over 34 grisly days. However, to keep a man artificially alive for a day, a month or a year without restoring him to health should not be the aim of medical art, for it doesn't benefit the patient, but his doctor. And the law should intervene.

Said a UPI dispatch datelined Madrid, November 14, 1975: "Franco today underwent his third emergency surgery in 12 days, a two-hour operation to repair his ruptured and bleeding stomach. The General was under sedation, a newly installed tube protruding from his abdomen to drain off fluid and blood from the rupture of stitches put in during an operation a week ago to remove most of his ulcerated stomach. His team of 32 doctors declared that his brain was still functioning but he needed machines to keep his body going." A respirator was meanwhile pumping air through a plastic tube into his congested lungs to keep him breathing, while a kidney machine cleansed his blood. A defibrillator was strapped to his chest to shock the heart back to work whenever it wanted to stop. A pump-like device was hooked up to keep his blood flowing. Eleven pints of blood were used in that last transfusion, bringing the total since the beginning of the crisis to 120 pints—enough to replace his normal body content 10 times. The doctors admitted that Franco was in great pain. But too much sedation would have speeded up his dying, which came at last to the tortured old man from what his heroic doctors, all raised on the vivisectionist principles, termed "irreversible cardiac failure."

It might very well be sheer coincidence, but Franco's father, who as a poor man had never had such a therapeutic arsenal at his disposal as his illustrious son, had reached the age of 86 without help, and Franco's grandfather had died ultracentenarian. That was before the era of medical "miracles," of course.

With the spreading of social services and health care, the kind of help Franco received from his regiment of doctors will probably soon be made available not only to the rich and the mighty, but also to the undistinguished poor, whether they want it or not: in the fall of 1975 an AP dispatch, under the title "Government Approves First Human Experiment Using Heart Pump," gave promise of more and more suffering for humanity, after having preventively brought untold suffering to animals.

So instead of putting an end to the experimental folly, American legislators, usually trend-setters for other countries' legislations, keep encouraging experiments on human beings by legalizing them more and more. If the trend is allowed to continue, we'll soon read headlines such as "AMERICAN GOVERNMENT APPROVES FIRST HUMAN HEAD TRANSPLANT EXPERIMENT." Which will mean the start of a new series of human sufferances—and the dying will find that Franco and Onassis got off easy compared to what *they* have to go through, when they will be as helpless in the hands of their doctors as the devocalized laboratory animals are today.

*   *   *

Is this, then, "the salon all resplendent with lights" that Claude Bernard had promised well over 100 years ago? One thing is sure: The animals are beginning to get their vengeance. Sad vengeance, not only for us, but also for them.

But what is worse, the dehumanization propagated

under the pretext of scientific research during the last century has spread to ours, getting tacitly accepted, with the complicity of the mass media, as a demonstration of intelligence and philanthropy: And it continues to proliferate in geometric progression, like the crazy cells of a cancer.

Current medical science, with its mechanistic conception of health, pretends to be illumined, but is barbaric and regressive, exclusively intent on perpetuating its errors, as did Galenism for 15 centuries. And the universities, luminous sources of humaneness and wisdom once upon a time, help propagate the new barbarism, spawned by the medical faculties, which instead of educating their pupils corrupt them.

If those in charge of public education and the mass media hadn't forgotten the civilizing duty of their mission, they would have kept in mind that the systematic cruelties that they are approving have been condemned by all the great men, including outstanding medical authorities, who are the only justification for the existence of the human species on earth. If our culture has a voice, it is theirs—and not that of the laboratory subculture.

Part Ten

CONCLUSION

As the spread of vivisection has been possible only through the conspiracy of secrecy and deception ("It's either a dog or your child, lady," and "It entails no sufferings at all for animals because of anesthesia"), it follows that the way to abolition is complete information, aimed not merely at a restricted circle of animal lovers, but at humanity at large.

Nothing could demonstrate better the urgent necessity for widespread information than a statement by Dr. Robert White in his already mentioned *American Scholar* article. "The American public," wrote the noted philosopher and monkey-head transplanter, "demonstrates its overwhelming support of medical research by annually contributing millions of dollars through direct federal financing and private subscriptions."

Surely most people who every year "demonstrate their support" by contributing to what is deceptively presented to them as "medical research" have no idea that their money goes either into animal tortures or directly into the vivisectors' pockets, and that they are financing deadly quackery to the detriment of true science.

Of course very large financial means will continue to be poured forth to keep the lid tightly on. All those who have so far produced, authorized and pushed medicaments advertised as harmless on the grounds of extensive animal tests but then proved responsible for malformations and cancers—those people will continue to wail that their opponents would rather see a baby die than a dog. And some mass media will still have an interest in glorifying present-day medical research based on the torture of animals, regardless of the fact that it will inevitably lead to more sufferings for mankind.

In Dickens' day, the advocates of child labor claimed to be humanitarians, and contended that its abolition would mean the end of civilization and the starvation of the masses, and that if substitute measures existed they would have been used. Similar arguments are being invoked by vivisectionists today, and were invoked by all those who wanted to perpetuate the slave trade, racial and sexual discrimination, and religious torture. Those who support vested interests that are responsible for severe injustice and cruelty always try to hide their crimes behind pseudo-humanitarian arguments; and many people believe them, simply because it is easier and seems safer to believe what one has been taught rather than venturing into intellectual independence. In fact conformism and inertia, not opposition, have always been the greatest obstacle to progress.

But the majority can't be fooled all the time. The winds of change are much keener today than when Vesalius revealed Galen's errors, and abolitionists do not intend to wait another century or two before today's medical "science" rights her errors.

We are in an age of unprecedented violence, of which the vivisectors set up an impressive example. Abolitionists are naturally opposed to violence, but that does not mean that they will stand forever idly by while others use violence. When we see a sadist maltreating a defenseless child, it is our duty to intervene, with violence if need be. In such a case violence becomes commendable. The same applies to vivisection.

"We are determined to let some vivisector have a taste of his own medicine, after we get our degree," a couple of Italian medical students told me, who were aroused by some of the experiments they were obliged to witness during physiology classes. "We might kidnap one of those birds and then do on him one of those experiments he is constantly performing on animals, allegedly for our benefit—like ligaturing his bile duct and then stimulating his gall bladder. And then we are going to ask him what he *now* thinks of vivisection."

Empty promises? Probably. But there are strong indications everywhere that the younger generation is just not going to stand by idly much longer. One Sunday in November of 1975, for the first time, a commando of young animal defenders, accompanied by a veterinarian, liberated some laboratory animals from their scientific torturers. They broke into the Neurophysiological Institute Marey, located at number 4 Avenue Gordon Bennett in Paris. That institute, belonging to the notorious *Collège de France* which was Claude Bernard's playground, specializes in "research on pain," using cats. Two of these unfortunate animals, which had been already so damaged that they couldn't be used for further experiments, had simply been left to starve to death in their cages. The vet estimated their martyrdom as having lasted between 30 and 40 days. The only thing their liberators could do for them was putting them to sleep. All the other cats were either nervous wrecks or totally insane. One kept hiding under the furniture and urinated constantly. All had electrodes implanted in their brains.

The laboratory could have brought charges of housebreaking and burglary, of course, but didn't. All they wanted was silence and oblivion. But the young people made sure to render the incident public. Thereupon the laboratory officials announced that their activity was "for the good of mankind," that they loved those animals and pampered them, and that *all the experiments on pain were totally painless for the animals involved.*

This called for an answer, so the commando broke into a laboratory of the CNRS—the so-called National Center of Scientific Research—located in Gif-sur-Yvette, a suburb of Paris. There they liberated more cats with part of their cranium sawed off and electrodes implanted in the brain, and brought them to a Parisian weekly, *Charlie Hebdo,* which organized an exhibit of the stolen cats for representatives of the press, radio and TV. They all reacted in the same manner: at first, incredulity, then profound indignation and disgust. Whereupon Dr. André Berkaloff, the "scientific director" of the laboratory's biological department, issued among other memorable statements the following: "As a consequence of this theft, the health of those cats is in jeopardy . . . . I only hope that they are going to be returned to us promptly."

In this case also the laboratory did not press charges. But the signs are increasing that the antivivisectionists will no longer permit silence and oblivion to prevail. There are more and more people who just don't like to think of the dogs that plead for mercy by licking the hands that cut them up, and they see no reason why human society should continue tolerating the presence of vivisectionists in their midst.

* * *

In Italy, the first act of violence came from the vivisectors. Following the stir caused by the appearance of this book in January 1976, several new antivivisection leagues had sprung into being in various Italian centers, to replace the existing, lame-duck organization and conduct intensive propaganda with the exhibition of laboratory pictures and salient passages from the book, and the revelation of the names and exploits of university vivisectors. In October of 1976, *La Nazione,* Florence's daily, reported a violent attack against the newly founded *LAN*—National Antivivisection League. Their offices had been set on fire and destroyed during the night, following a series of threatening phone calls and anonymous letters.

The answer came a few weeks later. On December 5, the same daily reported an attack against Florence's huge Medical Center of Careggi. Several gunshots were fired from the outside into the window of one of the vivisection laboratories while an illegal experiment on a dog was being performed there at night. Clearly, the attackers had received inside information. One bullet narrowly missed the performing vivisector. *La Nazione* published a letter it had received, signed "Front in Defense of Animals and Nature," which took credit for the attack, and promised more to come.

However, the problem will hardly be resolved by sporadic gun duels, though these might help awaken the sleeping majority to the realization of what is at stake. I was far more pleased when I received a request from a group of medical students from Naples University to lecture on the dangers of the vivisectionist method. The first of my lectures took place on May 10, 1977, in an auditorium of Anatomy of Naples' Second New Polyclinic, and I had the honor—perhaps I should say antivivisectionism had the honor—of being introduced to the two hundred students present by two faculty members of Naples University. One, a young professor of Microbiology, Gianfranco Tajana, the other the ancient professor of Surgery, Fernando de Leo, who is also chief surgeon at one of the most important city clinics, Ospedale Pellegrini.

After the lecture, one of the students announced that the hoped-for debate could not take place because not one of the vivisecting professors and students—the students who boasted of doing vivisections on their own—had accepted the invitation to attend. Signs had been posted for days in both Polyclinics requesting the vivisectors to show up, but the signs had been torn off again and again.

*   *   *

The vivisectors' insistence on operating behind inviolable doors is a good sign: It means that they know full well that once the people are informed, they will not stand for it; it proves that the moral sense is alive, even if, so far as vivisection is concerned, it has not yet awakened from the general anesthesia to which it is constantly subjected. Galen could cut up his victims in the public square. Today's vivisectors are obliged to hide. And the government agencies who protect them feel compelled to abet the prevailing secrecy and deception—in humanitarian Great Britain even more than elsewhere.

Actually, in writing my book I have often felt uneasy in having to present so many medical facts in support of my plea for abolition, for I couldn't help thinking of Shaw's recommendation of invoking humanitarian arguments exclusively. But then Shaw died before the Thalidomide and Stilboestrol and many other tragedies broke, confirming Bell's second law.

Actually, the fact that medical research has degenerated to the levels of quackery and crime, which instead of curing diseases causes them—at a profit—is secondary compared to the atrocious cruelty it represents, and to its inevitably corruptive effect on many members of the medical profession, to whom patients who are in fear or pain look up for help; but it offers the most useful tool so far in the revolt that must effect abolition. And that tool must be used, in conjunction with any other means that may be devised.

Charges must be pressed, not only against the manufacturers, but against the health authorities who have authorized the sale of drugs that cause human malformations and cancers after having been proved safe for animals. This has been demonstrated time and time again, by the so-called official science's own standards. The responsible parties must be brought to court, but judgment must no longer be left to their teammates, their accomplices, as happened in the Thalidomide trial.

The official document signed by Robert Miller and published by WHO, reported in this treatise along with an impressive list of warnings that had been sound —and disregarded—over the decades, proves that tragedies like the Stilboestrol case now in progress are due to the wrong reassurances obtained from animal tests; and it is the duty of the judiciary in the various countries to proceed against the responsible "health" agencies that approved and accepted a method of research that has long ago been proved wrong. Only thus can official medical research be brought to change its spots. Previous experiences have shown that even the most callous vivisectionists suddenly display very human sensitivity when they are hit, and hit hard, in their pocketbooks.

In contrast to their adversaries, the antivivisectionists want the truth out—and that's an enormous advantage. It's the vivisectors who want secrecy; who hire lobbyists to buy politicians, and pay journalists to blow smoke into the public eye; who barricade themselves in their laboratories and devocalize their victims. So others must cry out what the mutilated animals can no longer voice, and cause that movement of opinions invoked by Albert Schweitzer in his last message to the world, unmasking the impostors who set themselves up as the saviors of humanity, and getting rid of them by whatever means, until the prediction of Henry J. Bigelow, Harvard's late physiology professor, comes true:

"A day will come when the world will look upon today's vivisection in the name of science the way we look today upon witch hunts in the name of religion."

And such a day might come sooner than generally expected.

✗ APPENDIX

Book publishing is a slow procedure, and by the time I received the printer's proofs of this treatise, I had assembled enough new evidence of the unmitigated quackery and savagery inherent in today's pseudo-medical research to fill another book of equal length.

I feel I must mention at least a few of these new items, and to update, highlight or underscore what has already been said. They concern monkey-head transplanter Robert White, heart juggler Christiaan Barnard, Amnesty International, Human Guinea Pigs, the Laetrile case, and the latest drug scandal in West Germany.

* * *

Item One: I was in Rome when in the spring of 1977 Dr. Robert White pilgrimaged once more from Cleveland, Ohio, to the Holy City, for his traditional private audience with the Pope, a chummy reunion with his Italian confreres, and a well-publicized appearance on Italy's notoriously vivisection-friendly state-owned TV. This time Dr. White had brought along a film sequence showing one of his head-transplant victims, a moribund monkey from which the good doctor was trying to elicit some kind of reaction by prodding him in the face. That scene reminded me of a line in Dr. White's article in *Surgery,* which I mentioned in the part titled "Dehumanization": "The cephalons remained basically pugnacious in their attitudes, as demonstrated by their biting if orally stimulated." The monkey seen on Italian TV couldn't muster the strength to bite, no matter how persistently the surgeon was "stimulating" it, orally or otherwise; he just kept glaring at his tormentor, blood trickling continuously from his nose the while.

This was too much even for Italy's televiewers, who have never been known to waste much love on animals. This time they reacted with unprecedented indignation to Dr. White's revolting exhibition. The TV station was submerged with outraged phone calls, the newspapers with letters. Completely divorced from reality, like all vivisectors, Dr. White remained unaware of the public reaction he had caused. In a subsequent interview—and probably forgetting his earlier statement that the practical application of his experiments would have to wait some fifty years—he blithely announced that he was ready for a head transplant on man. All he was waiting for was a willing subject.

* * *

Item Two: In June 1977, at Capetown's Groote Schuur, Christiaan Barnard implanted in a ten-hour long operation the heart of a female baboon into the chest of a 25-year-old Italian woman, in addition to her own ailing heart. The rationale of the operation, as Barnard saw it, was to let the monkey's heart take over the work of keeping circulation going long enough to give the human heart a chance to rest and regain its strength.

Unfortunately the young woman—who for all we know might still be alive today without Barnard's experiment—was dead a few hours later.

Now question number one: Didn't Dr. Barnard know, as everyone who knows anything about anatomy and biology knows full well, that the heart is an organ which—contrary to the liver, for example—lacks the faculty to regenerate itself? So the experiment was silly, not to use some much stronger term. In fact the confraternity of surgeons minced no words saying so— as soon as the patient was dead.

Barnard had a brand-new alibi ready this time, at least to explain his patient's prompt demise: a baboon's heart is too small to keep up the circulation of a human adult, so the next time he was going to resort to a chimpanzee's heart, which is stronger.

Question number two: Wasn't Dr. Barnard aware of this anatomical fact before doing his experiment, having already massacred a large number of apes in his lifetime?

Or—question number three—doesn't all this prove once more that also for Christiaan Barnard experimentation on living organisms has become an obsession, a paranoid fixation devoid of all logical reasoning?

But there is more. Zurich's daily, *Blick*, reported on June 24 that during the operation the whole surgical ward of Groote Schuur shuddered again and again to the shrieks of the baboon lady, as her chest was being cut open and heart excised without the slightest anesthesia, because Barnard wanted to give to his patient a heart in perfect working order, completely free of any chemicals.

Now question number four: Was Barnard aware or not that baboons have an intelligence comparable to an approximately nine-year-old human and a much higher sensitivity, that baboons have gestures, reactions, social customs and even organizational talents comparable to ours, even if they don't organize sanguinary revelries like the clan of vivisectors?

Question number five concerns the moral law, which I have briefly discussed in another chapter. Couldn't it be a new evidence of the ineluctable moral law at work that at the comparatively early age of 53, Barnard's arthritis—in spite of all the experiments by his colleagues on the joints of millions of helpless animals to find a cure—had already progressed so far that he was unable to wield his knife for any length of time and had to pass it on frequently to one of his assistants, as the papers reported?

* * *

Item Three: This item demonstrates how far the miasmas of dehumanization have spread, as ever widening circles of people have been brainwashed into accepting the thesis that every kind of animal abuse is permissible, commendable, so long as it can be palmed off as "scientific," and even as a humanitarian activity. Those miasmas have engulfed even the London-based organization known as Amnesty International, which styles itself a humane society dedicated to the protection and liberation of political prisoners.

In the spring of 1977 Amnesty International admitted to having promoted experiments in which animals were submitted to burns with glowing irons and electric stimulation, in order to find out whether it is possible to torture prisoners without leaving telltale marks on their bodies. By AI's admission, the experiments had been conducted in Denmark at the organization's request "at the Institute for Internal Medicine in the Royal College of Veterinary Science and Agriculture with funding for expenses from the Danish Medical Research Council," which is one of Denmark's vivisectionist organizations.

The alibis were the typical ones used by vivisectors in all European countries where vivisection is "regulated" by law: The experiments were conducted on "anesthetized" pigs only; "every effort was made to ensure that the animals involved did not suffer;" "all laws governing experiments with animals in the country concerned were adhered to."

AI's official alibi when questioned by various antivivisection societies included furthermore the following statements: "The doctors wish to make it clear that they were not 'torturing' pigs. . . . The experiments in question occurred between February and November 1976. *If money for expenses is forthcoming* from the Danish Medical Research Council, the doctors will continue their work in September 1977."

Obviously, the AI officials were not aware that the animals' flesh reacts in an entirely different way to burns than does human skin, so that the results of those experiments were, like all animal experiments, not only useless but misleading. The Danish doctors involved certainly knew that, but to them this fact was clearly irrelevant—so long as "the money for expenses is forthcoming."

* * *

Item Four: This item could have been included in the chapter on Human Guinea Pigs. It also goes a long way toward showing to what point the dehumanization fostered by the vivisectionist propaganda that starts in the U.S. at early school age has progressed, not only in the medical world, but in the highest government quarters. It concerns information released from Washington, D.C., and reported among others by the *International Herald Tribune* (Aug. 17, 1977), in an article by Jo Thomas entitled "CIA Urged Use of Coma Victims." The writer warns us at one point that the documents available "were heavily censored before being declassified." But whatever is left over after the U.S. censor was through with his cutting (probably "for security reasons," the usual humbug) is chilling enough. The article opens thus:

"The CIA sponsored a six-year search for a 'knock-out' drug during which scientists were supposed to analyze spinal and other vital fluids from comatose and delirious patients hospitalized with terminal cancer, liver failure, uremia and severe infections, newly declassified records show.

"The project was designed to discover the biochemical mechanisms that cause delirium and to develop new drugs and techniques to produce 'maximum levels of physical and emotional stress in human beings,' the documents show.

"To keep their pool of human subjects and to continue the project's 'cover,' the researchers were also supposed to evaluate other effects of the drugs they were developing, such as their anti-cancer or cardiovascular effects.

"The CIA records show that this drug project lasted from 1955 to 1961 and cost $531,960. Funds went from the CIA to the Washington-based Geschickter Fund for Medical Research Inc.

"Although the records clearly describe the research proposed for humans and for parallel animal studies, only the results of the animal studies are described in detail. . . ."

This article shows the cynical deviousness not only of the CIA officials who conceived this project and many other similar ones, but also of the medical organizations like the respectable sounding Geschickter

Fund for Medical Research who were their willing accomplices, and probably got as much satisfaction—financial and otherwise—out of their "maximum stress" experiments on human beings as of the "parallel animal studies."

* * *

Item Five: Now we come to the Laetrile case. Laetrile is an extract from crushed apricot pits that releases tiny amounts of cyanide in the body. In large doses cyanide is a poison, but its propagandists claim that small doses of it are effective against cancer and tumors, and that thousands have been cured by it. Laetrile is not presented as a miracle drug but as a health food, which supplies vital substances lacking in the overly refined modern diet. Assuming that many cancers are simply "deficiency diseases," Laetrile is supposed to cure them in the same way that lime juice cures scurvy and whole grains cure pellagra.

The FDA, the AMA, the American Cancer Society have all joined in the cry of quackery and fraud (they should talk!), and forbidden the sale of Laetrile in the U.S. So now there is a lively black market for this product, and a steady pilgrimage of Americans who get the Laetrile treatment in Mexican clinics where the product is not outlawed.

Demonstrating in what low esteem the medical authorities are being held today, rumors are rife in America that they are fully aware of the curative properties of Laetrile, but there is far more money in it for them to outlaw it, and to sell it under the counter at a huge profit.

I am not going to express an opinion on this claim, nor on whether Laetrile can or cannot cure cancer. I only point out that so long as official medical science doesn't change its spots, the risk will subsist that vitally important drugs, a cancer cure for instance, will be withheld from the patients *simply because its effectiveness cannot be proven through animal tests,* just as dangerous drugs will inevitably keep coming on the market because animal tests have "proved" them to be safe.

Item Six: To what extent the drug industry, the most lucrative in the world, continually influences the decisions or non-decisions of the highest government agencies to the detriment of public health is shown once more by a recent article in the German news magazine *Der Spiegel* (Aug. 17, 1977), titled "Analgesica: The Time Bomb Ticks On."

It said that for years now the cancer researchers have known that one of the most powerful cancerogenic (cancer-causing) drugs is Dimethylnitrosamin, which occurs in all medicaments containing Aminophenazon. It can cause the dreaded agranulocythosis (a disease mentioned in this book). Besides being often a prelude to cancer, especially leukemia, agranulocythosis causes the disappearance of the white corpuscles in the blood, deriving from mutations in the spinal marrow, and thus impairs the organism's ability to fight off every kind of disease. This cancerogenic product is currently contained in about 200 drugs, including Pyramidon and Antipyrin, widely used in Europe against headaches, fever, and rheumatic pains. In the U.S., the Aminophenazon combinations have almost disappeared from the shelves because American manufacturers were obliged to print warnings in their descriptive leaflets. But American travelers abroad risk being sold these drugs, because the pharmaceutical lobbies in most European countries have managed, up to the time of this writing, to prevent any interference with the sale of these products.

The *Spiegel* article gave other disturbing information:

Menocil, a drug to curb appetite, caused uncounted deaths through high pressure in the lungs (*Cor pulmonale*) before the authorities felt obliged to ban it.

The use of purgatives, especially those containing Isatin and its derivatives, currently on sale, causes serious damage to the liver.

Analgesics like Thomapyrin or Gelonida, which contain Phenacitin, cause irreparable kidney damage after prolonged use.

Tranquilizers and sleeping tablets containing bromides, as do Staurodorm or Adalin, caused the death

of approximately 1000 people in the Federal Republic
alone in 1976.

Many other deaths have been caused by the anti-
diabetes Biguanid preparations, even though they
require a doctor's prescription. And yet the health
authorities (the *Bundesgesundheitsamt* or BGA, described as "notoriously friendly toward industry" in
the article) couldn't make up their minds to ban the
drug. They merely issued "recommendations" that it
should be prescribed only by doctors who have "particular experience" in the treatment of diabetes.

The article concluded that the manufacturers have
been given time to sell all their present stock of the
various concerogenic drugs and that the BGA has
promised to issue further "recommendations" some-
time soon, apparently banking on the claim of its
president, Pharmacology Professor Dr. med. Georges
Fülgraff, who had declared that, "The purely legal
proof of a direct damage from a medicament cannot
be brought."

* * *

Item Seven: This item concerns payments made to
U.S. lawmakers by organizations interested in keeping
the present fraudulent medical system going. I have
reported that American special interest groups "show-
ered a record $22.6 million on candidates for Con-
gress in 1976," and that the top donors were "the
Medical Associations" with $1,790,879, the Dairy
Committees following as poor seconds. I feel I should
enlarge on this information, giving a list of the political
candidates that were the beneficiaries of the Medical
Associations largesse, as revealed by *Time* Magazine
(Feb. 28, 1977). I advise that their names be remembered if ever they crop up among those who again
oppose any laws to abolish vivisection. They are:

Senate Candidates:

Vance Hartke (D., Ind.)	$245,700
Harrison Williams (D., N.J.)	244,373
Lloyd Bentsen (D., Texas)	229,299
John Tunney (D., Calif.)	219,419
William Green (D., Pa.)	216,660

House Candidates:

John Rhodes (R., Ariz.)	$ 98,620
Jim Mattox (D., Texas)	85,310
Mark Hannaford (D., Calif.)	81,368
Lloyd Meeds (D., Wash.)	80,078
Thomas L. Ashley (D., Ohio)	76,337

* * *

What can be done? What can the average citizen do to change the currently accepted and imposed method of pseudomedical research based on vivisection? The average citizen can do a lot—can in fact do all. The changes won't come overnight, but they will come inevitably. The average citizen can try to resist the brainwashing he is constantly subjected to through the overt and hidden publicity pandered consciously or inadvertently by the mass media. The citizen can try to stop ingesting the various patent medicines since they don't relieve headaches, stomach pains, liver, and kidney troubles or insomnia except, sometimes, temporarily, but are bound to aggravate the condition in the long run. And less money for the drug industry means less money for vivisection.

The average citizen will be amazed to discover how well he can live without the medicaments without which he thought he could not live. As has been sufficiently demonstrated through the documentation presented in this book, today's medicaments are not merely useless in the long run but highly damaging, owing to the erroneous basic research divised by the drug industry in its own interest and not in the public interest.

Those who feel they need medical advice should resort to the representatives of the alternative medicines—such as homeopathy, chiropraxis, herbal medicine, acupuncture, and the like. In fact any and every kind of "other" medicine is likely to prove more useful, and at any rate less harmful, than today's "official" medicine sponsored by the drug industry with the complicity of the university faculties.

The average citizen can and should spread the information received in this book.

The average citizen can write letters to the newspapers, and it won't matter much if most of them don't get published, as they will exert an impact on the editor none the less. If one letter arrives on a particular subject it rarely gets published. If they arrive by the hundreds, some of them are likely to get published. And one should keep in mind that sometimes a little spark will cause a great conflagration.

The average citizen should write repeatedly, relentlessly, to his or her government representatives. Americans have that great resort to fall back on—writing to their congressmen.

The average citizen should join the local or the nearest anti-vivisectionist society. There is the NAVS (National Anti-Vivisection Society) in Chicago, Ill., 100 E. Ohio Street. The American Anti-Vivisection Society, Suite 204, Noble Plaza, 801 Old York Road, Jenkintown, Pa. 19046. The United Action for Animals, Inc., in New York, N.Y., 205 East 42nd Street. There are many more. New societies spring into being from time to time. Some disappear when the founders, the driving force, die.

In several European countries, where vivisection is supposedly regulated by restrictive laws, some so-called anti-vivisection societies have been infiltrated at the top by the vivisectionist interests. Societies that have been thus infiltrated have opposed every initiative proposed by their own members.

For this reason I have founded the CIVIS, which is a Latin word on which the terms "civilization" and "civil" are based, but in this case stands also for *Centre d'Information Vivisectionniste International Scientifique,* which is French but understandable to everybody: a center for international, scientific information on vivisection. CIVIS is based at my home address in Switzerland, *7250 KLOSTERS,* Tal-Strasse 40, and its aim is to supply free, reliable information *to* the various anti-vivisection societies and *about* the various anti-vivisection societies: whether or not they are carrying their load—and especially whether they are actually trying to abolish vivisection and not trying to keep vivisection going.

APPENDIX
TO THE BRITISH EDITION

During the interval between the publication of *Slaughter of the Innocent* in the USA and in Great Britain, a year to the day, many new events have occurred confirming that present-day medical research is on the wrong track. In this period also, all over the world, a spate of drugs, all preventively tested on animals, had to be withdrawn from the market because they had turned out to be dangerous when administered to humans, very often creating new diseases.

Because of one such case, in the summer of 1978 a Tokyo court found three drug manufacturers—Ciba-Geigy Japan, Takeda and Takabe Seijaku—guilty of selling drugs that create a new malady called Smon, which causes paralysis, blindness and death, and sentenced them to pay 3.25 billion Yen to 133 plaintiffs.

At the same time Europe was worrying about a new malformation tragedy, which threatened to dwarf the Thalidomide disaster, in spite of all the new tests done on animals since then, specifically designed to discover any "teratogenic" (malformation-causing) effect of new drugs. Under suspicion was a synthetic hormone, Duogynon, manufactured by Schering in Berlin, who had already been obliged to withdraw this product from the markets of Great Britain, Sweden, Finland, Italy, Holland and Spain. While the German papers were reporting this, the Zurich daily *Tat* revealed that the Swiss licensee was planning to market the drug under a different name.

The world-wide worry about cancer has kept increasing abreast of the failure to check its increase by pouring more and more money into a type of research that has not changed over the past two hundred years. The "War on Cancer" begun as a PR-cause by the Nixon administration in 1971 was acknowledged lost in late May 1978. News of the defeat appeared on the front page of the *New York Times*, with Dr. Arthur Upton, Director of the National Cancer Institute, as herald of disaster. The rout was in the flow charts. A river of gold had been pumped into a mammoth establishment whose lush survival depended on the state of no-cure.

A few politicians are apparently beginning to discover the giant fraud behind it all. "I have the suspicion that we're losing the war on cancer because of mistaken priorities and mis-allocations of funds," said US Senator McGovern at a cancer hearing of the US Senate in the summer of 1978, adding: "There has been no lack of funds—it's almost $1 billion a year."

It is now generally acknowledged that 85 per cent of cancers are caused by environmental hazards, yet very little is being done in the order of prevention with this fact in mind. As Robert Houston wrote in a thoughtful article in New York's paper *Our Town* (3 September, 1978): "The most frightening notion in cancer research is in fact the prospect of the general resolution of the disease. A solution to cancer would mean the termination of research programmes, the obsolescence of skills, the end of dreams of personal glory; triumph over cancer would dry up contributions to self-perpetuating charities and cut off funding from Congress; it would mortally threaten the present clinical establishment by rendering obsolete the expensive surgical, radiological and chemotherapeutic treatments in which so much money, training and equipment is invested. Such fear, however unconscious, may result in resistance and hostility to alternative approaches in proportion as they are therapeutically promising. The new therapy must be disbelieved, denied, discouraged and disallowed at all costs, regardless of actual testing results and preferably without any testing at all. This pattern has in actuality occurred repeatedly, and almost consistently."

*   *   *

Last year, a German professor of law, Dr. Martin

Fincke of the University of Passau, wrote a book demonstrating that the entire medical profession should be brought to court on a charge of multiple murder.

In my country, Switzerland, I discovered what it is that has prevented animal experimentation being outlawed although it is used as an alibi to enable the drug industry to sell its damaging but lucrative products on a worldwide scale.

The Swiss government chose long ago to submit to an elementary form of blackmail. The chemical industry, being by far the most lucrative industrial complex, as in all industrialized countries, imposes its own dictatorship on the Government, using the following argument: "We are the top taxpayers in the land. We keep the State on its feet. We pay most of the salaries of you State officials. So we want to have a say in government policies. If you don't follow our advice—which is for the good of the people, anyway—or if you create difficulties of any sort for us, we will shut down our factories and move to some other country, which would welcome us."

In fact the Swiss chemical industry, of which the pharmacological is the most lucrative branch, holds the Government by the balls, and makes the most of it. Through the "advice" imparted to the Government, this industry has been dominating education (schools, universities) and the mass media (State-owned radio and TV) for well over fifty years. Through its influence on the educational system, with the enormous financial power it wields (commissions, advertisements for a wide spectrum of products from pharmaceuticals to fertilizers to cosmetics) and in alliance with its most effective agents, the Medical Associations, this industry has molded public opinion by an intensive brainwashing conducted relentlessly over a long number of years. Starting at school age and even before, within their families, the citizens are taught to believe in the magic power of Modern Medicine and in the other benefits of the chemical industry.

So they are persuaded to dash to the druggist at the first sign of a cold, which is just what the great majority of people will do—and never mind, for instance, the recent report of a special panel of the US Food and Drug

Administration which pointed out that while no medication exists that will cure or prevent the common cold, American pharmaceutical manufacturers manage to market some 35,000 different cold remedies, for which consumers shell out $735 million a year. Of course the British consumers, and consumers everywhere else, are hardly less gullible, and the manufacturers elsewhere hardly less guilty, than their American counterparts. Authoritative disssenters are simply outshouted, their voices drowned by the ballyhoo of the organized opinion-makers.

And yet a clear pattern of rebellion is beginning to emerge in several countries simultaneously, independently from one another, pointing to an impending showdown between the slowly growing number of responsible, clear-sighted individuals resolved to change the current system, and the destructive, self-annihilating policies of official power, of which vivisectionism is just one of the crudest aspects.

*   *   *

WINDS OF CHANGE

In Italy, where my earliest version of *Slaughter of the Innocent* appeared three years ago under the title *Imperatrice Nuda* ("Naked Empress"), some unprecedented practical results have already been obtained on the vivisection front, as a consequence of a nation-wide wave of public indignation, which included parliamentary interpolations. In 1977, illustrating their decision by citing passages of the book, which listed a number of drugs proved safe on animals but deadly for humans, several town mayors issued ordinances forbidding the customary delivery of pound dogs to the "scientific laboratories" that requested them. The example of the first mayor to sign such an ordinance, the Mayor of Voghera in Northern Italy, was soon followed by the Mayor of Milan, no less, which is Italy's industrial and vivisection capital, and then by several others, including the Mayor of Padua, a city famous for its medical university.

Although it is doubtful that vivisection has been substantially reduced as a consequence of these ordinances, since animals can still be obtained (though at a much higher cost) from breeding centres and on the black market, they represent a first, significant step forward: public officials, whose stay in office depends on votes, apparently well aware that their decision had the approval of the majority, have defied a century-old tradition. They have resisted all subsequent attempts by the vivisectionist confraternity to have those ordinances revoked, including an intensive, nation-wide propaganda campaign engineered by the Medical Faculty of Padua.

GREAT BRITAIN

The three principal anti-vivisection societies in Great Britain are, in alphabetical order, the *British Union for the Abolition of Vivisection* (BUAV), 47 Whitehall, London SW1; the *National Anti-Vivisection Society* (NAVS), 51 Harley Street, London W1N 1DD, and the *Scottish Society for the Prevention of Vivisection*, 10 Queensferry Street, Edinburgh EH2 4PG.

Not even the greatest optimist could claim that the considerable sums of money poured into these societies by Britain's anti-vivisectionists have yielded results to be proud of. Vivisection has not diminished in Great Britain over the past decades, neither in horror nor in scope. It would indeed be difficult to devise an experiment that would not be approved by the Home Office officials in charge of issuing permits to the vivisectors according to the Cruelty Against Animals Act of 1876. The Act has remained substantially unchanged ever since, in the name of progress and the good of mankind.

Far more notable results have been obtained in Italy in just a couple of years, with practically no financial support at all, just by arousing national indignation at all levels through information—with picket lines, posters and photographic exhibits of laboratory animals, denunciation of vivisectors on all levels, and no punches pulled. Specifically, single vivisectors, previously only known as respected MDs, and high government officials responsible for the practice were denounced to public opinion, and brought to court whenever possible. Anti-vivisectionist doctors, medical students and lawyers collaborated with the new leagues on these actions, which gradually snowballed, as a steadily growing proportion of the population became aware of the shameful activity inside the laboratories.

But all this seems to be considered slightly undignified by the British leagues. Ungentlemanly, really. "We like to denounce the sin, but not the sinners," was the way one of their officers put it when I questioned him; one of the many who seem to regard the anti-vivisection fight as a sort of elegant fencing duel among peers.

In fact the officers in charge of the British societies are as a rule extremely decent and well-meaning people, who conduct the fight with missionary zeal, sometimes at great personal expense and sacrifice, out of an ardent desire to reduce animal suffering; but frequently in the naive belief that such is also the vivisectors' aim, and that it is sufficient to draw a vivisector's attention to the existence of an alternative method of research, and he will then gratefully adopt this new method and thereupon leave the animals alone.

Out of this consideration all those societies have in recent years created "Funds for Humane Research" into which large sums of money have been pouring with which to encourage the use of alternative methods.

It is well possible that the donations that have enabled those funds to distribute large sums to "scientists" and "researchers" in an effort to persuade them to use some of the many alternatives extant instead of animals, have avoided a certain amount of animal suffering, even though the figures available don't point to any decrease of experiments on animals since those funds were set up. But one thing is certain: the existence of such funds will never bring about the abolition of vivisection. On the contrary: they lull the British public into a state of spurious optimism, deceiving the majority into believing that all it takes to stop vivisection is to pour more money into those funds.

One can't expect the average anti-vivisectionist to know more about medical art and research than the medical doctors themselves do, or to have escaped the general brainwashing to which the public is being subjected from on high; so no doubt there are many directors of the anti-vivisection societies who are convinced—in spite of massive proof to the contrary—that animal experiments *do* serve a scientific purpose, and that science must *first* find alternatives, and only *then* can animal experimentation be eliminated. But it's the other way round. Apart from the fact that alternatives already exist by the thousands, animal experiments must *first* be abolished by law, on the grounds of their degrading cruelty and fatal fallaciousness, and *then* the manufacturers who think that the 205,000 medicaments developed so far are not enough will have to use or develop other testing methods for the next 205,000 medicaments. And never mind the World Health Organisation's list, published in 1978, of just 200 medicaments that are fully sufficient for the world's needs, or the less than two dozen medicaments that Chile's former President Allende's medical commission, which had no commercial interests in the sale of drugs, had found to be the only ones with any demonstrable therapeutic value.

*   *   *

Unless or until a more active society springs into being, the three I have mentioned are the only ones anti-vivisectionists in Great Britain should adhere to—preferably to all three at once, in order to compare their activities. A tireless driving force behind British anti-vivisectionism has been for many years now the Rt. Hon. Lady Muriel Dowding, widow of the late Air Chief Marshal Lord Dowding, who had been persuaded by her to carry the fight right to the floor of the House of Lords.

There are other societies which sometimes effectively protect and benefit animals, but whose convictions in matters of vivisection are ambiguous or lukewarm at best. One of them is the powerful *Royal Society for the Prevention of Cruelty to Animals* (RSPCA), which lists Her Majesty the Queen as principal patron. This organisation pays mainly lip-service to anti-vivisectionism. Its annual report for 1977 officially stated that the society is "opposed to animal experiments which involve unnecessary repetitions or are for scientifically trivial ends . . . It is also opposed to the use of animals in the testing of inessential substances, such as cosmetics." Which means that it is not opposed to repetitions which the society (or the vivisectors?) consider "necessary", nor to experiments which the society (or the vivisectors?) do not consider to be "trivial", nor to experiments designed to test non-cosmetic substances—such as, say, drugs? Ambiguity will never do away with the shame of vivisection, but will perpetuate the profits of the drug industry forever.

One society that is not ambiguous so far as vivisection is concerned is the *Universities Federation for Animal Welfare* (UFAW), which denounces activist actions and issues publications authored by individuals with financial or research interests in vivisection. One of them is titled *The UFAW Handbook of the Care and Management of Laboratory Animals.*

And then there is the puzzling case of *FRAME* (Fund for the Replacement of Animals in Medical Research), an organisation I mentioned in the chapter "Alternative Methods."

When the magazine of Philadelphia's *American Anti-Vivisection Society* recently presented FRAME as an anti-vivisectionist organisation, FRAME protested, obliging the editor to publish a *Correction*: "... Mrs. Dorothy Hegarty, Chairman of the Trustees of FRAME, clarifies its position in the following letter: 'FRAME is not an anti-vivisection society nor is it crusading fearlessly against vivisection as stated ... It has never been our intention to expose the work of researchers in our literatures ...'"

FRAME has not attempted to explain how it ever hopes to do away, through alternatives, with the steadily increasing neuro-physiological experiments, for example, such as those described in the chapter "Profound Respect", in which animals serve as scapegoats, harassed with electric shocks until they become as insane as their tormentors. Only the law, and no alternative method, can put an end to this.

Small wonder that many vivisectors applaud initiatives such as FRAME, saying: "Contribute to FRAME, and get off our backs." And small wonder that many anti-vivisectionists in England are not happy with their societies, as I gather from quite a number of letters I've been receiving from British people, including physicians, who have managed to obtain the U.S. edition of this book. Their feeling can be epitomized by the following excerpt from a letter by a lady from Guildford, Surrey:

"After 32 years in the film biz, of hard slog and travel, have become increasingly aware of the dreadful hypocrisy and bull-shit that surrounds us all. Have on numerous occasions written letters to the papers re anti-vivisection and also marched the streets for signatures which, as you mentioned in your book, our "Iron Doll" turned down, through ignorance, of course, re the Thalidomide children. One has no appetite for enjoyment any more, being aware of what is really going on behind the scenes against our younger brothers—the animals. As one becomes increasingly sensitive and aware of the One-ness of All Life, one can't help looking at vivisection as an outrage perpetuated by sadistic people with greedy, sick minds deluding the public that they are 'scientists' with humanitarian principles. I have long been disenchanted with animal welfare groups in Britain as they are apathetic in action and long-winded in speech and print. I would like to explore the possibilities of seeing if a more active group could be created—'Abolition of Vivisection' rather than 'Anti' which should be spelt 'Auntie' in today's age!"

ACTIVISM IS BORN

In 1976, simultaneously with developments in France and Italy, a new organisation of urban guerrillas, known as The Band of Mercy, thrust itself into the sterile debate between supporters and opponents of vivisection in England. After a summer of isolated acts of violence against establishments known to breed laboratory animals, the organisation could claim a major breakthrough: they successfully burgled the London offices of the Research Defence Society, which is the vivisectionists' lobby group and exists mainly to promote the procurement and use of laboratory animals. The society's officials preferred to keep quiet about the break-in, their main concern being, as usual, to avoid any publicity. The public must not know that vivisection exists.

Having got hold of the files containing the membership records of the RDS, the militant group—which shortly afterward changed its name to Animal Liberation Front (ALF)—stepped up its activities, as indicated by the following brief excerpt from an article in *The Times*, of 12 April 1978, by novelist Maureen Duffy:

"Yesterday's illegality is tomorrow's accepted morality ... When change is too fast we experience disorientation leading to a conservationist backlash; when it is too slow, the frontrunners in the movement for change will be driven by frustration and the mounting pressure behind them to throw themselves at the barrier of inertia in an effort to move it ... In the period August 1976 to August 1977 there were ten raids on hunt kennels ... These activities were claimed by the amorphous Animal Liberation Front, described as 'not so much an organization as a state of anger and frustration'. The ALF claims 37 'hits' in the fourteen months ending in September 1977, and an estimated total of nearly £300,000 of damages. The chief subjects are the laboratory breeders and experimenters ..."

While others talked and wept, ALF acted in an unprecedented direct action campaign, with nothing to be gained for its members, much to be lost. In fact in March 1975, the newspapers had reported that two founders of the group had been jailed for three years for arson and damages in connection with their anti-vivisection activity: Ronald Lee, 23, a clerk, of Luton, and Clifford Goodman, a toolmaker, of Northampton.

Another member, Derek Cowell from Birmingham, told journalist Dick Tracy who interviewed him for *Musical World* (12 November, 1977): "ALF are organised in small groups around the country with a contact man in each area keeping in touch with the national leaders. Each job is planned to the last detail, and there's a strict code of conduct which states that nothing is to be stolen for personal gain."

If nowadays not many ALF actions get mentioned in the newspapers anymore it is because they have become fairly routine and no longer news, especially since it became the policy of the group to carry out lots of small raids rather than just a few big raids as before. "Numerous small raids," one member explained, "have the advantage of keeping lots of labs and breeders worried all the time. Their expenses for security have gone up tremendously and some smaller breeding enterprises have closed down altogether."

The Research Defence Society, 11 Chandos Street, London W1M 9DE, is in fact becoming worried and last year published *Guidance Notes on Prevention of Vandalism*, for all its correspondents in the United Kingdom and the United States.

ENCOURAGEMENT FROM USA

A powerful encouragement to British militants came from America, where the insane experiments on the sexual life of cats performed at the Museum of Natural History in New York were brought to a halt by a long-lasting wave of public protest, particularly noteworthy inasmuch as it achieved its purpose, stopping just short of actual violence.

Those experiments are briefly mentioned in the chapter "Sadism", and were still going on when I had to deliver the final manuscript to the American publisher. Half a year later, on my arrival in New York, I found that those experiments had been called off and the laboratory had been dismantled on orders of the Museum's director —even though similar experiments were going on simultaneously in about thirty other "seats of learning". How had they been stopped in New York? By public demonstrations which brought national attention to what went on in secrecy inside the respected institution.

They had been sparked by a New York high-school teacher, Henry Spira, who had been tipped off as to the existence of those experiments, and had obtained the vivisectors' original grant applications by invoking the little-known Freedom of Information Act. A perusal of those application forms showed how right I had been when I said at the beginning of this book that in matters of vivisection any exaggeration is not only superfluous, but impossible.

As "Principal investigator" on the applications was named one Lester B. Aronson, Ph.D., curator of the Museum's department of animal behaviour. Year after year—for fourteen years—he had applied for funds to purchase batches of three-month old kittens and of adult male cats. According to his own written statements, he intended to perform on them a series of mutilations, which included the "enucleation of both orbits" (removing the eyes), the surgical destruction of the sense of hearing and of smell, lesioning the brain, castration, and more exercises, allegedly designed to discover how all this would affect the sex-life of the victims. Apparently for variety's sake he also did some "terminal" (*i.e.* until death occurs) experiments in which the penis nerve was exposed and then submitted to electric shocks until "termination".

Statements in Aronson's application also contained references to the necessity of a "sound-retarded' testing room and of specially-built "transfer cages" for handling "violent animals".

In spite of these clear indications of almost unimaginable tortures to be uselessly inflicted upon innocent and highly sensitive creatures, Aronson and his assistant, Madeline L. Cooper, had no problem getting their projects funded every year, to the tune of almost half a million dollars all told, mostly with the support of the National Institute of Child Health and Human Development. Nor did they have any difficulty, when the case finally became a nation-wide scandal, in getting strenuous defence from influential personalities of the vivisectionist community, such as Dr. William Sadler, chief of the population and reproduction branch in the Child Health and Human Development Institute, who gave this evaluation, as reported by the *Christian Science Monitor* (20 September, 1976): "During my own investigation I couldn't find anything wrong. As far as we can determine, the animals are treated humanely and spared unnecessary suffering."

And in a long, highly ambiguous essay in *Science* (8 October, 1976), the prestigious, traditionally pro-vivisection journal of the American Association for the Advancement of Science, one Nicolas Wade wrote: "The allegations by the animal rights groups that the experimenters took a sadistic pleasure in the experiments is an obvious absurdity. Aronson says that surgery was conducted under anesthesia, as is customary." Wade did not try to explain what was the purpose of the "sound-retarded" testing rooms, or the necessity for the "transfer cages" specially built for handling "violent animals". And what about the post-surgical pains following the brief effect of anesthesia, assuming it was administered in the first place? And as later reports showed, some cats died, even before the experiments were completed, of urinary blockages—an extremely painful condition which in cats can result from torture or stress or improper diet.

The demonstrations were kept up during a whole year, and they included full-page ads in such papers as the *New York Times*, while placard-waving crowds picketed the Museum on every weekend, exhorting the visitors to keep away and to cancel their membership. The Museum symbolized millions of animals suffering repetitive tortures which add nothing of value to the sum of human knowledge, let alone medical knowledge; animal agony for the sake of profit, fame, or a sick kind of personal satisfaction. Thus the Museum became a national issue. The media started focusing their attention on it, Congressman Ed Koch discussed it twice on the floor of Congress, and with Congressman Biaggi he joined the demonstrators, who at times numbered as many as 1000 people. 121 members of Congress questioned the National Institutes of Health. Attacks were published in various papers, handbills were distributed, letters and telephone calls of harassment, some threatening, were directed at Museum employees and Trustees, pictures of the two main experimenters, Aronson and Cooper, complete with their telephone numbers and addresses, were circulated and sent to all their neighbours, and contributors to the Museum, particularly corporations and private foundations, were pressured in various ways, while hundreds of people cancelled their membership. Although the Museum's director announced that Aronson was going to retire anyway and thus end the experiments, it was certainly economic considerations that brought the desired result, for his decision came shortly after a lady had announced that she had modified her will, cancelling an important bequest to the Museum, and inviting other donors to follow her example.

*   *   *

On 3 May, 1978, I faced the Pope of American Vivi section, Dr. Clarence Dennis, well-known surgeon and vivisector, President of the National Society of Medical Research, which is the American counterpart of Britain's Research Defence Society, in a debate arranged by the Sherrye Henry Show on New York's WOR radio station.

Question: "Dr. Dennis, will you tell us what was the purpose of the cat experiments at New York's Museum of Natural History?"

Answer: "You remember that rape is a serious problem, and you know that there are abnormalities in sexual behavior that play a role in developing rape. I believe that what they were working on was to try to figure out, working with cats which in some respects have a brain that is comparable to the human—I know it's not nearly as complex but in many respects for this sort of purpose it is—and they were studying I believe with this end in view. This is what they have been working on for years."

(Word-for-word transcript from the original recording of the WOR Sherrye Henry Show programme.)

*   *   *

POSTSCRIPT

The Home Office is never very eager to release its "Return of experiments on living animals under the 1876 Cruelty to Animals Act", and so the latest figures available to me at the time of this writing are for 1976. They show yet another increase in experiments performed in Great Britain, to 5,474,739, the overwhelming majority done as usual without any anesthesia (the exception has become the rule!). They also showed an increase in the number of licences issued, 18,666, demonstrating how successful the Research Defence Society is in propagandizing the remunerative aspects of animal experimentation.

Klosters, 1 October 1978

INDEX

435